PUBLICATION DESIGN

PUBLICATION
DESIGN

THIRD EDITION

ROY PAUL NELSON
University of Oregon

wcb
Wm. C. Brown Company Publishers
Dubuque, Iowa

Designer: Roy Paul Nelson

Copyright © 1972, 1978, 1983 by Wm. C. Brown Company Publishers

Library of Congress Catalog Card Number: 82–73564

ISBN 0–697–04356–8

Second Printing, 1983

Printed in the United States of America   2-04356-02

FOR JOHN L. HULTENG

By Roy Paul Nelson

Publication Design
The Design of Advertising
Editing the News (with Roy H. Copperud)
The Fourth Estate (with John L. Hulteng)
Articles and Features
Comic Art and Caricature
Cartooning
Visits with 30 Magazine Art Directors
Fell's Guide to Commercial Art (with Byron Ferris)
Fell's Guide to the Art of Cartooning

CONTENTS

Seven: Magazine formula and format 130

Eight: The magazine cover 147

PREFACE

Publication Design deals with a continuing problem in journalism: how to coordinate art and typography with content. Through text and illustration, the book suggests ways to make pages and spreads in magazines, newspapers, books, and other publications attractive and easy to read. As a book of techniques, it directs itself to potential and practicing art directors and designers and to editors who do their own designing.

It also directs itself to journalists in general, trying to build in them an appreciation for good graphic design. While these journalists may not be called upon to actually design and lay out pages, they may have the responsibility for hiring designers and approving their work. A goal of this book is to help editor and art director work together more harmoniously. Friction exists between the two on many publications: the editor suspects that art and distinctive typography detract from articles and stories; the art director thinks of the editor as a visual illiterate.

The first edition of the book noted a scarcity of material on publication design and especially magazine design, but soon afterwards several excellent books appeared on the market. One came out just before this one and, by coincidence, bore the same title. The bibliographies at the ends of the chapters list those books along with the scores of books on narrower aspects of design, such as typography and letterform, most of them published within the past ten years.

This book differs from other books on publication design and layout in that it concerns itself as much with editing as with design matters.

As a textbook, it documents its information, where possible, and tries to keep in check its author's biases. Where the author lays down rules, he tries to offer reasons. But the rules of design in the 1980s become increasingly difficult to defend as art directors experiment, apparently successfully, with exciting new arrangements and styles.

Publication Design serves as a textbook or supplemental reading for students in such courses as Publication Design and Production, Graphic Design, Graphic Arts, Typography, Magazine Editing, Newspaper Editing, Picture Editing, Book Publishing, Publishing Procedures, Business and Industrial Journalism, Public Relations, and Supervision of School Publications.

In its early chapters the book deals with publication design in general; later chapters narrow in on magazines, newspapers, books, and miscellaneous publications, including direct-mail pieces. Magazines get a little more attention than other media because the magazine look has so dominated the thinking of publication designers in recent years. But with new sections on other media, this third edition better lives up to its billing as a guide to *publication* design, not just to magazine design.

Illustrations that served well in earlier editions remain, but many new ones appear in each of the chapters.

Since the publication of the first edition in 1972, the author has conducted a monthly column on design for *IABC News* (renamed *Communication World* in 1982), a publication of the International Association of Business Communicators. An occasional section in this new edition draws from material appearing in that column. Also, as was true of the first two editions, this one in its opening chapters relies in part on some informal research conducted under a grant from the Magazine Publishers Association.

PUBLICATION
DESIGN

Attenzione, a magazine for Italian-Americans celebrated for its design, devotes two pages to its table of contents and includes on those pages a masthead (far left) and, on both sides of the listing of articles, pieces of art, large page numbers, and blurbs about major articles and features. Paul Hardy is design director.

ATTENZIONE (USPS 483-930) is published monthly by Pauluzzi Publications, Inc. 60 East 49th Street, New York, NY 10017. Subscriptions $24.50 a year; USA, $27.50, Canada; $30.00 foreign (surface mail only). Controlled circulation postage paid at Milwaukee, WI and New York, NY. POSTMASTER Send address changes to ATTENZIONE, P.O. Box 941, Farmingdale, NY 11737. Copyright © 1980 by Pauluzzi Publications. Published in the United States. All rights reserved. Reproduction in whole or in part without permission is strictly prohibited. Member, Magazine Publishers Association. ABC membership applied for.

FASHION

THE HOUSE OF MISSONI

BY GWENDA BLAIR

Question: When is a sweater more than just a sweater? Answer: When it is an ultrachic knit inspired by folk designs and produced by Ottavio and Rosita Missoni in a small factory outside Milan. When it has the Missoni name on it, a winter warmer could sell for three hundred dollars in Italy, fifty percent more abroad, or even end up in New York's Metropolitan Museum of Art. And unlike the peasant traditions which have influenced the husband and wife team, the Missoni fashion imprint shows no signs of fading. The next generation of Missonis (sons Vittorio and Luca, daughter Angela, and daughter-in-law Susanna) is already geared to carrying on the firm's unique ability to combine flair and simplicity for the style-conscious.

Reversible tweed bouclé jackets are a highlight of the new fall collection.

Rosita Missoni designs the garments and oversees the family operation.

Ottavio, known to all as "Tai," creates the fabrics.

Vittorio, the oldest of the Missoni children, is in the financial and marketing end of the business.

Susanna, Vittorio's wife, handles the company's public relations.

Luca is his father's understudy in the area of fabric design.

Angela, the younger Missoni, has recently the firm and shows in pattern design.

Full-color silhouetted figures, a couple of other smaller silhouettes, a large photo showing jacket textures, and an across-the-page blurb give this two-page opener for *Attenzione* its impact. The article settles down to a four-column-per-page format (not seen) after this opener. Missoni is a classy sweater maker of Italy. The people shown are principals in the firm—all members of the Missoni family. *Attenzione* on many pages, as here, combines a Speedball-pen-like sans serif title face with a lightweight slab serif body face.

Books produced in fifteenth-century Italy, after movable type was perfected by Johann Gutenberg in Germany, are prized today by museums and collectors as art of a high order. Bibliophiles see in these books a design and printing quality not found in latter-day publications. Their excellence is all the more remarkable when you consider that the men of incunabula had to design their own types, cut them, make their own inks and in some instances their own papers, write their own books and do their own translating of the classics, set their own type, do their own printing, and sell their own product.

Or maybe that explains the excellence. With so proprietary an interest in the product, fifteenth-century artisans gave appearance and readability all necessary attention. But when the demand for printing grew, printers found it expedient to subdivide the work. Some designed and cut types—exclusively. Others set type—exclusively. Others ran presses—exclusively. Others wrote and edited copy, while still others took care of business matters. Specialization set in, and, inevitably, quality deteriorated.

By the time periodicals took their place alongside books as products of the press, page design was all but forgotten. Nobody elected to stay with the product through its various stages to see to it that it had, overall, the beauty and readability of earlier products of the press.

Then came photography and photoengraving. As art was combined with type on the page, the need for coordination of these elements became apparent. Because art, when it was used, tended to dominate the page, the people responsible for fitting type and art together became known, first, as art editors and, later, as art directors.

No one can say who functioned as the first publication art editor or art director. One of the first in this country, certainly, was Charles Parsons of the Harper & Brothers organization (now Harper & Row), publishers of books and magazines. It was Parsons who conceived the idea of gathering together a group of illustrators and schooling them in the needs of a publishing concern, and working with other artists on the outside as need for art increased at certain times of the year. He became a director of art.

Himself an illustrator of note, Parsons joined the staff at Harper's in 1863, serving twenty-six years. He directed artists for both the book- and magazine-publishing divisions of the company. Among his staffers were Winslow Homer, Thomas Nast, Edwin A. Abbey, and W. A. Rogers. Of Parsons, Rogers wrote: "Thanks to the clear vision and good common sense of wise old Charles Parsons, every man who came to Franklin Square [where the firm had

By the turn of the century, magazines were able to reproduce both line and halftone art, but real flair in design had not yet taken hold. This page from the April 1903 issue of *The Century Magazine* was typical. The look is more that of a book than a magazine. One article ends on this right-hand page, another begins. The only art is an ending decoration and an embellished initial letter.

Here she is: The Gibson Girl of an earlier era, admired, desired, and, by a jealous few, despised. The magazine illustrator and cartoonist, Charles Dana Gibson, made her one of the nation's most known symbols. This pen and ink sketch is from the old *Life*.

offices]—and it was the Mecca of illustrators in those days—was encouraged to be true to his own ideas, to develop his own style."[1]

So great was Parson's influence on commercial art of the late nineteenth century that artists referred to his department as "The Franklin Square School." As many as eight artists worked full time. Freelancers, including Frederic Remington and Howard Pyle, took on special assignments.

By the 1880s, Parsons was able to pay freelancers an average of $75 per illustration. For some works, he paid $150 or more.

Nearly all the illustrations had to be hand engraved on wood. It was after Parsons resigned in 1889 that photoengraving became a reality and illustration—including photos—became a vital part of most magazines. *Harper's Weekly* and *Harper's Magazine* were no longer alone as vehicles for illustrations. Every publication could run them.

Visual considerations for most publications in those days centered on the nature of the art they carried. The beauty and serviceability that could be derived from skillful and imaginative combinations of art with titles and columns of type had not yet been fully explored. Books were admired more for the fine craftsmanship that went into their manufacture than for the brilliance of their design. Nor was the small page size any inducement to do more than to give proper spacing to classic typefaces and to center titles and other display faces. The first magazines, with single- or two-column pages, adopted a book look. And the newspapers' only design concern seemed to be their hunt for bolder types, the better to make headlines stand out on the page.

A major influence on all graphic designers in the 1920s and 1930s was the Bauhaus, a school that preached "form follows function." The architect Walter Gropius founded the Bauhaus at Weimar, Germany, in 1919. Young architects and artists from all over came to live and study here. The idea was to deal with materials "honestly" and to bring the arts—all arts—together to serve "the people." The school also sought to bring art and technology together. Socialism was fashionable at the time among those who taught, and the place was run as sort of a commune. Even diet was controlled.[2]

Hitler closed it down in 1933, but not before its austere, geometric, modular, highly controlled look had taken hold around the world and especially in the United States, resulting in something called "the international style." Its faculty members scattered, many to the United States, where they took up teaching and greatly affected architecture here as well as graphic design.

Gropius became head of the architecture school at Harvard; Josef Albers started a Bauhaus-like school at Black Mountain College in North Carolina, then moved to Yale; Lazlo Moholy-Nagy opened the New Bauhaus in Chicago, which became the Chicago Institute of Design; Ludwig Mies van der Rohe became dean of Architecture at the Armour Institute in Chicago, which became the Illinois Institute of Technology.

1. Quoted by Eugene Exman in *The House of Harper,* Harper & Row, Publishers, New York, 1967, p. 107.

2. See Tom Wolfe's two-part series, "From Bauhaus to Our House," *Harper's,* June and July, 1981, or the book: *From Bauhaus to Our House,* Farrar, Straus & Giroux, New York, 1981.

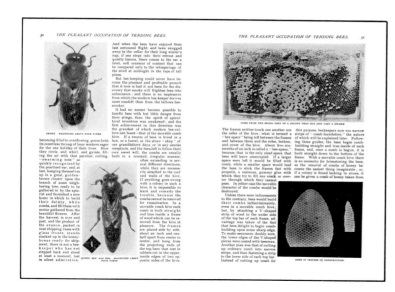

The design of magazines

The magazines which, as a group, pioneered in good design were, understandably, the fashion books—especially *Harper's Bazaar*.[3] It was in 1916, after it had been purchased by William Randolph Hearst, that the Russian-born L'Aiglon Erté, a designer for the theater, joined the staff. An illustrator in the manner of Aubrey Beardsley, Erté introduced an entirely new visual sensibility to the magazine.[4]

In 1934 another Russian-born designer, Alexey Brodovitch, became the art director, a position he held until 1958. He sought to give the magazine what *Print* magazine called "a musical feeling, a rhythm resulting from the interaction of space and time—he wanted the magazine to read like a sheet of music. He and [editor] Carmel Snow would dance around the pages spread before them on the floor, trying to pick up the rhythm."

At *Vogue* Heyworth Campbell was a force for innovative design. He served as art director from 1914 to 1928. Carmel Snow had been editor at *Vogue* before taking over as editor at *Harper's Bazaar* in 1932, no doubt bringing some of Campbell's design thinking with her.[5]

Another leader in magazine design was Dr. M. F. Agha, who, with a degree in political science, became art director of *Vanity Fair* in 1929. Allen Hurlburt, formerly director of design for Cowles Communications, has said this of Dr. Agha: "He entered areas of editorial judgment long denied to artists and created a magazine that brought typography, illustration, photography, and page de-

3. Some of what follows in this chapter and some of chapter 2 appeared in a different form in the author's *Visits with 30 Magazine Art Directors*, published by the Education Committee of the Magazine Publishers Association, New York. Copyright 1969 by the Magazine Publishers Association. Reprinted by permission.

4. See "Harper's Bazaar at 100," *Print*, September-October 1967, pp. 42–49.

5. From a letter to the author from Marcia R. Prior, instructor at Iowa State University Department of Journalism and Mass Communication, Ames, Iowa, Aug. 23, 1979.

Bernd Reuters, a German, did this perspective illustration for the July 1928 cover of *Motor* magazine. The centered logo is designed to look a little like an automobile's hood and grill, complete with headlights.

sign into a cohesion that has rarely been equalled. After exposure to the severe test of more than thirty of the fastest changing years in history, the pages of *Vanity Fair* remain surprisingly fresh and exciting."[6] Hurlburt gives much credit, too, to Editor Frank Crowninshield for his "rare discernment and good taste."

Unfortunately, *Vanity Fair* became a Depression victim; but Dr. Agha continued his association with the Condé Nast organization until 1942 as art director of *Vogue* and *House and Garden*. Many of today's top designers trained under Dr. Agha.

Brodovitch introduced to magazines the use of large blocks of white. For freshness, he used accomplished artists and photographers for kinds of work they had not tried before. At *Harper's Bazaar* he got Cartier-Bresson, Dali, Man Ray, and Richard Avedon to do fashions.

According to *Print*, Brodovitch "kept apprentices at his side much like an Old World master painter." He became famous not only as a designer but also as a photographer. He began teaching at the Philadelphia Museum in 1930, and among his students were soon-to-be magazine art directors Otto Storch, Henry Wolf, and Samuel Antupit and the photographer Irving Penn. Penn said: "All photographers are students of Brodovitch, whether they know it or not." Hurlburt adds: "This also applies to graphic designers."

"This disarming, glum, elegant, shy, incredibly tough artist made an impact on the design of this country that eludes description to this day," says a writer for *U&lc.* "Measured on the quality of his graphic performances and his contributions to the modern magazine alone, he must be ranked as the towering giant of our time. . . ." He was "the master craftsman who began it all."[7]

Gertrude Snyder in *U&lc.* said that Dr. Agha "forever altered the role of the editorial art director. . . . With innovative design, typography and layout, he shattered the restrictive style that was current." A native of Turkey, he was proud, arrogant, demanding. Nothing seemed to suit him. But he gained the respect of those who worked with him.

A colleague said of him that he was "kind to his inferiors." But "Everyone is my inferior," Dr. Agha once said, "so I'm kind to everyone."

A story Snyder tells suggests the opposite. A photographer showed his portfolio at *Vogue*. Someone brought him in to Dr. Agha.

"Where does this man work?"

"He works at Westinghouse."

"Tell him to continue to work at Westinghouse."[8]

Other trend-setters among magazine art directors in those days and later were Paul Rand, with *Apparel Arts,* and Bradbury Thompson, with *Mademoiselle* and several other magazines.

Still, the well-designed magazine was an exception. Well into the 1930s, most American magazines fitted themselves together,

6. Quoted from *Magazines: USA,* The American Institute of Graphic Arts, New York, 1965. See Cleveland Amory and Frederic Bradlee (Editors), *Vanity Fair: A Cavalcade of the 1920s and 1930s,* Viking Press, New York, 1970.

7. Jack Anson Finke, "Pro-File: Alexey Brodovitch," *U&lc.,* March 1977, p. 9. *U&lc.* beginning with this issue ran a series on famous designers and art directors.

8. Told by Gertrude Snyder, "Pro-file: Dr. M. F. Agha," *U&lc.,* December 1978, p. 5.

newspaper-style; when there was a column that didn't quite reach the bottom of the page, the editor simply threw in a filler. The job of any visually oriented person was primarily to buy illustrations, especially for the cover, and maybe to retouch photographs.

Two early-1930s books on magazine editing gave scant attention to art direction. John Bakeless in *Magazine Making* (Viking Press, New York, 1931) carried a six-page appendix on "Methods of Lay-Out." In it Bakeless discussed briefly a travel magazine that used "the daring device of running a picture across all of one page and part of another." The book itself mentioned "art editor" twice and recommended at least one such person for "a large, illustrated periodical." Bakeless said that magazines using no pictures "obviously do not require an art editor."

Lenox R. Lohr in *Magazine Publishing* (Williams & Wilkins Company, Baltimore, 1932) devoted a chapter to illustrations and another to "Mechanics of Editing" but in them he gave only six pages to Make-Up of an Issue."

One of the first non-fashion magazines to be fully designed was *Fortune,* introduced in February 1930 at a bold one dollar per copy. The designer was T. M. Cleland, who later set the format for the experimental newspaper *PM.* And *Esquire,* when it started in 1933, started right out with an art director. But he was a cartoonist, John Groth, who filled a good part of the first issue with his own cartoons.

In the 1940s Alexey Brodovitch designed a magazine that, with breathtaking beauty, showed other art directors what a well-designed magazine could be. Called *Portfolio,* it lasted three issues. That it was "ahead of its time" is probably an appropriate appraisal. In the late 1940s and early 1950s *Flair* (Louis-Marie Eude and later Herschel Bramson, art directors), although not universally admired by other art directors, encouraged format experimentation. It also was short-lived. In the early 1960s *Show,* with Henry Wolf as art director, shook up magazine design thinking. Allen Hurlburt observed: "[Wolf's] imaginative cover ideas and the precise simplicity of his pages have begun to influence a new generation of designers." *Show* soon died, too.

Stimulated by these thrusts, the well-established magazines began paying more attention to design. Hurlburt took over as *Look*'s art director in 1953 and gradually built the magazine, from a design standpoint, into one of the most admired in America. After the mid-1950s and "Togetherness," Herbert Mayes, the new editor of *McCall's,* let his art director, Otto Storch, have a free hand: what Storch did with types and pictures prompted all magazines to make themselves more exciting visually. Prodded by what Arthur Paul was doing in design with the upstart *Playboy, Esquire* redesigned itself.

Hurlburt has noted a change in the art director's function with the coming of television. Before TV, the function of the art director, in an agency or on a magazine, was simply "arranging things that were handed him." With story boards for TV, the art director provided ideas, and the copywriter filled in with words. The art director became more important. As his status improved in advertising agencies, it improved on magazines.

One of the important influences on magazine design in the 1960s in America was Push Pin Studios, New York. (A founder of Push Pin, Milton Glaser, was until 1977 design director of *New York.*) The organization was described by a magazine for the book trade as "one of the pioneering forces in developing an imaginative con-

Tadeusz Gronowski of Poland designed this busy art deco cover for the July 1928 issue of *Gebrauchsgraphik International* magazine.

The clean, orderly, and somewhat stilted Swiss Gothic look of the 1950s and 1960s continues to be popular with many magazines in the 1980s, including Soil and Water Conservation News. *For this and every spread in the magazine, the 2-inch sink and the thin horizontal lines remain the same. This spread accommodates two complete articles: one long, one short. The two heavy bars mark the articles' endings and lift out the legends about the authors. With organization this tight, it would be a good idea to add a line of copy to the second article and place the second legend parallel to the first legend. Also, the caption on the left-hand page would work better a little wider.*

temporary style that has had a major influence on the direction of current visual communications on an international scale."[9] The same magazine quoted the late Jerome Snyder, then art director of *Scientific American,* as saying that if imitation or plagiarism is any indication of flattery Push Pin "is by far the most flattered group in contemporary graphics."[10] "The growing reputation has allowed Push Pin the luxury of a healthy snobbishness in their acceptance of assignments, and potential clients have been conditioned into calling on Push Pin only when they were ready to accept the excellence of their work without too many suggestions for 'improvement,' " Henry Wolf wrote in the Foreword to *The Push Pin Style.*[11]

The individual who was most involved with the design direction taken by magazines in the 1960s and 1970s, most would say, was Herb Lubalin. Many younger designers can trace their design attitudes to his work. He was also a type designer and a typographer with an inventive flair, but he held readability to be more important than aesthetics. He designed or redesigned *Eros, Saturday Evening Post, Reader's Digest, Signature,* and *Sport,* among others. He also designed the logo for *Family Circle* and *Families.* He was editor of *U&lc.,* a magazine devoted to creative typography.

When he died in 1981, *The New Leader* devoted an obit editorial to him. He had redesigned the magazine in 1961, giving it a bold new look. He redesigned it again in 1969, to bring it up to date, making it one of the handsomest of the struggling opinion magazines. Lubalin also helped the magazine with some of its special issues and covers. *The New Leader* commented: "He worked with a speed and ease that awed his contemporaries, his left-hand scratches producing tissues that put other people's finished pieces to shame. He could make type talk and turn its thousands of faces into pictures. His own type creations married the classical to the modern with powerful clarity, extending his reputation worldwide."[12]

Also wielding influence on magazine design in the 1960s was Willie Fleckhaus, who art directed two magazines published in Europe, *Tuyonne* and *Twen.*

In the 1960s magazine design—a lot of it—was dazzling and spectacular, but it seemed *fitted on* rather than incorporated into the content. *Print* called the look "stupifying shallow." In the 1970s, magazines seemed to enter a new era: the emphasis was on content. *Communication Arts* and *Print* in 1970 both put out special issues on magazine design. Both were critical of what they had seen in the 1960s. The magazine industry, they agreed, was in a bad way because it had not adjusted to the times—not in content, not in design. Both agreed that flashy graphics often covered up for lack of solid content. Nor were the graphics of a kind to delight the eye.

The chief problems were those of slickness and sameness. *Print* said major magazines looked alike because their art directors played

9. "Louvre Holds Retrospective of Push Pin Studios' Graphics," *Publishers' Weekly,* April 13, 1970, p. 70.

10. *Ibid.,* p. 72.

11. Published by Communication Arts, Palo Alto, California, 1970.

12. "Between Issues," *The New Leader,* June 1, 1981, p. 2.

musical chairs, moving from magazine to magazine, "spreading their best ideas and perpetuating their worst mistakes." Dugald Stermer, ex-art director for *Ramparts,* was quoted as saying, "This makes magazines very inbred, almost incetuous."

Art Direction noted a "new graphics" in the early 1980s, saying it originated in this country in *Wet* in the 1970s and in Andy Warhol's *Interview.* It was inspired by Punk Rock and by a design movement at Basel, Switzerland. *Essence, New York,* and *Mademoiselle* were among magazines to pick it up. There were lots of lines and lots of dots, lots of mortises, lots of diagonals, lots of letterspacing. Designers of the old school saw it as a celebration of amateurism, with most of the standard rules of design gleefully broken.[13]

Just as the "new wave" defied design convention, it defied editorial convention by making editorial non-existent or secondary to advertising. The magazines' staffs designed much of the advertising—from specialty stores—and occasionally rejected ads that didn't meet design standards. Among these mostly-advertising magazines were *Manhattan Catalogue* (New York), *Boulevards* (San Francisco), and *Stuff* (Los Angeles). "People try to copy *Boulevards,*" art director Ross Carron said in 1980, "and art students seem to use it as a Bible. If they only knew how little time we put into it."[14]

The "new wave" subsided somewhat in the 1980s, but the fashion magazines, at least, continue to be trendy and experimental. What you see done with type and photographs in, say, *Mademoiselle,* you are not likely to see done in *Scientific American, Smithsonian,* or *Sports Illustrated.* "Fashion is concerned with style and change," says Judy Schiern Hecker, art director of *Young Miss.* It is not enough for an art director simply to go with current fashions in design. "You have to have a sense of what's in the air, a sense of what's coming. This has helped me to choose type with a special feeling."[15]

But "On the whole," said Henry Wolf in 1978, "I don't think it's a terrific time for us designers. We're lucky if there's a magazine out today which is as good as it was if it's been around for more than 10 years. If you look at *McCall's,* at *Holiday,* at *Esquire,* nothing is as good. It's all scaled down, all unified. . . . It's all very much what happened to American cars. In the 30's, they were wonderful. They generally made their own motors—Dusenberg, Pierce Arrow, Reo. Now they make one motor, and it fits the Chevrolet and Cadillac alike."[16]

Les Line, editor of *Audubon,* notes the "cookie-cutter layouts" used by many of today's magazines. Part of the problem lies with the economies today's magazines must take. "Magazines no longer have the luxury of taking a blank page, running a lettuce leaf in the corner and following that with a full page of salad," says Maxine Davidowitz, art director of *Redbook.* "Readers have less time. They want information, not just fluff."[17]

13. "The New Graphics," *Art Direction,* May 1980, p. 61.

14. *Ibid.,* p. 64.

15. Quoted by Karen Jacobson, *Art Direction,* May 1981, p. 69.

16. Quoted by Gertrude Snyder, "Pro-File: Henry Wolf," *U&lc.,* September 1978, p. 8.

17. "Many Magazines Today Look Alike, Designer, Editor Claim" *Folio,* April 1980, p. 24.

By the 1980s the fashion magazines, once the pacemakers in graphic design, had given in to the "new wave" look, a look demonstrated by these rough sketches—thumbnails—inspired (if that's the word) by pages in *Glamour, Vogue,* and *Mademoiselle.* Tilts, overlaps and mortises, dotted lines and bars, torn and odd-shaped color and tint blocks, mismatched typefaces, and general visual clutter seemed to be the order of the month.

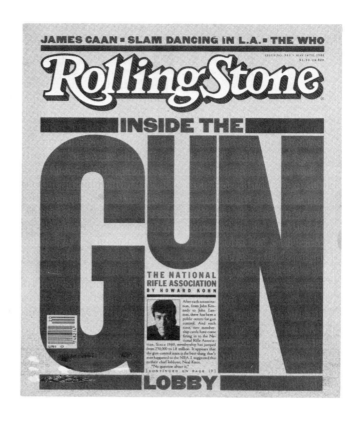

Phil Douglis, photographer and columnist, conducts one of his popular photography and design seminars for company magazine editors. Chris Craft took this bird's-eye-view shot of Douglis (left) showing editors how a specific photograph fits into a layout.

The hope of the 1980s probably lies with specialized publications. The editors of specialized magazines, realizing that their readers are accustomed to exciting visuals from sources other than magazines, attempt to make their magazines just as exciting to look at as the new films, the new products, the new paintings. These editors don't have to buck tradition. They serve homogeneous audiences. They have less to lose.

One specialized magazine that proved to be a trend setter was *Psychology Today.* In an early issue (January 1968) Nicholas H. Charney, editor and publisher, credited the magazine's "lively new look in graphic design" to its then art director, Donald K. Wright. "We think he was born with that bemused and faraway look. . . . He has an incredible mental file of graphic oddities. . . . And he is an unbudgeable perfectionist in seeking the precise scene to illustrate every article." By the time the magazine was eight issues old, the art director had (1) tranquilized rabbits to make them better models for the photographer, (2) traveled to Mexico to find some chessmen for special faces, (3) packed in to the desert, climbed mountains, traveled 100 miles along the railroad tracks "to find the necessary open land for just one photograph."

One of the most exciting groups of magazines to watch are the company magazines—sometimes called "house organs." Some of the very best graphic design is found in this group—and some of the very worst. In one respect, these magazines are an art director's dream. They carry no advertising around which editorial matter must wrap. The design theme can run through without interruption. That it does not do so in many company magazines can be laid to the fact that their budgets preclude hiring an art direc-

INSIDE THE GUN LOBBY

THE NATIONAL RIFLE ASSOCIATION
BY HOWARD KOHN

[CONTINUED FROM FRONT COVER]

"If it wasn't for you guys in the liberal press, the NRA would've closed up shop a long time ago. You guys like to have a big, bad villain. So presto, you make the NRA into a big, bad villain. To me, it isn't a villain at all. It's a paper tiger."
—an aide to Senator Edward M. Kennedy

Huey P. Long, 1935

From the Civil War statue at Scott Circle in Washington D.C. you can see the rise of gray-blue marble and tinted glass. The chrome calligraphy across its face reads THE NATIONAL RIFLE ASSOCIATION. In the basement there are soundproof target ranges. On the ground floor is a museum open to the public. The exhibits are kept under glass. Teddy Roosevelt's Winchester, a matched pair of percussion pistols, Erle Stanley Gardner's single-action Colt — they are masterpieces from history, objects of love.

Upstairs are the computers. Bank upon bank of computers. From them spit Mailgrams by the thousands, names and addresses peering urgently from windowed envelopes, and inside a plea from Neal Knox: Write! Write your congressman. Tell him you are watching. Don't let him screw around with your *right to bear arms!*

On a bright March morning, I signed the logbook for the security guard and took an elevator up to the seventh floor. Neal Knox waved me into his ample office — the kind a chairman of the board would have—but somehow he didn't look like he belonged there. He looked rumpled, rough-edged, the way old newspapermen sometimes do. "I gave some of the best years of my life to newspapers," he said. He had been the founding editor of *Gun Week* and the editor and publisher of two gun magazines.

"Sit down." His face was relaxed, a little puffy at the edges. Knox is an expert marksman, a two-time winner of national bench-rest rifle championships. While Knox is the man most responsible for modernizing the NRA, changing it from an association of sporting shooters into an often effective political weapon, he also remembers growing up in a time when the average boy learned how to whittle, how to play ball and how to fire a gun. In the early days of the organization, the typical NRA member lived far from the urban combat zones. He was a hunter. He shot rifles and shotguns. The new NRA member is likely to be a terrified city man with a pistol in a holster slung over his bedpost at night. He often joins to help Neal Knox scare the hell out of a few politicians.

In 1975, the NRA's board of directors created a lobbying arm, the Institute for

JAY MERRITT *provided additional research and reporting for this article.*

ROLLING STONE, MAY 14, 1981 : 19

tor; they remain undesigned. And many others are designed in outside shops, inhibiting thorough integration of design and editorial matter.

Of all magazine groups, the trade journals—or "businesspapers" as they are sometimes called—are probably the least design conscious. Excepting those going to physicians, architects, and similar professional groups, these magazines—especially the smaller ones—are "laid out" by editors rather than designed by art directors. Exceptions include McGraw-Hill's *Fleet Owner*.

"For many years publishers have used the words 'trade journals' as an excuse for poor taste and bad design," observes Bud Clarke, art editor of *Fleet Owner*. "The art editor or art director

Forestalk Resource Magazine,
published by the British Columbia
Ministry of Forests, uses a full-
color, full-bleed photograph for
an opening spread (above),
surrounding it with an interior
box and putting the title, byline,
and blurb at the upper right, all in
reverse. The spread below,
several pages into the article,
uses thin-line boxes again and a
heavy bar (in blue) above an
initial letter to match the one
over the title in the opening
spread. The designer arranges
the photos to make the boat
carry the eye to the smaller
ones. Ken Seabrook is art
director.

(Opposite page)
**To save space, *Harper's*, before
redesign in 1982, pushed small
art, usually in line, to outside
edges where margin space was
generous. You might think that
would have limited creativity. It
didn't. This series of right-hand
pages for Lewis H. Lapham's
article, ''Guilding the News,''
shows one arrangement that was
used, with blurb and art
clustered. The art, by Paul
Richer, cleverly emphasizes what
the blurbs say. Sheila Wolfe was
art director. (Copyright © 1981
by *Harper's*. Reprinted by
permission.)**

of these publications was either using the position as a stepping
stone to consumer books or semi-retirement. And in many cases
the editor wore two hats. . . . [The position of] art director was
an unnecessary expense.

"Now, however, times are changing. Our readers have more demands placed upon their 'free' time, i.e., TV. The reading they do
must be selective, interesting, and suited to their particular way
of life.

"This basically is why there is a small, but rapidly growing interest in design for the specialized reader. Many designers and art
directors today feel that trade publications are a rewarding end in
themselves rather than the means. Budgets and, of course, salaries
are growing along with this interest, and a new era of good taste
and design is emerging."[18]

18. Letter to the author from Bud Clarke, Aug. 17, 1970.

The design of newspapers

One man who has helped give newspapers better design is Edmund C. Arnold, former head of the graphic arts department of Syracuse University's School of Journalism now teaching at Virginia Commonwealth University. He has redesigned a number of major newspapers and served as consultant to the Mergenthaler Linotype Corporation. Carrying on the traditions established by John Allen and Albert Sutton in the 1930s and 1940s, Professor Arnold in his frequent lectures to conventions of newspapermen and in his numberless articles and books continues to pound home his admirable dicta: wider columns, no column rules, more white space, all-lowercase headlines. Still, with Arnold and other more recent designers, consultants, and educators working with editors in a period of rapidly changing typesetting and printing technology, newspapers continue to hold onto many of their old practices. Publisher Gardner Cowles put his finger on the problem a few years ago at a meeting of the William Allen White Foundation at the University of Kansas. "A good newspaper needs a good art director. When I say this, most editors don't know what I am talking about."

He explained that papers are laid out or made up by editors or printers with no art background or training. Other media would not think of assigning so important a task to people not equipped for it.

"On successful magazines, the art director ranks right below the top editor in importance and authority. He has a strong voice in helping decide how a story idea is to be developed. He suggests ways to give it maximum visual impact. He knows how to blend type and photographs so that each helps the other. His responsibility is to make each page come alive and intrigue the reader. Newspapers need this kind of talent. Too few have it."

Among papers that have employed art directors are the Chicago *Tribune*, New York *Times*, Providence *Journal* and *Bulletin*, Miami *Herald*, *Newsday* (Long Island), and *Today* (Cocoa, Fla.). *The Bulletin* of the American Society of Newspaper Editors in the early 1970s ran a report on the duties of art directors and concluded that any newspaper with a circulation of more than 50,000 needs the services of one. *The Bulletin* predicted that the idea of art directors for newspapers would spread.

But the concensus was that, by and large, newspapers still had a long way to go. Newspapers look as though they are appealing to readers 30 or 40 years ago, observed designer Peter Palazzo. "We're living in an age of audio-visually educated readers, and competing with much brighter visual products," said Thomas Winship, editor of the Boston *Globe*. "Too many papers look dull in comparison."[19]

When design help comes to newspapers it comes often these days from outside the fraternity. It comes from graphic designers with magazine or advertising agency experience who are fast enough and flexible enough to deal with multiple daily deadlines and late-breaking news and, more important, who are capable of making editorial as well as art and design decisions. It comes from graphic designers who are verbally as well as visually literate—people like Peter Palazzo, of whom more is mentioned in a later chapter.

19. "The Great Paper Chase," *Newsweek*, May 31, 1976, p. 73.

A news day like this, with all its memorable photographs, cries for dramatic treatment, and it gets it on a St. Cloud *Daily Times* front page. A severely horizontal photograph at the top contrasts with a larger, vertical photograph below, which contrasts with a small mug shot at the left. Two other small photographs complete the art on the page. The two heavy horizontal bars are in color. And some of the color shows up, too, in the insignia above "TUESDAY."

Evidence of growing interest in design among newspaper people can be seen in the founding in 1979 of the Society of Newspaper Designers. By 1981 the society listed 900 members. It publishes the *Journal of Newspaper Design.* Roger Fidler of the Knight-Ridder Newspapers edits another publication, *Newspaper Design Notebook.* The American Press Institute at Reston, Virginia, holds frequent seminars on newspaper design.

The design of miscellaneous publications

Regularly issued publications like magazines and newspapers account for only part of the money spent for printing and only part of the activities of editors, writers, designers, and artists. This book will deal also with a vast print medium sub-culture consisting of one-shots, infrequently issued publications, direct-mail pieces, and shoe-string operations.

The term "miscellaneous publications" hardly describes this

array of printed pieces, but no other term functions any better. Every conceivable format is involved; and few persons associated with print media escape producing such pieces. Nobody escapes reading them. Even regularly issued publications produce miscellaneous publications—to increase their audiences, to impress advertisers, to communicate with their employees, to comply with the law.

They range from elaborate printed pieces of cloth, leather, and materials other than paper to scruffy sheets of newsprint that are barely decipherable. They cost their sponsors anywhere from a penny or two to several dollars a unit. It is impossible to estimate the total funds going into these pieces, but the amount, if it could be calculated, would be staggering.

Every one of these pieces has to be designed.

Many of them are designed by people who don't know what they are doing. Others get the attention of the most accomplished designers.

Among them are some of the most beautiful and readable printed pieces ever produced. Some designers would rather work with miscellaneous publications than with periodicals because each represents a brand new challenge.

Rather than work with an established page size and an already contracted for paper stock, the designer often is free to set the size, pick the stock, and make any number of production decisions not usually made by the magazine or newspaper designer, or even the advertising designer.

Some of what falls into the miscellaneous-publications category qualifies as advertising, for it may be meant to sell a product, service, or idea of the sponsor. Such pieces can be called "direct advertising" or "direct-mail advertising." Other miscellaneous publications serve public relations purposes: improving employee morale, for instance, or impressing stockholders. If published by a non-profit organization, the piece may solicit funds or provide advice.

The most handsome of the miscellaneous publications originate in advertising agencies or public relations firms or departments. The art directors there may do the designing, or it may come from independent art studios or freelancers.

Too many miscellaneous publications—especially folders—originate with public officials or business executives and their secretaries, with no help from professional designers.

Both sides of a three-fold, eight-panel folder show how handling of photographs can bring unity to a direct-mail piece. The chopped corner look of the display type used for the title echoes the look of the heavy photo outlines. This is a two-color (black and brown) folder, with a wood texture built into the paper. Western Forestry Center is a forestry and forest industry museum.

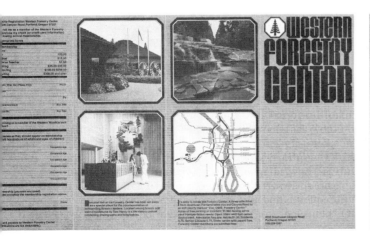

Emergence of publication design **13**

Literary Classics of the United States, New York, is republishing a series of important books by early American writers, all in a handsome, readable, standard format (5″ × 8 1/8″) worked out by Bruce Campell. This spread comes from the Herman Melville volume (1982). Good book design often asks only for careful choice of type, usually of modest size, and subtle and consistent spacing, with maybe a thin rule used here and there. Illustrations often are not necessary; in fact they could intrude.

The design of books

Although good design was very much a part of early books, it was forgotten as books became more readily available to the masses. Mechanical typesetting equipment and a great variety of new—and mostly vulgar—typefaces in the nineteenth century were partly to blame. Near the turn of the century, one man in England, William Morris, fighting the trend, revived the earlier roman types and brought hand craftsmanship back into vogue. But only a few books were affected. W. A. Dwiggins in 1920 observed that "All books of the present day are badly made. . . . The book publishing industry has depraved the taste of the public."

But design was returning to books. In England, people like Eric Gill, and in America, people like Daniel Berkeley Updike, Bruce Rogers, Will Bradley, Merle Armitage, and Thomas Maitland Cleland restored bookmaking to the high art it once had been. Dwiggins himself became a design consultant to Alfred A. Knopf, a publisher who then and now produces some of America's finest books, from the standpoint both of content and design. Adrian Wilson calls Knopf "perhaps the greatest influence on the making of books in America after World War I." From 1926 to 1956 Dwiggins designed an average of ten books a year for the publisher. "His salty typography and ornament were additional hallmarks of the Knopf firm, the assurance of an inviting page and pleasurable reading."[20] Others who designed for Knopf were Warren Chappell, Herbert Bayer, Rudolf Ruzicka, and George Salter.

These designers combined classic roman faces with appropriate decorative borders. Meanwhile in Germany the Bauhaus developed its revolutionary concept in graphic design. The Bauhaus look, applied to books, had a beauty that seemed particularly appropriate to the times.

20. Adrian Wilson, *The Design of Books,* Reinhold Publishing Corporation, New York, 1967, p. 23.

Still, to most publishers of popular books, design was not much of a consideration. In more expensive books, design played a role, but often it looked as if it were an afterthought, something tacked on just before the book went to press. For many books, no one designer took charge. "If the carpenter still determined our architecture, what would our buildings be like?" asked the book designer Ralph E. Eckerstrom.

With the coming of television, with increased competition from other media, with a growing appreciation of visual beauty even among the less sophisticated book buyers, this changed. Textbooks, especially, took on a more exciting look both on the covers and inside. One reason textbook publishers were willing to devote extra effort to design was that mass adoptions of these books were often dependent on their appearance. Furthermore, the average textbook enjoyed greater total sales than the average tradebook, which meant that more could be spent in anticipation of sales.

Some of the best design was found in the product of the university presses. Feeling less pressure than commercial publishers felt to show a profit, they could afford to devote a larger percentage of their budgets to design and printing.

Later chapters will concentrate on each of the publication categories—magazines, newspapers, miscellaneous publications, and books; but the next few chapters will deal with more general design matters. First a chapter examining the role of the art director on a publication.

Suggested further reading

Barthes, Roland, *Erté,* Franco Maria Ricci, Publisher, Parma, Italy, 1972.

Beisele, Igildo G., *Graphic Design Education,* Hastings House, Publishers, New York, 1981.

Bojko, Szymon, *New Graphic Design in Revolutionary Russia,* Praeger Publishers, New York, 1972. (Examples from the 1920s and 1930s.)

Chappell, Warren, *A Short History of the Printed Word,* Alfred A. Knopf, Inc., New York, 1970.

Ferebee, Ann, *A History of Design,* Van Nostrand Reinhold Company, New York, 1970. (Covers Victorian, Art Nouveau, and Modern styles.)

Hamilton, Edward A., *Graphic Design for the Computer Age: Visual Communication for All Media,* Van Nostrand Reinhold Company, New York, 1970. (By the art director of Time-Life Books.)

Meyer, Susan E., *America's Great Illustrators,* Harry N. Abrams, New York, 1978.

Perlman, Bennard B., *F. R. Gruger and His Circle: The Golden Age of American Illustration,* Van Nostrand Reinhold, New York, 1978.

Prohaska, Ray, *A Basic Course in Design,* Van Nostrand Reinhold, New York, 1980.

Reed, Walt, ed., *The Illustrator in America, 1900–1960s,* Reinhold Publishing Corporation, New York, 1967.

Spencer, Charles, *Erté,* Clarkson N. Potter, Inc., New York, 1970.

Thiel, Philip, *Visual Awareness and Design,* University of Washington Press, Seattle, Wash., 1981.

Yorke, Malcolm, *Eric Gill: Man of Flesh and Spirit,* Universe Books, New York, 1982.

The Push Pin Style, Communication Arts Magazine, Palo Alto, California, 1970.

Art Direction, New York. (Monthly.)

Communication Arts, Palo Alto, California. (Bi-monthly.)

Print, Washington, D.C. (Bi-monthly.)

Mary Lynn Blasutta, who studied with Milton Glaser in New York, nicely imitates the style of a colleague of Glaser's, Seymour Chwast, in executing this cover for *The Plain Dealer Magazine.* The butterflies coming from the stomach of the man tell you that, indeed, the poor fellow *is* "Scared Speechless." The cover and blurb refer to an article inside on "Speechmaking: How the Veterans Do It." Greg Paul is art director for this magazine published by the Cleveland *Plain Dealer.*

As art directors have moved up on publication mastheads—on some magazines to a spot just below that of the editor—they have become vaguely dissatisfied with their titles. No one has yet come up with a title that fully describes the art director's several functions: to buy and edit illustrations and photographs, choose typefaces, make production decisions, and design and lay out the publication. Titles in use include *art editor, designer, design editor, design director, design consultant, type director, production editor, graphics editor, picture editor. Art director* remains the most common title.

But *art director* does not connote a concern with type and design. *Art editor,* the preferred title of the 1930s and 1940s, is worse: it brings to mind a person who runs a section of the publication devoted to a discussion of painting and others of the fine arts. The old terms no longer seem adequate, especially now that some art directors are making editorial and management decisions.

Perhaps a publication should have two chief editors: a *verbal editor* and a *visual editor.* Maybe *editorial director* and *design director,* used on some magazines, represent the best combination of titles.

If a publication is large enough, its art director (or AD) is more an executive than a person who does the actual design work. A designer, working under the art director, designs and lays out the publication.

Samuel Antupit, once art director at *Esquire* and now director of art and design for Henry N. Abrams Inc., the book publisher, drew this distinction between a designer and an art director: "An art director, to distinguish him from a designer, must concern himself with converting the verbal into the visual by exploring and controlling the use of photography, drawing, painting, and typography within a magazine. By developing these elements he becomes a visual editor, interpreting and expressing the message of the magazine in visual terms. A designer is an arranger. He makes beautiful (if he's good) layouts which incorporate these elements. A designer's ultimate criteria, unfortunately, are the looks, not the meaning. A good art director may intentionally give the editor an ugly page if it best represents and expresses the material."[1]

Working with the art director or designer may be a pasteup artist, who puts type and art into final place for the printer. On many publications, the art director, designer, and pasteup artist are rolled into one person, who usually takes the "art director"

---

1. Samuel N. Antupit, "Laid Out and Laid Waste," *The Antioch Review,* Spring 1969, p. 59.

Art director Greg Paul picks a full-color photograph with a head-on goalpost for a two-page opener for *The Plain Dealer Magazine,* and puts his article title and beginning paragraphs smack-dab between the posts, along with a photo of the subject of the article: Brian Sipe, the Cleveland Browns' quarterback.

title. This book will use "art director" and "designer" interchangeably.

Some art directors are flirting with the term "communicator." "I put design way down the list of what I do," says Greg Paul, design director of *The Plain Dealer Magazine,* published by the Cleveland *Plain Dealer,* a 487,000-circulation newspaper. "I use design, but that's just a tool. I'm really interested in communicating with people."[2]

Assigning a job to an illustrator or photographer, Paul tries to allow a great deal of freedom. As a director of a weekly publication, he handles many features needing illustrations, and he doesn't have a lot of time. Relying only on his own creativity every week, he would soon run dry. Paul looks upon his freelance artists as collaborators.

He feels he can be a little experimental on a weekly because a weekly doesn't have the long life of a monthly. If he makes a mistake once in awhile, it isn't so serious. Paul spent some time as art director of a monthly, *Ohio* Magazine, between stints at the *Plain*

2. Jean A. Coyne, "Greg Paul," *Communication Arts,* May/June 1981, p. 16.

A big initial for the blurb at the top left, a heavy across-two-pages horizontal bar, and a mostly black photograph give this spread unusual strength and mood. It's a continuation from a previous page. Note the careful placement of the interior intitial letter, to the right of the man's eyes. Greg Paul art directed for *The Plain Dealer Magazine.*

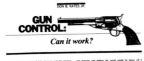

Thick horizontal lines and thin ones work together with repetitious art here to create a highly organized but pleasant motif for an article in *National Review* on gun control. Note the "no guns" sign with bullet holes in it. James W. O'Bryan is art director.

Dealer. Working on a newspaper magazine has its drawbacks: poor printing quality and paper, no binding, poor page trims, fast deadlines—but it has its rewards, too. His work has drawn national attention. And he has the satisfaction of doing a good job within the limitations.

Art directors are moving into areas that involve more than visual sensibility. They are interested in bringing *all* the senses into play—not just the sense of sight. The *feel* of the paper, for instance, is part of it. So are smells. A magazine—or a book for children—may want to make use of encapsulated fragrances.

The big-name clothing designers are not part of our study, but it is interesting to note that many of them have branched out into the perfume business—or at least lent their names to various fragrances. An AP writer noted that "Perfume is not only profitable; it doesn't have to be redesigned each season."[3] One designer has put his name on a brand of chocolates.

One for every publication

Ideally, every publication should have an art director. An art director not employed full time can be employed part time. An art director not part of the publication's own staff can be a freelancer or a designer attached to a design studio.

James W. O'Bryan, art director of *National Review,* runs a design studio in the building and treats the magazine as one client, although a very special one.

William Delorme handled *Los Angeles* from his studio miles away from the magazine's editorial offices. The magazine took 70 percent of his "working" time. He spent the other 30 percent on other graphic design assignments and on fine arts painting. "I put 'working' in quotes . . . because at least three weeks out of the month my time is my own. . . . The magazine work can be done at home in the evenings or on weekends. One week out of the month is practically round-the-clock labor on the magazine in order to meet printing deadlines." He visited the magazine for editorial conferences and to present his rough ideas and finished layouts. He saw photographers and illustrators in his studio.

Many company magazines are designed in this way, if not by studio designers, then by advertising agency art directors. But what about the small magazine that can't afford this help? And what if the editor doesn't want to—or can't—do his own designing?

Samuel Antupit, when he was with *Esquire,* said that if a magazine cannot afford an art director, it cannot afford to publish. Bernard Quint, then with *Life,* was less acrimonious. He suggested that an imaginative printer can do a lot for a magazine. Perhaps more than other magazines, the small magazine should look for such a printer and pay a little more for printing, if necessary. Quint felt that too many small publications are printed by printers who cut too many corners, making already dull periodicals even duller.

If a magazine cannot afford an art director, it should hire a designer temporarily to set a simple, standard format that an editor can follow. At the least, an editor without design expertise or without an art director should avoid oddball typography, tricks with photographs, and complicated layouts. Some of the best-designed magazines are the simplest.

3. AP dispatch, Eugene *Register-Guard,* May 3, 1978, p. 5D.

The art director's background

Schools do not offer adequate training programs for magazine and newspaper art directors and designers of books. The art schools—the commercial schools—are mostly advertising-oriented. The fine arts schools seem mostly interested in developing painters. The journalism schools—many of them—still think in terms of routine newspaper makeup.

Thus art directors come to magazines by circuitous routes. In the early history of magazine art direction, when the job involved primarily the purchasing of art work, they came largely from the ranks of illustrators. Even when type direction became a more important part of the job, the illustrator's background served an art director well. A good illustrator is as interested in the design of a painting as in the draftsmanship. The feel for design can be transferred from the canvas board to the printed page.

But today art directors increasingly come to magazines with backgrounds other than in illustration. They come with a more thorough knowledge of typography than their predecessors. Many neither draw nor paint. A few feel that a background in illustration would prejudice them in their art buying.

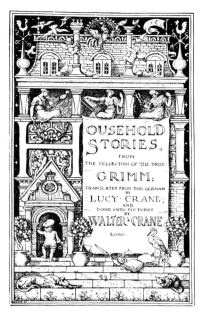

In every age designers have played with type to make illustrative art of it. In this example, from the year 1886, Walter Crane takes the first letter of the book title he is working with and makes it a unit in his drawing of a house.

John Whorrall, illustrator and art director for the *California Dental Association Journal*, uses the technique of Vincent Van Gogh to imitate a famous self-portrait, but with a slight change. Van Gogh is carrying dental tools on his pallet. The full-cover painting was used both on the cover and as a full page inside to illustrate an article by Woody Allen: "If the Impressionists Had Been Dentists," taken from the book, *Without Feathers.* From one of the "letters" to Theo: ". . . I asked Cezanne if he would share an office with me, but he is old and infirm and unable to hold the instruments and they must be tied to his wrists but then he lacks accuracy and once inside a mouth, he knocks out more teeth than he saves. What to do?"

The publication art director **19**

The industrial revolution brought the machine to typography and design, and pages began to look less decorative and more sterile. Eduard Bendemann in Germany was one designer who kept romanticism alive on pages he controlled. He designed this one in 1840. Observe how he has taken the basic design of his text or blackletter type (known as Old English) and applied it to the art and border elements on the page. This is a beautifully unified page. The decorative initial M, which juts up above the first line of body copy rather than down into the paragraph, is drawn in outline form to match the heading in the box under the figures.

Harris Lewine, an art director at Harcourt Brace Jovanovich, the book publisher, got into the business originally with a record company. He had no art background and certainly no ability to draw. ". . . I'm not [even] really a designer," he says. "At my best I function as a ringmaster. I'm not about to save the world for the sake of design." He gets his kicks as an art director "from competing—not with other ADs but, strange to say, with a [Milton] Glaser or a [Seymour] Chwast or whatever. How much of my idea do they use? . . . It's a matter of helping, pointing . . . [these illustrators and designers] in the right direction."[4]

On the other hand, Jean-Claud Suares of *New York* magazine illustrates as well as art directs. Once a week he does cartoon-like drawings for the op-ed page of the New York *Times*. He has illustrated (and designed) dozens of books as well, including a recent edition of *The Devil's Dictionary* by Ambrose Bierce. As an illustrator, Suares believes in a multiplicity of styles, even for a single assignment. *The Devil's Dictionary* shows his versatility. He started drawing at an early age, then stopped at 12 because "I didn't have the discipline," and later became an art director at the New York *Times*. He rediscovered drawing. "You know, art direction is working with other people's ornaments, and drawing is more yourself."[5]

Magazine art directors tend to come from the ranks of advertising agency art directors. They move into magazine work effortlessly. This is surprising when you consider the unlikelihood of an advertising copywriter moving into a magazine editorial slot.

On small magazines, art directors may even find themselves assigned the job of designing ads for small firms who don't have their ads prepared by or placed through advertising agencies.

Beyond page layout

Magazine art directors, like other journalists, have taken sides in the struggle for social, economic, and political changes. The art director for *National Review*, James W. O'Bryan, worked free at first because he shared the philosophy of the *Review's* conservative publisher, William F. Buckley, Jr. Dugald Stermer played the important role he did on *Ramparts* (years before he became art director of *Oceans*) because he believed in the leftist causes of that magazine. For the cover of one of its issues—in 1967—Stermer arranged for a photograph of four hands holding up burning draft cards. One of the hands was Stermer's. "If you're looking for an editorial in the usual place this month," said the magazine, "forget it. It's on the cover." The partners at Hess and/or Antupit, besides designing magazines and advertising and corporate pieces, handled a number of causes gratis or for low fees.

One thing becomes clear as you talk to art directors: they no longer are content merely to lay out pages. They argue—and the logic here is inescapable—that for a publication to be effective both verbally and visually, its art director must be involved in the planning as well as the production stages. Art directors on some of the

4. Kurt Wilner, "View from Above—Harris Lewine," *Art Direction,* November 1978, p. 69.

5. Kurt Wilner, "Too much Isn't Enough; J. C. Suares," *Art Direction,* May 1979, p. 84.

magazines, major and minor, regard themselves as operating on the same level as their editors. Some art directors report that if they didn't have a say about the policy their magazines adopt and the articles and stories their magazines accept, they would resign.

Richard Gangel, as art director of *Sports Illustrated,* was part of a triumvirate which decided policy. He saw his role as primarily journalistic. Dugald Stermer, when he was art director of *Ramparts,* said he wouldn't be content to be "just an art director." He estimated that 80 percent of his time on the magazine was spent on editorial matters, including fund raising. Kenneth Stuart, as art editor of *Reader's Digest,* checked articles before they were digested and suggested that certain sections be left in because they could be illustrated. Samuel Antupit on *Esquire* took an active role in accepting or rejecting manuscripts for publication.

Of course, someone has to have the final say, and that someone must be the editor. When Michael Parrish resigned in 1975 as editor of the weekly *City Magazine* of San Francisco, the San Francisco *Sunday Examiner and Chronicle* quoted a pleased art director Mike Salisbury as saying, "It's a really beautiful thing. We are all taking pictures, writing articles, and contributing in various ways. We don't have the traditional editorial hierarchy anymore." *City Magazine* didn't last long.

Not Just Jazz, a tabloid devoted to the artist, "whatever his chosen form," gives a page over to an interview with Tom Carnase, graphic designer known especially for his logos and his imaginative use of typography. Carnase is president of World Typeface Center, Inc., New York. (More *Not Just Jazz* examples later.)

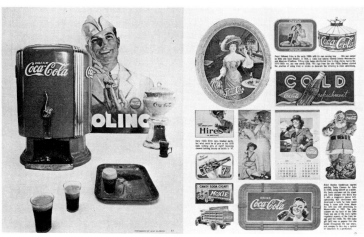

The Los Angeles *Times* once published a Sunday magazine called *West. West's* art director, Mike Salisbury, flew from Los Angeles to Atlanta to dig up the art for this article on Coca-Cola and its advertising gimmicks. "The signs, bottles, matchbooks, and trays—some of which are now collectors' items—are as American as . . . well . . . Coke itself," says the blurb. (The article is copyrighted by Lawrence Dietz. Used by permission.)

The publication art director **21**

Peggy Causgrove:
RESTORING LIFE TO A
CAROUSEL

"I was absolutely fascinated from the very first. Now I guess I'm hooked," said Peggy Causgrove, senior proof operator, Portland.

The source of Peggy's fascination is a menagerie of hand-carved, wooden animals. There are horses, camels, giraffes, an elephant, a dog, a fantastic dragon, and many more.

Along with her husband, Terry, and more than 50 other volunteers, Peggy is helping restore life and magic to an authentic, old carousel.

"Terry heard about the carousel at one of his monthly woodcarving association meetings. Duane Perron, the owner of the carousel, was there talking about it and asking for woodcarvers to help with the restoration," said Peggy.

Peggy went to the first meeting of the restoration group with Terry and said she fell in love with the whole idea right then.

"At the same time, I was also afraid to get involved because I have no talent. I don't carve or tolepaint. I hadn't even refinished an old piece of furniture before. And some of the animals are very valuable," she said.

But she did get involved and since May, 1980, Peggy has been working on one animal she selected that first evening — a simply-carved horse she

Peggy Causgrove and Angel.

calls "Angel." One or two nights a week, Peggy spends several hours in an old warehouse scraping, chipping, puttying and sanding her horse.

"Restoring these animals takes a lot of time and patience. Some of them are very elaborately carved and have jewels and real horse hair tails. We use everything down to toothpicks to clean the old paint off the wood. Some of the animals have had as many as 50 coats of paint," she said.

After the paint is carefully removed with liquid sander, and a photo history of the process is taken, the wood is puttied and broken pieces repaired. Then the bare wood is sanded and several coats of white basecoat applied.

"It took me about six weeks to sand Angel to the point where I could put on the first basecoat. Now I have three coats on and am ready to apply the final paint," Peggy said.

Supplies and tools for the restoration project are supplied by donors and Perron, who plans to refinish the animals as closely as possible to the original color and materials.

All of the animals represent the finest carvings of Charles I. D. Looff, a Dutch furniture maker and carver who worked in the U.S. at the turn of the century. The carousel is expected to be completed September, 1982, at which time it will be installed at the Willamette Center, downtown Portland.

When the time comes to part with Angel, Peggy said it will be hard, but she is anxious for "the day they turn it on. It's going to be beautiful."

"You can't believe how attached we've all gotten to these animals. I guess I'll never part with Angel entirely, there will always be that personal feeling," Peggy said.

Ordinarily, you design magazines in two-page units, looking for ways of uniting left pages with right pages. But when you have two facing single-page, unrelated articles, as art director Jeff Dayne has here in *FNB Statement,* you make the pages take on entirely different looks so the reader can easily separate them. The left page uses a center-everything approach and puts vertical lines at the left and right edges of the article. The right page features a title and some line art at the end rather than at the beginning of the article, but an initial letter gets the reader started at the right place. Chris Normandid is editor of this magazine published by the First National Bank of Oregon, now part of the First Interstate Bank.

Life with the editor

It is understandable that the relationship between the editor and the art director is sometimes strained. The one is word-oriented, the other visual-oriented, and the two orientations are not necessarily compatible. The editor may actually consider display typography and pictures intrusions on the text. Or the editor may expect the impossible of the art director, asking that a particular story and set of photos be fitted in too tight a space. The art director, on the other hand, may be more interested in showing tricks with type than in making the magazine readable. Or the art director may resort to the tired ways of laying out pages while the editor tries to move the magazine in some new direction.

Ideally, the editor and the art director should work as equal or near-equal members of a team, with the art director not only designing the magazine but also helping to make the decisions on editorial policy and content.

Art directors seem unimpressed by, if not hostile to, editors who have design backgrounds. Samuel Antupit thinks such editors, because their knowledge of design is likely to be superficial, are harder to work with than editors who know nothing about design and admit it. Editors who know design know only design clichés, he says.

Working with photographers and illustrators

Were you to become an art director or play at the role, you'd find yourself working part of the time as an art broker. It would be up to you to find the right illustrator or photographer for every cover, article, and story. Working for a magazine or book publisher, you'd deal mostly with talent outside the organization. This means you'd look at lots of portfolios put together by hopeful graduates of art schools. Perhaps you'd deal with artists' representatives. Working for a newspaper you'd probably deal with staff artists and photographers.

Some artists and photographers need a lot of direction. Others are more imaginative. You'll soon learn which freelancers need help, which ones should be left to their own devices. You will also learn that freelancers who perform well on certain kinds of assignments fail miserably on others. Your filing system will note strengths and weaknesses among your freelance contributors.

You will ask your photographers to give you full prints from their negatives so that you can, if necessary, do some cropping.

Mike Salisbury, when he was art director of *West*, late Sunday magazine of the Los Angeles *Times*, thought photos were easy to crop, retouch, or otherwise edit and often exercised his right to do

12

so. But he thought that illustrations shouldn't be changed. Nor did he request an illustrator to make changes after submitting the work.

If the illustrator is sufficiently dependable, the art director does not even ask to see roughs first. Frank Kilker, former art editor of *The Saturday Evening Post,* told the story of his acceptance of an illustration from a regular contributor, painted to fit a large area set aside for it in one of the layouts. But clearly, the illustration was not up to that artist's standard. Rather than throw it out, Kilker revamped the layout to make the illustration occupy a smaller space in the spread.

Assigning a job to an illustrator, you often specify a size and shape to fit an already existing layout. Seldom does the illustrator play a role in the selection of the typeface for the story title or in the placement of the title and body type on the page with the illustration. But of course art directors work differently with each of the various illustrators. An illustrator like Al Parker might well design the page or pages on which his illustration appears and incorporate the title into his painting.

Working with writers

When freelance writers submit articles for publication they often submit photographs, too. The photographs may be of only routine quality. It is up to the art director to select those that are usable and perhaps to ask that others be retaken. Sometimes the art director can improve the composition of the photographs by cropping them. Occasionally the photographs go on to illustrators to use as guides for paintings or drawings.

But freelance writers almost never have anything to do with the way their articles are laid out. Maybe publications should make more of an effort to cooperate with writers on design matters. In gathering examples of page design to be included in this book, this author found it necessary, after getting reprint permission from a magazine, to write to an author to get additional permission, even though the article would be reproduced in a size too small to read. It was a routine matter. But this is the note that came back: "I hope you don't think me a prig, but I must refuse your request. Each to his own taste—I happen to think the layout for my article . . . was an abomination. Title (not mine), blurb, pictures, and layout all worked together to violate the theme of my article. I cannot separate the layout from its purpose, and its purpose clearly was at odds with the text it supposedly was working with."

The freelancer's view of the art director

J. B. Handelsman, the cartoonist, showed what he thought of art directors (had one redesigned a magazine and closed out the gag cartoons?) with his picture of St. Peter standing at the gates of heaven talking to a worried-looking man on the outside. In back of St. Peter was an art director (you could tell he was an art director by his hair style and mod clothes). St. Peter was telling the man outside: "I'm terribly sorry. The art director thinks your ears are too big."

A certain uneasiness prevails where art directors or designers work with people supplying art to publications. Sometimes the artist benefits from the direction given; sometimes the artist feels frustrated.

University Review, published by the State University of New York, was one of the best-designed alumni magazines in the country in the 1960s. For this issue, designer Richard Danne reuses on the cover a portion of some inside art to create a tie-in of the cover with a lead article. The cover is in dark blue and light green. The inside pages are in stark black and white. The bottom of the copy block area remains constant while the art goes through an evolution right before the readers' eyes. Photographer was Herman Bachmann.

What is the photographer's idea of a good art director or designer? This question, among others, was discussed by three photographers at a meeting of the New York chapter of the International Association of Business Communicators.

Simpson Kalisher, whose work has appeared in many annual reports and other corporate publications, said, "For me, a good designer recognizes the integrity of an image. He doesn't crop and sacrifice an area either of color saturation or of grain. He also has a sense of the continuity of images when he puts a book together." Burt Glinn, whose photographs for the Magnum agency appear in many leading magazines, said, "You can be a good designer for the client and not for the photographer. But the best designer works for both of us." The designer should argue for what works, he added. ". . . I want . . . a designer who does not cave in at the first sign of opposition. For when a client loses sight of where he's heading, it's our job to try to bring him back on track." William Rivelli, for 20 years a photographer for corporate publications, felt that often design fails at the printing stage. Little money is left after design and photography are budgeted. "So many jobs are ruined by the printing, and that seems to me foolish. It's like throwing away all the money you've spent." Watching over the printing is just one of the designer's jobs.

In the world of annual reports, company magazines, and other corporate publications, Glinn counts about 30 "top level" designers. ". . . There are a lot of other good designers who are good with the scissors and they get their ideas from the first thirty."[6]

Realities of the job

On some magazines, the art director does not control the appearance of all the pages. James W. O'Bryan, for instance, used to do only the cover and the more important spreads for *National Review.* Recent art directors at *Esquire* did not do the covers: George Lois, an advertising art director and agency executive, did them. At *Newsweek,* art director Fred Lowry did not control the cover or the inside color section. When he was at *True,* Norman P. Schoenfeld, because of time limitations, found it necessary to leave back-of-the-book makeup to the printer, a practice common among

6. Robert A. Parker, "A Panel Discussion of Corporate Photography," *Communication Arts,* January/February 1982, p. 79.

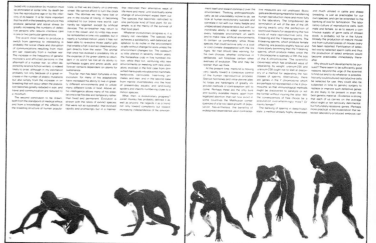

magazines and newspapers. In a way, you could say the whole of *The New Yorker* is put together in this way.

Raymond Waites, Jr., the innovative art director of the *United Church Herald* and later *A. D.,* found it necessary to include in his publication Polaroid shots taken by near amateurs.

When a magazine sees the need for a thorough revamping of its format, it is likely to call in an outsider to confer with its art director.

That he does not oversee *all* the pages; that he gives up control of the most important page of all, the cover; that he is willing to accept art and photography he knows to be inferior; that when redesign is considered it is some outsider who gets to remake the magazine—all this is rough on an art director's ego. There is, in addition, the problem of job burnout.

All too many magazine art directors lack a feeling of job security. Between the time the author conducted his research into the role of art directors on American magazines and published his report with the Magazine Publishers Association, a two-year period, at least seven of the thirty art directors he interviewed had moved. "The job-switching among editorial art directors resembles a game of musical chairs," Alexis Gelber noted in *Art Direction,* and then cataloged eight changes on major magazines in 1978.

Some of the changes obviously were forced by top management people looking for scapegoats for dwindling circulations and loss of advertising revenue.

Size of the art staff

On large magazines, the art director employs several assistants. When he was at *Life,* Bernard Quint had a staff of about twenty, not counting the picture editors. That *Life* came out weekly made so large an art staff necessary. Several persons were there to carry out the rough sketches of the art director, others to do keylines and assembly, others to handle production matters. *Look,* the bi-weekly, had about fifteen. The big monthlies operate with smaller staffs. Herb Bleiweiss, when he was with *Ladies' Home Journal,* had four assistants, but he used them in a way different from most art directors: he let each assistant handle all the details for a single article or story. It made for unity within a feature, but meant that the magazine lacked some unity overall.

Samuel Antupit, on his first stint with *Esquire,* had two assist-

By Frank J. Weinstock, M.D.

blackout

The eyes are really rather fantastic organs. They each receive an image, turn it upside down, flip it back over again, perceive, and combine the images—in color in daytime, black and white when it's dark—all, literally, in less than a blink of an eye! It's not surprising, therefore, that occasionally the system malfunctions. While a sudden loss of vision may not actually stem from the eyes themselves, it's frequently the first manifestation of a change there or somewhere else.

Sound complicated? It is, of course. But really, there's often quite a lot you can do to minimize the visual loss—and sometimes reverse it altogether—if you handle the problem quickly and correctly. And if there's nothing that can or/continued

A dramatic and powerful spread from *Emergency Medicine* making use of a large face in full color. The face is large enough and cropped close enough to run across the gutter. The size was necessary to make the fogged over eyes readable. The article starts out as reverse copy. Because this is an opening article occuring in the magazine after several pages of advertising, the editors run a small logo at the top.

ants and a secretary. In his opinion, "the smaller the staff the better." (These figures do not include artists and designers in the advertising and promotion departments.)

Emergency Medicine, one of the best-designed professional journals in the country, uses only two designers for its 240 to 250 pages per issue. Art director Ira Silberlicht says it can be done because the magazine is a "formatted book. There are a couple of typefaces that we use . . . we don't sit and design headlines in beautiful type and go crazy." The aesthetics and excitement come from theme art. Silberlicht wants a stay-the-same look each month to help readers segregate the magazine from the other couple of hundred in the field.[7]

Bringing in a consultant

It was a single-sentence letter: "How much would you charge us to review the last 10 issues of _____ and then meet with us to make recommendations for improving our design and format?" "The trouble with you, Ron," the designer wrote back (he happened to know the editor), "is that you beat around the bush. I had to read through your entire salutation before I came to the meat of your letter. . . ."

A pleasant enough start for a consulting job, and as it turned out, the results pleased all persons involved. The editor changed a few things, and the designer had the satisfaction of seeing the changes come about. But consulting jobs, both from the editor's and from the designer's standpoint, don't always work out as the principals hope.

7. John Peter, "The Top Ten Business Magazines," *Folio,* August 1976, p. 77.

No doubt editors who have used design consultants can catalog any number of complaints against them. Whether consultants are worth what they cost, in money and in the morale of the in-house designer, is subject to debate. But consultants have gripes, too. Among them, these:

1. The editor calls in the consultant not for fresh ideas but to substantiate some design biases.

2. A magazine is in desperate circumstances, and the editor knows that redesign can work a miracle.

3. The editor has read a book about design or heard a lecture by someone like Milton Glaser or Samuel Antupit. And now the editor knows what's "in."

4. The editor has just seen a magazine whose appearance is appealing. Can the consultant duplicate those looks?

5. The editor doesn't really want to change the appearance of the magazine, a look traditional if not outdated, but would like to try a type like Avant Garde Gothic (with alternate characters) for the headline schedule or titles.

6. Finally, the editor buys a handsome, well thought out format along with elaborate instructions about what to do in every conceivable situation and accepts the new design enthusiastically. Within a couple of months, though, the editor adds a different display face for a new standing column, say, and drops some italic in favor of boldface and decides to try initial letters for some of the articles. What happens then to the look of the magazine is similar to what happens to the appearance of a new, well-designed building when somebody starts placing crude, hand-painted signs above doorways and in windows.

An editor paying for a new design program ought to stick to it and check back with the designer when changes have to be made. Anyway, a design program submitted by an outsider should provide for future adjustments.

Editors of magazines bring in consultants to (1) do a hit-and-run job involving a study of past issues and come up with advice for basic changes to be made by the editor or an in-house designer, (2) do a full-service job, involving the selecting of types and the setting up of a basic design pattern or grid for the editor or in-house art director to follow, or (3) do the actual issue-by-issue design and layout of the magazine. In this final instance, the consultant becomes the art director, working for the editor on a freelance basis.

Freelance art directing

When the editor works with a freelance art director, as on a company magazine, frequent conferences may be necessary, not only to alert the art director to editorial complications but also to solicit advice. Art directors like to be involved in the editorial process. They do not want to be thought of as visual persons only.

But a great amount of the contact, typically, comes by phone. The art director may call in the middle of a pasteup to suggest a paragraph cut to make an article fit. This author, acting as a freelance art director, for some years designed a magazine 120 miles away from the editorial offices. Copy and photographs went back and forth by mail and Greyhound Express.

Lionel L. Fisher, editor of *Boise Cascade Paper Times,* had such a good relationship with his freelance art director, Joe Erceg of

Portland, Oregon, that he didn't even ask for thumbnails or roughs before final pasteup begins.

Some art directors carry the work to only a rough-layout, comprehensive, or rough-pasteup stage, leaving the final pasteup to a pasteup artist or to the printer. Whoever does the pasteup, then, simply follows directions. Perhaps the rough that this pasteup artist works from has all kinds of measurements and arrows and instructions marked in the margins. On the other hand, some rough pasteups are so neatly done they could almost stand in as camera-ready copy. They do not need instructions marked in the margins.

At any rate, somewhere along the line, *somebody* has to bother with exact fitting of lines of type and headlines and art onto the page. An art director who really cares about the product may insist on doing this final pasteup. There are always some last-minute, precise fitting decisions to be made. To a real art director, a half a point of space wrongly placed can ruin an otherwise good day.

The art director as illustrator

The smaller the magazine, the more likely the art director is to do his own illustration. Raymond Waites, Jr., prepared many of the illustrations for his magazine. Dugald Stermer did some illustrations for *Ramparts* while he was art director, causing Norman Rockwell to remark: "I didn't know he was a painter as well as an art editor. Boy, he has it both ways." In the 1970s Stermer made cover paintings for *Time*.

And for those who cannot draw, there is the camera. It was natural that art directors, working closely with photographers, should take up the tool themselves and do their own shooting. Perhaps the photographer missed a deadline. Perhaps the art director had a better feel for proportion than the photographer had. Otto Storch became so intrigued with the camera that he gave up his job at *McCall's* to go into film work. A number of other magazine-cover and interior shots have been taken by the sometimes magazine art director Henry Wolf.

Country Roads starts this article (and other articles in this issue) with initial art that acts as sort of an initial letter, getting the reader started. The small piece of art remains the same from article to article to unite an "on the farm" series. To tie these two pages together, designer George Watson of Ceco Publishing Company, which produces *Country Roads* for the Goodyear Tire & Rubber Company, runs a full-color silhouetted halftone across the gutter. The spread shows that you can sometimes run a title and blurb *below* the body of an article.

Some art directors arrived on magazines by way of careers as illustrators. Kenneth Stuart, former art editor of *The Saturday Evening Post*, later art editor of *Reader's Digest*, was one. But Stuart as art editor did not employ Stuart as illustrator. Those who use their own art in magazines have some misgivings about it; but for some magazines there is no budget for outside work. The art directors do what they must do.

But most art directors can't draw or paint well enough for publication. Samuel Antupit certainly does not consider himself an illustrator. "And I'm afraid to learn. I might be tempted to pick out people who did my kind of illustrating," he says.

Some art directors don't even design. They do only what their titles suggest: they direct. They feel their time is better spent working out solutions than actually executing them.

The art director as inventor

The best of the art directors develop a mechanical aptitude as well as a design sense. Sometimes the effect the art director wants can't be had with ordinary photographs of ordinary props.

For the first issue of the now-defunct *Careers Today*, published by *Psychology Today*, art director Don Wright, to illustrate "The University Womb," cut a womb-shaped hole in a piece of plywood; put supports under the plywood to bring it up from the floor; nailed sheets of clear mylar around the hole to form a well; filled the well with water; put a nude, sandled male in the well; and photographed the setup from the top.

The influence of advertising design

Magazine art directors take some inspiration from their colleagues in advertising art direction. Henry Wolf, who once left magazine art direction to become a principal in an advertising agency, thinks the best design these days can be found in the ads. Peter Palazzo, who designed *New York* when it was part of the New York *Herald Tribune*, thinks advertising has the best possibilities for graphic excellence.

Bernard Quint, formerly art director for *Life* and *McCall's*, thinks advertising design has had too much effect on magazine design. "The use of design for its own sake has increased in contemporary magazines in direct ratio to the lack of content."

When he was art editor of *The Saturday Evening Post*, Frank Kilker reported that whether or not a potential art director was acceptable to the advertising fraternity weighed heavily in the consideration of the editor who was doing the hiring.

Most art directors interviewed for the author's *Visits with 30 Magazine Art Directors* felt that advertising was setting the trends; magazine design was following. Herb Bleiweiss, of *Ladies' Home Journal*, thought otherwise. Mike Salisbury, of *West*, suggested that the trend-setting function moves back and forth between advertising and magazines, and that magazines would once again be in the forefront.

One thing all agreed on: advertising art directors are better paid. But in the opinion of Roger Waterman, who art directed *Kaiser News* and later *Chevron USA*, advertising art directors are under more pressure and therefore *should* be better paid.

The inside front cover and page of an issue of *Bell Telephone Magazine*, published by AT&T. "Priority," the feature at the left, spills over onto the table of contents page each issue. The nicely-designed table of contents uses lightface sans serif numbers at the left, boldface roman titles at the right. The lineup of editors and company officers appears immediately below. An illustration, part of a larger one on an inside page, completes the unit. Design of the magazine is by Eichinger Inc.

The exercise of taste

A new art director taking over a magazine immediately makes changes. What to the casual reader would seem unimportant might greatly disturb an art director: length of ruled lines, choice of body type, the logo, placement of captions, etc. "A change of editor or art director is reflected instantly . . . [a magazine's] pages," Henry Wolf points out. "A magazine is still largely the extension of an individual idea, a peculiar personal vision."

When Susan Niles moved up as art director of *Mademoiselle,* she changed the design to make it "cleaner, fresher, and younger." The covers became less poster-like, with colors more integrated. The "M" became much larger than the other letters in the logo. The January 1979 cover showed a woman wearing glasses, a first for fashion magazines, Niles thinks. "We're very natural here," she says. We're known for using real people as models. . . ."

While they would be slow to admit it, art directors in their choice of type and art and in their arrangement of these elements on a page lean heavily on what is fashionable. For a time the Bauhaus-inspired sans serifs are "in"; then the Swiss-inspired sans serifs.

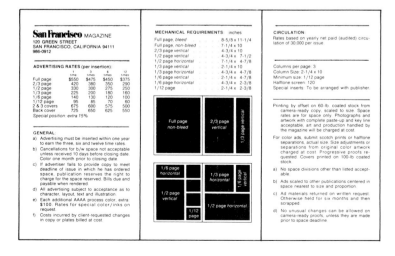

Inside panels of a *San Francisco* rate card designed by art director Dan Marr. Note his helpful diagrams of ad sizes.

Everybody bleeds photographs for a time; then suddenly, everybody wants generous white margins around pictures. Letterspacing is thought to "open up" the typography, making it more pleasant to read; then close fitting of letters takes hold, to make it possible for the reader to grasp whole words rather than individual letters. For a time, all space divisions are planned so they'll be unequal; then spaces are divided equally, and new magazines come out in a square format rather than a golden proportion size. For a few years, the look is austere, simple, straight; then swash caps and column rules and gingerbread prevail. It is the rare art director who can resist adapting current art trends to a design: witness the psychedelic look on magazine pages at the end of the 1960s. A few art directors break away, rediscover old styles, come up with unused ones; and they become the leaders. In a few months, others are following.

"Let us . . . not delude ourselves that we are lastingly right," cautions Henry Wolf.

Once in a while an art director decides to go with the banal, the obvious, or the discarded. An illustrator has passed his prime, his style outmoded. Very well, bring him back. He's the kind of an illustrator who would never have appeared in that magazine even when he was on top. But that makes him all the more appealing now. His shock value is worth a lot to the art director.

Or the art director picks one of the typefaces that, even when it was first released, was dismissed as gauche by discerning designers. The art director uses it now, smugly, cynically even.

A little of this goes a long way. The trouble with some magazines today is that their art directors, caught up in an anything-is-art mood, are breaking all the rules of typography and design. They insist on doing their own thing. Some of their experiments succeed, and less self-indulgent art directors probably will incorporate them into magazines of the future. But most of the experiments fail. They fail because the experimenters do not recognize *readability* as the one overriding requirement of magazine design.

Suggested further reading

Evans, Helen Marie, *Man the Designer,* The Macmillan Company, New York, 1973.

Glaser, Milton, *Milton Glaser: Graphic Design,* Overlook Press (Viking), New York, 1973.

Hillebrand, Henri, ed., *Graphic Designers in the U.S.A.,* Universe Books, New York, 1972–73. (Four volumes.)

———, ed., *Graphic Designers in Europe,* Universe Books, New York, 1972–73. (Four volumes.)

Nelson, George, *How to See: Visual Adventures in a World God Never Made,* Little, Brown and Company, Boston, 1977.

———, *George Nelson on Design,* Whitney Library of Design, New York, 1979.

Nelson, Roy Paul, *Visits with 30 Magazine Art Directors,* Magazine Publishers Association, New York, 1969.

Designers come to publications from different backgrounds. Some are ex-illustrators. Some are typographers. Some are editorial people doubling up on duties. Some get their experience with advertising agencies; some are more oriented to the fine arts. A few get along splendidly with their editors; they have mastered the art of compromise.

Compromise is important because design is largely a matter of reconciling editorial needs with visual needs, statement with white space, type with art. A series of compromises helps unify the publication.

Unity is one of the universal principles of design.

There are at least four others:

Balance; proportion; sequence; contrast.

We shall deal now with those principles, especially as they apply to magazines but also as they apply to other publications and printed pieces.

The principles of publication design

1. *Balance.* We start with the principle most respected by those who are unsure of themselves in the area of graphic design. The most obvious of the principles—and the least important—it states, simply, that what is put on the left half of the page must "weigh"

The handsome and expensive *Nautical Quarterly* is not afraid to take some chances on its square, glossy, full-color pages. This spread features two one-page profiles. Note the all-caps italic body copy (printed in a screened version of black) and the thin, slab serif all-caps titles. The name of the magazine in stenciled letters always appears at tops of pages. Creative director of the quarterly: B. Martin Pedersen.

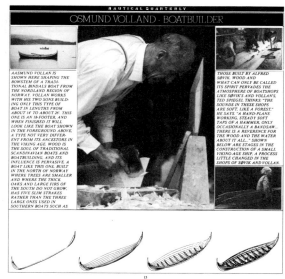

as much as what is put on the right half of the page. Or: what is put on one page of a spread must "weigh" as much as what is put on the facing page.

As a designer who is overconscientious about this principle, you can take the easy way out; you can *center* everything: the heading, the photo, the text matter. If a spread is involved, you can run the heading across the gutter so half is on each side. You put a picture on the left page and a picture of equal size across from it on the right page. If you run two columns of copy under one picture, you run two columns of copy under the other. The balance is bisymmetric.

For some articles, for some magazines, that solution may be a good one. Usually it is not.

With a little more effort, you can achieve balance that is asymmetric and therefore more interesting. You do this by putting a big picture on one page near the gutter and balancing it with a smaller picture at the outside edge of the other page. It is the principle of balance involved when a parent and child use a teeter-totter; the parent sits close to the fulcrum; the lighter child sits way out on the end.

The balance becomes more complicated as graphic elements are added. We shall not take the space here to consider the possibilities. Balance comes naturally enough as you move elements around and pull white space into concentrated masses. You feel the balance; and your intuition is all that is needed. Not confident, you may hold your design up to a mirror and check it in its reverse flow; this will quickly dramatize any lack of balance.

You work, then, with optical weights. You know from experience that big items weigh more than little ones, dark more than light, color more than black and white, unusual shapes more than usual shapes. You know, too, that a concentration of white space, because it is unusual, can itself be "heavy."

2. *Proportion.* Good proportion comes about less naturally. As a beginning designer you may be inclined to put equal space between the heading and the picture, between the picture and the

Another spread—an opening spread—from *Nautical Quarterly.* **The initial letter, in blue, is in stencil type to match the name running across the top. Oversize slab serif type makes the title stand out. The silhouetted fish contrasts nicely with the large painting on the left page. Designer B. Martin Pedersen is willing to run the text type across a page as a single column. A new paragraph is set off with a small box instead of an indentation.**

You get a good idea of what makes for a set of pleasing proportions by observing the ruled lines, added by this author, in the margins of this decorative title page designed near the turn of the century by Charles Ricketts at the Vale Press.

Design like this is hard to beat: clean, simple, direct—and classic. Palatino type is used throughout, and the drop from the top of the page to where the columns are—the sink—remains the same on the article's several pages. But the columns do not line up at the bottom. Barbara Edwards was editor (and designer) of *Old Oregon*, the magazine from which these pages were taken.

Collecting The Right Stuff

Nancy Woolum

Ed Kemp is bent on building a valid collection representing conservatism as an enduring political philosophy.

copy, and between the copy and the edge of the page. Your margins become monotonously the same.

Better proportion comes from Nature. The circumference of the tree trunk supersedes the circumference of the branch. The distance between the tip of the finger and the first joint is different from the distance between the first joint and the second joint.

In designing publications we also have the inspiration of the "golden section" (or "golden mean") of the fine arts. It provides that the lesser dimension in a plane figure is to the greater as the greater is to the sum of both; or, the dimensions are in a 0.616 to 1.000 ratio. Roughly: 2 to 3. We base page size—of typing sheets, of books, of magazines—more or less on this ratio. We find the ratio more interesting, less tiresome, less obvious than a simple 1 to 1. We avoid 2 to 1, 3 to 1, and 4 to 2 ratios, because they are merely variations of 1 to 1. They divide into equal portions. We avoid cutting pages visually into halves or quarters. We avoid running pictures that are perfectly square because the ratio of width to depth is 1 to 1.

In designing an issue of a magazine you might well vary the space between pictures as you move from page to page. And the space between title and article start on one spread may be different from what it is on another spread. But with these varying proportions you would maintain consistent spacing where distances are meant to be equal, as in the separation of subheads from the body of an article, and captions from their pictures.

The page margin for many magazines is narrowest between inside edge of copy and gutter, wider between top of copy and top of page, wider still between outside edge of copy and outside edge of page, and widest between bottom of copy and bottom of page.

Total picture area for most publications takes up more space than non-picture area; or it takes up less space. The ratio is seldom 1 to 1.

3. *Sequence.* You do not leave to chance the order in which the reader perceives the items on a page or spread. You know the reader ordinarily starts at the top left of a page or spread and moves to the bottom right. Arranging the elements so they read from left to right and from top to bottom is easy enough; but it limits design flexibility.

The reader also has a tendency to move from big items to smaller items, from black to white, from color to noncolor, from unusual shape to usual shape. You find it possible, then, to begin your design *anywhere,* directing the reader to the left, the right, the top, the bottom—in a circular motion, diagonally, whatever way you wish. Diminishing visual impact does the job.

You direct the reader, too, through the use of lines, real or implied, which carry the eye as tracks carry a train. The pictures themselves have direction or facing; as surely as if they were arrows, they point the way. This is why you would always arrange a major mug shot so that the subject looks into the text.

You try to arrange photographs so that an edge or a force from one photograph flows into an adjoining one. The curve of an arm, for instance, if carried over to the next photograph would merge into the roll of a hill. This happens without regard to what may be the outer dimensions of the photographs; one photograph might be considerably larger than the other and not aligned with it.

Or taking a line from within the picture—say the edge of a building—you extend it (without actually drawing it) and fit against it another item—say a block of copy. Or taking the hard edge of a picture and extending it, you fit another picture against it somewhere across the page.

And do not discount the possibility of actually *numbering* the pictures. If chronological order is all-important, as for a step-by-step illustrated article on how to build a guest house, you may not find a better way for handling sequence.

Developing sequence from spread to spread is also part of the assignment. Which leads to another principle.

4. *Unity.* The typeface must look as if it were designed to fit the style of the illustration. It must fit the mood of the piece. The overall effect of the spread, of the entire article or story, of the entire magazine must be one of unity, of harmony. The pieces, the pages belong together.

Ideally, all typefaces in a magazine come from the same family. Ideally, all art is furnished by the same artist or photographer.

Heavy rules or borders ordinarily call for boldface sans serifs. Bold sans serifs call for line drawings with plenty of solid blacks.

Thick and thin rules call for modern romans. Modern romans call for well-ordered photographs, or clean line drawings, arranged in severe horizontal and vertical patterns.

And pattern concerns the designer. Stepping back, you contemplate the overall effect. No longer looking for individual trees, you survey the forest. Does it all seem to fit together?

The pattern may be loose, tight, bulky, smooth, rugged, soft, loud, dark, light, hard, straight, rolling, changing, any number of things—but the pattern is unmistakably there.

You take a major step toward unity when you push your white space to the outside edges of your spreads. This teams photographs with other elements so that they work together. When large amounts of white space seep into the center, there is an explosion, sending the elements off in all directions. White space on the outside edges should be there in unequal concentrations, in conformance with the principle of pleasing proportion.

5. *Contrast.* Expressed negatively, the principle is Contrast. Put positively, it is Emphasis. Either way, something on the page or on the spread stands out from all else. What stands out is probably the most important item on the page. It is probably the item the reader sees first.

You achieve contrast or give an item emphasis by making it bigger than anything else there—blacker, more colorful, or more unusually shaped. Or you get it by causing all other items to point to the item or by putting it in a different setting, giving it different texture, or otherwise making it seem out of place.

This is important: only *one* item—or one cluster of items—dominates. When you give graphic emphasis to several items, they all compete for attention, frustrating the reader.

The principles in perspective

No doubt you would find that designing a publication is not as simple as the preceding section indicates. Nor do practicing designers pay a great deal of attention to these principles. Perhaps they could not state them if asked. Certainly they would not give them exactly as they are given here.

Still it is a worthwhile list to contemplate. The amateur designer, or the editor who has the design job by default, especially, should give the principles some attention.

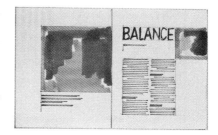
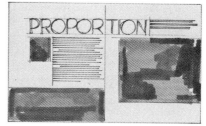

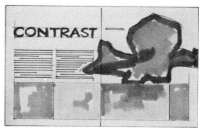

Each of these five rough sketches (thumbnails) of magazine spreads shows a design principle at work. (The sketches appeared originally in the author's *Communication World* column.)

All the principles of design described in this chapter are incorporated by Don Menell, assistant art director of *Look,* in this single page. It is the opening page of a two-page article that starts on a right-hand page and ends on the (next) left-hand page. Menell combines roman display type with sans serif body type, adds column rules, and carefully fits the type around the illustration. The illustration ties in beautifully with the title, carrying the reader down into the article and dividing the page pleasingly. Note that the hand both holds a pill and forms into the symbol for "okay." The ring on the finger, faintly seen, is a nice added touch. (Reproduced by courtesy of the editors. From the June 30, 1970, issue of *Look* magazine. Copyright 1970 by Cowles Communications, Inc.)

Popular Photography combines three same-size pictures and one big one, all in a square format, with some column rules for an opening spread in the back of the book. The main picture is cropped to lead the reader down the teeter-totter to the beginning of the article's title. Art director George N. Soppelsa was able to retain formally balanced-sections (the title and the right-hand page) in an informally balanced context.

No medication is foolproof, but taken with your doctor's advice…

THE PILL IS SAFE

BY EDWARD T. TYLER, M.D., WITH ROLAND H. BERG

The boxing of articles appeals to many art directors, just for the visual order it brings. In this right-page opener, the subject matter calls for a box—or wall; so the visual treatment is all the more appropriate. To tie the title with the initial letter, the designer uses a chiseled-out style for both. The original employs a second color, maroon, in solid and two different tints arrived at by screening. Only the area outside the box—or wall—is white. (Courtesy of *Liberty,* "A Magazine of Religious Freedom.")

THE WALL
By Michael J. Exner

Playground seesaw becomes moving platform from which to shoot action scene of person on the other end.

The ups and downs of camera movements

… ON SEESAWS, SWINGS, AND SLIDES

BY BOB DUNCAN

PHOTOGRAPHS BY HARVEY V. FONDILLER

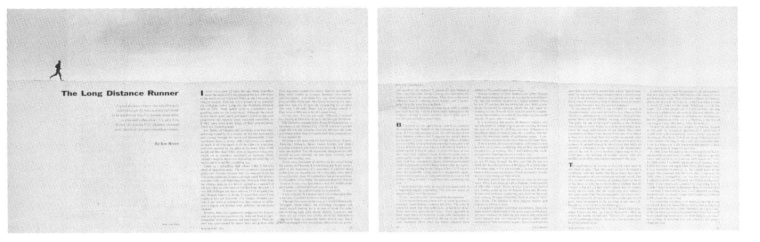

They represent a starting point.

It may have occurred to you that the principles are contradictory. How can you have unity, for instance, when you insist on setting up one item to contrast with others? And doesn't use of unequal space divisions break up the sequence?

The challenge in the list lies in knowing when to stress one principle, when to stress another. Obviously they can't all be applied in equal measure. When one principle does not seem appropriate, you should not hesitate to abandon it.

Trends in design

Graphic design accommodates to trends in fashion, architecture, the fine arts, the political climate, culture in general. What strikes us as a good page now might not strike us that way ten years from now, or even next year. At times in the history of the graphic arts, a cluttered, busy, crowded page, overly decorated, has impressed designers if not readers. Even today, such a page is good, under certain conditions, simply because it is different from others. The principle of contrast—contrast with other designs—gives the page respectability.

But the main thrust of design today is toward simplicity. The reader simply does not have time to browse and hunt.

So as a designer you give the reader a few elements per page or spread as you can. Instead of many small pictures—two or three large ones. Instead of three columns to the page—two or one. Instead of a multi-decked heading—a single title. Instead of a three-line title—a title in a single line.

Even when you have a half dozen or more photographs to work into the design, you can organize them into one mass, butting them together so they make either a true rectangle or a square.

Some designers organize all the elements so that they will form three basic areas of unequal size separated from each other by unequal distances.

Two basic approaches

A designer takes one of two basic approaches to publication design. The first approach goes like this: Each picture, each caption, each title, each block of copy falls into a consistent pattern to unify

This two-spread, four-page article from *Old Oregon,* an alumni magazine, is held together by a single photograph, full bleed on all pages. The designer, Stan Bettis, who took the picture, uses part of it for one spread, part for another. He runs the photo in a light tone so he can surprint the title and body copy. Note how the runner and the title move the reader to the initial letter that begins the article. The horizon line in the photo carries the reader from the first spread to the second.

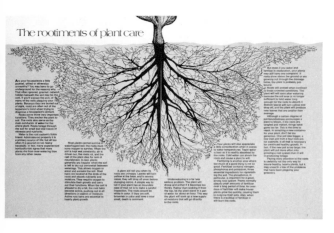

The rootiments of plant care

For this spread (an article complete on the two pages) the editor puts the title and plant trunk aboveground and everything else below. A tint block of black serves as the underground area. It is light enough to allow the boldface copy to be read easily. The short segments relieved by the root system also make things easy for the reader. The editor gives in to the urge to use a pun: "rootiments." (Used with permission from *Ralston Purina Magazine.*)

the publication. The look is orderly. The reader feels secure and knows what to expect.

The second approach provides great variety, page after page. The reader prepares for a series of surprises. Using this approach you would worry about unity, but only within a given article or story. You would feel that the nature of the article or story should dictate the choice of typeface and illustration.

One writer characterized the two styles as Bauhaus/Swiss Design and Push Pin. Bauhaus/Swiss Design, as he saw it, was spare, functional, austere, uncluttered. It made use of a grid. It seemed particularly appropriate for corporate publications. The second style, popularized by Push Pin Studios, was more inventive, combining many styles, including decorative. In the Push Pin style there was often a touch of humor, a whiff of nostalgia. It seemed particularly appropriate to magazine covers, posters, and advertising.[1]

A magazine may have elements of both approaches, but one approach should predominate. One may be more appropriate than the other for a given magazine, but properly handled, either approach can work, regardless of magazine content.

1. *The ordered approach.* Herb Lubalin called *Scientific American* "the best designed magazine in America." *Sports Illustrated* has impressed many art directors as a magazine of great beauty. The magazines have this in common: they are highly organized, almost predictable in their approach to design. Each uses a single typeface for all major titles. Each makes limited use of ruled lines to set off some of the type, but otherwise, each avoids typographic frills. The art directors frame their pictures nicely in white. They avoid crowding. A look of quiet luxury results. More important, readers can get through their articles, look at their pictures, unhampered by visual pyrotechnics.

Don't be misled by the simplicity of the look. The subtle relationship of spaces is not easy to duplicate. Still, of the two basic approaches, the ordered approach is the one that should be used by the editor-without-an-art-director. Ideally that editor should call in a consulting art director to set up a format, choose the types, and draw up a set of instructions and diagrams on how to handle special features and standing departments. Then the editor takes over.

Two other magazines stand out as unique examples of the ordered approach. *The New Republic* from 1959 to 1967 was about as ordered as any magazine could be, and handsome for it. Noel Martin, brought in as a consultant for a complete format redesign, chose a roman typeface, Palatino, designed in 1950 by Hermann Zapf. Looking very contemporary, Palatino nevertheless draws its inspiration from the early Venetian types. It suggests a happy blend of tradition and progress. Martin used it not only for main titles but for subtitles, credit lines, body copy, the logo—everything. He permitted typographic variety only through varying the sizes and combining uprights with italics. The editors never varied Martin's simple two-column pattern until someone there, unfortunately, decided to jazz up the magazine with boldface versions of the type (most type designs lose their beauty when their strokes are thick-

1. Harold T. P. Hayes, "The Push Pin Conspiracy," *The New York Times Magazine,* March 6, 1977, pp. 19–22.

ened) and with an angular script that for some column headings occasionally ran on a diagonal. The magazine made some rather substantial changes again with the Sept. 9, 1981 issue, getting rid of the two rectangular blocks that used to flank the logo, changing the logo to outline letters, and making other adjustments but staying with the Palatino type.

The New Yorker's design is so ordered as to be nonexistent. A cartoonist back in the early 1920s, when it was founded, designed its display face, and the magazine has never changed it. It uses a few spot drawings and, of course, those celebrated gag cartoons to provide occasional graphic oases, but otherwise its "designer" simply pours the editorial material into the holes left over by the advertising. There is no opening display for any of the articles or stories. The advertisers love it, because it makes their insertions, always well designed anyway, striking by comparison.

2. *The diversified approach.* Whereas the ordered approach virtually guarantees reasonably good design, even for magazines with limited resources, the diversified approach works only when directed by a professional designer. Its success depends to a considerable extent on violations of traditional principles of design.

In the diversified approach, the designer may arrange elements to create a large void on one side of a page, purposely disturbing the reader in order to focus attention on an article which deals, let us say, with student unrest. Out goes balance.

Or the designer uses square- rather than rectangular-shaped photographs. The reasoning may be that for this particular set of photographs, cropping to squares brings out the best composition. Or the designer chooses a permanent square page format, as Herb Lubalin did for *Avant Garde,* to make the magazine stand out from all others. Out goes standard proportion.

Or the designer doesn't care in which direction the reader goes. The designer scrambles the picture because there is no correct order. The effect need not be cumulative for the article: it is no how-to-do-it. Out goes sequence.

Or the designer wants to show the complicated strategy of a single football play, as *Esquire* did in one of its issues. Samuel Antupit ran a chart showing all players on both sides, officials and coaches, fans in the stands, the press corps, the stadium and scoreboard, with labels and captions and directional lines and boxes fighting for attention with the article itself and its title. Out goes simplicity.

Or the designer is dealing with an article that makes five or six main points, equally important. No one item should stand out. This calls for a series of equal-size pictures. Out goes contrast.

And yet in each case the designer maintains a semblance of each of the design principles. The concentration of white space is itself "heavy," and tends to counterbalance the dark elements on the other side of the page. Square-shaped photographs appear on a rectangular page. Scrambled pictures precede a column of type that moves in the conventional way from top to bottom. Visual confusion is confined only to the display types. One cluttered article fits into an issue filled otherwise with pages stark and clean. Even-size pictures, no one of them standing out from the others, form one large mass that overpowers a smaller copy block, providing contrast to the page after all.

It would be more accurate to say that the designer using the diversified approach does not so much ignore design principles as emphasize one over the others.

creditline

VOL. X NO. 1   JANUARY 1981

Welch succeeds Jones as GE Chairman on April 1

John F. Welch Jr.

New Service Award Program

Big S&SP 'Payout' on the way

This medallion will be the focus of the revamped Service Award Program.

Creditline, an eight-page magapaper published by General Electric Credit Corporation, uses a double three-point-design approach for one of its covers. You see three pieces of art (if you count the logo as one piece) and three boldface headlines. One piece of art is large and round rather than rectangular to bring variety to the page. And one of the headlines is smaller than the other two. Furthermore, one headline is a two-liner, one a one-liner, and one a three-liner. A clean, interesting page with plenty of white space to keep the reader relaxed. That blank space at the upper right will carry the address sticker.

Gombl mjnet
with hoving abx
the wmbjde

A rough layout by this author for
a one-page article in a tabloid
takes a tightly organized
approach to design.

The diversified approach is the experimental approach. And experiment is best conducted by those who are grounded in the fundamentals.

Two of the most honored practitioners of the diversified approach were Allen Hurlburt of *Look* and Otto Storch of *McCall's*. *Look's* imaginative handling of photographs in sequence caused *Life* to revitalize its appearance. *McCall's* brought new life to the women's magazines.

Some observers feel the diversified approach makes things difficult for the reader. But "It is more interesting for the reader if the visual pace of the magazine varies," Storch said. "Some pages can be quiet and others bold, some restful and others exciting, some with pictures dominating the layout and others with no pictures at all."

The diversified approach works best for large-format publications. The *Digest* size of some magazines tends to cramp the style of the freewheeling designer.

Visualization

As a designer taking on a magazine assignment, you would first make a decision on format (chapter 7). Then you would decide which of the two basic approaches to design to take: the ordered or diversified.

Already you have placed some limitations on yourself. Additional limitations may come from the editor. You get a manuscript of, say, 2,500 words, a title, and four photographs, and five pages in the magazine where you can put them. You make of this what you can, deciding which photograph to play up, how far down on the page to start the article, where subheads will go, how much white space to allow. Other articles will follow. And similar restrictions will accompany them.

In this case you are not much more than a layout artist. You get some satisfaction out of fitting these things together, but clearly, you are not fully engaged in graphic design.

Far better is the arrangement whereby you plan the issue with the editor, helping decide subject areas for articles and stories. Occasionally you may plan the art and lay out the pages before the article is written; the article then is tailored to fit.

Art director Greg Paul takes the
diamond-shaped window and
repeats it on the opposite page,
at the same level, to unite the
two pages. Paul has also
coordinated the underline, main-
title type, and initial letter. *The
Plain Dealer Magazine* article
celebrates a now-gone diner in
Cleveland. The painting by John
Baeder is from the book *Diners*
(Harry N. Abrams, Inc., New York)
and is copyrighted.

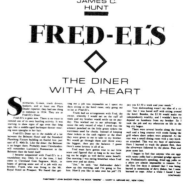

BY
JAMES C.
HUNT

FRED-EL'S
◇
THE DINER
WITH A HEART

The last two pages of a four-page "Commentary" article in *Bell Telephone Magazine*. The title is "On Regulation," as the folio line at the top reminds readers. The folio line and the two initial letters are in red, forming a triangle of color. The spread features *both* initial letters and a blurb, plus a photograph, to keep the design active. The initial letters take scattered placement: one is low on its page, the other one is high; one is in a middle column, the other is in a left-hand column. Each of the pages in the article is surrounded by a thin-line box, and each of the columns is fenced in by the same thin lines. The heavier bars, used above and below the blurb, take their thickness from the black box that signals the article's end. The top bar lines up with the top of the photograph, helping to unify the two elements.

Most important in the visualization process is the setting of the mood. You decide: photographs or drawings or no art at all? color? sans serif or roman type for the title? two-column or three-column pages? initial letters or subheads?

Realism might be better served through photography. Clarity might be better served through drawings. Color has psychological effects. Sans serifs may say "now"; romans may say "yesterday." Wide columns may suggest urgency, but narrow columns may be more immediate. Initial letters can be decorated to suggest the period of the piece.

You consider all of this, keeping in mind, always, production problems likely to result. Color adds to costs. Wide columns take more space because type has to be set larger.

Designers faced a difficult assignment in the mid-1960s with the "Death of God" debate. Nearly every magazine dealt with the matter; the question was: how to illustrate it. Designers could run mug shots of the theologians quoted, but these would not make very good opening spreads. And photographs of God Himself were hard to come by. Most designers took this way out: beautiful display of the article titles in old roman type. This seemed appropriate to the mood. *Time* (April 8, 1966), doing a major story on the debate, settled, for the first time in its history, on an all-type cover.

Whether art follows copy or copy follows art, the two must work in harmony. An article on the hippies of the 1960s features psychedelic lettering and art. An article about the computer age appears under a title set in a typeface we associate with punch cards. One on the navy appears under a title done in stencil letters. An article on the population explosion swells out to the edge of a crowded page.

The art accompanying the article should say the same thing the title says. For an article on "The Hectic Life of a College President," for instance, you would not select a routine shot of a well-dressed executive, hands folded, behind a cleared-off desk. For fiction, you would use a drawing or painting for the opening spread; for nonfiction, photography. For fiction, you can reach deep into the story for a scene to illustrate. The scene need not be thematic. For nonfiction, the main piece of art should *typify* what's in type.

Hi-Lines, published for
employees of Saskatchewan
Power Corporation, Regina, uses
a consistent design approach to
unite this cover with inside
pages. The pages are heavily
framed with color or tone, with
art allowed to break through to
give the pages some variety. On
one of the inside pages, part of
one photograph extends into the
frame of the other. Captions are
reversed in the maroon color
areas.

As a designer you normally would read the manuscript before
it is set in type to decide what kind of typographic and illustrative
treatment it should have. You may have a copy made for the illustrator, who can then decide on which illustration technique to
use.

With some idea of what the picture or pictures will be, and
knowing how much space the manuscript will take, you begin with
a series of thumbnail sketches of the pages, toying with space divisions. When you have thumbnails that show promise, you redraw
them actual size so that you can begin figuring exact dimensions.

Mike Salisbury, when he was art director of *West,* told how he
did it: "I don't rework any layouts. The first ideas I sketch out are
usually the ones produced.

"I work very loose and spontaneously, trying to keep a good
pacing of layout styles throughout the book.

"The less attention I give a layout's styling the better it will
look.

"I spend more time getting the proper photos, illustrations, and
research material organized. The layout is usually secondary in
importance to the material used in the layout."[2]

In some cases, especially for letterpress books, you would do
your designing with galley proofs and photostats of the art, cutting
and pasting and moving items around until they give the fit and
the look you desire. You may ask the editor to cut down or increase
wordage as an aid to fitting the manuscript to the page. You enjoy
true luxury when you act as both editor and designer: you can do
the cutting and the padding then exactly where you need it, when
you need it.

Design clichés

In what may be misguided enthusiasm for one or the other of the
design principles, or because of his lack of knowledge of what good
design is, amateur designers make a number of mistakes, and make

2. Letter to the author from Mike Salisbury, November 27, 1970.

them consistently. Perhaps the designers have seen design solutions, like them, and used them in new situations even when they don't fit. The solutions have been used to death.

Writers have their "tired but happy"'s and "last but not least"'s; designers have these:

1. *Picture cutouts.* Amateur designers seem to think that pictures displayed in regular rectangle or square shapes bore the reader. They may. But only because the pictures themselves are boring. Cutting them into circles or triangles or stars or whatever will not make them better pictures. If the pictures are good to begin with, such cutting will stunt their impact, ruin their composition, and demoralize the photographer who took them.

2. *Tilts.* Closely related to Cliché No. 1 is the practice of putting a picture or a headline on a diagonal. Presumably, the designer feels this will make it stand out from others. It will, but at the expense of causing the reader irritation.

The introduction of the diagonal suggests movement. The picture is falling. The reader gets caught up in this phenomenon at the expense of giving full attention to what the picture actually says. Readability suffers.

More defensible is the practice of putting the entire contents of the spread on a single or on parallel diagonals. The designer should have a good reason for doing this—a reason better than "to be different."

3. *Vertical typography.* The designer has a deep vertical space left over and a title to fit in, therefore runs it with the letters on top of each other in succession down the page. The title is unreadable; and the designer has probably run it in type larger than necessary.

The designer would save white space and make the title more readable—make it stand out better—by decreasing its size and running it in usual left-to-right form at a strategic spot near the article's beginning.

4. *Mortises.* Seeing an expanse of picture that is all sky or all foreground, some designers, prompted perhaps by a lack of space elsewhere, cut out a block and put type there. The block may be completely surrounded by photograph, or it may be at an edge or corner. Wherever the mortise is located, it usually hurts the composition of the picture and cheapens the page.

The mortise is slightly more defensible when another photograph rather than type is placed into the cut-out portion of the original photograph, providing for a picture within a picture. *Look* used this technique effectively.

5. *Overlaps.* The designer runs type for a heading partly in the white space next to a photograph and partly in the photograph itself. As it passes from white space to photograph, the type can remain black (surprint). Or, as it makes the crossing, it can change to white letters (reverse printing).

The designer resorts to this cliché for two reasons: (1) to save space (perhaps the heading is too wide for the space allotted to it) and (2) to draw type and picture together (the principle of unity). But the space saving comes at the expense of a visual interruption where the type crosses over. And the unification of type and photo comes at the expense of photo clarity and beauty.

The list of clichés could be expanded. For instance, it would be easy to make a case against all reverses and surprints. Designers too often resort to these—at some expense to readability.

A set of boxes sometimes can best organize a page of miscellaneous items. In "Futurescope," a full-color page from *Johns-Manville Future,* the designer uses different typefaces for each feature and where necessary wraps copy around the art. The all-the-way-across-the-page heading, the black border, and the same-style drawings help unify the page that otherwise might have been a hodgepodge.

Occasionally, a venturesome designer goes slumming among the clichés, picks one out, and lends some dignity to it. In good hands, even a cliché can please.

Rules, bars, boxes, and other delights

Sorting through typical newspapers, you can pretty much tell the modern from the old-fashioned by the lack of column rules. Get rid of column rules, editors figure, go to all-lowercase heads, and change the nameplate from Old English to, say, Bodoni, or, if you are really daring, go to Helvetica, and you put your newspaper among the avant-garde.

What the newspaper throweth away, the magazine picketh up. Or: One medium's garbage is another medium's treasure.

Column rules are big news in magazine design, now that art directors have rediscovered them. And when rules are not enough, there are bars. Nice, thick bars. Some magazines combine thick bars with thin rules. The bars can be used, for instance, as horizontal underlines or overlines, the thin rules as column or story separators.

When he was art director of *New York,* Milton Glaser brought the Scotch rule back into general use. Many magazines copied the look. A Scotch rule consists of a thick line sandwiched between two thin lines.

And for many editors and art directors, the box is a staple of design, especially when several vaguely related items appear on a page or spread. Boxes may be built from single-width lines, decorative lines, or sets of parallel lines (like Scotch rules). You can also get a box by running a tint block in gray or color under a unit of type.

Lines, bars, boxes, and other typographic gimmicks can help sort things out for the reader. But they can become clichés. One day, perhaps, magazine editors and art directors will grow tired of them and toss them aside, where young newspaper art directors (or makeup people) will rediscover them, and a new trend will come to newspaper design. In fact, looking at the handsome special sections of the New York *Times* and other important newspapers, you get the impression the trend has already begun. The ruled lines in this reincarnation run horizontally rather than vertically.

The swipe file

A cartoonist copies the cross-hatched, carefully controlled lines of David Levine, and his colleagues, if not his readers, will spot the plagiarism. An illustrator copies the delicate line, the flat colors, and the decorative look of Milton Glaser or the virile, freshly painted look of Al Parker, and fellow painters will see at once the influence of the master. In practice the appropriation of another person's style or technique seldom results in work that is the equal of the original.

In the area of graphic design, lifting ideas comes easier and with less stigma attached, although a few designers are beginning to copyright their work. The copyright law, which has long protected original writing and art, has recently been interpreted more broadly to include design. Joan Stoliar is thought to be the first designer to copyright a book design (*Illusions* by Richard Bach, Delacorte

Press/Eleanor Fried, 1977). The design, such as it was, for *Paul McCartney: Composer/Artist* (Simon & Schuster, 1981) was copyrighted. But the U.S. Copyright Office, after a two-year study, decided it would not give protection to graphic design.

Anyway, it is difficult to successfully trace design to its source. It is the rare designer who is not influenced—and not just subconsciously—by the work of other designers. Nor is this bad. The innovators—Allen Hurlburt, Dugald Stermer, Henry Wolf, Peter Palazzo, Paul Rand, and the others—have doubtless had great influence on the look of magazines other than those they've designed, and they must be pleased to have played a role in upgrading the general level of graphic design; they do not have exclusive interest in any one solution, anyway. Their great satisfaction lies in moving on to unexplored design plateaus.

Even these designers maintain swipe files—printed portfolios of prize-winning work, if not the more obvious folders of clippings. All designers and editors should build up their own collections of designs that please, inspire, and, most important, communicate clearly.

There is such a thing as creative copying. As a beginning designer you can't get much satisfaction out of lifting a spread, whole, out of one publication and putting it down in your own magazine with a mere substitution of pictures and wording. You will try to change facings and picture sizes, adjust title length and placement, and so on, not solely to disguise the fact that you lifted the design, but to try to improve on it. You should use another's design primarily as a starting point. And you should remember that good design is tailored to the needs of a specific article or story.

You will draw inspiration not only from other graphic designs but from architectural structures, oil paintings (they are designed, too), and, of course, Nature's landscapes.

You may find some stimulus from that classic set of ready-made designs: the alphabet. An *L* or a *U* or an *A* or an *R*, or a number, or one of the letters turned sideways or upside-down might suggest a pattern for a page or spread. Of course the reader will not see the letter or figure. As a designer you will not be bound by it. You will merely use it as a beginning.

Obviously, much of publication design springs from advertising design. Advertising designers, probably more than publication designers, take chances with graphics. As a publication designer who borrows from advertisers you will be keeping abreast of graphic design trends. You should remember, though, that many of these "trends" will turn out to be short-lived fads.

Redesign

When editors think Redesign, they should think beyond typefaces and uses of art. They should start with basic size and format. They should reexamine their typesetting systems, their printing processes, their paper stock. They should even rethink their publications' purposes.

One major reason for rethinking design for a consumer magazine is to better attract potential advertisers. Advertisers like to appear in handsome and contemporary settings. Good-looking magazines are likely to impress the media buyers at advertising agencies. These people face bewildering choices from among the scores of competing magazines in any one field. Obviously they

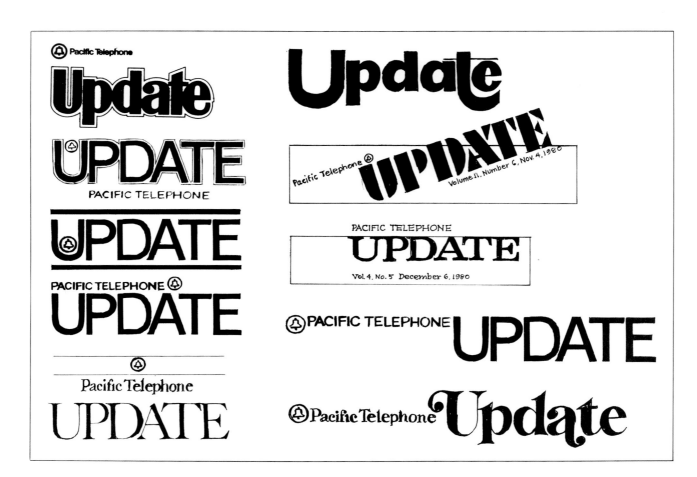

Sometimes an editor flirts with the idea of changing basic design, looks over suggested changes, then decides to stick with what has worked well enough in the past. A logo change is especially agonizing because of the investment of time it represents and its recognition value. The editor of *Update,* a tabloid for employees of Pacific Telephone, asked to see some logo ideas from this author/designer, and decided, finally, to stay with the logo it had (the first example shown) because it seemed to fit the format best after all.

can't read all the magazines thoroughly to determine editorial content and meanings. But they can *look* at the magazines.

The major newsmagazines did some redesigning in the late 1970s to give themselves more of a contemporary look. *Time* hired Walter Bernard, former art director for *New York,* who chose a slightly different typeface for headlines, introduced secondary headlines, and made wider use of thin rules. The magazine said it was after "a simpler, cleaner-looking environment" for its full-color pictures, by now widely used on its pages. The new look started with the Aug. 15, 1977 issue. You might want to examine this and compare it to the previous issue.

Prompted by *Time, Newsweek* brought in outside help and redesigned itself in 1979, using several new typefaces. Sections started with an elbow-like arrangement, with "NEWSWEEK" running up the side. Small boldface initial letters appeared frequently in the magazine. But the look was gimmicky, and *Newsweek* went back to a look closer to what it had been.

Feeling the need of a change in format, the editor and art director may find, on getting into it, that the old way of doing things wasn't so bad after all. A case in point is *Advertising Age.* In 1966 it called in John Peter to consider changing its looks. At first, Peter offered a multitude of suggestions for changes. "But the more he and our editors discussed the matter, the more they all agreed that only a minimum of change should be made—that basically, the typographic dress we've been using for 15 years or more was still pretty sound," the magazine said in a 1967 statement. A weekly, the magazine is really a news magazine; and so it wants a newspaper look.

Peter did do these things:

He eliminated column rules.

He modernized the logo, using a condensed Clarendon, a better looking slab serif type than the more standard slab serif the magazine had been using.

He modernized (read that: *simplified*) the standing heads.

In 1971 *Advertising Age* made another modest change by substituting a modern sans serif for the slab serif it had been using for its heads. It has made a few other changes, but it still has its original *Advertising Age* look.

Christianity and Crisis is another magazine that thought it needed a complete change, and then decided against it. The magazine gave full freedom to two designers to make major changes. The changes they recommended were trivial. They came up with a new logo and a new masthead, and that was about all. One of the designers, Robert Newman, said: "While all avenues were open, we decided not to change it very much. We concluded that the magazine is what it seems to be, which is rare and a virtue in typographic design."

A redesign job, when it is attempted, usually takes a period of several months while the designer learns all about the editorial processes of the publication (every publication develops its own routines) and finds out about the typesetting and the printing facilities available. Decisions must be made to cover every contingency, guidelines laid down to be followed more or less permanently by persons who may not have had a hand in the setting of the design. Henry Wolf reported in 1978 that he had "a two-year engagement to redo *House Beautiful*."

The time to redesign is when a publication is still successful but not looking the part. Waiting until their publications are slipping, editors wait too long. Beautiful new design can't hide a lack of editorial vitality.

It is better, probably, for editors to change their publications' looks gradually as the times change. Too abrupt and far-reaching changes could lose some loyal followers. Readers tend to be conservative in matters of design. They like the familiar.

The secret is to hold on to old readers with familiar typographic landmarks while luring new readers with innovation.

Looking back on the demise of the original *Saturday Evening Post* just after its radical design changes, James W. O'Bryan, art director of *National Review,* says, "I . . . believe that . . . [most] magazines become familiar habits to readers, and when you radically change the book you really upset the reader and cause in some special type magazines—actual resentment. Perhaps *T.S.E.P.,* was old fashioned, but, by God, it was what the reader enjoyed."

He adds: "Here at *N.R.* we've made many changes since I first became A.D., but I try never to make a *drastic* change, one that will upset anyone, and yet even the subtle, almost imperceptible occasional changes do cause the letters of protest to come our way."[3]

Redesign leads to redesign. *Esquire* modernized its look in the

3. Letter to the author from James W. O'Bryan, June 10, 1981.

1970s with new management, then in 1980 changed its mind with still newer management. The magazine resurrected its distinctive script logo, causing art director Alfred Zelcer of *TWA Ambassador* to observe: "To revert to [the old logo] from a 'contemporary' face-lift is truly courageous. . . . In a business that becomes more bottom-line oriented every year, it gives me a sense of well-being to know that integrity and primal love of magazines is not a thing of more civilized, past times."[4]

The tools of design

Tools used by designers range from ordinary writing pencils to felt- and nylon-tip pens and markers used on anything from newsprint to illustration board. Starting out making thumbnail sketches, you may want to use a ballpoint or nylon-tip pen or a Rapidograph on sheets of cheap typing paper. Moving to actual size roughs, you might want to work on sheets in a layout pad or tracing pad.

You probably would want to draw small rectangles for all the pages of your publication to plan content in sequence. Then you'd do more careful, actual size rough layouts that deal with design aspects.

In most cases you would not carry any of your rough layouts to the finished look of comprehensives (or comps) of the kind produced by advertising agency art directors for their clients.

To indicate copy, you'd draw or scribble a pattern of parallel lines. To indicate titles and headlines, you'd rough in the letters by size and weight if not by their actual design. In indicating art you would try to distinguish, through the choice of tools you use, between line drawings and continuous tone art (photographs and paintings).

Markers, which come in warm and cool grays as well as colors, are particularly useful for indicating photographs and paintings. Some markers on some surfaces bleed or spread and seep through to the other side. It is a good idea to test them on extra sheets before using them on your layouts. You can spray Blair Marker Fix onto your sheets before laying on a color and respray between color applications. The product prevents bleeds, keeps the colors from fading, and gives your paper a good surface to receive the color.

Suggested further reading

Adams, Robert, *Creativity in Communications,* New York Graphic Society Ltd., Greenwich, Connecticut, 1971.

Arnold, Edmund C., *Arnold's Ancient Axioms,* The Ragan Report Press, Chicago, 1978.

Berryman, Gregg, *Notes on Graphic Design and Visual Communication,* William Kaufmann, Inc., Los Altos, Calif., 1979.

Booth-Clibborn, Eduard and Daniele Baroni, *The Language of Graphics,* Harry N. Abrams, New York, 1980.

Davis, Alec, *Graphics: Design into Production,* Pitman Publishing Corporation, New York, 1974.

Donahue, Bud, *The Language of Layout,* Prentice-Hall, Englewood Cliffs, N.J., 1978.

4. In a letter to the editor of *Esquire,* May 1980, p. 6.

Evans, Harold, *Editing and Design: A Five Volume Manual of English, Typography, and Layout,* Heinemann, London, 1972–.

Felton, Charles J., *Layout 4: Printing Design and Typography,* Charles J. Felton, St. Petersburg, Florida, 1970.

Gill, Bob, *Forget All the Rules You Ever Learned About Graphic Design, Including the Ones in This Book,* Watson-Guptill Publications, New York, 1981.

Goodchild, Jon and Bill Henkin, *By Design: A Graphics Sourcebook of Materials, Equipment and Services,* Quick Fox, Inc., New York, 1980.

Hanks, Kurt, et al., *Design Yourself!,* William Kaufmann, Inc., Los Altos, Calif., 1977.

Hartmann, Robert, *Graphics for Designers,* Iowa State University Press, Ames, Iowa, 1979.

Hofmann, Armin, *Graphic Design Manual: Principles and Practice,* Reinhold Publishing Corporation, New York, 1965.

Hurlburt, Allen F., *Publication Design,* Van Nostrand Reinhold Company, New York, 1976. (Second Edition.)

———, *Layout: The Design of the Printed Page,* Watson-Guptill Publications, New York, 1977.

———, *The Grid: A Modular System for the Design and Production of Newspapers, Magazines, and Books,* Van Nostrand Reinhold, New York, 1978.

———, *The Design Concept,* Watson Guptill Publications, New York, 1981.

Jussim, Estelle, *Visual Communication and the Graphic Arts,* R. R. Bowker Company, New York, 1974.

Karo, Jerry, *Graphic Design,* Van Nostrand Reinhold Company, New York, 1975.

Kince, Eli, *Visual Puns in Design,* Watson-Guptill Publications, New York, 1982.

Maier, Manfred, *Basic Principles of Design,* Van Nostrand Reinhold, New York, 1977. (Four volumes based on the program at the School of Design in Basel, Switzerland.)

McConnell, John, ed, *Design and Art Direction,* Hastings House, Publishers, New York, 1974.

Muller-Brockmann, Josef, *Grid Systems in Graphic Design,* Hastings House Publisher, New York, 1981.

Munce, Howard, *Graphics Handbook,* Northlight/Van Nostrand Reinhold, New York, 1982.

Rand, Paul, *Thoughts on Design,* Van Nostrand Reinhold Company, New York, 1971. (Second Edition.)

Silver, Gerald A., *Graphic Layout and Design,* Delmar Publications, Albany, N.Y., 1981.

White, Jan V., *Graphic Idea Notebook,* Watson-Guptill, New York, 1980.

———, *On Graphics: Tips for Editors,* Lawrence Ragan Communications, Inc., Chicago, 1982.

Wilson, Noel Avon, *A Journalist's Guide to Graphic Design and Planning,* William F. Wilson Memorial Publishing Fund, 1311 Kolb Drive, Jefferson City, Mo., 1975.

Print Casebooks 4, Print Magazine, Washington, D.C., 1980–81. (Six Volumes.)

FOUR: PRODUCTION

"**Y**ou don't simply read *Aspen* . . .," said one of its promotion pieces, "you hear it, hang it, feel it, fly it, sniff it, play with it." *Aspen* was "the magazine in a box," a collection of odds and ends that portended the end to magazines as we had known them: the simple flat, two-dimensional storehouses of printed information, opinion, entertainment, and advertisements. But it was *Aspen* that expired. Traditional-format magazines lived on, in spite of the fact that Marshall McLuhan, in the 1960s, forecast their demise. A number of them died, that is true; they tried to serve audiences which were too diverse, audiences which television could better accommodate. But those that narrowed their focus found receptive audiences and advertisers willing to spend money on their pages.

Despite some widely heralded improvements in technology—even in printing technology—the actual job of producing magazines as well as other publications remains pretty much unchanged.

This chapter deals with production: the activity necessary after editors have done their editing and art directors have laid out the pages. Defined broadly enough "production" includes the laying out of the pages (but not the actual designing of the publication).

Art directors need a knowledge of production in order to (1) get the effects they want and (2) cut down on costs. Most publications have a production director or editor who acts as a sort of middleman between the art director and the printer.

The main consideration in production is printing.

Gutenberg and before

Johann Gutenberg in Germany did not invent printing; the Chinese beat him to it. He did not invent movable type; the Koreans beat him to that. But, unaware of what Koreans had done, Gutenberg worked out his own system and introduced it to the Western world. He designed his types, taking as his model the black, close-fitting, angular calligraphy of the lowlands; carved them; punched them into metal to make molds; and cast them. The characters could be stored in individual compartments and used over and over again. Until then, printing had to be done from wood blocks into which characters were carved, in relief. Once used, the characters served no further purpose.

Before printing of any kind there were the scribes, working alone, who copied manuscripts by hand. When many copies were needed, a group of scribes would sit together in a semi-circle around a reader. The scribes wrote while the reader dictated. This produced several copies of a manuscript at a time. This was Middle Ages mass production.

Printing processes

The printing process Gutenberg used is still very much alive. We call it *letterpress:* printing from a raised surface. It is the process used by a few large daily newspapers and by some large magazines, like *Time, Newsweek,* and *U.S. News & World Report.* Other processes are *offset lithography* (printing from a flat surface) and *gravure* (printing from tiny wells incised in a metal plate). Offset is the almost universal printing process for company magazines and specialized magazines as well as most newspapers and most books; gravure is the process for large, generously illustrated magazines like *Seventeen* and the syndicated Sunday supplements like *Parade* and *Family Weekly.*

In the late 1970s a number of magazines previously printed by letterpress switched to gravure because it could give quality reproduction to photographs on cheaper, lighter paper. Gravure uses a 175-line screen for halftones compared to letterpress's 120-line screen for magazine printing. And gravure presses turn faster.

Experts say that at a 4,000,000-circulation a magazine should consider gravure.[1] When *Mademoiselle* switched from letterpress to gravure, art director Susan Niles found it took some getting used to. "You can't make corrections at the last minute, for instance, so it's more demanding. But you get wonderful photographic quality."

Many magazines use more than one printing process for a single issue. *Better Homes & Gardens, Family Circle,* and *Woman's Day* are part letterpress, part gravure. *Reader's Digest* is part gravure, part offset.

If you want to know what printing process a magazine uses, look it up in *Consumer Magazine and Farm Publication Rates and Data* or *Business Publication Rates and Data,* monthly publications of Standard Rate & Data Service, Inc. Under Entry 15 for each magazine you will find mechanical requirements and printing process listed.

Some printers insist that offset lithography can't match letterpress for quality, especially if a coated paper stock is used. In letterpress, halftones can be beautifully crisp, type can be remarkably defined.

A disadvantage of letterpress is the high cost of photoengraving. If a magazine is heavy on art and the press run is small, it is likely to find that offset lithography is a more appropriate printing process. So far as small magazines are concerned, letterpress is competitive only when pages are made up mostly of type.

The type most often used in letterpress printing is set by one of the "hot type" composition systems: foundry (the system Gutenberg used), Ludlow (used primarily for headlines), Linotype and Intertype systems (used for body copy), and Monotype (used for high-quality letterpress printing). All of these systems can be used for offset lithography, too, after a first "printing" is made (or after a repro proof is pulled); but offset lithography has the additional advantage over letterpress of being able to use any of the "cold type" composition systems besides: hand lettering, hand "setting" of paper type, typewriter composition, photolettering, and photo-

This diagram shows how offset lithography works. The plate wraps around cylinder A and picks up ink and the dampening agent from the rollers above. The plate transfers its image to the rubber blanket on cylinder B, which in turn transfers it to the web of paper delivered by cylinder C. Cylinder D delivers the paper from the press.

1. "Magazines Switch to Gravure Printing," *Folio,* June 1978, p. 31. "Gravure" is commonly used now for "rotogravure." There is a slower, better quality form of gravure—"sheet-fed gravure"—used for a few expensive art or photography books but not for magazines.

Before the turn of the century, the process of engraving for reproduction in magazines involved enough hand work — enough artistry — to merit two signatures or credit lines: one for the illustrator, one for engraver. This illustration appeared in *Frank Leslie's Popular Monthly Magazine.*

typesetting. Before cold type composition can be used in letterpress, it must first be converted to a photoengraving.

Offset, because of relatively low "getting ready" costs, is the process for all small-circulation publications.

A big advantage of offset, especially for newspapers, is its ability to reproduce photographs—especially color photographs—clearly, even on poorer quality paper. But that advantage can be a disadvantage if you don't have good photographs to start out with. One fuzzy photograph shown on a page with several outstanding ones will look out of place. Letterpress on newsprint tends to bring all photos down to an average level, so the poor photograph is not so disturbing.

Magazine art directors prefer offset lithography to letterpress because with offset lithography they have firm control over the precise placement of each element on the page. In letterpress, the printer uses the art director's *rough sketch* or *rough pasteup* only as a guide. In offset the printer takes the art director's *finished pasteup* (also called *camera-ready copy,* or *the mechanical*) and actually photographs it. (Everything in offset is photographed, including the type.) But this means that someone on the magazine—the art director, the art director's assistant, the production editor, or pasteup artist—has to do a finished pasteup: a tedious, demanding, time-consuming job. (Gravure requires a finished pasteup, too.)

What an offset publication turns over to the printer is what the printer prints, exactly—crooked lines and columns, uneven impressions on the repros, smudges, and all. It is safe to say that the editor of an offset publication has more production headaches than the editor of a letterpress publication.

Newspapers generally operate their own printing presses. Magazines and book publishers hire the printing done. Magazines enter into long-term contracts with printers. Book publishers may dicker with printers for each book published. Some magazines leave the pasteups to their printers. The printers get rough or finished layouts or dummies to use as guides.

A study of offset magazines, especially the smaller company magazines, suggests that editors do not know how to take advantage of the flexibility of the process. They either treat their magazines as though they were produced by letterpress, and as a result their magazines look stilted—or they overreact: tilting pictures, cutting them into strange shapes, drawing unnecessary lines around them, fitting crude cartoons onto the page, and in general making their magazines look like the work of amateurs.

The revolution in printing

Carroll Streeter of *Farm Journal* sees the day when his magazine will custom build each copy to fit the special needs of each subscriber: what that subscriber wants will be recorded on electronic tape, and a computerized bindery will pick up only materials that interest him.

Less dramatic changes in format have taken place already. Printing and typesetting technology has brought great fidelity to the printed page, better color, more flexibility. Some of the newest magazines are coming out in a square rather than in the usual rectangular format. Gatefold covers and center foldouts and booklets bound within magazines are commonplace. *Venture* used three-dimensional color photographs on its covers. *Aspen*, you remember, put itself in a box. *American Heritage* wrapped itself in hard covers. Some publishers have flirted with the idea of "video magazines" to take advantage of the video cassette and cartridge markets.

New technology has been made necessary by rising costs of traditional printing processes and by the increased amount of information that has to be recorded. The cost of composition is particularly prohibitive. By the mid-1960s many U.S. dailies had gone to computer composition. Computers produced tape that was fed into linecasting machines, quadrupling the speed of setting.

And computer editing was at hand. That was a system whereby copy was first typed into a computer, which hyphenated it, justified it, and fitted it into a layout. The layout was presented to the editor as a TV image. The editor used an electronic pointer and a keyboard to rewrite and rearrange the material.

The system moved to actual type after the editing was done, thereby eliminating any resetting. And if offset lithography was the printing process, hot type composition was eliminated altogether. Under the system, pages could be transmitted instantaneously via facsimile to regional printing plants.

By 1970 *Life* was using an Editorial Layout Display System (ELDS).[2] ELDS was a 7,000-pound electromechanical optical system with a screen, a table-top instrument panel, and some powerful transistorized equipment. Using projectors and computers, it edited, recorded, and printed layouts on demand.[3] It gave the art director immediate visualization of various layout ideas, in full color and in actual size.

It worked this way: the art director mounted all elements in the layout on 35 mm slides and slipped them into the machine. The machine held ninety-nine of them, plus a basic library of typefaces and a layout grid.

Using the instrument panel, the art director could call any combination of elements into position, enlarge any of them, crop any of them—and work anywhere on the spread. Operators could be trained to use the machine in about two hours.

In 1977 *Reader's Digest* went to a computerized system that had the magazine's staff perform some functions normally associated with a typesetting house. *Digest* personnel put text material on computer tapes in binary coding suitable for driving the phototypesetters at York Graphic Services, where the type was set and typeset page negatives made.

Newspapers, which had long ignored the revolution taking place, suddenly joined in. Papers all over the country in the 1960s and 1970s switched from letterpress to offset, to cold-type composition, and to computer technology.

The Pasadena *Star-News* (to name one paper) in 1981 announced its plans for the installation of a pagination system (set up by Information International, Inc.) to handle halftones and line art as well as headlines and text matter. Pages were to be made up by operators in the news and advertising departments on video display terminals. In this system, a scanner digitizes photos and

When *Northwest,* magazine section of *The Oregonian,* was a letterpress operation, editor Joe Bianco had to settle for bold, flat colors and a poster format. This example shows that the poster approach to covers can result in excellent design. The artist: E. Bruce Dauner.

2. "Art Direction Enters New Age as LIFE Begins Layout by Machine," *Publishers' Weekly,* July 6, 1970, pp. 28,29.
3. *Ibid.,* p. 28.

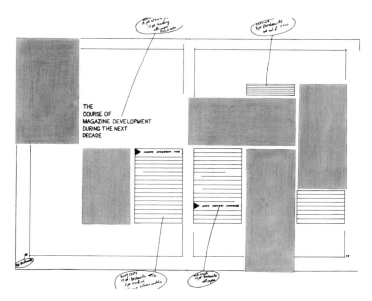

Early in the term of his Publication Design and Production course at the University of Illinois, Prof. Glenn Hanson distributes copies of manuscripts and asks students to copyfit them and incorporate them into page design. This is a first effort by student Ralph Sullivan: a spread involving five photos. The student writes notes in the margins to indicate his preferences in type styles and sizes. This is a rough layout. For a more comprehensive layout, he would be expected to omit the black outlines around the copy blocks and, using the drawing tools available to him, make the rectangles of gray actually look like photographs.

line art and stores them in disk memory while the system accepts and stores data from a text editing system. Any of this material can be displayed on the terminal, and the operator can then jump stories, rehyphenate, rejustify, edit, expand, cut, tighten, space out, etc. The system then allows for the transmission of completed page layouts to a unit that makes the film for platemaking.[4]

At the start of the 1980s it was possible, through the new technology, for a publication to create full-color art with a keyboard and a cathode-ray tube, using 128 colors. The future promised, among other wonders, programmed formats. The choices for art directors appeared to be endless. Everything could be done quicker and, on balance, more economically. Of course it all meant greater pressures on art directors. In many instances they had to make decisions in a hurry and stick by them. "Speed is becoming an element of talent," *U&lc.* observed in its "Vision '80" issue.[5]

Some of the new equipment can be operated by non-designers. But where taste and judgment are involved, designers themselves have to step in. Designers insisting on traditional approaches—designers who avoid the new machinery—will be at a disadvantage compared to more experimental designers who welcome the changes.

One big problem with the new technology is that it changes so fast. A printing establishment or a type house that installs new equipment finds that it becomes outdated in just a few years. The 1980s promised a bewildering lineup of printing, typesetting, and picture-reproduction methods and machines.[6]

Typesetting

The types of the early printers were set by hand. Today we still set some types this way. But, thanks to Ottmar Mergenthaler's invention (1884) and some follow-up inventions in both America and Great Britain, most types are set now by machine.

4. "Pasadena Star-News Buys $2 Million Pagination System," *TypeWorld,* June 26, 1981, p. 13.

5. *U&lc.,* June 1980, p. 39.

6. Prof. Harold Wilson of the University of Minnesota has put together an excellent collection of slides on *The New Technology of Print Media,* available from National Scholastic Press Association, Minneapolis, Minnesota.

Hand-set types (foundry type and Ludlow) and machine-set types (Linotype, Intertype, and Monotype) were all developed for letterpress printing. The later printing process, offset lithography, brought about new methods of typesetting. Type produced by these new methods is called "cold type."

Cold type systems have cut typesetting costs in some cases to one-fourth of what they would be by "hot type" systems; they have broadened considerably the art director's choice of faces and given everyone great flexibility in designing pages.

Printers and typesetters do not agree on the meanings of the various terms used in cold-type composition. But here are some generally accepted definitions:

Cold type refers to any method of type composition other than hot type. It was the obvious term to use when offset lithography came on the scene to do away with the necessity of using foundry type and the product of the Linotype, Ludlow, and Monotype systems, although all of these systems *can* be used in offset if desired. The type is "cold" because hot lead is not involved anywhere in the process.

Photocomposition as a term covers much but not all cold-type composition. It includes phototypesetting and photolettering, both of which require photographic paper.

Phototypesetting refers to systems which set line after line of text matter. A computer often is involved.

Photolettering refers to systems that set only display type, often in single lines or strips.

Pagination refers to systems that can produce complete pages of text and display type along with art. No pasteup necessary.

Strike-on composition refers to text matter produced by typewriter-like machines (and typewriters themselves). No photography is involved at this early stage in the production process.

Unfortunately, some of the cold-type composition systems have resulted in inferior typography, especially where strike-on composition is involved. The problem is especially noticeable in narrow-width columns of copy where justification of the right-hand margin is involved. Uneven spacing between words is something to watch for and eliminate.

Some typewriter-composers produce letters designed to fit a sin-

Roger Waterman's full-color comprehensive rough layout of a spread for *Chevron USA* along with the two pages as they actually appeared in the magazine. The typed note pasted down at an angle on the right-hand page is a reminder to the designer to make some adjustments: *"HAWAII"* is to be smaller and in heavier type. And "Motorambling in" is to be bigger. The reproduction does not show it clearly, but the smaller photo is marked to be recropped and lifted slightly on the page. Most magazines do not require so high a degree of finish for rough layouts.

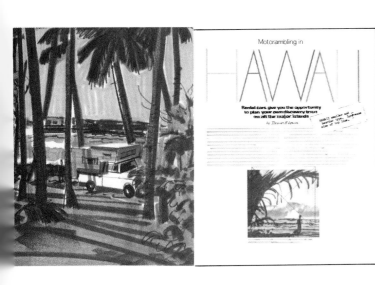

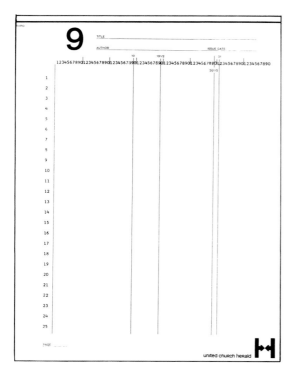

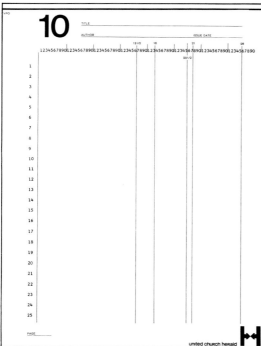

gle width or, at best, three or four widths, whereas in their ideal state letters occupy a great variety of widths.

Most newspapers set their own type. They always have. First they set type by hand, using foundry type. Then came Linotype machines. The Linotype machines gave way to various cold-type systems with the coming of offset lithography. Magazines, which used to have all their type set by outside houses, are now installing their own typesetting systems. A *Folio* survey of 559 magazines in 1980 showed that half of them set type in-house. Even book publishing houses are doing much of their own typesetting now.

Where magazines *don't* set body copy in-house, they often set their own headlines and titles on photolettering machines. Some art directors and designers use press-on or dry-transfer letters, the kind you can buy in sheets at art-supply stores.

Computer typesetting

When type was set only by hand, a speed of one character per second was possible. Mechanical typesetters increased the speed to five characters per second. Photographic typesetters since World War II brought it up to 500 characters per second. By the end of the 1960s electronic-computer typesetting could reach a speed of 10,000 characters per second.[7]

Many of the new typesetters relate to computers which take care of justification and its necessary hyphenation. The new typesetters also offer kerning (fitting letters together so that their spaces overlap, or, as one typographer describes it, "nesting . . . letters to avoid typographic gaposis"), hung punctuation (punctuation placed outside the edges of a copy block), and minus leading (less than normal spacing between lines). Of course they also offer the qualities standard typesetters have always offered—like letterspacing and regular leading.

Some newspapers now own typesetters that compose not just by columns but by pages. Printers of magazines are experimenting with similar typesetters.

OCR (optical character reader) scanners can read typed manuscripts and feed what they read directly into typesetting equipment. This means no additional keyboarding, as at a Linotype machine. Direct-entry typesetters in 1977 were available at around $10,000 where earlier they cost as much as $200,000. And a secretary or office worker could operate the machines.

Computers have changed—and will change—typesetting procedures for publications, but they won't change the basic role of the art director, which is to pick the right types and the right art and put them together to give the best possible display to editorial matter.

Copyfitting

Most editors find it necessary to determine, before the type is set, how much space it will take in the magazine. Essentially, copyfitting involves these five steps:

1. Decide on the width of the columns in print.
2. Consult a character-count chart (available from your type

7. Gerald O. Walter, "Typesetting," *Scientific American,* May 1969, p. 61.

house) to find the number of characters you can get in that line width in the typeface you want to use.

3. Set the typewriter margins for that number of characters.

4. Type your copy, going only slightly under or over that count for each line.

5. Count the lines in your typed manuscript. You will know from previous settings how many printed lines you can get in a column.

On most publications there is considerable adjusting of copy during the layout or makeup stage. Lines are added or deleted, art is enlarged or reduced—all as part of the copyfitting process. One of the pleasant outcomes of the current practice of allowing columns to run to uneven lengths on pages in magazines and even books is that copyfitting becomes less of a problem.

Copyfitting for titles and headlines become less a problem of counting and more a problem of tracing off letters from existing alphabets and estimating space to be occupied. Increasingly, editors and art directors are asking typesetters to set to fit in the typeface chosen.

The point system

The typesetter or printer uses *points* to measure type sizes, *picas* to measure column widths. There are 72 points to an inch. There are 12 points to a pica, hence 6 picas to an inch.

The point system is not universal. America and England use it; the countries on the Continent do not. There the Didot system prevails (points are slightly bigger). Now it looks as if all of us will be moving, gradually, into the metric system for measuring type (as for measuring everything else). Already a few type manufacturers are measuring their types in centimeters.[8]

Getting along with the printer

Understanding the printing processes will keep the art director from asking the impossible of the printer. It will also open his eyes to printing's possibilities. But Alfred Lowry, art director of *Newsweek*, thinks there is such a thing as knowing *too much* about printing. If you think an effect can't be had, you won't ask for it.

Every art director should know at least enough about printing and production to be able to converse intelligently with the printer.

On any publication, the printer and art director must reconcile differences resulting from a pragmatic approach to the job on the one hand and a visionary's approach on the other. Frequent consultation is necessary.

If the printer and the editor and staff members sit down and reason with each other, explain to each other their needs and limitations, and talk frankly about costs, and if each side is willing to compromise, the relationship between editor and printer can be pleasant enough. Too many editors (and art directors) arrive at some arbitrary effect or size and hold out for it, despite the fact

(Opposite page)
Typical typing sheets used by a magazine in preparing its copy for the typesetter. One is for copy that will be set in 9-point type, the other for copy that will be set in 10-point. The typist chooses the vertical line at the right that represents the correct column width and ends each line of typing as close to that line as possible. The numbers going down the side at the left quickly show the editor how many lines the copy will take when it is set in type.

8. Sandra B. Ernst, "Measuring Column Inches in Centimeters," *Art Direction,* March 1977, pp. 68, 69. Her article contains tables showing conversion of metrics to points, points to metrics.

that with slight modification, the time involved in production (and hence the cost) could be greatly reduced.

Ideally, printing offices and editorial offices should be in the same city, but for reasons of economy, publications tend to let out contracts to printers in other parts of the country. For instance, many of the magazines edited on both the East and West Coasts are printed in the Middle West.

In seeking out a printer it is important to find one interested in innovation. Settling for the printer who comes in with the lowest bid may not be the most economical way of publishing.

Every printer has certain strengths, certain idiosyncrasies. Every printer has a preferred way for the editor to mark and prepare copy. An unhurried discussion at the start and frequent conferrals with the printer over the year will do much to ease production problems on a publication.

Choosing paper

Working for a newspaper you lose little sleep in your choice of a paper stock. You pick a newsprint sheet, and pick it once, and worry only about its skyrocketing costs. Working for a magazine or book publisher or designing direct-mail, your choices become a little bewildering. There are so many possibilities. For a magazine, usually, you chose once and live with it. For books and direct-mail pieces, you make new choices constantly.

Four considerations should guide the editor and art director in their choice of paper stock.

1. *The look of the paper.* How does its brightness, color, and texture match the mood of the publication? Offset papers as chosen by editors of magazines are usually washday white, but they don't have to be. An off-white or even a light cream-colored stock has a richer appearance.

If the publication contains mostly photographs, whiteness of the paper *is* important. You want as much contrast as possible between the ink and the paper.

For special issues or for special sections, a colored stock can be arresting. It is cheaper than using a second color in printing, but with pure white gone, the art director faces a problem in giving photographs their best display.

As for texture, coated glossy, or smooth papers best display photographs; coarse paper best displays type. But a face like Bodoni works best on coated stock because of the fine detail of the thin strokes and serifs.

Some editors and art directors change stock from issue to issue and even use more than one stock in a single issue.

Some editors like a paper stock with a noticeable pattern in it: like a stipple. Those editors should remember that the texture stays constant as the size of the sheet increases or decreases. The pattern may look innocuous enough on a large-size sheet, but when the sheet is cut down to page size, it may be too intrusive. Such a pattern would be better in an *Life*-size magazine than in a *Reader's Digest*-size magazine. Better to avoid it altogether.

2. *The feel of the paper.* Does the editor want a rough feel or a smooth one, a soft feel or a hard one (a paper can be both rough and soft, or smooth and hard), a thick sheet or a thin one?

An interesting fact about roughness: it can carry the feel of cheapness, as in the paper that was used by the old pulp magazines, or the feel of quality, as in an Alfred A. Knopf book printed on antique paper. The feel of the paper does tell the reader something about quality.

Most people like the feel of coated or polished stock, and that may be reason enough for editors to choose it—if they can afford it.

With respect to thickness: an editor may prefer a thicker sheet so that the publication will appear heftier. The name for such a sheet: high-bulk paper. A 60-pound sheet in one paper may be thicker than a 60-pound sheet in another simply because the one has been bulked. A paper's pound designation is determined by taking 500 sheets in the manufacturer's basic size—25 × 38 for book papers—and weighing them.

3. *The suitability of the paper.* Is the paper heavy enough to stand the strain of continued use? Ordinarily, the editor chooses for the cover a stock that is heavier than for the inside pages.

Is the paper permanent? A newspaper, quickly discarded, can go with newsprint. A scholarly quarterly, which will be bound and used for years by researchers, needs a longer lasting stock.

Is the paper suitable for the printing process? Papers manufactured for letterpress equipment will not work for offset. Offset needs a paper stock that can adapt to the dampness of the process and that will not cause lint problems. Letterpress needs a paper stock that isn't too crisp. the various textures, smooth and rough, are available in both letterpress and offset stock.

What typefaces should be used? Old style romans call for an antique stock, modern romans a glossy or polished stock. But most papers offered for magazine printing are versatile enough so that, within reason, any type can be used.

Does the editor need a paper with high opacity? Or can the paper be more transparent? If photographs are a consideration, or if masses of dark inks will be used, the editor will have to have an

A crowded two pages from the old *West* magazine (Mike Salisbury, art director). The art is by James McMullan of Visible Studios Inc., New York.

Teller, published by the Royal Bank of Canada, combines colorful art and typography for lead articles with a more subdued look for standing features. This news section makes use of horizontal lines, sans serif headline faces, roman body copy, and numbered pictures. Part of the magazine is printed on glossy white paper; this section, and several other news-oriented sections are printed on dull-finish, blue-tinted stock.

Bell Telephone Magazine uses a second color—baby blue—boldly here to contrast one page with the other, to make two words in a title stand out, and to unite a left-hand page with a right-hand page. The initial letter starting out the article picks up the color of the page opposite. It offers the only color on that right-hand page, making the contrast between the two pages all the more startling. The shadow letters in the title nicely lend themselves to this color treatment.

opaque paper. For good reproduction of photographs editors of magazines should use at least a 40-pound stock, but to fight rising costs, some have gone to lighter papers.

It is possible that as an editor you would want your paper stock to look inexpensive. If your publication goes to members of an organization or to the public supporting you through taxes, you might not want to convey the feel of quality and expense.

4. *The cost of the paper.* Paper cost represents a major production cost to all publications. The Magazine Publishers Association estimates that for a small magazine, paper represents 18 percent of operating costs; for a large magazine, 30 percent. The cost of the paper itself is only part of it. The cost of mailing comes into the picture, too. The heavier the paper, the more it will cost to mail copies of the magazine. A slight reduction in paper weight can mean thousands of dollars difference over a period of a year in mailing costs. An editor choosing between two papers should have the printer make up dummies of each to take to the post office for a consultation.

A magazine doesn't have to use high-quality paper to look well designed. *Rolling Stone* proved that, followed by *Rags* (no longer published). Using newsprint, *Rags* in 1970 was able to print and mail copies at less than 10 cents each.

The Economist, published in London, uses a Bible paper, at least for its U.S. edition, presumably to cut postage costs but perhaps for prestige reasons, too. A daily newspaper in Italy, *Giornale di Pavia,* printed bright color photographs on polyethylene. You could read this paper in the pouring rain, and when you were through you could shake it out, fold it up like a handkerchief, and put it in your pocket. You could also use the paper as a makeshift raincoat.

You can buy paper in rolls or sheets. Those who produce direct-mail pieces and small magazines usually buy sheets. When you buy fewer sheets than the standard number in a paper merchant's package you often pay a 25 percent markup penalty. Paper merchants justify this by pointing out that partially-used packages complicate their storage problems and sometimes result in deterioration of stock.

Turning to color

From the time it was possible, color in printing has played an important role in the growth of many general-circulation and specialized magazines. American Business Press, the organization of trade journals, found in a study conducted in 1980 that 90 percent of its members use color on their editorial (non-advertising) pages. The magazine world's interest in color was spurred in the 1960s with the coming of color to television and with the coming in the late 1950s of Hi-Fi and later SpectaColor to newspapers.

Newspapers fought back with color photography in their news coverage. But with their better paper stock and less hurried production deadlines, magazines clearly had the color advantage over newspapers.

For small magazines wishing to use color, the obvious printing choice is offset, especially when lots of art is also a consideration. With offset, some small magazines enjoy R-O-P (run-of-press) color. That means they don't have to plan their color only for certain pages.

There seems little doubt that color can increase a publication's audience. The *National Star,* right after going to full color in 1975, experienced a 12 percent rise in newsstand sales.

But cost is always a factor. A second color throughout can increase the printing bill for a publication by 25 percent. Full-color can double that. So art directors should know what they're doing when they use color. Otherwise, they should leave experimenting to others. It is a good idea to build a file of the uses of color by others. Study that file. And profit from the mistakes and successes it shows.

One thing you should remember about color: when you see it in isolation, it looks one way, when you see it next to another color, it takes on a different look. Another thing: it looks one way on antique or uncoated stock, another way on coated stock.

If you cannot afford color on a regular basis you can use it on occasion, as when you put out a special issue or special section. The use of color helps say "special."

Because of costs, color in some magazines has been more the tool of the advertising than of the editorial department. The hue and placement of color may be dependent upon decisions made by the advertising department in response to insertion order specifications from advertisers. The editorial department gets a free ride, provided it uses color only on pages in signatures carrying color advertisements.

But editors and their art directors these days are demanding more of a say about where and when to use color.

Not that editors and art directors are wholly sold on color. Some feel that the additional money spent on plates and color printing could be better spent on additional black-and-white pages. Nor are all artists sold on color. Henri Cartier-Bresson, a founder of the Magnum photographic agency, told *Time:* "I don't like color. By the time it goes through the printer, the inks, and the paper, it has nothing to do with the emotion you had when you shot it. Black and white is a transcription of that emotion, an abstraction of it." Irving Penn, another great photographer, said: "I don't think I have ever seen a really great color photograph." Penn's reservations about color stem from his belief in photography as an *art* form. He thinks that photography in its purest form must deviate from realism. And color is realism.

The way to check transparencies is to put them out on a light table and look at them through a magnifying glass. (Photo by Seldon Dix. Courtesy of *Time* Magazine.)

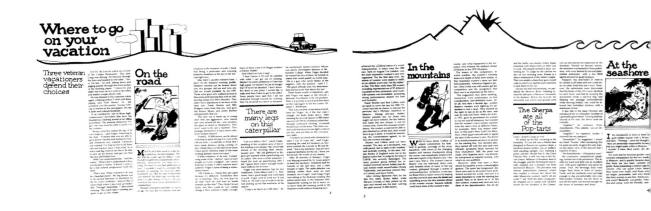

William Hamilton Jones, editor of the Yale alumni magazine, also has strong reservations about color. "My own feeling about a second color is that it's usually a waste of time and money to use it." He says people don't use a second color imaginatively. "They use it in a way that's repetitious. You know, your headline is already bigger than any other type on the page. And if you put it in red besides, you really aren't serving any useful function." Or people use a second color as a tint block behind a picture or as a duotone. "It's a cheap way to call attention to your photograph. . . . It doesn't serve any positive function."[9]

One of the problems is that the editor and art director do not plan an issue of the magazine for color. When color becomes available in one of the signatures, the art director hastily finds some way to use it. Color is *added* to a page or merely *substituted for black*. It is not integrated as part of the design. Hence the many titles in color, blurbs in color blocks, photos in duotone. In some instances, line artwork is added to a page simply to make use of the color. John Peter of John Peter Associates, Inc., magazine consulting firm, calls this the "we-got-it-why-not-use-it" approach to color, an approach that leads to results "that are usually regretted by the time the issue is off the press." He advises: "When in doubt about using color, stay with black and white."[10]

Spot color

What Jones means by *second color* is *spot* or *flat color:* color laid in pure, solid form somewhere on the page as an area of emphasis. It is a "second" color because it is used in association with black or some other color. It involves an additional press run (or a press capable of printing two colors at once).

Some ways the art director can use a second color:

1. *For type.* Color is better for display sizes than for body sizes. When used for type, the color should be on the dark side. A bright red is all right. Yellow does not work. Sometimes it is a good idea to run only one word in a title in color to give it emphasis.

If you reverse a title (run it in white) in a dark area, say in a black part of a photograph, you can run color in the reversed area, in which case the color can be a light color, like yellow.

2. *For photographs.* The best way to print a black-and-white

9. William Hamilton Jones in an untitled interview, *Alma Mater,* April–June 1969, pp. 68, 69.
10. John Peter, "Second Color," *Better Editing,* Spring 1968, pp. 9, 10.

photograph is in black ink on white paper. When you print a photograph in a color, say green, you diminish the tonal scale; the lighter the color, the less scale you have, and the less detailed your photograph will be. If you must print your photograph in a color, you should choose one that is close to black, like dark brown, dark blue, or dark green. If you want the photograph merely as a decorative element or as a backdrop for copy printed over it, then you can print it in a light color.

If you want the complete tonal value plus the mood of color, you can print the photograph twice, once in the color and once in black. This requires two plates printed so that the dots of the black plate register just to the side of the dots in the color plate. We call this kind of halftone a *duotone*. (Example: you might want to use a brown duotone when you have an old-time photograph to reproduce.) You can also run a black-and-white wash drawing as a duotone. And you can apply the color used in the duotone as ordinary spot color elsewhere on the page or signature.

It is possible to take an ordinary black-and-white photo and *posterize* it for a run in black and one or more spot colors. The printer shoots it for line reproduction, dropping out the middle tones. He gives it more exposure for the color plate, less for black. In the printing, the black covers only some of the area printed in color.

It is also possible to print part of a photograph in black, part in a second color. If you have a mug shot, for instance, you can run it as a silhouette, dropping out the background; and in that white area you can print your second color, making a regular rectangle of the photograph. You can also reverse a circle, arrow, or number on a photograph, if one of these is needed, and fill it in in color.

3. *For line art.* A drawing can be printed in the second color, or it can be printed in black with second color used to fill in certain areas.

Second color has special value in charts, graphs, maps, and tables. The color clarifies and emphasizes.

4. *For lines, boxes, and blocks.* Lines in black or in color, horizontal or vertical, help organize and departmentalize a page. Putting a box around a word in a title, or a section of an article, makes it stand out. Or you can use a box to completely surround an article or story.

One excellent use of a second color is as a solid-color or tint block to serve as a backdrop for line artwork. Allen Hutt made good use of a second color—a light yellow—in his book, *The Changing Newspaper* (Gordon Fraser, London, 1973). The newspaper pages he showed were all on faded yellow. The color made the examples stand out from the white pages without the use of boxes. And the faded yellow look seemed appropriate to the look of newsprint.

A block of color can be in a solid or a tint version of that color. Over these blocks you can run titles, body copy, or even photographs. If the blocks are dark enough, you can reverse type in them. A *photograph with a tint block* is different from a *duotone* in that the dot pattern in the former is even and consistent. The photograph with a tint block doesn't have as much contrast as the duotone. It looks as if it were printed on a colored paper stock.

Spot color can involve more than a second color. It can involve all the colors, as in the Sunday comic sections of newspapers. What's needed then are separate pieces of art for each of the primary colors plus black, separate plates, and multiple printings. The art in two-, three-, or four-color spot color work in most cases requires line reproduction.

Process color

A much more expensive form of color is *process color*, necessary when the magazine has full-color paintings or photographs to reproduce. In four-color spot color, the magazine supplies separate art (called *overlays*) for each of the four plates. In process color it supplies only the one piece of art; the printer (or photoengraver) must separate the colors photographically, through use of filters, and painstakingly reconstruct them for the four negatives used to make the four plates.

You have three basic color separation systems to consider: conventional, direct, and scan.

In the conventional system, a process color camera copies the original color painting, photo, or transparency and makes four exposures—for printing in magenta, cyan blue, yellow, and black inks. The continuous-tone negatives later are screened before being used to make the plates. Before they are screened, the negatives can be reworked by highly skilled artists to correct the color. A little more correction can be done after the screening through a process known as dot etching.

Direct-screen separations call for halftone screens being placed over each piece of film in the photocopying of the art. This takes

A typical magazine layout sheet or grid presenting two facing pages in actual size. Each page can accommodate either a three- or four-column format. The tiny marks at the bottom left and right are for page numbers. The white lines in the grayed area are the edges for bleed pictures. This sheet can be used for both the rough layout and the pasteup. Some magazines design their layout sheets to show number of lines per column.

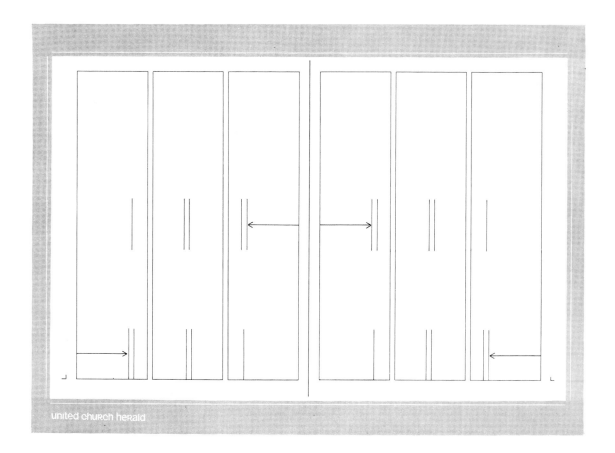

united church herald

less time, but you lose some in quality. You can dot-etch only then, and dot etching is more limited than reworking of continuous tone negatives.

The third system, color-scanner separations, involves laser beams. The art is wrapped around a scanning drum. A light-sensing stylus travels the length of the drum while it rotates. Each of the primary colors is sensed and the information fed to a computer, which sends it to another stylus that emits light to expose a film. That light is screened, so you get already-screened film, as in the direct-screen process.

Of the three processes, color scanning, so far as the editor is concerned, is the least expensive. But it has some limitations. The original art cannot exceed a certain size and it can't be done on illustration board or anything that can't be wrapped around a cylinder. But, "Generally speaking, you can get high quality separations using any of the three systems. . . . The results depend, of course, on the skill of the camera or scanner operators and the amount of corrections you need performed."[11]

For best printing results for color photographs (and you should refer to them as *color* photographs rather than *colored* photographs; the latter suggests color is added after the picture is taken, as in the tinting of photographs) you should supply your printer with transparencies. The printer shouldn't use color prints unless they are all you have. They do not reproduce as well, and the printer charges more to handle them.

In working with transparencies, you should use the same kind of transparency viewer at every step of the reproduction process. It is necessary that everyone who makes a judgement about the transparency make it using the same kind of viewer. To expand this advice a little: you should inspect transparencies, color prints, artwork, proofs, and press sheets under identical lighting conditions in order to maintain control of the work, especially color quality. (Printers urge that one person—preferably a production chief—have full authority on production quality control for both the editorial and advertising sides. Printers find it frustrating to get instructions from one person and final okays from another. One often does not agree with the other.)

You should not ask your printer to enlarge more than five times the original negative. A 2 1/4 × 2 1/4 camera is better for color than a 35 mm, so far as picture reproduction is concerned. A 4 × 5 or an 8 × 10 is best, but of course such cameras are too cumbersome for most publications work.

Coated, or at least a calendered, stock is best for reproducing color photos and probably black and white photos, too, especially if the printing process used is letterpress. If the publication's process is offset, the smoothness of the stock is not so important a factor in photo reproduction.

Laying out the pages

Whether you provide camera-ready copy or merely rough layouts or pasteups to your printer, you or your art director will have to work out the arrangement of articles, stories, and features on the

11. Jeffery R. Parnau, "The Basic Guide to Color Separation," *Folio,* August 1981, p. 82. See his complete article, pp. 81–93.

The Crime Of Punishment

various pages of your magazine, issue after issue. We call this arrangement the *dummy*. In the preceding chapter we went into design considerations for the dummy; in this chapter we will consider the mechanics.

The problem, of course, is to fit all the items, editorial and advertising, together so they will look good and read easily. It is impossible to tell someone who has not done it before exactly how to do it; fitting a magazine together is something one does by instinct or feeling. No two persons do it exactly the same way. There is a good deal of trial and error to the procedure, even for professionals. As a designer you will try one thing, discard it, and try another. When you see the proofs you still will not be satisfied, and you'll probably adjust them, even at that late date.

Almost every magazine has a two-page layout sheet, or grid, on which to arrange layouts. These sheets can be used for both the rough dummy and the finished pasteup.

You can either draw in, roughly, the titles and art, or you can paste into place, also roughly, the galleys and photoprints of the art. If you use galleys, they will be a second set, marked with numbers to show the printer from what galley forms the various articles and stories were taken. The first set is used for proofreading.

The ads are already blocked in. What's left is what a newspaper person would call the "news hole," what a magazine person might call the "editorial hole." The hole consists of a number of beautifully blank spreads ready for your artistry.

The main chore lies with the several major items that start in the front half of the book. A certain number of pages have already been set aside for each item. By previous decision, some items will occupy several pages, some will have one or two. Some items are to begin on a right-hand page, and some on a left-hand page. You often start with this already given.

You have a choice of three basic approaches:

1. *Start from the front.* You figure out where you want your opening art, and how big, and where you want your title and blurb, and then take what space you need for such display, and trail the article column by column through the remaining space. If you run over, you ask the editor to cut. If you're under, you increase the size of the art in front or add art to the body.

2. *Start from the back.* Assuming the publication does not use fillers, you start with the tail end of an article and work forward, allowing for subheads, if that is the magazine's style. The design at first is only tentative; if galleys are used they are fastened down with small dabs of rubber cement. The amount of space between where the feature is supposed to begin and where the first paragraph happens to land is the amount of space available for title, blurb, and art. If it's not very much, you may use it all right there

at the opening. If it is considerable, you will move part of the article forward and put additional art into the space thus opened up.

3. *Work backward and forward from the middle.* This results in a better designed feature, usually, and, more than the other two approaches, requires coordination between editor and designer. The designer is as concerned with the looks of the back half of the article as with the opening spread. Some designers run their big art near the middle rather than at the beginning.

You can best estimate how much space the title type will take by actually lettering it. You indicate body copy by boxes or by a series of parallel lines. How do you know exactly how many lines of type the article will take? You use one of several copyfitting systems[12] or, better, you ask your editor to have all manuscripts typed at preset widths on calibrated copy paper. (See earlier illustration.) On most magazines a little editing at the proof stage is necessary for a perfect fit.

Some editors and designers, recognizing that such last-minute editing is a disservice to the writer and possibly the reader, have gone in for pages whose columns do not necessarily line up at the top or bottom.

Company magazines designed by advertising agencies or design studios and some other magazines require much more finished dummies or layouts—"comprehensive roughs" or "comps," in the language of advertising. The designers treat their editors as though they were clients. A comp leaves little to the imagination; design that doesn't work can be corrected before type is set and pictures are taken. But comps take time, and designers who do them command high fees. Comps are out of reach of most magazine editors.

Instead of using a preprinted grid sheet, the designer doing a comp or even a carefully drawn rough layout is likely to use tissue or tracing paper. For many, many years the drawing and lettering were done in pencil and chalks; now felt-tip pens and markers are the preferred medium. These come in a wide variety of colors and in various shades of gray, both warm and cool.

Martin Baskett's solution was to stretch the title across a two-page spread and use the first and last *T*s as prison towers. The typeface, Bolt Bold, in all caps nicely supports the wall behind. The barbed wire at the top of the wall adds an authentic note.

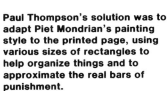

Paul Thompson's solution was to adapt Piet Mondrian's painting style to the printed page, using various sizes of rectangles to help organize things and to approximate the real bars of punishment.

Doing the pasteup

If the publication is printed by offset or gravure, you or your designer carry the layout to a higher level: the pasteup. Using rubber cement or a waxing process, the designer—or a pasteup artist—fastens everything into place: reproduction proofs of titles and text and any actual-size line art. Line art that is to be reduced along

12. Like Glenn Hanson's *How to Take the Fits Out of Copyfitting,* The Mul-T-Rul Company, For Morgan, Colorado, 1967.

These two separate carryover spreads from *Go,* the Goodyear tire dealers' magazine, show how photographs can be clustered to form one irregularly shaped unit, with copy wrapped around. The art shape for each spread is interesting without detracting from the photographs. And the bringing together of the photographs eliminates clutter and gives the small photographs bigger impact than they would have as scattered units. (Larry Miller is editor; Robert R. Wise is art director.)

with photographs and paintings are submitted to the printer separately.

Photographs can be handled in either of two ways. They can be prescreened as Velox prints and pasted down with the type as though they were pieces of line art, or they can be shot separately as halftone negatives and "stripped in" by the printer. You get better fidelity, usually, using the "stripped in" process, but sometimes, as when you have many small photographs on a page, the use of Veloxes is practical. You can also easily retouch a Velox, bringing out highlights.

So far as copy is concerned, pasteup offers the desirable restriction of no last-minute partial leading between lines to even out a column. It is a lot of trouble for a pasteup artist to cut lines apart and respace them. (By contrast, it is a simple matter to extend a story set in hot type; your printer simply puts leads between lines.) That with cold type you can't lead at the last minute means that you won't have unequally leaded stories side-by-side in the publication, and that makes for consistency of pattern—a good thing in design.

In doing a pasteup you trim pieces of copy to within a quarter or, better, an eighth of an inch of the print. You can use a single-edge razor blade or an X-acto knife on a self-healing plastic cutting board. Moving the pieces to position, you may want to use tweezers rather than your fingers. This will keep smudges off them. To save wear and tear on artwork that may go through several hands, and perhaps also to protect the pasteups themselves, you may want to do flaps. These are overlays fastened down at the backs of the pieces and folded over to cover the working surfaces.

Some pasteup artists like to work at light tables, with light coming from below frosted glass to aid in the lining up process. Others prefer ordinary drawing tables with T-squares and triangles. Doing pasteup work you should be particularly concerned about exact and even spacing. You will find a pair of dividers almost indispensable. Where you want to repeat a measurement, you set it once against an original measurement, and the sharp points help you mark it off elsewhere.

It is not a good idea, usually, to do your design thinking while you do the pasteup. You should do a rough sketch or comprehensive first or, at least, a rough pasteup. Then, after you have moved things around to your satisfaction you turn to the final pieces. You want to handle them as infrequently as possible.

Some patching on the final pasteup may result in shadows cast which will be picked up by the camera. These must be opaqued by the printer on the negative. You will see where the printer overlooked a printed shadow on the Van Dyke proofs, and you will circle the error for correction. Rubber cement residue can cause these unwanted marks, too.

Careful pasteup artists pasting down thick copy sheets like to skive the edges with a knife or emery board to eliminate the shadows. Some pasteup artists outline edges of thick copy sheets with a buildup of white opaque paint after the sheets are in place.

Wrapping it up

The production phase ends with the publication's being readied for distribution to the reader.

The publication distributed to the reader via the mails often goes in a wrapper of some kind: a paper sleeve, an envelope, even a box.

A sleeve might fully cover the face of the publication, as for a thick saddle- or side-stitched magazine, or it might cover only a part of the publication, as for a thin one that is folded vertically down the middle before the sleeve is fitted on. Some magazines, mailed flat, go out in transparent full wrappers that protect copies from rain and also allow subscribers to recognize their magazines at once when they arrive. A few magazines wrap themselves in extra covers, perhaps of kraft paper, which as four-page extra signatures are saddle-stitched on. They carry the address label, and they can be torn off when the magazines arrive to allow subscribers to fully appreciate well-designed front covers unmarred by stickers or rough handling in the mails.

Too often the wrapper is overlooked in planning. The art director should be as concerned about its design—about its form and typography—as about the magazine itself. The wrapper is the reader's first contact with each issue as it arrives.

Keeping costs down

To keep printing and production costs down, Roger V. Dickeson, president of Printing Efficiency Management Corporation, offers these suggestions:

1. Cut the publication's trim size, if only slightly. The trimming can save both paper and postage costs.

2. Decrease the paper weight.

3. Come to an understanding with your printer as to exactly what quality you expect and are willing to pay for. Dickeson says that many editors unknowingly add about 10 percent to their printing costs through "extended press makereadies, press running waste, 'make goods,' unnecessary time spent in endless argument and discussion, sending representatives to the printing plant to 'approve' press forms."

Dickeson says requirements for paper, film, and ink—all three—should be worked out ahead of time.

4. Follow the schedules set up with the printer. The editor who doesn't "must pay a premium for any delay time he causes."

Dickeson points out that dailies and weeklies work more efficiently with printers than monthlies do. There appears to be a law in operation here: ". . . production inefficiency expands in direct relationship to the time interval between publication dates." What happens is that the rhythm is lost.[13]

Suggested further reading

Arnold, Edmund C., *Ink on Paper 2,* Harper & Row, Publishers, New York, 1972.

Benevento, Frank S. and others, *Art and Copy Preparation, with an Introduction to Phototypesetting,* Graphic Arts Technical Foundation, Pittsburgh, 1976.

Berg, N. Edward, *Electronic Composition: A Guide to the Revolution in Typesetting,* Graphic Arts Technical Foundation, Pittsburgh, 1976.

13. Roger V. Dickeson, "You *Can* Reduce Print Costs," *Folio,* August 1981, pp. 68 ff. Dickeson offers additional suggestions in this article, including the publisher's supplying of paper to the printer and better money management.

Borowsky, Irvin J., *Handbook for Color Printing*, North American Publishing Company, Philadelphia, 1977. (Revised Edition. Charts showing combinations in two-color printing.)

Brownstone, David and Irene Franck, *The Dictionary of Publishing*, Van Nostrand Reinhold, New York, 1982.

Cardamone, Tom, *Mechanical Color Separation Skills for the Commercial Artist*, Van Nostrand Reinhold, New York, 1979.

————, *Advertising Agency and Studio Skills: A Guide to the Preparation of Art and Mechanicals for Reproduction*, Watson-Guptill Publications, New York, 1970. (Revised Edition.)

Clements, Ben and David Rosenfield, *Photographic Composition*, Prentice-Hall, New York, 1974.

Cogoli, John, *Everything to Know About Photo-Offset*, North American Publishing Company, Philadelphia, 1973.

Cooke, Donald E., *Dramatic Color by Overprinting*, North American Publishing Company, Philadelphia, 1974.

Craig, James, *Production for the Graphic Designer*, Watson-Guptill Publications, New York, 1974.

Demuney, Jerry and Susan E. Meyer, *Pasteups and Mechanicals*, Watson-Guptill Publications, New York, 1982.

Favre, Jean-Paul and Andre November, *Color and Communication*, Hastings House, Publishers, New York, 1980.

Field, Janet N., ed., *Graphic Arts Manual*, Arno Press, New York, 1980.

Gottschall, Edward, *Graphic Communications '80s*, Prentice-Hall, Englewood Cliffs, N.J., 1981.

Graham, Walter B., *Complete Guide to Pasteup*, North American Publishing Company, Philadelphia, 1975.

Gross, Edmund J., *How to Do Your Own Pasteup for Printing*, Halls of Ivy Press, North Hollywood, Calif., 1979.

Hill, Donald E., *The Practice of Copyfitting*, Graphic Arts & Journalism Publishing Company, Huntsville, Alabama, 1971.

Jauneau, Roger, *Small Printing Houses and Modern Technology*, The Unesco Press, Paris, 1981.

Kleper, Michael L., *Understanding Phototypesetting*, North American Publishing Company, Philadelphia, 1976.

Kuppers, Harald, *Color: Origins, Systems, Uses*, Van Nostrand Reinhold Company, New York, 1973.

Levitan, Eli L., *Electronic Imaging Techniques*, Van Nostrand Reinhold Company, New York, 1977.

Lewis, John, *The Anatomy of Printing: The Influence of Art and History on its Design*, Watson-Guptill Publications, New York, 1970.

Memme, Susan, *Teach Yourself to Fit Copy*, Sunrise Communications, Box 1452, Brea, Calif. 92621, 1980.

Mintz, Patricia Barns, *A Dictionary of Graphic Arts Terms*, Van Nostrand Reinhold, New York, 1981.

Moran, James, *Printing in the Twentieth Century: A Penrose Anthology*, Hastings House, Publishers, New York, 1974.

Proudfoot, W. B., *The Origin of Stencil Duplicating*, R. Fenton, Publisher, New York, 1973.

Quick, John, *Artists' and Illustrators' Encyclopedia*, McGraw-Hill Book Company, New York, 1977. (Second Edition.)

Rasberry, Leslie, *Computer Age Copyfitting: A Method of Using the Small Electronic Calculator*, Art Direction Book Company, New York, 1977.

Seybold, John W., *Fundamentals of Modern Composition*, Seybold Publications, Inc., Box 44, Media, Pa. 19063, 1977.

Sanders, Norman and William Bevington, *Graphic Designer's Production Handbook*, Hastings House, Publishers, New York, 1982.

Sharpe, Deborah T., *The Psychology of Color and Design*, Nelson-Hall Co., Chicago, 1974.

Simon, Herbert, *Introduction to Printing*, Faber & Faber, Inc., Salem, N.H., 1980.

Simon, Hilda, *Color in Reproduction: Theory and Techniques for Artists and Designers*, The Viking Press, New York, 1980.

Stevenson, George, A., *Graphic Arts Encyclopedia,* McGraw-Hill Book Company, New York, 1979. (Second Edition.)

Turnbull, Arthur T. and Russell N. Baird, *The Graphics of Communication,* Holt, Rinehart and Winston, New York, 1980. (Fourth Edition.)

Van Deusen, Edmund, *Computer Videographics: Color, Design, Typography,* CCC Exchange, Box 1251, Laguna Beach, Calif. 92652, 1981.

van Uchelen, Rod, *Paste-up: Production Techniques and New Applications,* Van Nostrand Reinhold, New York, 1976.

Graphics Master 2, Dean Lem Associates, P.O. Box 25920, Los Angeles, California, 90025, 1977. (Expensive all-purpose reference book on production, printing, color, typesetting, copyfitting.)

Halftone Reproduction Guide, Halftone Reproduction Guide, P.O. Box 212, Great Neck, New York 11022, 1975. (More than 1,200 different effects using two-color printing.)

Paste-up Guide, Portage, P.O. Box 5500, Akron, Ohio, 1976.

Pocket Pal: A Graphic Arts Digest for Printers and Advertising Production Managers, International Paper Company, New York.

The cover and two nonconsecutive spreads from a 24-page 8 1/2 × 11 booklet, *Managing the Great American Forest,* published by American Forest Institute, Washington, D.C. The story starts on the cover. The 2 1/2-inch sink inside remains constant, with an occasional jutting up of a headline. To encourage reading, the booklet offers its copy in almost display-size bold-face slab-serif letters, with columns unjustified. Each page features art in black and a second color: green. In the second spread, where a section of the story ends, the designer uses a portion of the illustration from the earlier spread, but enlarged and made into a silhouette.

THE
RUGGED
INDIVIDUALS

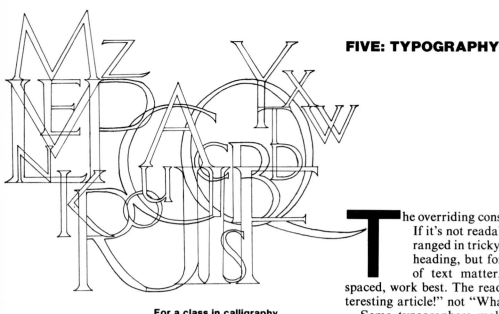

For a class in calligraphy, Joanne Hasegawa, student at the University of Oregon, creates an experimental design with old style roman letters in various sizes. A feel for letterform should be part of the training of every potential art director.

The overriding consideration in typography is readability. If it's not readable, it's not good typography. Type arranged in tricky formation may work for an occasional heading, but for most headings and for long columns of text matter, the traditional types, traditionally spaced, work best. The reader's reaction should be "What an interesting article!" not "What interesting typography!"

Some typographers make a point of distinguishing between readability and legibility. Legibility has to do with the ease with which the reader distinguishes one letter from another. Readability, a broader term, has to do with the ease with which the reader takes in a column or page of type. Readability also has to do with the way the story or article is written.

Readability, from a typographic standpoint, is affected by these factors:

1. *The style of the typeface.* Familiar styles are usually the most readable.

2. *The size of the typeface.* Within reason, the larger the face, the better.

3. *The length of the line.* Comfortably narrow columns are better than wide columns.

4. *The amount of leading (pronounced "ledding") between lines.* Most body sizes can use at least one and probably two points.

5. *The pattern of the column of type.* It should be even-toned.

6. *The contrast between the darkness of the type and the lightness of the paper.* The more contrast the better.

7. *The texture of the paper.* It shouldn't be intrusive.

8. *The relationship of the type to other elements on the page.* The relationship should be obvious.

9. *The suitability of type to content.* The art director should exploit the "personality" of types.

Of course, it isn't all that simple. More on readability later.

Type development

The early types were designed to approximate the handwriting— the calligraphy—of the countries in which they developed. The first German types of Gutenberg and his followers in the fifteenth century were harsh, black, and closefitting—the German blackletter we today mistakenly refer to as "Old English." (A more accurate term for these types is "text," taken from the "texture" of the page, with its heavy, woven look.)

In Italy the faces were lighter, more delicate, after the Humanistic hand of Petrarch. These types were the forerunners of what we today call roman (small *r*) types.

During the first two centuries of printing in Europe (1450–1650) these two faces—blackletter and roman—were used extensively. One other took its place beside them . It was italic, a slanting type introduced by Aldus Manutius in 1501.

The advantage of italic, as Manutius designed it, was that it was close-fitting. That meant you could get more type per page. That was important because paper was expensive. And italic looked more like handwriting, which added to its desirability.

Categories of type

There are many ways to classify types. If you were to classify them from an historical standpoint you would do it one way. If you were to classify them from a utilitarian standpoint, you would do it another.

Type in a small size (up to 14 points) is *body type*. Type in larger sizes (14 points or more) is *display type*.

While many faces come in both body and display sizes, some come only as body types and others come only as display types. In a face designed for both categories you can detect subtle changes as it moves from the large to the small. For instance, the interior area of the loop of the "e" has to be proportionately larger in the smaller sizes of a face. Otherwise it would fill in with ink.

The body faces are divided into *book* faces (the most common faces and the faces used for texts of magazines) and *news* faces. News faces have been especially designed for fast, relatively inexpensive printing in small sizes on newsprint. They are bold faces, essentially, with large x-heights.[1] They do not come in display sizes.

We can break down typefaces, body and display, into several broad categories, sometimes called "races":

1. *Roman.* These faces have two distinguishing characteristics: (1) thick and thin strokes and (b) serifs at the stroke terminals. Where the differences in the strokes are minimal and where serifs blend into the letters, the romans are "old style"; where the differences are pronounced and where the serifs appear almost tacked on as an afterthought, the romans are "modern." In-between styles are "transitional."[2]

2. *Sans serif.* Sans serif types came along first in the early 1800s and were revived by the Bauhaus in the 1920s. Their strokes are essentially of the same thickness. There are no serifs at the terminals. More recent sans serifs, with slight differences in stroke thickness and with a slightly squared look, are called "gothics" or "grotesques."[3]

3. *Slab serif.* Slab or square serif types have even-thickness strokes as on the sans serif types, and serifs as on the roman types. The most beautiful of the slab serifs, because they lean toward the romans, are the Clarendons. Slab serifs were developed in England at a time when the country was fascinated by Egyptian culture, and the term "Egyptian," for no particular reason, was applied to

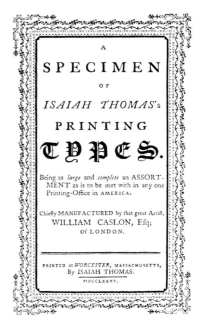

A printer or typesetting house offers customers a type specimen book to use, with available types shown in complete alphabets and in a variety of sizes. One house in New York, Photo-Lettering, Inc., shows samples of close to 10,000 faces. Typesetting houses of an earlier era, when type was all foundry type, had fewer faces to show, but those houses put out books, too. This is the title page of the book offered by Isaiah Thomas, printer at Worcester, Massachusetts. The year was 1785.

1. The x-height is the height of the lowercase "x."

2. The term "roman" is used by some printers to designate all upright types (as opposed to italic—or slanted—types).

3. The word "gothic" has been applied to many new—and hence controversial—types, including the type we know as Old English.

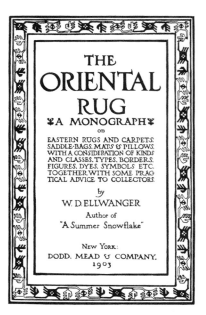

Hand lettering put inside a border that looks like the border of a fine rug makes this exquisite title page from 1903 say "rug" twice, verbally and visually.

them. Many of the slab serif faces are named after Egyptian cities. These faces have also been referred to as "antiques."

4. *Ornamental*. To keep the list workable, the author lumps a number of faces under this one category. There are the text or black letters (Old English), the scripts (which are intended to look like handwriting), and the gimmick letters (made to look like logs, pieces of furniture, etc.).

In each of the major categories are hundreds of sub-categories, sometimes called "families." For instance, in the sans serif category are such families as Franklin Gothic, Futura, Helvetica, News Gothic, Record Gothic, Spartan, Tempo, Trade Gothic, Standard, and Univers. You order types by family names such as these. Each of the types represented by these names usually comes in several varieties.

One of the interesting features of Univers is that the designer of the face, instead of giving the various versions descriptive names like "light" and "heavy" and "expanded," gave them numbers. He reserved odd numbers in Univers for upright letters, even numbers for italics. One of the recent families among the sans serifs is Avant Garde Gothic, designed by Herb Lubalin and Tom Carnase for International Typeface Corporation. The face is named after *Avant Garde,* drawing its character from the logo for that magazine. The face, available in several weights, is noteworthy for its close-fitting characters, its large x-height, and the unusual number of ligatures and alternate characters.[4]

Not only will you find it difficult to distinguish among the various families (exactly how does Granjon differ from Janson?), you also will have difficulty distinguishing among variations within the family. Linotype's Garamond differs from Ludlow's Garamond which differs from the Garamond issued by a foundry type manufacturer. The Mergenthaler Linotype Corporation has two kinds of Garamond: regular and Garamond #3. Garamond #3 is very similar to a version of Garamond offered by Intertype, but Linotype's regular Garamond is quite different from the other two.

More recent faces have been designed exclusively for one company or the other. Caledonia is exclusively Linotype. Century Schoolbook is an Intertype exclusive. But successful faces inspire imitators, and correctly identifying faces these days becomes almost impossible. For instance, Palatino, produced by Mergenthaler Linotype and by Berthold, comes from other firms as Paladium, Andover, Elegante, Malibu, Patina, and Pontiac. These faces differ very slightly from Palatino. Times Roman comes also as Times New Roman, Press Roman, London Roman, English, English Times, and Pegasus. Helvetica comes also as Helios, Newton, Vega, Claro, Corvus, Geneva, and Megaron.

Most families of type come in more than one weight (light, regular, bold, ultrabold) and more than one width (regular, expanded, condensed).

The italics

Although from an historical standpoint italics deserve their own category, typographers do not consider them as a category, major or otherwise. The reason: italics have become more a style varia-

---

4. A ligature is a combination of two or more characters designed in a way to make them one unit.

tion than a type in their own right. Almost every face has its italic version.

For some types the italics are exactly like the uprights, but slanted. For other types, the italics are quite different—so different, in fact, that they appear to be of a different design. Many art directors prefer italics different in design from their uprights because then they are more useful as contrast types.

Italics, as conceived by Manutius, were narrower than the uprights, but in some faces today they are actually wider. In Linotype and Intertype faces they are equal in width to their uprights. That's because both the upright and the italic version of each letter are on the same mat, one underneath the other.

Because they are designed on a diagonal, italics tend to project a mood of restlessness or haste. Italics are not quite as easy to read as uprights. Art directors find italics useful for captions, for emphasis in body copy, for foreign phraseology, and for names of publications, plays, ships, and works of art. Used column after column, solid italics can be fatiguing. Nor does the reader appreciate them as occasional paragraphs in body copy; when readers move back into the uprights they get the optical illusion of reading type that bends over to the left.

When you underline a word in a manuscript, you are telling the typesetter to set the word in italics. You should make sure italics are *available* in that face; if not, the printer may set the word in boldface. It is a mistake to set names of publications in boldface.

An illustration from a whimsical ad sponsored by Quad Typographers, New York. The company has matched typefaces with illustration styles. These characters supposedly attended the typesetting company's "posh Fifth Anniversary Party." From left: European industrialist Claude Graphique, society columnist Lightline Gothic, impresario Futura Black, Baroness Excelsior Script, health faddist 20th Century Ultrabold, unidentified maid (her face is the company insignia), Texas tycoon Windsor Elongated, underground film star Prisma, Italian futurist designer Sig. Modern Roman No. 20, former channel swimmer Samantha Smoke, and her escort, Seventh Ave. mogul Max Balloon. Concept and design by Peter Rauch and Herb Levitt; illustration by Tim Lewis.

It makes them stand out unnecessarily from other words. If no italics are available, names of publications should be set in ordinary uprights.

Some magazines run the names of publications in italics but they run their own names, when they're mentioned in the copy, in caps and small caps. Like this: PUBLICATION DESIGN.

Small caps, only as tall as the x-height of the letters, are also useful for jobs ordinarily assigned to full-size caps: for instance, headlines quoted from newspapers and telegrams from letters-to-the-editor writers.

Character in types

Some types are versatile enough to be appropriate for almost any job. Others are more limited in what they can do. But all have some special qualities that set them apart. Art directors are not in agreement about these qualities, but here are a few familiar faces (sub-categories or families, if you prefer), along with descriptions of the moods they seem to convey:

1. *Baskerville*—beauty, quality, urbanity.
2. *Bodoni*—formality, aristocracy, modernity.
3. *Caslon*—dignity, character, maturity.
4. *Century*—elegance, clarity.
5. *Cheltenham*—honesty, reliability, awkwardness.
6. *Franklin Gothic*—urgency, bluntness.
7. *Futura*—severity, utility.
8. *Garamond*—grace, worth, fragility.
9. *Standard*—order, newness.
10. *Stymie*—precision, solidarity.
11. *Times Roman*—tradition, efficiency.

These qualities, if they come across to readers, come across only vaguely. Furthermore, a single face can have qualities that tend to cancel out each other. (Can a type be both tradition-oriented and efficient?) While you should be conscious of these qualities and make whatever use you can of them, you should not feel bound to any one type because of a mood you want to convey.

Assume that you are designing a radical, militant political magazine. Baskerville seems an unlikely choice for the title face. And yet Dugald Stermer used it successfully at *Ramparts* while Kenneth Stuart was using it, also successfully, at *Reader's Digest,* a magazine near the opposite end of the political spectrum.

Sometimes the best answer to the question "What type to use in title display?" is to go with a stately, readable type—like Baskerville—and rely upon the *words* in the title to express the mood of the piece.

Type revivals

What may be good for one period of time in typography may not be good in another. Type preferences change. Types come and go—and come back again.

A case in point is Bookman, rediscovered in the mid-1960s as a display face. Bookman is a face adapted from an oldstyle antique face of the 1860s. It is like Clarendon, but it has more roundness.

At the turn of the century it had become so popular that a reaction set in against it. Designers began to consider it monotonous. It was kept alive by offset and gravure, because its strong lines and serifs stood up well in that kind of printing. (The old *Collier's* magazine used it.) As these processes became more sophisticated and better able to handle more fragile types, Bookman died out.

In revival, it gives display matter a solid, strong look. In its italic

Baskerville
Bodoni
Caslon
Century
Cheltenham
Franklin Gothic
Futura
Garamond
Standard
Stymie
Times Roman

Some familiar typefaces whose moods are described in the text on the opposite page.

HAVE YOU VISITED A MOOSE LATELY?

In an era of diminishing ranges, Western reserves are the best places to find our wildest animals—moose, bear or bison

by Joe Van Wormer

One sunny afternoon last September, five moose, three bulls and two cows, walked out of the timber to feed in willow-covered Pelican Creek marsh in Yellowstone National Park. In a matter of minutes excited visitors blocked a nearby road to take advantage of this rare opportunity to see and photograph specimens of our largest deer. Because big game species are generally both shy and scarce, there aren't many places where they can readily be seen at close range. However, in a few areas they have lost most of their fear of man. Yellowstone National Park is one such place. I have never failed to see moose there.

Chevron USA's art director, Roger Waterman, for this right-hand page opener, was able to come up with a typeface that perfectly matched his drawing of a moose. Or maybe it was the other way around: he drew his moose to take on the look of the type.

version, with swash caps, it has a charm that has captivated some of our leading designers. (See the *New York* logo in chapter 8.)

Other types that have made a comeback in magazine design include Cooper Black, Cheltenham, and Futura. In the 1970s Souvenir, a bowlegged roman type, came on strong, both as display and body copy. In 1977 TypeSpectra, a type-design house, introduced Souvenir Gothic (below), a sans-serif version. In an advertisement to art directors, TypeSpectra said: "When you order Souvenir Gothic you are certain of getting the original . . . because months will pass before the round-cornered misaligned, pirate copies come out." The type-designing industry is plagued by imitation.

Souvenir Gothic.

The variety of typefaces

In all, you face a choice of several thousand typefaces. And if you can't find exactly what you want from one of the houses supplying photolettering, you can take a standard type and doctor it, coming up with a title like this one used by *Pacific Powerland,* a publication of Pacific Power & Light Company, Portland. "More dramatically than words," went the lead of the article underneath, "the parched mudflat pictured on the cover tells the story of an unprecedented six-month drought in much of the region served by Pacific Power." The texture in the letters duplicated the texture in the picture.

DROUGHT!

Eventually, you will develop strong prejudices against many typefaces, strong preferences for others. You may conclude that only a few fit your publication. And you will change your mind from time to time as to which ones those are.

Because he worked for a magazine that ran articles on subject matter that "ranges literally from pickles to politics," Herb Bleiweiss, art director of *Ladies' Home Journal,* used a great variety of typefaces, as many as thirty in a single issue. ". . . An art director must let a natural variety develop without preconceptions which might limit effectiveness," he said. He even tried running headlines or titles that were smaller than the body type. Once he had a heading set on a piece of acetate and frozen into a cake of ice. That was for a feature with the title: "Work Wonders with Canned and Frozen Poultry Products." Resting on top of the ice were assorted products.

An art director like Herb Bleiweiss can get away with such innovation, but the beginning art director is wise to stay with only a few faces in traditional arrangements. A magazine's pages can easily turn into what Will Burton has described as "visual riddles." The reader will not have the patience for them.

What type to use

As an art director you select your types largely on the basis of personal preference. Still you have some rules to go by.

"Objective research has produced few dramatic results," said Herbert Spencer, "but it has provided a wealth of information about factors of typography which contribute to greater reader efficiency, and it has confirmed the validity of many established typographic conventions, but not of all."[5]

Among findings verified by research are these:

1. All caps slow reading speed. They also occupy 40–50 percent more space.

2. Italics are harder to read than uprights.

3. Very short lines—and very long lines—are hard to read.

4. Unjustified lines do *not* hurt readability, especially now that we are getting used to them.

Most art directors decide on a body type and stick with it issue after issue. Occasionally an art director runs a special article in a different face or uses one face for articles and another for standing features like columns and departments.

In making your original choice for body type or types, you will take paper stock into consideration. For instance, old style romans work better on rough paper stock; modern romans reproduce best on smooth or coated stocks.

The choice of typeface should also be influenced by the printing process to be used. Some of the Bodoni faces, because of their hairline serifs, do not show up well in offset. Typefaces in gravure tend to darken; hence for a text face you might not want to start out with a type already boldface. That everything in gravure is screened, including the type, suggests you would want to use a face without frills.

Once you make your choice of type or types for body copy, you live with it for a period of several years, perhaps even for the duration of the publication. Choosing type for titles, on the other hand, represents a continuing problem. You might well choose a different type to match the mood of each article.

That the display type does not match the body type shouldn't bother you. But you should see to it that the various display types for a spread come from the same family. The display types should be obviously related and perfectly matched. If that's not possible, then they should be *clearly* unrelated. You should not put display types together that are *almost* related. *Almost* related types create the illusion that a mistake was made in setting.

You could combine an old style roman with a sans serif very nicely, but you would almost never combine an old style roman with a modern roman.

You-can't-go-wrong types

Every art director has a favorite typeface, and one favorite may differ radically from another. Most art directors, however, could agree on a half dozen or so faces that form the standards against which other types are measured. A Basic Seven, so far as this author is concerned, would include these:

GREECE
JAMAICA
Ceylon
China
MEXICO
Tahiti
Canada
Ireland
Scotland
Denmark
Japan
PORTUGAL
BRITAIN

Some attempts by art directors to find typefaces or letterforms appropriate to specific countries or places. Do they work? Well, if they do, they work in some cases because art directors have used them in the past to do similar jobs. In a few cases, you could say the types are appropriate because of how they evolved. For instance: the "GREECE" imitates early Greek letters, when they were scratched with a stylus on a wax tablet; the "China" has a Chinese calligraphy look; the "Ireland" stems from Irish calligraphy (semiuncials); the "Denmark" comes in the text or blackletter that developed out of the European lowlands.

5. Herbert Spencer, *The Visible Word,* Hastings House, Publishers, New York, 1969, p. 6.

ABCDEFGHIJKL
MNOPQRSTUV
WXYZ
abcdefghijklmnopq
rstuvwxyz
1234567890

ABCDEFGHIJ
KLMNOPQRS
TUVWXYZ
abcdefghijklmno
pqrstuvwxyz
1234567890

ABCDEFGHIJ
KLMNOPQR
STUVWXYZ
abcdefghijklmn
opqrstuvwxyz
1234567890

ABCDEFGH
IJKLMNOP
QRSTUVW
XYZ
abcdefghijkl
mnopqrstuv
wxyz
1234567890

1. *Baskerville.* This face ranks as one of the most beautiful ever designed. It comes now in many versions, but it was originally designed by John Baskerville, a British calligrapher, around 1760. Considered a threat to Caslon when it was introduced, Baskerville represented a break with the past, a move to a more modern look. It is a transitional face, more precise than the old style romans but not so precise as Bodoni.

A "wide set" type, it needs some leading. It looks best on smooth paper.

A quirk in the design results in a lowercase *g* with an incomplete bottom loop.

2. *Bodoni.* Italian designer Giambattista Bodoni drew some inspiration from Baskerville as he created Bodoni, a beautifully balanced if severe face, with marked differences in the thicks and thins of the strokes and with clean, harsh serifs.

The face looks best on slick paper and must be properly inked and printed. It is a little difficult to read in large doses. Like most faces, its beauty is lost in its bold and ultrabold versions.

3. *Caslon.* To most printers over the years, Caslon, designed in the eighteenth century by the Englishman, William Caslon, served as the No. 1 typeface. The rule was: "When in doubt, use Caslon."

The most familiar example of old style roman, this face still enjoys wide use. It has been described variously as "honest," "unobtrusive," and "classical."

Its caps, when you study them, are surprisingly wide, and its cap *A* seems to have a chip cut out of its top. The bottom loop on the lowercase *g* seems small. Otherwise, the face has no eccentricities.

4. *Craw Clarendon.* Clarendon faces are a cross between slab serifs and old style romans. The serifs, heavy as in slab serif letters, are bracketed, as in roman. They merge into the main strokes.

The first Clarendons appeared in England in the middle of the nineteenth century. Two recent versions are Hermann Eidenbenz's (1952) and Freeman Craw's (1954), the most popular.

5. *Garamond.* This face was named after a sixteenth-century French typefounder, Claude Garamond, but it was probably designed by Jean Jannon. Equipped with unpredictable serifs, it is, nonetheless, beautiful and readable. It is a rather narrow face with a small x-height. It can be set solid.

6. *Helvetica.* Three great gothic faces came out of Europe in 1957: Univers, from France, designed by Adrian Frutiger; Folio, from Germany, designed by Konrad Bauer and Walter Baum; and Helvetica, from Switzerland, designed by Mas Miedinger. Clean and crisp, they look very much alike.

Helvetica, introduced in America in 1963 in body and display sizes, is perhaps the most available of the three. Unlike Univers, it is a close-fitting type, even on the Linotype. Like all the newer gothics, its rounds are slightly squared, and its strokes vary just a bit in thickness. The terminals on letters such as *e* and *s* are cut on the horizontal, aiding in readability; in all a handsome, modern face.

It comes in light, regular, regular italic, medium, bold, bold compact italic, regular extended, bold extended, extra bold extended, regular condensed, bold condensed, and extra bold condensed. The example shown here is Helvetica Regular.

7. *Times Roman.* Sometimes called *New Times Roman* or *Times New Roman,* this is the face designed by Stanley Morison

for *The Times* of London in 1931. It is very much a twentieth-century type, not a revival, good for all kinds of jobs, although it is more of a body than a display face. Essentially an old style roman, it could, with its sharp-cut serifs, be classified as a transitional face. A peculiarity is the rounded bottom of the *b*.

Its large x-height makes some leading necessary. With its bold look, it was first a newspaper face, becoming popular later as a magazine and book face, particularly in America.

Allen Hutt says Times Roman is not always a good body face for newspapers because it requires good press work.[6] In 1975 *The Times* discontinued its use of Times Roman as a text face.

All of these faces came along before the cold-type revolution, when it was easy enough to tell one face from another because there were only a couple of hundred to choose from. But these faces are as useful—and up to date—as they ever were, and they are available in cold type as well as hot type, in a much greater variety of sizes and weights than before. You may find, however, that some of the newer types designed for cold-type setting have characteristics of these types with flourishes to make them even more useful or to give them late-20th century distinction. They will carry names quite different from the names here, of course.

What to tell the typesetter

Sending copy to the typesetter or printer, you would in most cases specify the following:

1. Point size.
2. Name of the typeface.
3. Weight of the typeface, if other than regular (light, book, medium, bold, demibold, ultrabold, black).
4. Style, if other than upright (italic, condensed, expanded; it could be both italic *and* condensed or expanded).
5. Amount of leading between lines (the art director should specify "set solid" if no leading is desired).
6. Width of column (in picas).
7. Amount of letterspacing, if any.
8. Any special instructions on paragraph indentions and margins (flush left? flush right?).

Copyediting marks will take care of such matters as occasional use of italics, small caps, etc.

To save space this book will not reproduce the various copy-reading and proofreading marks used to communicate with the typesetter and printer. These marks, basically standardized, are shown in most good dictionaries, style books, editing books, and type specimen books.

Copyediting marks are made right on the original copy, which has been double spaced—triple spaced if for a newspaper—to provide the necessary write-in area. Proofreading marks are made in the margins of galley or page proofs.

One piece of advice is in order here: Both copyreading and proofreading marks should be made with a soft pencil to facilitate

ABCDEFGHIJKL
MNOPQRSTUV
WXYZ
abcdefghijklmnop
qrstuvwxyz
1234567890

ABCDEFGHIJK
LMNOPQRSTU
VWXYZ
abcdefghijklmno
pqrstuvwxyz
1234567890

ABCDEFGHIJ
KLMNOPQRS
TUVWXYZ
abcdefghijklmno
pqrstuvwxyz
1234567890

6. Allen Hutt, "Times Roman: A Reassessment," *The Journal of Typographic Research,* Summer 1970, pp. 259–70.

erasures. The copyreader or proofreader sometimes has second thoughts about changes made.

Title display

Titles for magazine articles differ from newspaper headlines in that their shape and placement are not dictated by a *headline schedule*. Only the designer's lack of imagination limits what may be done.

Many art directors fail to take advantage of the greater flexibility magazines have over newspapers. The trade magazines, especially, seem wedded to old newspaper ideas about titles or headlines. They use the same old flush-left, multi-line settings. Even the jargon of the headlines is the same. On the other hand, some magazines resort to so much typographic and design trickery that their readers become bewildered. And that isn't good either.

Only rarely should you make a title curve, dip, slant, overlap, pile on, or turn sideways. It should remain on the horizontal. A good starting point could be to design a title that occupies a single line of type in a size only slightly larger than the body copy. Perhaps it would be set in the same face as the body copy. The reader, then, finds it possible to take the title in as a single unit, not having to jump from one line to another. The title would be like a sentence taken from out of the copy and made larger for easy access.

How Foremost-McKesson is working to turn the energy problem into an energy project

If you think death and taxes are all that are certain, think again.

The energy crunch, it would seem, is here to stay.

While it's true that everybody's talking about the energy shortage, who's doing anything about it? Well, it turns out, there's a good deal of activity at Foremost-McKesson operations across the country.

Back in 1975, the corporation launched an energy management pro-

operation. A special fund of $2 million was allocated, to be divided among the units. In addition, a move began to phase out current Foremost-McKesson company automobiles and replace their fleet of 1800 vehicles with smaller, "X-body/6 cylinder" passenger vehicles. That step alone is expected to yield a 30% savings in energy.

"People didn't take the energy crunch too seriously until gas got expensive," Art said. "Some of the language of energy conservation is too technical, but the huge impact of gas prices is easy to relate to."

As the energy-saving proposals began to roll in from every unit of the company, they were reviewed by Joe Maldari, chief engineer and coordinator of the special energy committee.

introducing the steam formerly lost to help heat the raw products, more energy is being conserved.

The Dairy Division, which had already been using thermal recompression systems, asked that they convert to a mechanical recompression system. This costs more than the thermal variety, but results in a considerable increase in energy savings. The dairy plant at Hughson, California now operates with this improved system.

The Water Division came up with a real winner, which proved that the best ideas are often the simplest. By replacing all the 5-gallon glass bottles with plastic ones, a double energy savings will result, in the amount of heat used to sterilize them and in the amount of fuel used by the delivery trucks because of

the ideas are kooky, but we're glad to get them all."

One not-so-kooky idea came directly from the federal government's Department of Energy. They suggested that Foremost-McKesson reactivate a hydro power unit at the Appleton, Wisconsin facility of the Food Ingredients Division. More than 70 years ago, energy for the plant, then a paper mill, was provided by a water wheel. Since then, it has been converted to conventional electric power. Now, the DOE's notion is being considered, and the water wheel is being dusted off for still greater energy savings.

What's in the future for energy conservation? Solar power, for sure, according to Joe Maldari, but it may be somewhat down the road. "It's still far

Need a lift?

Tired of driving to work with just the company of a distant disc jockey? Pool it. Check bulletin boards at work, in your local markets and ads in local papers, or put up your own notice to join others headed in your direction. And remember, carpools can be more than just a way to work.

Consider these tips, then into the pool!

Make a commitment. Be dependable so you can feel comfortable depending on others.

Be on time. Inform the driver when you won't be riding, and notify the group if you're having difficulty meeting your driving schedule.

Be considerate. Keep in

mind the needs, likes and dislikes of others in your carpool, and agree in advance about rules on smoking, stopovers for personal errands, etc.

Keep your car in top shape. Preventive maintenance is your carpool's extra insurance.

Drive defensively, but gently! Don't change lanes unnecessarily, maintain a moderate speed for gas conservation and safety, obey all traffic laws, and pay attention to the cars around you.

Cruuunch!!!

gram to comply with the government's request that everyone—and every company—do whatever possible to cut down on the use of energy. That meant turning off lights whenever possible, insulating pipes, holding down heating and air conditioning to a frugal level, and retraining truck drivers to improve driving habits.

Still, many people didn't take the "energy shortage" too seriously back then, perhaps because people were just too accustomed to an endless supply of fuel to imagine it could ever run out. But the corporation tightened its belt, and as a result managed to reduce its energy/productivity ratio by an amazing 16% over the last four years.

Last January, Art Weiner, vice president and director of procurement, transportation and engineering, was named to spearhead a special energy project. As a first step, Art requested suggestions from each operating unit of Foremost-McKesson on how they could employ new energy reduction equipment in their

"Because of the increased unit cost in doing business," said Joe, "we asked our people to contribute suggestions for cutting expenses as well as saving energy. As a result, one of the important changes we've made is in the purchase of our own storage tanks for gasoline and diesel fuel. This will enable our fleets in the Drug, Chemical and Wine & Spirits Groups to fill their tanks from our own pumps."

Not only will this save the company money in buying fuel at a wholesale rate, noted Joe, but it will also help relieve the congestion at the filling stations in every community.

Ideas that related strictly to energy-saving measures came from virtually all corners of the corporation. From the Food Ingredients Division came the notion of incorporating "heat savers" on the evaporators used in drawing off water from raw food products. Food Ingredients is also considering the installation of thermal recompression systems into its evaporators. By re-

the reduced weight. The plastic containers will also eliminate the glass breakage problem, while making life easier for the route salespeople who deliver the huge bottles of Alhambra, Sparkletts and Crystal Water.

At Mueller's, the macaroni makers suggested that their ovens be converted to microwave, similar to the ovens used by Foremost-Gentry for vegetable drying. That way, the final steps in drying the macaroni products could pick up some extra points in energy conservation.

Since the Drug & Health Care, Chemical and Wine & Spirits Groups are primarily distribution operations, the logical energy-saving ideas have come from finding ways to save energy while warehousing or transporting these goods to market. Air locks have been installed on loading platforms to keep warm air from escaping from the warehouses during loading operations.

"This program has started a feeling of real enthusiasm," Joe said. "Some of

too expensive. Solar units alone cost about $10 a square foot, and it takes about 1,000 square feet for an average house. Add in the cost of the rest of the equipment needed, and it just isn't yet a practical matter to convert. Project those costs into industrial use, and you have the same problem on a larger scale."

Joe believes that eventually the cost of solar systems will come down as the cost of conventional energy increases. "Somewhere the lines will cross, and we'll be in a solar age," he predicted.

Perhaps the most realistic comment on the energy situation comes from Art Weiner. "We may be looking forward to an era of changing lifestyles, accompanied by profound shifts in attitudes and buying habits, as Americans come to realize that the tight supply and high cost of energy is a fact of life and become more willing to focus on the problem."

So, if you hear some strange noises in the night, you can relax. It's the sound of our energy crunching.

6

For some magazines, this style works very well, page after page. For other magazines, a more lively arrangement would be necessary. Not only would titles be broken up into two or more lines; they would also be set in type considerably larger than and different from the body copy.

The mood of the article could dictate the choice of title typeface, and that choice might vary greatly from article to article in a single issue.

Sometimes you may choose to vary the typeface—or at least the size—*within* the title. Let's say one word in the title should stand out over the others. You can bring out its importance in many ways: by setting it in a different face, a different size, a different weight; by printing it in color; by putting a box around it or underlining it; by reversing it in a black box or a color block; by separating it from the other words with a small piece of art; by showing it in perspective; by running it out of alignment. The important thing to remember is: only that one word should get the treatment. When two different words are made to stand out they cancel each other out.

Should you want to innovate with the entire title, you can try setting it in giant letters; building it with letters cut from a photographic background; surprinting or reversing it in a photograph or tint block; wrapping it around a photograph; arranging the lines in a piggyback fashion; nesting the lines partially inside other lines; fitting them inside the text; alternating the letters in black and color; superimposing them—the list is endless.

When *Sunset* sets a title in giant letters, it screens the letters to gray to keep them from looking cheap or loud. Another idea is to set giant-size titles in lowercase. Lowercase letters are more complicated in design and hence more interesting to view in large sizes.

Titles should ordinarily be set in lowercase anyway, with only the first word and all proper nouns capitalized. Lowercase is easier to read than all caps because lowercase letters are easier to distinguish from one another. Also, lowercase is easier to read than caps and lowercase because caps and lowercase cause the eye to move up and down, like the springs on a car moving along a bumpy road. Besides, writing caps-and-lowercase titles takes longer than writing all-lowercase titles: the title writer faces a complicated set of rules on which words to capitalize, which ones to leave lowercase.

When you have a multi-line title to deal with, you can show it flush left, flush right, or centered. It is not a good idea to run it flush left-flush right. To make it come out even on both sides usually takes some fancy and unnatural spacing. The most intriguing multi-line titles are those set in a staggered pattern to form an irregular silhouette. The lines should be kept close enough together so the title reads as a unit.

In multi-line titles it is almost never desirable to single out one word for emphasis. Asking the reader to jump from line to line is interruption enough. Asking acceptance of a change in type style in the middle of it is asking too much. If you *must* have one word in a multi-line title stand out, you can put it in a line by itself, and without changing the typeface. To make it stand out more, in a flush-left title, you can run it a little to the left of the axis.

In planning a multi-line title, you should pay more attention to the logic of the arrangement than its looks. It is desirable, of course, that lines be reasonably equal in length, but it is more important by far that they be easily read.

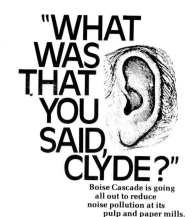

"WHAT WAS THAT YOU SAID, CLYDE?"

Boise Cascade is going all out to reduce noise pollution at its pulp and paper mills.

By Linda Miller

Sometimes an art director incorporates a piece of art with the article's title. Art director Joe Erceg does it here for *Paper Times,* using some public-domain art. The title type wraps around the ear, and the blurb takes its place just below. A little extra space separates the byline from the title-blurb unit. Ragged-right and -left setting work for both title and blurb.

Running a heading up the side works in this case because the "E" seen this way really looks like the "STEPS" of the heading. Just below the heading you see some subheads (out of context) which also are a bit playful, combining art with type. In actual use, of course, each of the subheads would have a number of short items underneath them. These examples are from *Seafirst News* published by Seattle First National Bank.

When the title comes as two sentences, you cannot very well separate them with a period (unless the publication's style is to end titles with periods), so you have to resort to some other device. You can use a semicolon, if you are designing for a newspaper; you can use a typographic dingbat at the beginning of each sentence; you can use some extra white space; you can change to another typeface or size for the second sentence; you can change to color; you can change the position.

Newspapers standardize their headlines, consistently using the same typeface and line arrangements, but once in a while in a spirit of playfulness they doctor the type or go with a different face. The staid *Wall Street Journal* for a feature on the return of calligraphy in the U.S., used real calligraphy for its headline and byline.

Practices to avoid in titles and headlines

In their drive to be different, people who plan titles for magazine articles and headlines for newspaper stories resort to practices that can prove embarrassing on publication or alienate the readership. Using a dollar sign for an *S* in a headline over a story on spending, for instance, is by now a cliché. Putting hyphens between letters in "STRETCH" has been tried too many times. Causing a headline to cross over into a photograph, there to be lost in a busy pattern of tones, brings regret later.

Here are some other practices you might want to avoid as you work with display type:

1. *Using kickers.* Kickers are small, short, second-thought headlines that appear just above main headlines. When kickers are used to categorize pieces—to tell the reader, for instance, that what follows is "An Editorial"—they probably serve a useful function. But when they are there simply to give readers more display type to look at before reading the stories, they only add clutter to the pages.

2. *Lining up headlines on the diagonal.* You may have seen those old newspaper head schedules (or "hed" schedules) that showed all kinds of geometric contortions headlines could fit into. And in those days, the typical newspaper headline consisted of several "decks," each with its own shape. One of these shapes was called the "stepline." Each line of that head indented itself slightly from the line above. In other words, the headline flushed itself against a diagonal axis.

A lot of today's publication editors seem moved by diagonal axes. They understand that a diagonal thrust means action, as opposed to static vertical and horizontal thrusts. But is that kind of action necessary in a headline? There is a dated look to such a headline. The standard flush-left or each-line-centered arrangement works just as well while looking contemporary.

3. *Incorrectly spacing the letters.* While it had been widely criticized, the trend to closefitting letters probably has resulted in increased readability. Now instead of seeing only letters, readers see words and phrases. But closefitting can be overdone. Get the letters too close together, and they merge, making ligatures that are not graceful but, instead, hard to read. And, of course, the pattern of the headline becomes spotty.

In closefitting as in regular fitting, you have to make some allowance for optical illusions that occur as certain letters take their places next others. You need to add a little space here, take away a little space there. Your spacing becomes optical, not mechanical.

4. *Failing to space properly between lines.* Your spacing between lines of a headline should be consistent. But again, it may have to be optical rather than mechanical. A line with several ascending strokes, or descending strokes, may create an optical illusion in spacing. As a designer, you have to compensate for such spacing, making necessary adjustments to please the eye.

5. *Misusing the flexibility of offset.* In the old days of letterpress, you couldn't use a headline with a too-long count because you couldn't fit it in. The leads and rules made it impossible for the head to spill over into the margins. Now, with mere pasteup, you can cheat. You see such cheating occasionally in *Editor & Publisher* and especially in weekly newspapers. Ignoring margins when it happens to be convenient brings inconsistency to a publication.

Blurbs

"Blurb" is another one of those elastic words in journalism, taking on any number of meanings. Magazine article titles printed on covers are blurbs. Excerpts taken out of articles and run in larger-than-body-copy type, one or more to a spread, to (1) break up gray areas of type and (2) stop readers who maybe didn't stop at the article titles, are blurbs, too. Blurbs are also secondary titles adjacent to main titles of articles. Newspaper people would call them "second decks" or "second banks."

Magazines run blurbs either above or below the titles, almost always in smaller type. Often they are longer than the titles, running for several sentences. They offer necessary elaboration on titles that may be more clever than illuminating.

A designer can get too tricky with type, making things difficult rather than easy for the reader. The problem here is compounded by a rather unpleasant typeface, a slab serif with the playful characteristics of Avant Garde Gothic. The overlapping only adds to the confusion.

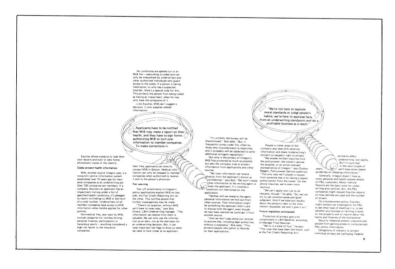

An unusual way to dramatize interior blurbs within a spread. Actually, they aren't blurbs so much as parts of the article writ large. The magnifying-glass motif is set up on the opening spread (on the previous two pages) where a detective is shown, page high, inspecting the title of the article, using his glass. The title is: "Right to Privacy—at What Price?" Notice the generous amount of white space on this spread and the building of the columns from the bottom. Notice, too, that this continuation does not begin immediately in the left-hand column. It waits a column. The spread is from *Integon Listener,* a bimonthly published by Integon Corporation, Winston-Salem, North Carolina.

Punctuation up close

You may find it easier to make a punctuation mistake in a headline or title than in the body of an article. Punctuation may seem unimportant as you write a heading to fit a layout and pick the appropriate typeface, but a wrong or omitted mark can completely alter your meaning.

You can trace many punctuation errors in headings and copy to carelessness and haste. And you can trace some to ignorance.

When you get right down to it, punctuation is mostly a matter of common sense and rhythm. Punctuation is an art; it is impossible to reduce the art to an easy set of rules.

| Listen. Can't you hear the ocean.
didn't invent it ... we | **DDB,**
COPY, | **theme:**
fades;
men: |
| **"A magazine**
'The
disappointing."
SELVES"
send 'em | experienced it—for 47 years
ALL-AROUND
24-hour
non·stop | |

Punctuation errors occur both in choice of marks and in the way they are displayed. Even the best publications and the most affluent advertisers let the errors slip by. The "Listen. Can't you hear the ocean." example with the missing question mark comes right out of a recent full-page ad in *The New Yorker*. With punctuation not fully understood, no wonder some writers turn to the Walter Winchell-like practice of using three periods (second example).

Editors and designers who set their own headings with press-on or dry-transfer type sometimes have trouble placing the comma properly. It should always snuggle up close to the word just ahead of it. The "9"-shape comma with its big head (as in the "DDB" example) is easy enough to place, but what about the wedge-shape comma available in some of the sans serifs? Sometimes it's hard to figure where the tail is. You see proper placement of the wedge-shape comma in "COPY."

Colons and commas should have their lower unit line up at the base line, their upper unit at the top of the x-height of the letters. In some faces, though, where the x-height is deep, the upper unit may be lowered, as in "men." You don't want a lot of space separating the two units.

Headlines and titles can use double or, to save space, single quote marks. Interestingly, some faces give you the bulb above and the tail below while other faces give you a "6"-shaped mark, with the bulb below.

The period and comma always go inside the ending quote marks. In body copy sizes, the quote marks immediately follow the punctuation mark. In display type, you can pile the quote marks on top of the period.

If the title consists of several flush-left lines, you may elect to put the quote marks outside the line of the axis. This is called "hung punctuation," and it results in margins that appear more straightly cut. It works for body copy, too, and includes all marks of punctuation that occur at the edges of copy blocks, but not many magazines and certainly few newspapers can afford the luxury of that kind of setting.

As art director you would be careful to put in apostrophes where they're called for. The word is *it's* when *it* and *is* are contracted. Only the possessive is *its*. The possessive for *men* is *men's*, never *mens*.

An apostrophe always faces the same way, whether used at the beginning, middle, or end of a word.

Finally: the dash and hyphen. Both these marks should fit rather tightly against the words they follow and precede. The dash is considerably longer, at least as wide as the capital *N* or, better, the capital *M*. The dash is also thinner than the hyphen. Both should be placed somewhere below the top of the x-height of the letters.

Sometimes you can take liberties with a hyphen, as in "nonstop." The designer here decided that a slab-like hyphen would not fit the character of the very round, thick-and-thin letters.

The late Carl Dair made an interesting contribution to the typography of punctuation. He introduced for body copy an upright, straight line, the height of the x-height, set off with extra white space, to help readers make a distinction between a broken word (broken because it wouldn't fit at the end of the line) and a compound word (like *world-wide*). He used the ordinary hyphen for compound words only.[7]

Another punctuation contribution comes from American Type Founders Company, which introduced the interabang, special punctuation combining both the question mark and the exclamation mark (for use in such sentences as "Are you kidding?").

Body copy

In choosing a typeface for body copy, you are not quite so concerned with the beauty of the face as when you choose display type. Your primary concern should be: Is the type readable column after column? Further: What kind of pattern does the type make over a large area? The pattern should be even-textured, not spotty.

You see how important consistent spacing is when your typesetter puts a little too much space between the "e" and "r" in "therapist" or brings the "n" and the "i" too close together in "the pen is. . . ."

In newspapers, at least, the trend has been to wider columns and consequently slightly larger typeface. In one comparison of narrow to wide settings, Prof. Lloyd R. Bostian of the University of Wisconsin found that on an 8 1/2 × 11 page, a single wide column, provided it had some white space to set it off, could be as readable as two narrow columns.[8]

A wider column produces shorter paragraphs, and this in itself may aid readability.

Most art directors prefer roman to sans serif faces for body copy simply because readers are used to them. Novelty hurts readability. But as sans serif finds increasing acceptance among readers of avant-garde magazines it will find increasing acceptance among readers of all magazines. As a matter of fact, sans serif has in recent years become almost commonplace as body copy for many company magazines and some general-circulation magazines.

Dog 'n pony
CASH N' CARRY
HEAT n EAT
rhythm 'n' blues
Cook'N' Clean
Sugar 'n' spice

Which of these abbreviated "and"s is correct? Only the last one. The first example leaves out the second apostrophe (you need two, because both the *a* and *d* are missing). The second example leaves off the first apostrophe. The third example doesn't carry any. The fourth example uses single quote marks rather than apostrophes. (The first mark, you can see, turns inward; that means it's not an apostrophe.) The fifth example capitalizes the *N*. It should not be capitalized. "Sugar 'n' spice" wins. But why not use an honest "and" and be done with all the apostrophes?

---

7. See how the system works in his book, *Design with Type,* University of Toronto Press, Toronto, Canada, 1967.
8. See Lloyd R. Bostian, "Effect of Line Width on Reading Speed and Comprehension," *Journalism Quarterly,* Summer 1976, pp. 328–330.

in profes...

Can you spot the problems with these body-copy excerpts from various publications? The first example shows uneven spacing between letters. Compare "Bully" with "filled." The *pattern* of the setting is faulty. The second example shows a publication name in boldface type. The machine setting this type, apparently, does not have italics available. The editor underlines the name of a publication on the manuscript and gets not italics but the only alternate characters available: boldface. Should the name of a publication jump out from the page? Not unless you run a column about the media. When italics are not available you should treat names of publications as you would ordinary proper names. No underlining on the manuscript. This excerpt also shows too much space between words. The third example shows unequal spacing between two of the lines. The makeup artist needs to measure accurately the distance between lines when patching copy. The fourth example shows a subhead with too little space above and below. The subhead doesn't stand out enough. It is lost between the paragraphs, even though it's in boldface.

One objection to sans serif used to be that it was too "vertical"; it did not have serifs to help move the reader horizontally across the line. But the newer sans serifs feature terminals that are sliced horizontally, and this tends to do the job serifs do. Also, the strokes of the newer sans serifs vary slightly in thickness, just as roman strokes do; sans serif type now is less monotonous in large doses.

Sans serifs, because of their solid character, are especially recommended where printing quality is inferior. Types with intricate serifs need superior printing in order to reproduce well.

Art directors have also changed their minds about unjustified lines. More and more magazines (but few newspapers) use them. Advertisers in their copy often get away with unjustified *left-hand* margins. Magazines avoid this. In magazine editorial matter, the lack of justification occurs on the *right*. In long blocks of copy, readers need a constant margin at the left to which they can return, line after line.

Some types need more space between words than others. Expanded types need more space between words than condensed types. Types with large x-heights need more space between words than those with small x-heights.

The spacing between words should never exceed the space between lines.

Copy needs extra spacing between lines when

1. the type has a large x-height;
2. the type has a pronounced vertical stress, as with Bodoni and with most of the sans serifs; and
3. the line length is longer than usual.

If copy is set in a single width, leading should be consistent throughout. It is best to specify the amount of leading before copy is set, as: "Set 10 on 12" (which means, "Set it in 10-point type on a 12-point slug.") Adding leading between lines afterwards costs more.

If you want a highly contemporary, crowded look, you might consider the possibility of *minus*-leading. This means setting a point size (say 10-point) on a smaller body (say 9-point). You would do this only when you have a face with a large x-height (with short descenders). And you would do it for a minimum amount of copy because minus-leading is hard to read.

Many art directors no longer consider a widow—a less than full-length line at the top of a column in a multicolumn spread—as the typographic monstrosity it was thought to be. But when a widow consists of a single word or syllable, the leftover space is great enough to spoil the horizontal axis at the top of the columns. The art director then should do some rearranging of lines to get rid of the widow.

But readers appreciate an occasional oasis deep into long columns of copy. Art directors supply it with subheadings or—better still—just a little extra white space. Sometimes an initial letter helps.

Subheads

Subheads—small headlines within the columns of copy—give readers a place to catch their breath. Subheads make the copy look less foreboding. They divide it into easier—shorter—segments.

They take the form usually of independent labels or sentences, summarizing what is to follow or teasing the reader to carry on.

To set them apart from the body copy, you would put extra space above and below, especially above, and you would set them in boldface type, possibly in the same face and size as the body copy. Or you might set them in all caps, small caps, or italics. You could center them or run them flush left. Designing a book, you might choose to put them in the margins.

Book publishers, in contrast to magazine editors, set up a couple of levels of subheads, the more important ones appearing in a bolder type or centered in the column. The book you are now reading, however, uses a single level of subheads.

Some newspapers have adopted a style of subheads that puts the first few words of a paragraph in all-caps, boldface type. The subhead is not a separate line. A little extra space separates the subhead from the paragraph above. The advantage of this system is that you don't have to write the subhead. It is already written. The disadvantage is that you find it harder to eliminate or add subheads after the copy is set.

Whatever style you choose, you should place subheads at several places in your article, not just in one place. A single subhead suggests too much of a break. The reader may get the impression that you are announcing a new article. If your article appears to be too short to carry more than one subhead, don't use any.

Editors who do not have a news-oriented content tend to avoid subheads. In place of subheads these editors use initial letters, blurbs, or merely units of white space. Some editors feel that small photographs or art pieces strategically placed serve as subheads.

Initial letters

An oversize letter used at the beginning of an article or story and at each of its breaks can help get readers started and rekindle their interest as the story progresses. When using initial letters, you should go to the face of your title, not the face of your body copy.

It is called a two-, three-, four-, or five-line initial, depending upon how deep in lines it is. It can be bigger than the title-type size. You may find it desirable to help readers make the step down from the initial to the body copy by giving them the remainder of the first word and maybe another word or two in all caps or small caps. And you will probably want your body copy to fit snugly around the initial. Sometimes this takes some fancy work by the composing room.

You might want to consider using initial letters that project out or up from the body copy rather than fit down into it, in which case you can move the letters toward the center of the columns. You may also want to use initial words instead of initial letters. *Go,* the Goodyear tire-dealer magazine, doesn't use initial letters but does start its articles off with one complete line of boldface type in sans serif, where the remainder of the body copy is in roman and in a size slightly smaller than the boldface lead in. *The New Era,* a publication of The Church of Jesus Christ of Latter-day Saints, uses a small version of its cover logo as an "initial letter" for each of its major articles. It ends each article with yet a smaller version of the logo.

Initials really become interesting when you contract to have them drawn to fit the mood of an article. For instance: you ask an artist to construct the initials out of cartoon figures and props, perhaps adding a second color. One of the charms of Hendrick Wil-

An initial letter can be more than a mere piece of type set large. This one is drawn, and it is as much a gag cartoon as an initial letter. Now as an editor all you would have to do to use this is make sure your article on sleep starts out with a word beginning with *Z* and maybe straighten out the big letter.

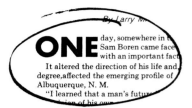
Some of the ways magazines handle initial letters, both at the beginnings and in the interiors of articles. The first is a two-line initial in a three-line setting. Several words in caps ease the reader from the initial into the text. The second use boldface type to make the bridge, and carries the boldfacing all the way across the first line. The third uses an initial word. Not a bad idea, unless you happen to begin an article with "Paleontography" or something similar. The fourth, an interior initial, does not ask for any extra space between itself and the previous paragraph. Note that the copy fits around the initial. The fifth, also an interior initial, juts up from the line. The sixth illustrates what to do when you start out with a direct quote. You use quote marks in the initial size, not in the body-copy size. Some designers leave off the beginning quote marks in a situation like this. That works, too.

lem van Loon's illustrated histories published in the 1920s and 1930s were the initial letters he drew for chapter openings.

For an article entitled "It's a Dirty Job . . . But Somebody's Gotta Do It," *Not Just Jazz* separated sections, not with initial letters or subheads, but with finger prints and smudges. *New York* used blocks of the kind babies play with for initial letters in an article on babies born to older couples.

It would be foolhardy to pick one style as being superior to others, or to argue that using initial letters in the first place is preferable to bypassing them. It comes down to being a matter of one person's taste matched against another's.

One thing is certain: initial letters poorly planned look a lot worse than standard openings and white-space interior rests. And it probably is true that to work well, initial letters should work boldly.

When used in two or three places on a spread as interior rests, they should be spaced so that distances between them vary. And ordinarily, they should not line up horizontally. They should succeed in dividing the columns of a spread into unequal takes.

Having settled on the kind and placement of initial letters, you had better sit back and give the spread some study. Do the letters by any chance spell out some word your readers may find offensive? You may have to make some last minute changes, just as you would make if, on looking over the final page proofs, you see an ad placed right next to editorial matter that makes a contradictory point.

You don't have to confine initials to body copy. Editors and designers have used them in headlines and titles, blurbs, and even captions.

Article starts

Sometimes the design of a magazine page confuses readers, making it difficult for them to know where to start the article. For instance, the title may be off to the right. Do readers start right under the title, then, or do they move over to the left and start there?

If titles fit immediately above the first column of copy, no special typographic treatment is needed. The first paragraph can be set indented to look like the other paragraphs.

But in other cases, the readers need help. One solution, of course, is to use an initial letter. Even if the spread has several, readers will pick up first the initial letter at the far-left point. Another solution is to line up the columns evenly across the top. Readers will see that the columns are related and start with the one at the extreme left. Still another solution, less often tried, is to put a small piece of art near the start, to sort of point to the beginning.

For many magazines, the best way of saying "Here is where the article starts" is to set the first paragraph without an indentation. The "indenting," which is nothing more than an arresting of reader

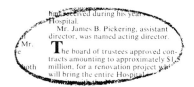

attention, anyway, has already been done by the title, these editors feel.

If as art director you have reason to doubt that readers will begin articles where they should, you should redesign the page. Getting readers started is a chief function of page design.

Captions

In some quarters the caption has fallen from favor. The advertising-design look so prevalent in company magazines, for instance, tends to regard the caption as nothing more than visual clutter. So art directors—some of them—talk their editors out of captions. In the classroom the caption often disappears simply because the student, preoccupied with title and picture placement, forgets to plan for it.

Some photographers applaud the no-caption practice. They argue that captions are redundant. Considering what some captions are made to say by editors, maybe the photographers are right.

Still, looking at the matter from a reader's standpoint, you have to conclude that the caption is necessary for a full understanding of the photograph except in those cases—rare in news oriented publications—where the photograph's purpose is merely to establish a mood. An operating rule ought to be that the editor should include a caption unless there is a compelling reason to leave it out.

Captions give photographs an additional dimension.

They can tell what happened before the picture was taken. Or what happened afterwards. If the photograph itself is something of a mystery, a caption can clear things up.

Mug shots almost always need captions. When a publication runs a mug shot with a standing column, the reader can't tell whether the picture is of the columnist or the person being written about unless the shot carries a name.

Caption designing takes two basic approaches: either the captions appear adjacent to the pictures they describe or they gather themselves together in a group and key themselves to the various pictures in the spread. You do not necessarily have to use numbers to key the captions. You can key through description. *Integon Listener,* published by the Integon Corporation, Winston-Salem, N.C., in one issue showed photographs of a business executive alone at his desk talking into a phone, the executive shaking hands with visitors, and the executive playing shuffleboard with his family. The caption off to the side reads: "Despite his busy schedule, Ed Collette believes in making time for people, whether it's a customer or employee on the phone, a group of new fieldman like these from Provident Life, or his own family, including wife Evelyn, daughter Gayle and twin grandsons Johnny and Jerry."

Haste in caption writing can lead to embarrassments. *National*

P E O P L E

DON'T BE A STATISTIC

THEY'RE IN BUSINESS

All-cap titles or headlines showing spacing possibilities. The first uses letterspacing. The second uses normal spacing between letters. The third uses tight spacing between letters, which in most magazines these days is normal spacing. Note the tight spacing between words, too.

Review spotted this correction in *Community Life:* "Mai Thai Finn is one of the students in the program and was in the center of the photo. We incorrectly listed her as one of the items on the menu."[9]

Art directors like the cluster-caption idea because it allows them to butt pictures against each other, bleed them, and in other ways better display them. Using a cluster caption, you don't have to plan for just the right space between the pictures to accommodate the various captions. You bring the captions together in a block.

But where names are involved, readers no doubt prefer captions right next to each picture for ready reference.

If your caption seems to be off to one side and not obviously connected to the photograph, your solution is *not* to include an arrow that points the reader in the right direction. Your solution is to redesign the page.

Captions right above or below photographs should appear in the same widths as the photographs—or narrower. You would not want to run them wider. Some art directors like to run captions at a standard width regardless of how wide the photographs are. This does help simplify the design and speed up the typesetting. You always know how wide to set your captions.

Photographs that stand by themselves—photographs not there to illustrate stories or features—need not only captions but also their own headlines, however small.

Some editors seem to feel that caption writers should even out the last line each time so that it is fully filled and flush with the other lines. This is folly. The time spent counting characters and rewriting to make that last line fit can be spent better on other editorial matters.

Bylines

The New Yorker places bylines at the ends of articles or stories, apparently in the belief that readers should get into editorial material without regard to who wrote it. Most magazines, if they use bylines, place them at the beginnings. Some magazines run bylines well removed from the titles of articles and right next to the articles' beginnings.

Bylines are set in type smaller than that used for article or story titles but larger, usually, than type used for body copy.

Some magazines combine bylines with blurbs about the author. Example: "Mathew S. Ogawa shows how after-midnight broadcasts are reaching Japanese youth." In this kind of arrangement the author's name is set in italics, boldface, all-caps, or even underlined to make it stand out. Other magazines run blurbs about the authors in small type at the bottoms of article openings, sort of as footnotes. Still others run separate columns combining information about all the contributors.

Credit lines

Some magazines run credit lines in a box on the table of contents page or somewhere else in the magazine. It is surprising that companies granting permission to reprint photographs or other illus-

9. "The Week," *National Review,* July 24, 1981, p. 818.

trations would settle for that kind of credit. Few readers study such a box to find out who took what picture.

The more common practice is to run credit lines right next to the photographs, whether they be original or borrowed. Credit-line type is usually smaller than caption type, to keep the two entirely separate; often a sans serif type is used. Some magazines run credit lines up the sides of pictures to keep the lines from interfering with captions.

Credit lines can be reversed or surprinted inside the photographs at their bottom edges.

If a magazine does not want to be bothered with separate settings for credit lines, it can run them as last lines of captions, set off by parentheses.

When one photographer takes all the pictures or one illustrator does all the sketches for a feature, a single byline rather than credit lines may be called for. The photographer's or illustrator's byline may be slightly smaller than the author's and placed away from the story's opening.

It may be that credit lines are getting out of hand. *Communication Arts* under a photograph of Kinuko Y. Craft, a magazine illustrator, runs this one: "Photograph by Byron Ferris, print by Rob Reynolds." Now all we have to know is who wrapped the package to mail it to the editor.

In-Service Training and Education, now *Health Care Education,* uses type only to create the art that starts off this article on "hospitalese." Everything here, including body copy, is in sans serif type. The deep blurbs on each page help unite the pages.

Typographic endings

Like a good cup of coffee after a meal, some writer has said. That's what an article's ending should be. The reader should feel the end of the article or story and then move away inspired, shocked, amused, instructed, perhaps even intent on some course of action.

Many editors feel that the writing alone may not be enough to signal that the encounter between the writer and reader is over. Some typographic accessory should announce, in effect: this is The End. This is especially true now that so few magazines provide a cushion of fillers at the ends of articles. They end at the bottom of pages.

The standard typographic device is the small, square box, available on any linecasting machine. Some magazines design their own end device and see that it is made available to the typesetter. The ending device may be a tiny version of the logo or, simply, the word "End."

A book needs none of these devices to end a chapter. A little leftover space does the job.

Suggested further reading

Bain, Eric K., *Display Typography: Theory and Practice,* Hastings House, Publishers, New York, 1970.

Biegeleisen, J. I., *Art Directors' Book of Type Faces,* Arco Publishing Company, Inc., New York, 1976. (Revised and Enlarged Edition.)

Biggs, John R., *Letter-forms & Lettering,* Pentalic Corp., New York, 1977.

Chadbourne, Bill N., *What Every Editor Should Know About Layout and Typography,* National Composition Association, 1730 N. Lynn St., Arlington, Va. 22209, n.d.

Cirillo, Bob and Kevin Ahearn, *Dry Faces,* Art Direction Book Company, New York, 1978. (Shows 1000 faces available from manufacturers of dry transfer letters.)

Craig, James, *Phototypesetting: A Design Manual,* Watson-Guptill, New York, 1978.

———, *Designing with Type,* Watson-Guptill, New York 1980. (Revised Edition.)

Ernst, Sandra B., *The ABC's of Typography,* Art Direction Book Co., New York, 1978.

Haley, Allen, *Phototypography: A Guide to In-house Typography and Design,* Charles Scribner's Sons, New York, 1980.

Hopkins, Richard L., *Origin of the American Point System for Printers' Type Measurement,* Hill & Dale Press, Terra Alta, West Virginia, 1976.

King, Jean Callan and Tony Esposito, *The Designer's Guide to Text Type,* Van Nostrand Reinhold, New York, 1980.

Lawson, Alexander, *Printing Types,* Beacon Press, Boston, 1971.

——— and Archie Provan, *Typography for Composition,* National Composition Association, 1730 N. Lynn St., Arlington, Virginia, 22209, 1976.

LeWinter, Renee (Compiler), *Directory of Evocative Typography,* GAMA Communications, P.O. Box 597, Salem, N.H. 03079, 1980.

Lewis, John, *Typography: Design and Practice,* Taplinger, New York, 1978. (Revised Edition.)

Morison, Stanley, *A Tally of Types,* Cambridge University Press, New York, 1973. (Covering types designed by Morison.)

———, *Selected Essays,* Cambridge University Press, New York, 1982. (Two volumes; expensive.)

Ogg, Oscar, *The 26 Letters,* Thomas Y. Crowell Company, New York, 1971. (Revised Edition.)

Rehe, Rolf F., *Typography: How to Make it More Legible,* Design Research Publications, Indianapolis, 1974.

Rosen, Ben, *Type and Typography: The Designer's Notebook,* Van Nostrand Reinhold, New York, 1976. (Revised Edition.)

Ruder, Emil, *Typography: A Manual of Design,* Hastings House, Publishers, New York, 1980.

Soppeland, Mark, *Words,* William Kaufman, Inc., Los Altos, Calif., 1980. (Unusual drawings of 110 words.)

Updike, Daniel Berkeley, *Printing Types: Their History, Forms and Use,* Dover Publications, New York, 1980. (Reprint of the Harvard University Press classic.)

Zapf, Hermann, *About Alphabets: Some Marginal Notes on Type Design,* M.I.T. Press, Cambridge, Massachusetts, 1970.

The Type Specimen Book, Van Nostrand Reinhold Company, New York, 1974. (544 faces, 3,000 sizes.)

The University of Maryland proves that a student handbook can be interesting and well designed. This spread, representing two of 54 pages, shows the design used: three columns per 8 × 10 1/2 page with several pieces of funky art on each spread. The art varied in size, but all of it was in the same style. Note the use of both horizontal and vertical rules and the large page numbers. Main headings are in all caps, secondary headings are in caps and lowercase, but all in the same type. Two colors are used throughout, with an additional feeling of color achieved through screening. Roz Hiebert edited, Heidi Kingsley designed, and Russ Fleury compiled.

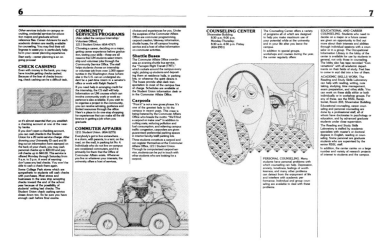

Art in a publication can either stand by itself as a separate feature, with or without a caption, or work with text matter as an illustration. Art that stands by itself often originates outside the editorial offices. It may be submitted as something of a surprise to the editor or art director. Illustrative art, on the other hand, is commissioned by the editor or art director, who wants it for one or more of these reasons:

1. To create a mood for a cover or feature.
2. To merely decorate a cover or feature.
3. To amplify or explain what's in a title or headline or what's in the text.
4. To fill space when words fall short.

And there is a less common reason:

5. To add something new to a title, headline, or feature. "I really think photography should give an article an additional dimension," said William Hamilton Jones, the alumni editor quoted earlier. "You can follow one line of thought in your text and you can deal with another in your visual material, and they will reinforce each other and each will add to the dimension of the other." An interesting idea, but dangerous; for you may end up confusing your readers. The art may compete with the feature instead of working with it. Illustrative art should make a story or concept more vivid, not more complex.

The art of photography

The halftone process for reproducing photographs was developed in the 1880s. One of the first magazines to use halftones regularly was the *National Geographic,* beginning in 1903. But *Life*'s contribution to the development of photography in magazines was undoubtedly greater than *National Geographic*'s. Started in 1936 as a sort of illustrated *Time, Life* gradually changed from a news magazine to a magazine of special features. More than any other publication it developed the idea of photojournalism: great photographs taken on the spot, where and when important things were happening. Sometimes the photographs merely reported, sometimes they expressed a form of opinion. Often their greatness was accidental.

For many years the photograph, like the painting or drawing, was used merely to *illustrate* an article or story. It still is used that way. But in the 1930s some editors, especially those at *Life,* worked out an additional use for photographs, putting them into a spread or a series of spreads and letting them tell their own story, sometimes without captions. The photo essay was born.

Photographer Chris Craft catches five-year-old Danny Om in action at a Karate class. The blurred look was deliberate, but Craft wanted enough clear focus to show that the child was Oriental and to make readable the name on the belt. This was shot in a not-very-well-lighted studio with tri-X film.

95

This 12 × 6 magapaper uses a silhouetted photograph for one of its covers, allowing a couple of the heads of the runners to overlap the big logo, which is printed in a second color. (Reprinted by permission of *Touche Ross Life,* June 1981, published by Touche Ross & Co.)

Like a piece of prose, a photo essay has a story to tell or a point to make. The pictures all revolve around a central theme. They may be uniform in size, or they may vary greatly in both size and shape. There is always a key photograph for the series, but there may be a sub-key photograph for each spread, too. It is up to the art director to unify the photographs.

Any combination of pictures is likely to say something different from what each picture by itself says. The sum is different from its parts. As an art director you must share with the photographer the responsibility for developing the theme of the essay. The order of presentation and the juxtaposition of one picture with another greatly affect what the essay says.

The new photographic equipment available makes all kinds of effects possible. "There's an embarrassment of riches as far as lenses are concerned," says Jean-Claude Suares, art director of *New York.* "What you see now is a lack of discipline in the use of lenses, to the point that photographers are getting everything in one picture. . . . The best example is Douglas Kirkland—his kind of pictures." Such pictures seem "right," but there are too many of them. For contrast, Suares looks for "wrong" pictures, just as among illustrations, he looks for "crazy stuff" instead of slick drawings.[1]

Robert N. Essman, art director of *People,* notes a deterioration in photography submitted to magazines. Photographs to him these days seem too precious, as though they were taken for museum showing rather than for publication. And often when the pictures are good, the focus is bad. "Why not focus clearly?" he asks. "Is there a course being given somewhere that now teaches one how to take out-of-focus pictures?"

The magazines' infatuation with blurred photographs in the early 1970s became the subject of some satire in *Saturday Review.* "What has happened," wrote Dereck Williamson, ". . . is that the improperly exposed and badly focused photograph has become Art. The bad picture is now good, and the good picture is bad. For amateur 35-millimeter photographers like myself, this is distressing news. For years I've been culling my slides and throwing away Art.

"Many of my mistakes would now be worth big money in the modern magazine market place."

He cites a number of his culls, including "One Tennis Shoe, with Kneecap," "Child Unrolling Agfachrome at High Noon," and "Daughter's Birthday Party with Failing Flashcube." His "Giant Redwoods and Finger," had it been sent to a magazine, would have been accepted and probably captioned: "A personal statement of the photographer concerning man's ruthless attitude toward his environment."[2]

There are still plenty of art directors who insist on sharply focused, well-lighted photographers. Editors and art directors like them because they say things that need to be said. And they are readily available. While only a few persons can turn out usable drawings or paintings, almost anyone can turn out publishable photographs, not the kind that would delight the heart of a Harry Benson, perhaps, but publishable nevertheless. To many, photography represents "instant art"; and everyone can participate. Out

1. Kurt Wilner, "Too Much Isn't Enough; J. C. Suares," *Art Direction,* May 1979, p. 87.

2. Dereck Williamson, "Shutter Shudders," Phoenix Nest column of *Saturday Review,* December 5, 1970, p. 4.

of thousands upon thousands of routine photographs, there just have to be some that, if they don't qualify as works of art, at least have enough clarity or meaning to justify reproduction in some publication.

More and more publications these days expect their editors or writers to take their own pictures. "We can't afford to hire a freelance photographer when the writer is on location in the boondocks," says Joe Ruskin, photography director at McGraw-Hill Publications Company. "It's too expensive to hire a photographer just to take one picture a day." At *Construction Equipment Maintenance,* a Cahners Publishing Company magazine, one of the first questions editorial job applicants face is: "Can you take pictures?"[3]

Among the most popular courses offered on college campuses these days—and in the high schools, too—are the courses in photography. Moholy-Nagy once said, prophetically: "The illiterate of the future will be the man who does not know how to take a photograph."

This photo is an editor's delight, because the photographer (Chris Craft) has purposely left a lot of white sky onto which columns of type can be superimposed. The photograph could be run as a full-page bleed, with the rounded art at the bottom of the page serving as a silhouette, providing a nice contrast to the straight columns of type.

3. "More Editors Trained to Take Photos," *Folio,* January 1981, p. 19.

Photographer Chris Craft had to take off her shoes and get up on a counter to take this bird's-eye shot of the Governor of Oregon, Vic Atiyeh, cutting a ribbon at a bank opening. She used a wide-angle lens to bring in the background. Too often routine shots like this, necessary to a publication, are made from usual vantage points with no attempt to really compose them. The bold-shapes and darkness in the foreground add dimension to this picture.

In a confrontation shot like this one, much depends upon the expressions a photographer is able to capture. People here are objecting to herbicide spraying. That's a Bureau of Land Management official at the left who is weathering the protests. Peter Haley of the *Daily Tidings* of Ashland, Oregon, took the picture.

Deciding on photographs

You should make sure the photographer fully understands any assignment and knows how the pictures will be used, whether for illustration or essay purposes.

   If you want to emphasize height, you should direct the photographer to take the picture from a worm's-eye angle. If you want to show an item in context with its surrounding, you may ask for a bird's eye view.

   Often a photograph does not tell the complete story unless scale is included. A photograph of a tree seedling may not mean much unless a knife or shovel or some other item whose size is understood is included in the picture. When *Posh,* the quarterly published by

Peter Haley used a fisheye lens
to make this routine shot
memorable.

A hilltribe woman on her way to fish in Northeastern Thailand waters. Native dress like hers with its bright colors and shoulder designs served as inspiration in the West for fasionable evening coats in the early 1980s. Photographer Steven R. Lorton, an editor at *Sunset,* decided a head-on pose would best show off his subject. The short depth of field puts detail where it should be in the photograph.

P & O Lines, Inc., ran an article on sculptures in miniature, the art director saw to it that photographs showed the various pieces held in hands. Closeup shots were made from different angles to heighten interest.

As art director you should insist on a wide selection of prints. Contact sheets are good enough. You can study the prints with an 8-power magnifier. You should ask for more blowups than you can use—three or four times as many—because no matter how well you read the prints, you'll see new things when they're bigger. You should have some choices at that level, too.

On some publications you can't afford the luxury of choice. Small publications often settle for the single picture or two that

To make one dancing couple stand out at a fiddlers' association dance, John Bauguess shoots from above and arranges things into a sort of "T" formation, showing only parts of the dancing couples in the background. Effective silhouetting of the centered couple and subtle expressions add to the readability and enjoyment of this exceptional piece of art. © by John Bauguess.

are available. As art director you would have to use a picture you know is inferior; but it is the only one that is available to you. A way to minimize the poor quality is to run it small.

Sometimes you have two or three excellent shots, but there is not much difference among them in camera angle, camera distance, or subject matter. You should resist the impulse to use them all. Redundancy spoils good photography.

There is some merit, however, in using a series of similar shots of an individual who is the subject of an interview. A series of photographs tells the reader more about the interviewee than a single photograph can. Besides, the several similar pictures give the reader a feel of visual continuity.

When you need a mug shot to go with an article or story and you have several to choose from, you should select the one that has an expression appropriate to the mood of the article. The reader can't help being puzzled when seeing the victim of a tragedy wearing a silly grin. At the least the caption should explain that the picture was taken on some earlier occasion.

There is plenty of room for innovation.

If you want to stage a photograph to represent something that happened earlier and to people not available to the photographer, you can arrange the scene mostly with backs facing the camera and, to protect your integrity, include the line under the photograph, "A re-creation of an actual event."

Color photography vs. black-and-white

For certain kinds of magazines—those dealing with exquisite scenery and luxurious travel, for instance—full-color photography is a must. But full color is expensive.

Another problem with full-color photography is that it makes *everything* look beautiful. By focusing close, the photographer makes the pattern and the splash of color more important than the content of the picture. Ugly things, like filth washing up on a river bank, become works of art to be admired. For this reason, even when you can afford color, you may choose to stay with black-and-white for some of your features.

Black-and-white photography has some advantages.

Lou Jacobs, Jr., who conducts a New York *Times* column on photography, says that, at least in the darkroom, photographers can maintain better control and manipulation of their work when they work with black-and-white pictures. You also have a greater choice of film speeds. "And with black-and-white you don't have to worry about distorted color from mixed light sources." Even photographers who consider themselves more artists than journalists often turn to black-and-white "because of the creative and artistic controls available, and because the prints are more permanent than color prints."

Jacobs adds: "Once you get really immersed in black-and-white photography you will also become aware of the ways you see people, places and things differently . . . [from what] you do in color."[4]

Photographic clichés

While any pose, from any angle, with any focus, can find a place in today's publications, certain pictures, at least in ordinary usage, should be avoided if for no other reason than that they have been used too often. These pictures include the following poses:

1. people shaking hands during award ceremonies.
2. public officials signing proclamations and other papers.
3. people studying documents.
4. people pointing to maps, to trees, to anything.
5. committees at work.
6. public speakers at the rostrum.

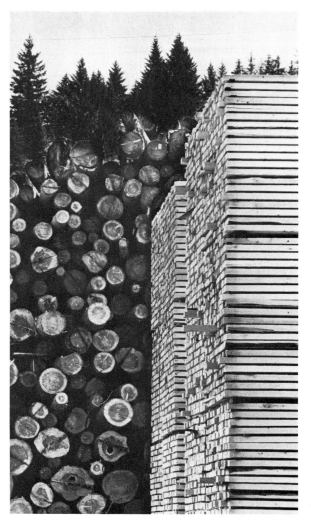

Pattern often is enough to make a photograph interesting. Peter Haley took this shot for the Salem (Oreg.) *Statesman-Journal* to illustrate a feature on high interest rates and how they were resulting in stacked up inventories for the forest products industries.

4. Lou Jacobs, Jr., "A Fresh Look at Black-and-White," New York *Times,* Jan. 31, 1982, Section 2, p. D37.

The accepting-the-award picture will, unfortunately, always be with us, and in many cases it will be in a form no less awkward than this.

But even the photographic cliché has its place in well-designed publications. The fact that a picture may be "Camp" might be reason enough to run it. Or maybe the nature of the article calls for a photograph that, under other circumstances, would be considered as too stilted to use. Art directors seem more willing than in the past to run group shots, with subjects looking straight ahead into the lens of the camera. The Western Art Directors Club in a publicity stunt got away with a photographic cliché when it sent out a formal group shot of newly-elected officers. All persons but one were looking straight ahead into the camera, painfully serious. One, in the middle of the front row, had his back facing the camera. He was the outgoing president.

William H. Neubeck, editor of the New Jersey *Herald,* a small daily, makes a case for the familiar and discredited group shot. Neubeck is tired of the outside expert—someone, say, from a 200,000-circulation paper—holding up such a picture as a horrible example. Such experts "may know a lot about photography or graphics, but few, it seems, know very much about community newspapers." Readers of community papers like to see pictures— even group pictures—of people they know. "I suppose we could arrange the [fire department] chief, deputy chief, et al., around one of the fire engines or sliding down a fire pole (if we could find a firehouse that still has a fire pole). But after doing that once or twice, wouldn't the novelty have worn off?"[5]

Handling photographs

When finally laying out the pages, you work with 8 × 10 glossies. Using a grease crayon, you make your crop marks in the margin. You do not write on the backs of photos for fear of denting the front surfaces. Dents, bends, and folds show up in the final printing.

You should be particularly careful in your handling of transparencies. When a black-and-white print is lost, a new one can be made easily. But when a transparency is lost, all is lost.

A right-hand page opener for an article in *Bell Telephone Magazine* on government regulation. The black border is appropriate in view of the word "Strangling" in the title. Further dramatizing the concept of strangling is the twisted shape of the phone, accomplished by heating it in an oven and working it over before taking the photograph. To tell readers that the article really starts on the next page, the editor, after the italicized blurb, runs the word "continued."

5. William H. Neubeck, "Would *You* Use This Photo?" *The Bulletin of the Society of Newspaper Editors,* February 1981, p. 52.

In indicating sizes to the photographer or printer, you always give width first, then depth. (The British do it just the opposite.) You can make sure there is no misunderstanding when you write down a size by marking a short horizontal line above the width and a short vertical line above the depth.

Cropping photographs

Most art directors feel they can improve on the original composition of photographs, dramatize them, make them more "readable," change the emphasis, by cropping—cutting away unnecessary detail and background. This is the age of the closeup.

Much of this cropping is good. But some of it is unnecessary and, worse, destructive of good photography. What appears to be monotonous background or foreground may be vital to a photograph's proportion.

In cropping a mug shot you would ordinarily leave a little space above the head and a bit of the chest showing. The sketch below

shows a wrong—an uncomfortable—cropping. It is never a good idea to crop exactly at the neck for a mug shot or at the ankles for a full-figure shot. And on a full figure, you should leave a little foreground for the feet.

When you have mug shots from several sources, with faces in several sizes, you should crop them so that the faces line up in the same sizes, the same amount of bust showing. The rough sketch here shows the right and wrong way of handling this. The even

handling establishes a relationship among the people shown and puts them on the same level.

The art of cropping affects the electronic media as well as the print media. When Dan Rather succeeded Walter Cronkite as anchorman for CBS, the camera moved back to keep him from dominating the screen, as Cronkite had done. It was one thing for the kindly, everybody's uncle to be seen up close like that; it would be something else for the more austere Rather to be so close. But by 1982, with viewers used to Rather, the camera moved in again, making Rather's handsome face even bigger than the craggy Cronkite's face had been.

Doctoring photographs

Inexperienced art directors often cut photographs into odd shapes because squares and rectangles are "monotonous." These art directors make the mistake of thinking that readers are more interested in shape than in content.

Nothing—nothing—beats the rectangle or square as a shape for a photograph. A circle, a triangle, a star, a free form—these may have occasional impact; but as a general rule, they should be avoided. If you want some added impact you can crop your photographs into extremely wide or tall rectangles.

A silhouette halftone—the reproduction of a photograph in which a figure is outlined against a white background—provides an effective change of pace for the art director. The silhouette is much preferred to the photograph with doctored edges because it does not represent shape for the sake of shape; it emphasizes content. A single silhouette can be used for contrast on a spread of photographs that are rectangles and squares.

If you feel that one element in a picture should "walk out" from the rest of the picture, you can put that element—or part of it—into a silhouette and square off the rest of the picture. You can also box in the white area of the photograph.

When silhouetting (also referred to as outlining) a photograph, you may find it necessary to do your own cutting or opaquing. You should be sure the figure or object in the photograph is large enough to take the silhouetting. You should avoid intricate silhouettes, such as a woman with windblown hair.

The silhouette in photography often comes naturally, without any need for doctoring. It starts with the photographer taking the picture so that the subject—say it's a businesswoman hailing a taxi—is mostly in dark tones against a light background. There are few in-between tones.

Silhouette photographs, provided you don't overuse them, can dress up a publication. Such photographs are more decorative than informative. They work especially well as covers or introductions. As an art director you would try to select silhouette photographs with low vantage points. Such photographs better display the subject against, say, the sky. One way for a photographer to take a silhouette photograph is to get the subject to block out the sun, thus allowing light to fill in all around her.

Bleeding photographs

Bleeding photographs—running them off the edge of the page—tends to dramatize them and make them appear larger than they really are. Not only does a bleed picture occupy extra white space that would be used as margins; it also seems to stretch beyond the page. There is no optical fence to contain it.

Generally speaking, only large photographs should be bled. It is never advisable to bleed small mug shots. Nor is it necessary,

To illustrate an article on how to "deal" with customers swarming the marketplace "after a long winter's sleep," *Go,* the Goodyear magazine for tire dealers, came up with this photograph taken by Don Landstrom, an amateur magician. The article discussed a nationwide "Goodyear Cuts the Deck and Deals" promotion. Because few magicians or even gamblers are able to shuffle cards like this, Landstrom drilled a hole through the center of the cards and threaded them with a string to "enable the cards to follow a predetermined path from the top hand to the bottom," according to editor Larry Miller.

Because this nearly full-page photograph appeared on a left-hand page of a college magazine, the editor flopped it to make it face the gutter. But in the process he made a left-hander out of singer-guitarist Ric Masten, changed the arrangement of strings on his guitar, buttoned the man's shirt the wrong way, and moved the pocket over to the other side. It would have been much better to let the picture face off the page. The flopping was made all the more ludicrous by a picture elsewhere on the spread that showed Masten playing the guitar in his normal way—from his right side.

Captions under or right next to photographs make things easy for the reader, but it is sometimes necessary, from a design standpoint, to run photographs together as a unit, uninterrupted by type. These beautiful full-color photographs form one bleed unit on the right-hand page of a two-page spread; only a thin white line separates them from each other. This reproduction may not show it clearly, but the one caption for the pictures appears on the left-hand page, about in the middle of the third column, in a slightly smaller, different type, printed in blue ink. Nor was it necessary to number the photographs so that the caption could point to them. The caption starts out this way: "Clockwise from upper left:.." The pages, part of a six-page article are from *Exxon USA*, published by the Exxon Company, U.S.A., Houston. Downs Matthews, editor; Richard Payne, art director.

when you use bleeds, to bleed consistently throughout the magazine. Sometimes a combination of bleed and nonbleed pictures is best.

It is not a good idea to bleed photographs that are outlined with thin black lines. When you bleed such a photograph, you lose some of the outlines and introduce some inconsistency.

You must order your halftones with an extra one-eighth to one-quarter inch strip (final halftone size) for each edge that bleeds. Because extra trimming may be involved and an oversize sheet must be used, the printer may charge more for bleed pages.

Art directors favor bleeding for a while, then abandon the practice, then pick it up again.

Flopping photographs

You may be tempted occasionally to flop a photograph—change its facing—if it seems to point off a page. But this is tricky business.

Flop a portrait, and the part in the hair is on the wrong side. The suit is buttoned on the wrong side. If a sign is included in the picture, it will read from right to left.

Scholastic Editor once ran a photograph of the cover of *Onondagan,* the yearbook of Syracuse University. On the yearbook's cover was a picture of a light switch turned on. The "ON" in caps showed plainly (*On* is a shortened version of the yearbook's name). But for the sake of a facing, the editor of *Scholastic Editor* flopped the photograph. And the "ON" came out reading "NO."

Arranging photos on the page

It might be useful here to consider chapter 3's design principles as they apply to the use of photographs.

To bring order to your pages, you should use fewer pictures—perhaps fewer than you would consider desirable—and you should use them in large sizes. A large photograph is many times more effective than a smaller one. The impact does not increase arithmetically; it increases by geometric progression.

Big photographs also save money. It costs as much to take a small picture as it does to take a big one. As much thinking and effort go into a small picture.

For the sake of unity, you should bring related photographs together in your layout. Organization for content is more important than organization based on the way photographs happen to face.

When you use several photographs per page or spread, you should place the closeups at the bottom because this conforms more naturally to the way we see things in perspective. You should keep your photographs all the same size—or you should make them obviously different in size. You want to avoid making them almost—but not quite—equal. In most cases you would have some large, some middle-size, some small photographs; and you would combine squares with rectangles, and among your rectangles you would have some horizontals and some verticals.

It is not a good idea to run full-page pictures on both left- and right-hand pages, especially if they bleed on three sides and run into the gutter. The two then appear to be a single, massive photograph. A small band of white should separate them at the gutter.

Here is a summary of techniques for combining several photographs on a page, unifying them and yet allowing them to stand separately:

1. *Run a small band of white between them.* The band may vary in width, or it can stay the same throughout the spread. Art directors used to prefer separations of no more than an eighth of an inch, but now they seem to prefer a wider band: a quarter of an inch or more.

2. *Butt the photos up against each other.* This works well if the photos are of different sizes; some of the photo edges will be printed against a field of white. Some art directors like to run a thin black line where the photographs join.

3. *Overlap the photos.* This means cutting mortises into photos and slipping portions of other photos into the holes. The overlap can fit snugly. Or it can have a small white line around it to help separate one photo from the other.

Overlapping is not always desirable because it calls attention to shape rather than content. When you overlap, you get photos that are *L*- or *U*-shaped. This spoils the composition of the photos, even when what is mortised out appears to be unimportant foreground or sky.

The usual overlap allows only one of the photographs to print in the shared area. For an unusual effect you can print one photograph in black, one in color, without bothering to mortise; you can let them both show. Or you can print one photograph in one color, one in another, and where they overlap you will get a third color.

4. *Fit one photo inside the other.* You can do this when the center of interest of the base photograph is concentrated in one area. Your base photograph would be one you would otherwise crop. The smaller photo would fit into an internal mortise. Again it could fit snugly, or it could carry a thin white outline.

Photographs or illustrations?

In a review of *America's Great Illustrators,* Tom Wolfe points out that "The period 1880 to 1930 was the half-century in which the magazine industry grew up and boomed, and magazines became

In this set of nine faces, used on the cover of a college catalog, designer Jim Bodoh of the University of Oregon was careful to pick faces to represent all classes of students. The faces started out as regular photographs, but the reproduction called for was line. Then, on his prints, Bodoh did some retouching to dramatize some of the shapes. And of course he gave careful attention to cropping in every case.

In this shot of country women fishing in central Thailand, Lorton puts a participant with a winsome look in the foreground and concentrates on her. There is enough action around her to keep the picture interesting. Those are sheets of plastic the women are wearing as raincoats.

the dominant form of popular entertainment. Magazine illustration idealized and reshaped popular taste in a way that film and, to some extent, comic strips would after 1920."

The early magazine illustrators worked without the stigma of being "mere illustrators." The split between fine art and commercial art had not yet occurred. "So much of the most prestigious painting of the 19th century was itself illustration. . . . As late as 1900 artists moved back and forth from easel painting to commercial illustration without any real sense of crossing a boundary line," Wolfe adds.[6]

Early in this century magazine illustrators became important persons in building circulations for magazines. People became much more familiar with art in magazines than in museums. The most popular magazine artist of all, of course, was Norman Rockwell, who did a total of 317 covers for *The Saturday Evening Post*. One estimate had it that each of his covers was seen by 4,000,000 persons.

Illustrators whose work appeared *inside* the magazines became popular, too. Charles Dana Gibson, who drew for *Life, Collier's,* and *Harper's Weekly,* set the standard for the beautiful girl in America. Stephen Becker in *Comic Art in America* said that "From the early nineties to the First World War, the Gibson Girl was the American ideal: women imitated her, men desired her."

Newspapers employed illustrators, too, but, facing tight deadline schedules, relied on their own staffs rather than on freelancers. Big newspapers employed teams of artists, some of them cartoonists.

Illustrators enjoyed a "golden age" in the 1930s, 1940s, and early 1950s. But in the mid-1950s, their magazine market shriveled. Magazines were hard-hit by that new medium, television, and in their search for a new identity they turned to the camera. Fiction was no longer a major part of magazines; nonfiction seemed better served by photographs. Illustrators, if they got magazine assignments at all, had to offer something the camera could not. One illustrator, Mark English, remarked that "The camera has helped the artist see the direction he shouldn't be going in." Newspapers already had abandoned their large art staffs for teams of photographers.

No doubt about it: the camera put many illlustrators out of work. Art directors preferred photographers because they were more realistic, when realism was important; and they were more readily available and at less cost. Furthermore, the photographer gave the art director a choice of many poses and scenes.

But there is some evidence that the illustration has made a comeback. Donald Holden, art book editor for Watson-Guptill Publications, observes that photography "is becoming a very fatiguing medium." Art directors are constantly looking for new ways to use the camera; using it in focus, using it out of focus, changing the angle. "I sense a certain desperateness in their efforts," he says. ". . . The fatigue factor may force the art director to rediscover illustration."

Fiction did not return to magazines but think pieces multiplied, and illustrations seem better suited to these than photographs.

6. Tom Wolfe, "Golden Age," *The New York Times Book Review,* June 4, 1978, p. 45.

"Although concept photography can be employed it's usually easier to draw symbols than to photograph them," says designer John Peter. Peter observes that the new illustrations devote themselves to spirit or mood. The old illustrations dealt only with narrative or incident.

Illustration has become especially popular with the newly launched magazines, many of which need special identity.

And many different styles find favor with art directors these days. Some styles are merely revivals; others appear to be innovative, even shrill. Magazines and books, especially, hold many visual surprises for readers. Illustrators now are willing to experiment.

In his days on *Look,* Allen Hurlburt preferred photographs to illustrations, but *Look,* like *Life,* was essentially a photographic magazine. Even on *Look,* Hurlburt saw situations where illustrations were called for. For instance: carrying a camera sometimes can be dangerous or even illegal, or sometimes it is difficult or impossible to gain model releases. An example of Hurlburt's imaginative approach to illustration was his commissioning of Norman Rockwell to do a series of paintings on integration. Hurlburt reasoned that because Rockwell had so long been trusted and admired by the middle class as an upholder of traditional American values, his work in this area would be all the more effective.

Now that we have some photographers who have abandoned realism for abstraction and we have some painters who have come back to realism—in some cases to superrealism—the line between photography and illustration is blurred. It's still the policy of most art directors to order photography for nonfiction and illustrations for fiction, but that is no hard-and-fast rule. An obvious exception is the use of cartoons to illustrate a piece of nonfiction on, say, human foibles.

So the only answer the art director can give to the question, Should we use photographs or illustrations? has to be: It depends.

For this shot, Lorton steps farther back to put his subjects into better context with the landscape and to better show off the fishing gear. Note the strong diagonal thrust running from upper left to lower right.

Realism or abstraction?

The penchant for realism in art goes back a long way. The closer a piece of art was to real life, the better. *Time* tells the story of Zeuxis, fifth century, B.C., Greek artist, competing with another

Nation's Cities uses a piece of line art to supply visual interest to a right-hand opener, and then, where the article continues, reuses part of the art to help the reader adjust to the new page. Actually, the magazine reuses two parts of the art—the bottom five figures and two more figures ahead of them in the line. Art directors are Louise Levine and Evelyn Sanford.

Art 109

The correct way to put a contact lens in your eye: how would you show it? Artist Sarah Qualey for *Rochester Methodist Hospital News* uses pure line, and chooses a side view. She also moves in close. A line drawing like this can be more explicit than a photograph.

artist to see who could paint the most realistic picture. When his painting of grapes was unveiled, birds flew down and pecked at them. Surely he had won. But when the judges started to unveil the other painting, they were stunned. *The veil was the painting.* Zeuxis had fooled the birds, but his opponent had fooled the judges.

The coming of photography in the 1800s brought into question the idea that art was imitation. The camera was an instrument that could do the job better. Many artists then assumed a new role. Art became more than imitation; it became something with a value of its own.

Abstraction followed. Not that artists had not worked in abstractions before. But now abstraction became a dominant movement in art. Eventually, almost anything could pass for art: pieces of junk, objects that moved, combinations of common artifacts.

Not everyone was impressed. A writer in *True* told the story of a man who told Pablo Picasso that he didn't like modern paintings because they weren't realistic. When the man later showed Picasso a snapshot of his girl friend, Picasso asked: "My word, is she really as small as all that?"

With the Armory Show in 1913, when modern art made its debut in America, artists favoring realism as an art form went into a decline, as far as the critics were concerned. But the average person continued to admire the Norman Rockwell kind of artist. Late in his career, perhaps because Americans then enjoyed what *Newsweek* called the "vogue for the old," partly because Andrew Wyeth had made realism respectable again, Rockwell staged a comeback in the magazines. Several books came out offering his collected works—at premium prices. Even the critics reassessed the man.

Art as it has appeared in magazines has been slow to give up realism. Only in recent years have magazines made the move toward abstraction. But now the leaders among them and the smaller, specialized magazines, too, seem willing to experiment with any art form that can stand up to the printing process.

It would be difficult—certainly this book will not attempt it—to make a case for one kind of art as preferable to another. There is a place for all kinds of art in American magazines. For some magazines, for some articles, for some audiences—realism works better. In other circumstances, abstract art would be preferable.

Sources of illustrations

One of the notable advantages of offset lithography is that almost anything from almost any source can be reproduced with little or no additional expense. In fact the flexibility and adaptability of offset has tempted editors of marginal publications to steal printed photographs and artwork from more affluent publications. The only reason these editors are not prosecuted is that their publications attract virtually no attention outside their own limited audiences. But clearly they are violating the law if the material they appropriate is copyrighted, and often it is.

There are enough low-cost art and photographic services around to make such illegal activity unnecessary, even for the most mendicant of editors.

Up until 1978, any art published in books or magazines that were 56 years old or older could be clipped and used with or without credit at no cost to the user. After 56 years the original copyright (granted for a 28-year period) and the second and final copyright (granted for another 28-year period if it was applied for) had expired. The art had fallen into the public domain.

Now, because Congress changed the copyright law to make it conform to the law in other countries, things are more complicated. Editors and art directors are still free to lift material from publications whose copyrights expired before 1978. But material whose copyright periods extend beyond January 1978 and material copyrighted since then come under a different ruling: the copyrights last for the lifetime of the holders and for fifty years beyond that.

Still, plenty of material remains in the public domain. And if it is not yet there, you can always contact the owner and get permission to use it, possibly paying a small fee for the privilege. Also in the public domain are most government publications.

While the price is right for public-domain art, the dated look of much of the material may be a problem.

If you can't find what you want from public-domain sources you can turn to any of the hundreds of picture agencies and stock-art houses, to government agencies, to chambers of commerce, to trade and professional organizations, to businesses, to libraries, to historical societies, to other publications who sell or loan prints, or to publishers who make clipbooks available.[7]

Dover Publications, 180 Varick Street, New York, New York 10014, remains a leader in this field, with its Pictorial Archives Series of inexpensive collections, mostly of public-domain art. Dover does ask that you use no more than a half a dozen pieces for any one job. This is to prevent people from republishing and marketing the books. Hart Publishing Company, Inc., 15 West 4th Street, New York, New York 10012, has recently entered the field

7. See listings in *Literary Market Place*, *Writer's Market*, and *Photographer's Market*.

You have to move in close and get just the right lighting to show that someone is wearing a contact lens. And that is what photographer Jim Bambenek did for this *Rochester Methodist Hospital News* cover photo. Editor-designer Bev Parker bleeds the photo all around and finds just the right place to reverse the title and blurb. This is a black-and-white publication.

The all-caps title for Lee Guthrie's article in *The Plain Dealer Magazine* is treated as a rebus, with small pieces of art inserted. That the art, both in the title and outside, is dated adds to the feeling of nostalgia here. Greg Paul art directed.

FORGOTTEN THINGS THAT WILL BE REMEMBERED ALWAYS

BY LEE GUTHRIE

THANKSGIVING, 1945

Childhood's memory is capricious. Sometimes the most important events of our young lives sink without a trace into that vast cavern of myth, fairy tale and nightmare known as the unconscious. Other times, a seemingly innocuous occurrence reverberates down through the years out of all proportion to its apparent importance.

That November I was eight years old. The war was over at last, and the Allied victory meant that I no longer had to walk to school in darkness: from now on, daylight saving time would be a summer phenomenon.

In parochial schools then, the school day began with 8 o'clock Mass. Last year when I had left my house at 7:30 for the mile-long walk to school, it was still dark. Only as Mass was ending, only at the Agnus Dei, did the tall stained glass windows on the Blessed Virgin's side of the church begin to glow with the morning sun.

That morning was a Friday. I had to carry a four-layer chocolate cake to school along with the Baltimore catechism and my lunch pail and I was glad it wasn't dark.

The cake would be won that night by a neighbor at a special Thanksgiving festival to be held in the school gym. The festival, with its cake and turkey raffles, with the beer and cotton candy and apple cider and doughnuts for sale, would pay for the special dinner that was being held in the auditorium just across the playground.

This was November, 1945, and most of the men from St. Columba parish who had fought in the war were home now. Whoever decided such things had decreed that the parish would stage a feast of celebration that its sons were home at last. The killing was over, the U. S. was the most powerful country in the world and we would see to it that no one would ever again be stupid enough to start another war. Who could doubt it?

After dinner in the auditorium, which was strictly for the newly-discharged soldiers and their families, they would come over to the gym to meet old friends and to see if their luck would hold on the turkey wheel.

It was hard to assimilate. My war was the one that was fought on the screen of the Park Theatre by William Bendix and Lloyd Nolan in Guadalcanal Diary and by Raymond Massey and Humphrey Bogart in Action in the North Atlantic. Only slowly did I begin to understand that night, amidst the gaiety and the cotton candy and the cigar smoke, that these thin and haggard men actually had been in "the war" along with John Wayne and

A sample drawing from "Human Relations," one of scores of clip books available from Volk Studios, one of the better stock-art houses. Editors can purchase clip books by subject area for a few dollars each, and each book contains about two dozen drawings from which to choose. There are no limitations on how they are used, or on frequency of use. Of course, no editor or advertiser who uses the Volk service, or some similar service, gets exclusive rights to the material.

with some first-rate collections centering on, for instance, Chairs, Weather, Dining and Drinking, Trades and Professions, and Animals.

Art Direction Book Company, 19 West 44th Street, New York, New York 10036, publisher of *Art Direction* magazine, publishes and distributes a number of clipbooks of public-domain art, including the *Ron Yablon Graphic Archives* covering Nature, People, Things, and Typography & Design.

Calling itself "The World's Leading Publisher of Copyright Free Archive Material," The Dick Sutphen Studio," Box 628, Scottsdale, Arizona 85252, offers editors books of both old art and new material, including illustrative cartoons "in numerous sizes and categories."

Among organizations offering a regularly-issued clipboard service are Volk Studios, Pleasantville, New Jersey 08232, and Dynamic Graphics, Inc., 6707 N. Sheridan Road, Peoria, Illinois 61614. The work from these and similar organizations is contemporary, executed by a variety of artists in a kind of house style: adequate, slick, and not particularly exciting.

In addition to stock-art organizations you have hundreds of stock-photo organizations and agencies at your call. Some specialize; others offer a great variety of photographs. Harold M. Lambert Studios, Inc., Philadelphia, for example, has on hand some 500,000 black and white photographs and 50,000 color transparencies. Rental fees vary, depending upon intended use.

A stock-art house differs from a stock-photo house in that once you purchase the clipbook or service from a stock-art house you are free to use it in any way that you wish and as often as you wish. A stock-photo house ordinarily grants you one-time use.

A problem with both of these sources, of course, is that ordinarily you would not get exclusive use. You face the chance that some other publication will show the same material.

Art from within

Accessible as it is, public-domain or stock art does not often exactly fit your needs. So when possible—when you can afford it—you order art to fit. Or you go to a staff artist or photographer. Or, if you have the necessary talent, you do the work yourself.

On smaller publications editors often do their own photography. The favorite camera is the 35 mm, single-lens reflex with interchangeable lenses. If the camera has some automatic features, so much the better.

Most editors/photographers prefer using fast film—Tri-X—and doing their photography, even their inside photography, in natural light. Getting the subject well lighted and in focus is only part of the challenge. What really separates the amateur photographer from the professional is the composition of the photograph. It should not be necessary to improve the photograph's composition through cropping, although if the photograph can take some cropping it becomes a more versatile element in the hands of an imaginative art director looking, say, for a deep vertical or wide horizontal to add interest to the page.

By taking many more pictures that you would want, you are likely to come up with at least a few that work well. You would ask for contact prints from your developer and mark the promising ones for enlargement.

If you have a staff artist or photographer, you would make assignments as you would with a freelancer. The chief advantage is that the staffer will be readily available and at a comparatively modest cost. But there has to be a continuous flow of work to make such an arrangement pay off.

Art from freelancers

Freelancers are everywhere. Once the word gets out that your publication is in the market, you will face a steady stream of them—illustrators and photographers nervously clutching their portfolios of examples. "Sorry—what's the name again?—we really don't have many assignments that call for charcoal renderings of nudes." In case you don't find the freelancer you want, you can turn to several directories now available.

One way to arrange for photographs in a faraway section of the country is to line up a member of the American Society of Magazine Photographers—easy enough to do if you refer to the *ASMP Book,* an annual that lists the organization's members. ASMP's address is 205 Lexington Ave., New York 10016.

It is one thing to select prints or drawings from among those submitted on speculation. It is another to choose a photographer or illustrator from among those available and send that person off on an assignment. A portfolio may not be representative of what an artist can do under adverse conditions.

Another problem has to do with deadlines. You can't be sure that a new artist will deliver the work on time. So you tend to stick to a small stable of freelancers with whose work and working habits you are familiar.

Samuel Antupit says art directors have been negligent in developing new talent. They should be willing to try the work of the lesser-knowns, he argues. Only the small specialized magazines seem willing to heed his advice, if for no other reason than that they can't afford the big names.

The big magazines have shown some interest in using name artists in unfamiliar roles. Herb Bleiweiss, when he was art director for *Ladies' Home Journal,* used photographers on assignments they had not tried before. "These people when working in a new area approach problems with a fresh eye," he said. When *LHJ* ran Truman Capote's "A Christmas Memory," Bleiweiss used a painting by Andrew Wyeth to illustrate it.

The usual procedure is to give the illustrator a copy of the manuscript with a request for a series of rough sketches. From these the art director orders the finished drawings or paintings. At *Fleet Owner,* illustrators are required to read articles thoroughly before illustrating them. Daniel P. Eigo, editor, says this practice not only aids creativity; it also helps the magazine avoid publishing off-target or misleading artwork.

The art of compromise

Working with artists and photographers you are likely to face some tensions. An artist or photographer is never quite as awed by a deadline as an editor or art director is. Nor does the artist take kindly to changes in submitted work, however necessary they may be from an editorial standpoint. So far as the artist is concerned, the editor and art director always want the work yesterday and

Let's say your subject is "love," and you need an illustration. You could use a piece of public-domain art like this. It appeared originally in *Werbezeichen: An Album,* Munich, n.d.

Popular in literary and book-review magazines and in newspaper "forum" sections or on op-ed pages is line art with scratchy shading and barely defined features. Such art carries the feel of sophistication. This example by Sovetskii Khudozhnik comes from *Album: Fifty Years of Soviet Art: Graphic Arts,* Moscow, n.d.

seem to change their minds about what they want after the final art is in.

Paul Hightower, a participant in a University of Iowa Visual Scholars Program, offered these tongue-in-cheek distinctions between editors and photographers. An *editor,* he said, "leaps tall buildings in a single bound, is more powerful than a locomotive, is faster than a speeding bullet, walks on water, dictates policy to God" while an *assistant editor* "barely clears a thatched hut, loses a tug of war with a hand car, can fire a speeding bullet, swims well, is occasionally addressed by God." A *copy editor* "makes high marks on the wall while trying to leap tall buildings. . . ." And the *photographer?* "[He] Lifts buildings and walks under them, kicks locomotives off the tracks, catches bullets in his teeth and eats them, freezes water with a single glance, *is* God."[8]

In any kind of skirmish, the art director, doing the buying, has to have the last word. This does not mean that the two—art director and artist—cannot work together harmoniously. But the art director has to be something of a public relations person and personnel director, seeing things from the artist's viewpoint. The art director may find that a hired photographer has much more to offer than an ability to follow directions. A good photographer may have ideas for illustrating the story or article that the art director has not thought of. The art director should be willing to listen to suggestions and consider alternate shots submitted by the photographer. The photographer often finds new illustrative possibilities at the scene, not envisioned when the two worked out plans for photographic coverage.

The art director owes it to the photographer to explain the nature of the article or story being illustrated, the reasons for the pictures, their intended use and placement, and the nature of other art for that issue. Often the art director provides the photographer with a rough layout of the pages when the assignment is given.

One continuing problem centers on the ownership of negatives. Does the buyer own them? Or does the photographer? What happens when the editor needs another print or wants to re-use the photograph in another issue or another publication? Freelancers like to hold onto negatives and get paid for each additional use, of course; but some editors manage to buy all rights to photos and negatives. Walter F. Giersbach, manager of international communications for The Dun & Bradstreet Corp., New York, operates this way:

"I have stopped short of having each still photographer sign over all rights to our company, but there is a clear verbal understanding that we own negatives and prints, can reorder prints for internal non-commercial use at a fair market price, and that negatives will be filed by the photographer or a laboratory that meets with our approval."[9]

Settling on rates

The staff artist or staff photographer works on a regular salary, so rates are not a problem. The freelancer works differently. Rates are negotiable.

8. Reported by *Journalism Educator,* April 1977, p. 64.
9. Walter F. Giersbach in a letter to the editor, *IABC News,* May 1981, p. 23.

The freelance illustrator may be attached to a studio or work independently. The freelancer is often willing to accept less for work for a publication than for an advertising agency, simply because publication work seems more gratifying.

The usual procedure is to give the illustrator a copy of the manuscript with the request for a series of rough sketches. From these the art director orders the finished drawings or paintings desired, specifying any necessary changes. Often the publication and the illustrator settle on a price in advance. Sometimes it's a matter of saying, "We have $250 to spend on a cover illustration. Interested?"

Rates vary widely.

The bigness of the publication makes a difference. Geography makes a difference, too. Freelancers can't charge as much in Provo as in San Francisco.

Often freelancers ask for a deposit or advance on a job. And they sometimes specify to what use their work may be put. Any further use may be subject to additional payment.

Tad Crawford and Arie Kopelman in *Selling Your Graphic Design and Illustration* (St. Martin's Press, New York, 1981) say that a full-color illustration used in a national consumer magazine will cost from $500 to $1,500. For a regional, trade, or small company magazine the same illustration might cost $300 to $850.

In case you have to buy freelance design, you can expect to pay from $25 to $75 an hour. A freelance pasteup artist will charge from $12 to $35 an hour.

Crawford and Kopelman are talking about real professionals. Beginners in small markets are likely to work for considerably less. They should be willing to work for less because they make more mistakes and often exhibit less flair. On the other hand beginners do not want to ask too little for their work or they will be marked as amateurs.

As a group, photographers seem to have standardized their rates more than other artists have. Still, routine photography, if you are willing to settle for it, is probably the least expensive custom art you can buy. First-class photography, on the other hand, comes high. A professional photographer will charge a magazine at least $200 a day plus expenses. The rate may go higher if a large number of prints from the shooting are used.

Many artists, designers, and photographers working as freelancers hire agencies to represent them, find assignments, and dicker on prices. One way for an artist or photographer to make it is to come up with a name that will be remembered. A photographer in San Francisco contributing to *Artbeat,* an "independent arts newspaper," calls himself f. Stop Fitzgerald.

". . . Each story calls for its own individual technique," says Robert Quackenbush, who did the illustration for this right-hand opener for *Clipper.* "For this reason, I experiment with many mediums and tools to find the 'right' technique for a story." Note how well the art here is integrated with the display type: each has a bold, hand-carved look. (Reproduced by permission from *Clipper* Magazine, published and copyrighted by Pan American World Airways.

Where to put your art

Ordinarily art, in a large size, would start out an article or feature. Smaller pieces might scatter themselves throughout the piece. Sometimes it is a good idea to let pieces of art evolve as the article progresses. In a magazine, for instance, each right-hand page might show the subject in a progressively more advanced stage.

Sometimes you might want to hold off your impact art until the reader turns the opening page, and then you hit hard. Or you might want to sandwich the article between impressive opening and closing art, perhaps art that hold a one-two or before-and-after punch.

To cut down on units on a page, you might want to incorporate the title with the art, making a single visual unit.

Where space is a problem and one big illustration does not seem appropriate, you can order small drawings made, all the same size, to be used as inserts. Each of these drawings might occupy half-column squares or rectangles, the copy wrapping around them.

Using art imaginatively

The usual procedure is to do the article or story first, then go out after the pictures to illustrate it. But sometimes it's better to do it the other way around: tell the story in pictures, using words only where facts or statistics are not clear without them.

What the art director tries to do is come up with the one visualization that will tell the story immediately and forcefully. One indication of Otto Storch's genius was the illustration he commissioned for a *McCall's* article on infidelity: a big red apple with a couple of bites taken out of it. Nothing else.

When Herb Bleiweiss of *Ladies' Home Journal* had the job of illustrating a feature on women's nightgowns, he didn't show the women in just typical poses; he caught them in action, including one woman being rescued from a burning building.

For a feature on builds of athletes, *Esquire* showed actual-size photos of biceps of Arnold Schwarzenegger, the neck of Mean Joe Greene, the forearm of Rod Laver, the hand of Robyn C. Smith, and the thigh of Pele.

For an article entitled "What To Do in Case of Armed Robbery," *Go*, Goodyear's dealer magazine, showed a frightening close-up of a gun pointing straight out at the reader.

For a feature on "9 Ways to Beat Winter," *Small World*, the magazine for Volkswagen owners, showed a drawing of a VW, head on, enclosed in giant earmuffs.

For an article on "Marijuana as Medicine," *Psychology Today* showed a young, mustached patient in bed, looking a little spaced out, being fed intravenously. On close inspection the reader could see that the "jar" was a marijuana plant.

To illustrate the title "Aging is Coming of Age: Society Scraps

Pennzoil Perspectives, an 11 × 13 monthly, lets art dominate these two pages, part of a seven-page article on the interest-bearing NOW checking accounts offered by banks. This all-in-line drawing by R. Edwards helps the copy make the point that the NOW accounts lure people as bait lures fish. (Reprinted by permission. © 1981 Pennzoil Company, Houston.)

a Stereotype," Polly Pattison, designer for *Soundings,* published by Pacific Mutual, came up with this photographic idea: a rocking chair crammed into a garbage can. It was part of a one-two visual. It followed a cover that showed a rocking chair in a more traditional lace-curtain setting.

To go with a feature on privacy (and the lack of it), Ted Thai for *Time* posed the chairman of a government privacy commission so that he could be photographed through a keyhole. The portrait, then, when it ran in the magazine was framed with a keyhole-shaped black border.

To illustrate the title, "Libel Law 1980: A Map of Tricky Territory," Ann Green for *Publishers Weekly* drew a "map" of no particular territory or shape, showing crisscrossing roads dotted with "cities" like "New York *Times* v. Sullivan" and "Wolston v. *Reader's Digest,* Inc."

To promote an article recognizing the emergence of a "hardline culture" at the beginning of the 1980s, *Esquire* ran a picture of John Wayne, with wings, waste deep in clouds. The blurb read: "Somewhere the Duke is Smiling."

When *Parade* ran Jane Fonda on its cover it showed her angry, her fists clenched. And rightly so, for the cover blurb read: "Jane Fonda: Why Is She Hollywood's Angry Woman?"

Loring Eutemy's illustration for an article in *Ladies' Home Journal,* " 'My Husband Thinks He's My Father,' " showed a wife in a baby carriage and a husband looking proud and tickling her under her chin.

Sometimes it is a good idea is to concentrate on texture rather than form. If the subject is "Forests," you can make a rubbing or painting from a piece of bark and use it as a piece of line art. If the subject is "Accidents," you might make a rubbing or printing from a piece of bandage cloth.

But the style or technique of illustration doesn't have to have an obvious connection with the subject matter. Art Young, the socialist cartoonist, used an outdated drawing style, not unlike that of a crude woodcut, to fight capitalism and social injustice. Young considered the matter later in one of his autobiographies. "Here I was, a man commonly thought to be 'ahead of the procession' in ideas, who was for progress and change, and with little reverence for tradition, and yet my style was 'archaic,' reminiscent of the ancient past."[10]

Nor does the artist have to use traditional media. Art directors recently have encouraged their illustrators to experiment. The collage has lately become popular: the pasting together of fragments of art, already printed art, or papers and textiles. These can be used to form an abstraction or something that, viewed from a distance, looks quite representational. Some art directors are even using photographs of pieces of sculpture done especially for their magazines. For a cover on "Suburbia: A Myth Challenged," *Time* used a color photo of a needlepoint picture.

What kind of art the you settle for depends upon what you want your art to do. Do you want it to be informative? Then you ask for realism, either in photographs or illustrations. Do you want it to supply mood for the article or story? Then you ask for abstraction, something as simple, say, as a black border to symbolize death.

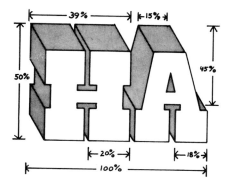

John Simon in one of his theater columns in *New York* makes the point that critics should not feel obligated to report on the length or loudness of the laughter of the audience for any given play. "For that you could install laugh-and-applause meters in the theatres and publish graphs instead of reviews." To illustrate the column, Beth Charney letters a laugh complete with some imaginary measurements.

10. Art Young, *On My Way,* Horace Liveright, New York, 1928, p. 193.

Dan Mindolovich, using a quick, sketchy style, created this cartoon illustration for a column analyzing Garrison Keillor's tongue-in-cheek campaign for "shy rights." What you see is a cartoonist, with portfolio, afraid to enter an editor's office. Mindolovich is a Portland, Oregon, graphic designer and cartoonist.

Do you want it simply to decorate your page? Then you ask for ornament.

The job often requires some kind of art that suggests universality. A single individual on a cover of a recruitment piece, for instance, might turn off readers who don't fit the mold. So you might want to work for some kind of a montage. Then the problem becomes one of quotas. Both male and female must be represented, for instance; and so must members of several races. Perhaps both young and old should be there. These days special efforts must be made in many situations to get members of minority groups up front.

You have to exercise some restraint in depicting money. *Time* has faced problems with the Treasury Department because it has shown realistic portrayals of money for what the department considers "decorative or eye-catching purposes," which are not allowed, instead of for educational or newsworthy purposes, which are allowed. The law is designed to discourage counterfeiting. You should be especially careful of size. If you have a question, get an opinion from the Department before publishing.

Involving your reader

How often have we been disappointed when a radio announcer whose voice we've admired shows up on the TV screen! The person doesn't look at all as we imagined. If it's possible to leave the "illustrating" to the reader, the art director should do it. Charles Schulz will never show us the inside of Snoopy's doghouse. We can be grateful. We already have our own ideas of what it looks like.

The art director can directly involve the reader in the use of illustrations. *Playboy* ran an article on possible winners of a presidential election. On a left-hand page was a painting of the president seated at his desk. A blank white box blocked out his head. At the right were portraits of the various candidates boxed in with dotted lines. It was a sort of do-it-yourself spread; the reader presumably was tempted to cut out one of the faces and paste it in place.

Using cartoons

The cartoon continues to play an important role—sometimes diversionary, sometimes propagandistic—for many publications. Newspapers run *editorial cartoons* on their editorial pages to bring current events into sharp, if distorted, focus. And they give over most of a page daily to a selection of *comic strips* purchased from feature syndicates.

Gag cartoons are largely the province of magazines. Where editorial cartoons and comic strips are done on a salary or contract basis, gag cartoons are done on speculation by freelancers. The cartoon editors on magazines buy them occasionally, paying from $10 to $200 or more for each one, and keep them ready to drop into holes in the back of the book. These cartoons are used primarily as fillers. But *The New Yorker,* the magazine that really developed this art form in America, continues to use gag cartoons as a principal element of editorial display.

A fourth kind of cartoon is the *humorous illustration* used as any illustration might be used for stories, articles, or features deserving of a light touch.

You can tell that *Plain Dealer Magazine* art director Greg Paul has been a cartoonist. Rain coming down from inside an umbrella but from nowhere else has long been a favorite device for cartoonists. Paul directs the use of the gimmick here in an eerie painting by Theo Rudnak. The leaning, half floating pose contributes to the mood.

A number of magazines prefer reprinting editorial or gag cartoons from other publications to originating their own. They may have to pay a fee for this, but the fee is likely to be less than the price of original work. The reasoning: let some other editor be the talent scout. The editor who reprints assumes that the cartoon appeared in a publication not likely to have been seen by present readers.

Time and *Newsweek,* when they reprint editorial cartoons from newspapers, often add color, something easy enough to do. A staff artist makes an overlay for each color desired. The newsmagazines also occasionally break a reprinted editorial cartoon into two parts and run the parts at opposite ends of a page.

Editors, even those running the original cartoons, are all-too-willing to tamper with a cartoonist's caption—to omit it when it may be necessary to the meaning or to change its wording. It is one thing to change a few words of a manuscript without consulting its author; it is another to change a word or two in a four- or five-word caption. A "minor" caption change may represent a 25 or even 50 percent change in the cartoonist's "manuscript." In this writer's editorial-cartoon days, editors went so far as to completely reverse the intent of the caption—from, say, something negative to something positive—without so much as giving him a chance to change the expressions on the faces. One way a cartoonist can fight this kind of editing is to change the caption to a conversation balloon and put it inside the drawing. At least that makes things more difficult for the nitpicking editor.

Editors should understand that there are two kinds of captions for editorial cartoons: those that represent further comment of the cartoonist and those that represent conversation coming from someone within the cartoon—from the one character with his mouth open. Only in the latter case should quotation marks be used.

In gag cartoons—as distinguished from editorial cartoons—the caption (or gag-line) always carries quote marks. Captions without quote marks—descriptive captions—belong above a cartoon. Captions in quotes go below.

Other suggestions editors should consider in their use of cartoons:

1. Avoid cropping a cartoon. If it is well drawn—and why buy it if it is not?—it has been deliberately composed for a square or vertical or horizontal showing. An expanse of "unused" fore-

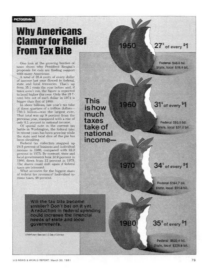

ground in a farm scene, for instance, should not be an open invitation to change a vertical into a horizontal.

2. Do not reduce the cartoon to a size where the reader has to strain to get its message or enjoy its hilarity. The move to miniatures has made a mockery of the comic strips in our newspapers. In magazines it is better to run one or two generous-size gag cartoons than a half a dozen postage-stamp ones.

3. Don't consider the cartoon as simply a change of page-texture, a visual oasis in a landscape of body copy. Treat it as you would any other feature in your publication. Subject it to the same rigid test of usefulness to the reader as you would a piece of copy. Thanks to paper patches and white paint, a cartoon can be corrected by its originator as easily as a piece of copy can be corrected by a writer.

4. Guard against too big a dose of cartoons for a single issue. The magazine that brings a half a dozen gag cartoons together on a single spread or the newspaper that crowds several editorial cartoons onto the editorial page is not giving any of the cartoons much chance to make its point. You can make more of a case for bunching *illustrative* cartoons, because they often are more decorative than anything else. They do not compete with one another in the messages they bring.

The value of charts, graphs, tables, and maps

When the text matter deals with statistics, you can amplify, clarify, or summarize them with charts, graphs, or tables. Purely abstract thoughts and information already simple enough to understand do not lend themselves to charts, graphs, or tables, but almost everything else does. What you need to look for is what Matthew P. Murgio in *Communications Graphics* has described as a "visual handle."

You can use a *flow chart* to show how machinery works, an *organization chart* to show how a company functions, a *line graph* or *bar chart* to show growth in numbers over a given period of time, or a *pie chart* to show percentages of a whole.

Ordinary charts and graphs are clear enough, but an artist can heighten their impact by changing them to what *U.S. News & World Report* calls Pictographs: drawings in which lines, bars, or circles have been converted to representational art shown in perspective. For instance, people can be shown in place of bars or a silver dollar in place of a pie chart. But when using Pictographs you must make certain the scale is not distorted.[11]

You can make a *table* more useful by careful organization of material and skillful use of color, tint blocks, and rules. You can add drama to a *map* by showing it in perspective, by showing its topography as well as its outline, or by simplifying and stylizing its outline. It may even be desirable to distort a map to make a point (provided the reader understands), as an airline did in its advertising to dramatize the fact that its fast planes had brought Europe and America close together.

Hendrik Hertzberg built an entire book around a single graph—page after page of dots, one million of them. "This book is a yard-

---

11. See Darrell Huff's *How to Lie with Statistics,* W. W. Norton & Company, Inc., New York, 1954.

It may look a bit complicated at first glance, but this two-page Pictogram—a vertical bar chart—shows clearly, year by year, how much of a federal deficit there was under each President, from Hoover to Reagan. That Reagan was just beginning his term gave him a question mark, partly above, partly below the base line. In the original, the deficit spending bars are in red. (Reprinted from *U.S. News & World Report,* Jan. 19, 1981 issue. Copyright 1981, U.S. News & World Report, Inc.)

stick, a ruler divided into a million parts instead of a dozen," he said in his introduction. "The chief value of the book is as an aid to comprehension, and to contemplation. By riffling slowly through its pages, the reader may discover precisely what is meant by one million." At various intervals the reader finds a blank spot where a dot is supposed to be; a line runs from that blank spot out into the margin, and there the dot is reproduced with a caption. Dot No. 2, for instance, represents the "Population of the Garden of Eden," Dot No. 46,399 the "Number of times the word 'and' ap-

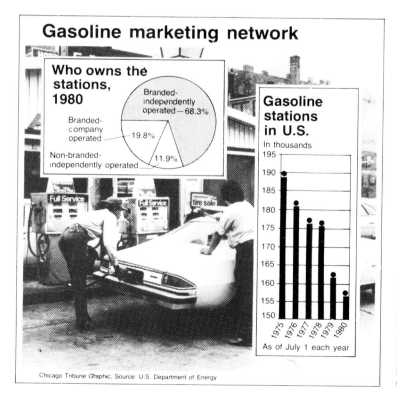

The Tribune Company Syndicate circulates charts and graphs and other Chicago *Tribune*-prepared graphics to newspapers subscribing to this special service. The example here combines a pie chart with a bar graph to show (1) ownership of gasoline stations in the United States and (2) the decline of stations since 1975.

This Chicago *Tribune*-prepared line graph shows (1) production of U.S.-built cars, (2) production of Japanese-built cars, and (3) number of Japanese-built cars sold in the United States. That the two solid lines are converging shows immediately the problem the U.S. auto industry was facing in 1981, when the chart was drawn.

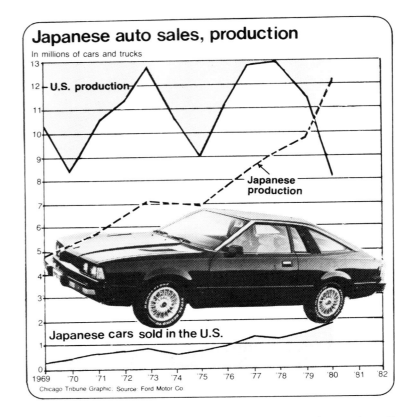

Japanese auto sales, production

In millions of cars and trucks

U.S. production

Japanese production

Japanese cars sold in the U.S.

1969 '70 '71 '72 '73 '74 '75 '76 '77 '78 '79 '80 '81 '82

Chicago Tribune Graphic. Source: Ford Motor Co

pears in the King James Bible," Dot No. 407,316 the number of "U.S. soldiers killed in World War II."[12]

To illustrate "What a Way to Make a Living," an article about the injuries suffered by the running backs in professional football, *Sports Illustrated* ran a drawing of a player, standing, facing to the front. The various injuries to the players were listed at the side. Ruled lines connected the various listings to various parts of the body, allowing readers to see at a glance where the concentration of injuries was. The diagram in a minimum amount of space summarized information that, in ordinary prose, would have taken a lot more space and told the story a lot less vividly.

It is possible to make a chart out of an ordinary photograph. Suppose you want to illustrate an article on high school dropouts. You can take an ordinary shot of students walking in a school hallway, and white-out a scattered portion of them in proportion to real drop-out numbers.

Style in art

Art style preferences change—for magazine art as well as gallery art. At the turn of the century the look was Art Nouveau: sinuous, decorative, curvy. Art Nouveau took its patterns and motifs mostly from nature, but it was also influenced by Japanese art, by the drawings of William Blake, by Persian pottery, and by other sources. Flowers and flowing hair were often a part of the look. Hippie art of the 1960s can be traced to Art Nouveau.

An example of Art Nouveau. From *The Studio.*

12. See Hendrik Hertzberg, *One Million,* Simon & Schuster, Inc., New York, 1970.

Art Deco was a style popular from about 1910 to 1940, with revivals of interest since. It affected architects as well as graphic and industrial designers. You can see it in the Chrysler Building and Radio City Music Hall in New York. It made wide use of geometric forms. Some people refer to it as "modernistic" or "skyscraper modern." It was a stern reaction to what some considered the excesses of Art Nouveau.

In the 1920s the Bauhaus made its influence felt; the look was orderly, geometric, functional. The Bauhaus look never did die out. It took a slightly more elegant turn in the 1950s with the introduction of Swiss design: the magazine page was still tightly organized, but some of the stiffness was gone.

Art Nouveau made a comeback in the 1960s, as did almost every art style. The 1960s were a decade of revival and experimentation. Among the new styles: Op Art, with its illusions in color and shape; Pop Art, with its attachment to the comic strip and high-Camp packaging; and the psychedelic look, with its sliding blobs of color in weird combinations, its illegible typefaces expanded, condensed, and contorted to fit curved spaces. More recently "new wave" and "punk" styles have made themselves felt, especially in the fashion magazines. With so much freedom in art and design these days it is hard to separate one style from another. We have lived through a lot of crossover.

Art techniques

Preferences in technique change, too. Brush painting, pallet knife painting, wash drawing, line drawing, scratchboard drawing, pencil drawing, felt- and nylon-tip drawing: they all have a place. Some

A line drawing is not just a line drawing. You see here three different kinds of line drawings done by one artist, Don Thompson, for one issue of *Aramco World Magazine.* Each illustrated its own article. The top illustration, one of several done in that style for an article, has a sketchy look. The lines seem to be scrubbed onto the paper quickly. (You see the illustration greatly reduced.) The tightly drawn second example has flat, decorative look. The third, with its calligraphic look, qualified as a stylized drawing. It is the most abstract of the three.

techniques require tight handling, some a loose flair. Every imaginable tool is used on every kind of surface. In the 1960s, for instance, many illustrators were working in washes on glossy paper not meant to take washes. This resulted in tones that seemed to shrivel, like water on an oily surface.

Print expressed concern that illustrators are preoccupied with techniques—at the expense of content. Maybe so. But illustrators need to constantly experiment with their styles and techniques, and art directors should encourage them to do so.

Design of the art

Art directors cannot agree what style is best for magazines or what techniques best do the job. They cannot agree on whether art should be realistic or abstract. But they can agree on this: *The illustration should be well designed.* The principles of design which govern the arrangement of type and illustration on a page or spread also govern the placement of figures, props, and background within an illustration. Every illustration, from the crudest cartoon to the finest painting, should be well designed.

To most art directors, design in illustration is more important than draftsmanship.

Planning the art's reproduction

In working with line art, you should see to it that for a single feature it all takes the same reduction. This is desirable not only to save costs but also to keep consistent the strength of the artist's line. It is not a good idea to use both fine-line art and thick-line art in the same feature. This means that you must decide where you want big art and where you want small art before giving out your assignments.

Line art—and halftone art, too—generally turns out best when reduced to about two-thirds of original size. The slight imperfections or irregularities are thus minimized. For a change of pace, however, you ought to try *blowing up* in size your line artwork. This adds greatly to its strength and sometimes gives the art a refreshingly crude, bold look it doesn't have in its original state.

One of the advantages of line art over halftone art is that line art, at least when it is run actual size, always comes out as the art director expects. With a halftone, you can never be quite sure.

Art directors soon learn that a photograph that has the necessary qualities to hang in an art gallery is not always the photograph that reproduces well. Some art directors feel that a photograph a little on the gray side reproduces better than one a little on the black side. Sometimes the photoengraver or offset cameraman can bring out a gray photograph by overexposing it; there is not much they can do with an already overexposed print.

You must choose your photographs not so much on the basis of how well they look in hand as on the basis of how well they will reproduce. Only long experience with photographs can really teach you this.

In the days of letterpress newspapers, printers used coarse screen halftones—made with 65-line screens—in order to get impressions on newsprint stock. Offset lithography allows the use of much finer screens, even when rough paper is used; and this means better fidelity in the reproduction. No longer can you get away with crude

Walt Whirl, magazine and advertising illustrator, uses an ordinary pencil to make this sensitive line drawing. He combines a fine outline with areas of texture, letting the edges of the texture areas define some of the outline of the figure. He distorts the perspective in order to create tension in the drawing.

retouching on a photograph. Nor is it necessary. With the use of 35 mm. cameras, editors and art directors now have plenty of prints to choose from.

Polaroid has made it possible for photographers working for off-set publications to produce their own prescreened halftones, ready for pasteup as line art. It makes available a camera that houses its own screen in any coarseness, from 45 to 133 lines. The Polaroid camera is not an ideal camera for newspaper or magazine work—it is bulkier than a 35 mm, does not have the accessories, and the pictures it produces are sometimes flatter than those made with other cameras—but for small weekly newspapers, especially, the prescreen feature may more than compensate for these disadvantages.

While the usual halftone for both letterpress and offset appears in a dot pattern, newer developments in both photo preparation

One way an artist can get tone into a line drawing is by doing the art in ink on textured paper and then using a grease crayon for shading. This is Horace Greeley, drawn by the author on Garco No. 12 paper.

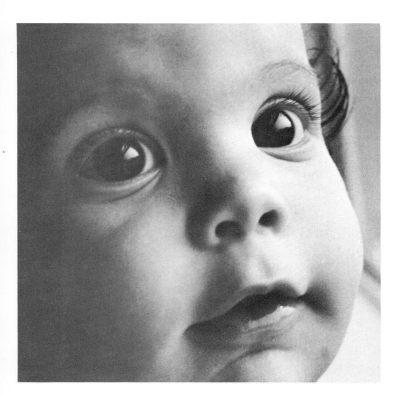

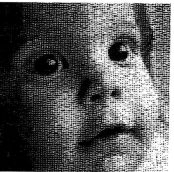

The original photograph printed as a normal-screen halftone and, in a smaller size, four line art conversions: random dot (top left), spiral (top right), mesh (bottom left), and wavy line (bottom right). (Courtesy of Line Art Unlimited, Princeton, New Jersey.)

and photo reproduction make possible halftones in various line patterns and textures. *Newsweek,* when it did a cover story entitled, "Does TV Tell It Straight?" ran photographs of four TV newsmen—all in ruled-line halftones. Because the photos were cut to a shape resembling a TV screen, the pattern related the halftones even more meaningfully to the subject.

Turning to the print to be reproduced, you should remember that the closer it is to the original, the better. If you must turn in a copy, turn in a first copy. A copy of a copy is never as good as a copy, and a copy is never as good as the original. Have photographs made from original negatives; don't make copy prints from photographs unless you don't have access to original negatives.

Once in a while you may have to use an already printed halftone, clipped from a newspaper, magazine, or book. You can treat

To execute this small-town winter scene, Prof. Glenn Hanson of the University of Illinois Department of Journalism uses nylon-tip pens and, finally, some Zipatone at the top for the sky. Hanson's composition leads you right into the center of the picture. He makes use of a low horizon line to give you almost a worm's-eye-view. He provides three distinct textures: the Zipatone dot-pattern, the tree-top lace-pattern, and the horizontal-line pattern for the shading on the buildings and the shadows in the snow.

such art as line art, because the screening has already been done. Sometimes you can improve a coarse-screen, already printed halftone by reducing it, thereby making the screen finer. If the screen is already fine or the print indecisive, the printer may have to rescreen the halftone print.

In rescreening, the platemaker must avoid a moire pattern—a sort of swirl—in the final print. Sometimes you get a moire pattern even when working with an original photograph, as when a figure in that photograph wears a suit or dress with a pronounced pattern. The platemaker may be able to eliminate the moire in a second shooting by adjusting the angle of the screen.

Art directors have a number of ways to turn an ordinary photograph into something that looks like the work of an illustrator or painter. The most common practice—it has almost become a cliché—is to make a line reproduction from the photograph, rather than a halftone reproduction. The platemaker simply handles the photograph as if it were a line drawing, avoiding the use of a screen. What happens is: all the middle tones of gray drop out. You get a high-contrast print—stark, dramatic, bold. And sections of it, if desired, can easily be painted out or retouched. A variation is to take the bold line art and screen it to, say, 60 percent of black, or combine it with a block of solid second color.

You can get an unusual effect, too, by ordering this halftone in a jumbo size screen, so that the dots are much larger than normal. From a distance, the art looks like a photograph. Up close, it looks like a piece of Pop Art.

Art teacher Marilyn McKenzie Chaffee shows how to make a realistic portrait by pasting down pieces of black paper where she wants deep shadows and pieces of printed body copy where she wants lighter shadows. The technique is particularly appropriate for this portrait: it is of Graham Greene, the writer.

Is art necessary?

Not every article and story needs art in the traditional sense. Carefully selected display typography, tastefully arranged with generous amounts of white space, can be art enough.

Some subjects simply do not lend themselves to art. A subject can be too momentous, too tragic, too lofty to picture. In this case art would be at best redundant, at worse anticlimatic.

And when as art director you can't afford art or you find only mediocre-quality photography for a feature, you should be willing to design your pages without art. A quiet, even stilted spread is preferable to an amateurish one.

Suggested further reading

Beakley, George C., *Freehand Drawing and Visualization*, Bobbs-Merrill, Indianapolis, 1982.

Benson, Harry and Gigi Benson, *Harry Benson on Photojournalism*, Harmony Books (Crown Publishers), New York, 1982.

Borgman, Harry, *Art & Illustration Techniques*, Watson-Guptill Publications, New York, 1979.

Cardamone, Tom, *Chart and Graph Preparation Skills*, Van Nostrand Reinhold, New York, 1981.

Chernoff, George and Sarbin Hershel, *Photography and the Law*, Chilton Book Company, Philadelphia, 1971. (Fourth Edition.)

Cherry, David, *Preparing Artwork for Reproduction*, Crown Publishers, Inc., New York, 1976. (From the standpoint of a British artist.)

Craven, George M., *Object and Image: An Introduction to Photography*, Prentice-Hall, Inc., Englewood Cliffs, N.J., 1975.

Crawford, Tad, *Legal Guide for the Visual Artist*, Hawthorn Books, New York, 1977.

Croy, O. R., *Croy's Camera Trickery,* Hastings House, Publishers, New York, 1977.

Curl, David H., *Photocommunication,* Macmillan Publishing Co., Inc., New York, 1978.

Curtis, Seng-Gye Tombs and Christopher Hunt, *The Airbrush Book,* Van Nostrand Reinhold, New York, 1980.

Dalley, Terence, *The Complete Guide to Illustration and Design: Techniques and Materials,* Chartwell Books, Inc., 110 Enterprise Ave., Secaucus, N.J. 07094, 1980.

Davis, Phil, *Photography,* Wm. C. Brown Company Publishers, Dubuque, 1981. (Fourth Edition.)

Douglis, Phil, *Communicating with Pictures,* Lawrence Ragan Communications, Inc., Chicago, 1979.

Editors of Eastman Kodak Company, *The Joy of Photography,* Addison-Wesley, Reading, Mass., 1980.

————, *More Joy of Photography,* Addison-Wesley, Reading, Mass., 1981.

Edom, Clifton C., *Photojournalism,* Wm. C. Brown Company Publishers, Dubuque, Iowa, 1980. (Second Edition.)

Evans, Harold, *Pictures on a Page: Photojournalism and Picture Editing,* Wadsworth Publishing Company, Belmont, Calif., 1979.

Feininger, Andreas, *The Color Photo Book,* Prentice-Hall, Inc., Englewood Cliffs, N.J., 1970.

Evans, Hilary, *The Art of Picture Research,* David & Charles, London, 1980.

Fincher, Terry, *Creative Techniques in Photojournalism,* Lippincott & Crowell, Publishers, New York, 1980.

Geraci, Philip C., *Photojournalism: Making Pictures for Publication,* Kendall/Hunt Publishing Company, Dubuque, Iowa, 1978. (Second Edition.)

Graham, Donald W., *Composing Pictures,* Van Nostrand Reinhold Company, New York, 1970.

Gray, Bill, *More Studio Tips for Artists and Graphic Designers,* Van Nostrand Reinhold, New York, 1978.

Herdeg, Walter, *Graphis/Diagrams: The Graphic Visualization of Abstract Data,* Hastings House, Publishers, New York, 1982. (New Edition.)

Hurley, Gerald D., and Angus McDougall, *Visual Impact in Print: How to Make Pictures Communicate: A Guide for the Photographer, the Editor, the Designer,* American Publishers Press, Chicago, 1971.

Hutter, Heribert, *Styles in Art,* Universe Books, New York, 1977.

Jacobs, Lou, Jr., *Free Lance Magazine Photography,* Hastings House, Publishers, New York, 1970. (Revised Edition.)

Kemp, Weston D., *Photography for Visual Communicators,* Prentice-Hall, Englewood Cliffs, N.J., 1973.

Kerns, Robert L., *Photojournalism: Photography with a Purpose,* Prentice-Hall, Englewood Cliffs, N.J., 1980.

Kobre, Kenneth, *Photojournalism: The Professionals' Approach,* Van Nostrand Rinehold, New York, 1980.

McDarrah, Fred W., ed., *Stock Photo and Assignment Source Book,* R. R. Bowker Company, New York, 1977. (Guide to photos available from 6,000 sources.)

McMullan, James, *Revealing Illustrations,* Watson-Guptill Publications, New York, 1981.

Meyer, Hans, *150 Techniques in Art,* Reinhold Publishing Corporation, New York, 1963.

Mills, John Fitz-Maurice, *Studio and Art-Room Techniques,* Pitman Publishing Corp., New York, 1965.

Murgio, Matthew P., *Communications Graphics,* Van Nostrand Reinhold Company, New York, 1969. (Charts and graphs and other visual presentations.)

Nelson, Roy Paul, *Cartooning,* Henry Regnery Company Publishers, Chicago, 1975.

————, *Comic Art and Caricature,* Contemporary Books, Inc., Chicago, 1978.

Philippe, Robert, *Political Graphics: Art as a Weapon,* Abbeville Press, New York, 1982.

Pollack, Peter, *The Picture History of Photography,* Harry N. Abrams, Inc., New York, 1970. (Revised Edition.)

Porter, Tom, and Bob Greenstreet, *Manual of Graphic Techniques for Architects, Graphic Designers, and Artists,* Charles Scribner's Sons, New York, 1980.

Rhode, Robert B., and Floyd H. McCall, *Introduction to Photography,* Macmillan Company, New York, 1976. (Third Edition.)

Rodewald, Fred C. and Edward Gottschall, *Commercial Art as a Business,* Viking Press, Inc., New York, 1970. (Second Revised Edition.)

Rosen, Marvin J., *Introduction to Photography,* Houghton Mifflin, Boston, 1982. (Second Edition.)

Rothstein, Arthur. *Photojournalism,* Amphoto, Garden City, New York, 1974.

————, *Photojournalism,* Amphoto, Garden City, N.Y., 1979. (Fourth Edition.)

Schuneman, R. Smith, ed., *Photographic Communication: Principles, Problems, and Challenges of Photojournalism,* Hastings House, Publishers, Inc., New York, 1972.

Sheppard, Julian, *Photo Design Methods,* Hastings House, Publishers, New York, 1970.

Snyder, John, *Commercial Artists Handbook,* Watson-Guptill Publications, New York, 1973.

Snyder, Norman, ed., *The Photography Catalog: A Sourcebook of the Best Equipment, Materials, and Photographic Resources,* Harper & Row, Publishers, New York, 1976.

Sontag, Susan, *On Photography,* Farrar Straus and Giroux, Inc., 1976.

Swedlund, Charles, *Photography: A Handbook of History, Materials and Processes,* Holt, Rinehart and Winston, New York, 1981.

Thompson, Philip and Peter Davenport, *The Dictionary of Graphic Images,* St. Martin's Press, New York, 1980.

van Uchelen, Rod, *Say It with Pictures,* Van Nostrand Reinhold Company, New York, 1979.

Vestal, David, *The Craft of Photography,* Harper & Row, Publishers, New York, 1975.

Wakerman, Elyce, *Air Powered: The Art of the Airbrush,* Random House, New York, 1980.

Art Books, 1950–1979, R. R. Bowker, New York, 1979. (Listing of 37,000 books on fine and applied arts, including design.)

For this inside spread in a 16-page, two-color, 8 1/2 × 11 recruitment booklet, designer Jim Bodoh reuses a large photo he had used in an earlier spread. But this time he chops it into squares, and in some of the squares he inserts new, smaller pictures. The reader recognizes the original photo, though; it contains the three large faces and arms and shoulders that connect them. The College of Education, University of Oregon, is the publisher.

Art **129**

David Brier, art/design director of *Not Just Jazz*, uses horizontal bars and his own abstract, silhouette illustration to top the first page of an "Innerview" with the owner of a musical instrument company. The title wraps around the piano to make one unit of the bars, title, and art. Randy Fordyce is publisher of the eight-times-a-year tabloid.

What *Publication Design* has observed and advised so far applies generally to all the print media. Now in this chapter and in two chapters to follow the book concentrates on magazines. Later chapters will deal specifically with newspapers, miscellaneous publications, and books.

"A magazine is a collaborative effort involving various people, philosophies, talents, and imaginations," observes Ruth Ansel, art director of *The New York Times Magazine*. "One never really works alone [on a major magazine], the way a painter in a studio does. You have to be open to respond to the changing accidents of the moment, and to trust your instincts. . . . One's work is never like it's imagined in one's head. It's either better or worse. The creative process consists of a constant balance between assimilation and selectivity. An idea comes from absorbing the events around you."[1]

The magazine's formula

Every magazine has its unique mixture of articles and stories. We call this its *formula*. Most editors do not put their formulas down in words, but they and their staff members have a general understanding of what kind of material the magazine should run.

Anthony A. Lyle, editor of the *Pennsylvania Gazette*, an alumni magazine, after an informal study of that branch of publishing, found some interesting goals expressed by editors. One said, "We strive for a delicate balance of predictability and surprise. . . ." Another said, "As the only University publication which consistently reaches alumni, it is also used to help maintain the integrity of alumni address files."[2]

A prime consideration is: what is the purpose of the magazine? Does the magazine, like *Ladies' Home Journal* or *Iron Age*, exist to make money? Does it, like *The New Republic* or *National Review*, exist to spread ideas? Does it, like *Ford Times* or *Friends*, exist to do a public relations job? Does it, like *The Rotarian* or *Junior League Magazine*, exist to serve members of an organization?

Keeping the purpose in mind, the editor of any magazine works out a formula that best serves an intended audience or, in some rare cases, a formula that perpetuates an editor's strong convictions.

1. Quoted by Alexis Gelber, "Ruth Ansel, 1978," *Art Direction*, September 1978, p. 78.
2. Anthony A. Lyle, "It Was Written," *Pennsylvania Gazette*, June 1978, p. 2.

The bigger the magazine is to be and the more that is invested in it, the more likely the editor is to rely on opinion research of the intended audience when implementing the formula. The object is to win as many readers as possible within the area the magazine has staked out for itself.

Since the advent of television, magazines by and large have given up the idea of serving large, general audiences and moved into areas of specialization. It is hard to think of any interest area that is not served by a magazine or a set of magazines. David Z. Orlow, in a satire in *Folio* on the trend to put together magazines to appeal to ever more specialized audiences, suggests *Death*, "the magazine of the inevitable." As a character in Orlow's story explains it, it would be a picture magazine "featuring the most dramatic aspects of the subject—obscure diseases, dramatic accidents, berserk assassins, disasters, wars, and things like that." The magazine would be "absolutely lurid with respect to photography while at the same time absolutely nonemotional with respect to copy." It would be a magazine to appeal to a generation brought up on media violence.

"True enough, the reader time per copy may be only three minutes due to reaction to some of the better pictures, but word-of-mouth will make it the best pass-along book since the advent of beauty parlor magazines."[3]

The *National Lampoon* offered a couple of other possibilities for specialized magazines: *Guns and Sandwiches* and *Negligent Mother*.

Even magazines that operate in the same area have subtle differences that distinguish their formulas from one another. *Harper's* is more politically oriented than *The Atlantic; The Atlantic* is stronger in literature. *Time* and *Newsweek* are more liberal, less business-oriented than *U.S. News & World Report*.

When rock music lost some of its fascination, *Rolling Stone*, its bible, changed editorial direction somewhat, concentrating more on articles dealing with politics, culture, and lifestyles. It also sought to erase its earlier anti-establishment image. "We have never been an underground publication," editor Jann S. Wenner is quoted as having said. "We have always said we wanted to make money."

The New Yorker worked out a formula that puts it into a unique category: humor mixed with social consciousness; great reporting done in a casual and sometimes rambling style; stories that have no endings; and, of course, the best gag cartoons anywhere. *New York*, a newer magazine some people may confuse with *The New Yorker*, really has quite a different formula: a merging of the so-called "new journalism" with helpful advice on how to survive in Manhattan.

Reader's Digest is another magazine with a unique formula: dogmatism, conservatism, optimism—and, some would say, simlistic solutions to complicated problems. It is among the most consistent of magazines. Its formula has not changed basically since it was started in the early 1920s, nor, with one of the largest circulations of any magazine, is it likely to.

The Number 2 magazine in any field is the one most likely to change its formula. When *Playboy* outstripped *Esquire* in the mid- to late-fifties, *Esquire* dropped the nudes and turned to more serious matters. When the women's magazines were locked in a death

The front page of a newsmagazine tabloid published by West High School, Iowa City, Iowa. That's the logo at the upper right, with the dateline and other information at the upper left. The article's title is below, hooked up with the art. The uncluttered look continues inside.

3. David Z. Orlow, "The Magazine of the Inevitable," *Folio*, January 1977, pp. 22, 23.

Ordinarily content would dictate design, but sometimes you have to do designing first. Here is one of several spreads designed by the author to help the editor of a new Crown Zellerbach magazine decide on a format before material for his first issue was completed. This article was to be about a fish hatchery, but the title and blurb were not yet written, and photographs were not yet available. At least placement, margins, and sizes could be indicated. And a few strokes from a felt marker, if nothing else, could show where photos (one square, one widely horizontal) would go. Because the letters in "HATCHERY" were to be so large, the designer lined up the tail of the Y—not the Y itself—with the right-hand margin of the far-right column.

struggle in the mid-1950s, *McCall's*, second to *Ladies' Home Journal,* tried to spread out to include the entire family, calling itself a magazine of "Togetherness." The formula didn't work, and today *McCall's* and *Ladies' Home Journal* are very close again in formula.

The formula remains pretty much the same from issue to issue. If a magazine feels it is losing its audience or if it wants to reach out for a new audience, it changes its formula. Sometimes the change is gradual. Sometimes—especially if the magazine is desperate—the change is sudden.

The magazine's format

When a magazine changes its formula it also usually changes its *format.* The format is the *looks* of the publication: its size, its shape, its arrangement of copy and pictures on the page. Format includes design. Sometimes a magazine changes its format, or at least its design, without changing its formula.

Some magazines are best suited to visual excitement and novelty. Others are best suited to visual order.

Which means that magazine design boils down to two main schools, both with respected followings. The visually exciting mag-

A two-page spread, part of a magazine tabloid designed by student Chris Barnes for a daily newspaper. The left page carries the conclusion of an article on field burning; the right page begins a regular feature called "Outings." As Barnes conceived the design, the regular heading each week would be large; the pertinent headline ("Inner Tubing Down the Santiam") would be smaller. She used three-column format throughout. She chose to cluster her right page photographs (which she indicated with gray felt markers) rather than scatter them. The single caption covering the three photographs when finally written no doubt would take more space than is shown here.

azines are represented, among others, by *McCall's,* a pioneer in that kind of design, and the fashion magazines. The highly ordered magazines are represented by *Sports Illustrated* and *Scientific American.* This does not mean that a magazine needs to belong exclusively to one school or the other. *Sports Illustrated,* for instance, within its ordered format, has much excitement in art and photography. It does mean that a magazine should be mostly one, or mostly the other.

The first thing an editor and art director must decide, then, is What kind of a look are we after? The purpose of the magazine should have something to do with the kind of look they settle for.

A magazine published to make a profit must lure and hold the reader with visually exciting pages. Illustrations are a must. These days such a magazine almost has to use color. "But all the visual excitement in the world cannot mean very much unless a magazine is relevant. It must serve a purpose, be useful and valid, and reflect the constant shifts and changes of its readers," says Ruth Ansel.[4]

A magazine published to disseminate ideas can exist with a more austere format as, for example, one finds in *Foreign Affairs.* Its readers already believe; they don't have to be pampered. Such magazines generally will settle for a coarse, sometimes cheap paper stock and pages unrelieved by illustrations.

A magazine published to do a public relations job needs a glossy appearance, if it is to go to outsiders; if it is an internal publication, it can be more homey.

A magazine published to serve members of an organization must

Management Update, a monthly 11 × 16 magapaper published by the Dun & Bradstreet Corporation, uses two-deck flush-right headlines at the sides of stories, as this double spread shows. The publication combines rectangular photographs with silhouetted photographs to bring variety to its pages. On the right-hand page, the photographs partially overlap.

4. Quoted by Alexis Gelber, *op. cit.,* p. 81.

The Visiting Fireman, published biweekly by Fireman's Fund Insurance Companies, San Francisco, uses the one-extra-fold tabloid format. You see here the 7 1/2 × 11 front page along with the 11 × 15 second front page. The first one acts more like a magazine cover, the second more like a newspaper front page. As you unfold to the second front page, of course, you turn the publication ninety degrees. The original comes in black plus a second color. Note the thin lines that separate each line of the headlines. Ken Borger, a freelancer, is the designer.

watch closely what it spends. If the members of the organization pay fees to belong, and the members are cost-conscious, they are not likely to appreciate getting an overly pretentious publication.

But purpose is only one factor in deciding format. Policy is another. Two magazines have as their policy the spreading of ideas: the one is leftist and activist; the other is moderately Republican. Will the same format serve both? Possibly. But if the tone of the articles is different, it seems reasonable to expect a difference, too, in the setting in which these articles are presented. Are there angry, vitriolic typefaces available for headlines? There are. And what about artwork: are some drawing styles more militant than others? See the work that appeared in the 1930s in *New Masses.*[5]

While opinion research may dictate in part a magazine's formula, it has little to do with deciding a magazine's format. Format is still largely a matter of personal preference, taste, and intuition; and that's what makes format so challenging a topic.

Basic formats

Publications appear in a variety of formats, the most common of which are these:

1. *Magazines,* consisting of a series of bound pages that have been printed in multiples of four, eight, sixteen, or thirty-two (these are called "signatures"), then folded down to size and trimmed.

2. *Newspapers,* consisting of a series of oversize sheets folded down the middle to make four pages. Each set of four-pages loosely houses another, which loosely houses still another, etc. An occasional loose sheet is included. A newspaper that is bulky enough divides its sets of pages into sections. The pages are so large that,

5. A source is Joseph North, ed., *New Masses: An Anthology of the Rebel Thirties,* International Publishers, New York, 1969.

for delivery, the entire newspaper has to be folded once and then opened up when the reader gets to it.

3. *Tabloids,* consisting of a series of unbound oversize pages that are about half the size of regular newspaper pages.

The tabloid *Rolling Stone* used to give itself one extra fold to appear as an 8 1/2 × 11 magazine on the newsstand, but by 1973 the publication had become too thick to take the folding. From then on it appeared as a regular tabloid. But the idea caught the fancy of other editors, especially editors of company and alumni tabloids, and the Rolling Stone fold has become almost a generic term.

4. *Magapapers,* combining qualities of both newspapers and magazines and looking a bit like tabloids, but printed usually on quality stock. Often they consist of only four pages. This format has become a favorite with editors of company publications for employees.

5. *Newsletters,* consisting often, but not always, of 8 1/2 × 11 sheets printed inexpensively and stapled at the top or side. Related to this format are all the formats that have been developed over the years by direct-mail advertisers.

Anything goes

Conditions beyond the control of the designer may dictate the choice of format. When a strike in 1964 made a regular magazine impossible for Vail-Ballou Press, Inc., Binghamton, New York, a printing and manufacturing firm for the book trade, it brought out its house organ in galley proof form as an emergency measure. The "publication" was 5 × 21, single column. The format seemed particularly appropriate for this particular company. The circulation, after all, was only 600.

Editor L. Jeanette Clarke said at the time: "No company should feel that if it can't have a breath-taking, expensive magazine, newsletter or tabloid it should have none at all. To a large extent employees are captive readers." She said that because her readers are curious, they don't have to be lured by fancy trimmings.

Another strange format was introduced by *Datebook,* a teeny-boppers' magazine, now defunct. To create the effect of two magazines in one, *Datebook* carried a front cover at both ends. The teen-age reader worked her way through half the magazine, came to an upside-down page, closed the magazine and turned to the other cover, and worked her way through that half.

Foreign Policy uses a tall, slim format: 4 1/2″ wide by 10 1/8″ deep. That means, of course, one column per page. Why that size? "We wanted a distinctive magazine that was easy to read and put in a pocket," answers editor Bill Manyes.[6]

Format innovation was one of the selling points of *Flair* when it was being published in the early 1950s. The editors constantly titillated readers with die-cut covers, inserts of sizes different from the page size, sections inside the book printed on unusual paper stocks, and so on. These practices live on in other magazines, but the editor who resorts to them is advised to check first with the post office, where regulations change frequently on what is allowed under second-class and bulk-rate mailing permits.

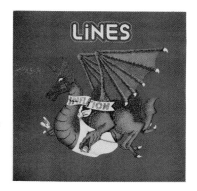

The square—or near-square—format is popular with many editors. Here's a beautifully simple brown and yellow cover for the square-format magazine *Lines,* published by Reliance Insurance Companies. An explanatory note inside the front cover explains: "The inflationary 'dragon' is still lurking nearby—preying upon the homes and businesses of underinsured policy-holders. The story on page 2 explains what Reliance is doing to help its agents 'slay the dragon.' "

6. Quoted by John Peter, "The Leading Edge," *Folio,* September 1980, p. 146.

Page sizes

Phil Douglis, photographer and columnist, thinks the magazine format's chief advantage over the newspaper, newsletter, and magapaper format is "the ability to relate pictures to each other as a sequence over a series of pages, alternately withholding them from our view and then revealing them, carrying the reader through a visual process not unlike the frame-by-frame and scene-by-scene method of cinema."[7]

Magazines come in three basic sizes:

1. *Life*-size, roughly 10 1/2 × 13. *Life* popularized the size with its founding in 1936, and many other magazines went to that size before paper prices and postage rates forced their scaling down. *Ebony* used the size until early 1982, when it dropped down to *Time*-size. (At that time it also went from letterpress to offset lithography.)

2. *Time*-size, roughly 8 1/2 × 11. By far the most popular size for magazines.

3. *Reader's Digest*-size, roughly 5 1/2 × 7 1/2. Other magazines using *Reader's Digest* size are *TV Guide* and *Forum,* which calls itself "The International Journal of Human Relations." *Science Digest,* a digest-size magazine from 1936, went up to an 8 1/2 × 11 size in late 1980 in an attempt to change its image. It also went from newsprint-like paper to slick paper. "The introduction and success of *Omni* had proven that people will buy a full-size, slick science magazine at the newsstand each month," John Peter, a design consultant, observed.[8]

These three sizes aren't the only ones. A company magazine might come in a 6 × 9, 7 1/2 × 9 1/2, 7 × 10, 8 1/2 × 13, or a 9 × 12 size. The size would depend upon the equipment the printer uses and the availability of paper stock.

Ries Cappiello Colwell, an advertising agency, conducted a study of magazines in 1978 and found nine different sizes. Not one magazine actually used an 8 1/2 × 11 size: "8 1/2 × 11" magazines turned out to be 8 1/8 × 10 7/8, 8 1/4 × 11 3/4, 8 3/16 × 10 7/8, or some other size close to any of these.

Magazine pages are almost always vertical. A magazine not dependent upon advertising should consider the novelty and even the design advantages of an 11 × 8 1/2 page. Opened out, the magazine would be unusually horizontal.

A few magazines in recent years, along with some books—particularly art books—have gone for a square format. *Avant Garde,* an 11 × 11 publication, was one. But a square format can mean paper waste. If a magazine is big enough, it can special order paper to size. If not, it can do what *Avant Garde* did: use the paper waste—the odd-cut sheets—for direct-mail advertising campaigns.

One of the most handsome of the square-format or near square-format publications is *The New York Times Book Review* with its horizontal rules and generous use of art. *Harper's Bazaar* also comes close to being a square format magazine, but it is something of a hodgepodge, hardly the trend setter it once was.

7. Phil Douglis, "How Magazine Pages Help Sequence Pictures," *IABC News,* October 1976, p. 3.

8. Quoted in "Publishing Goal Should Precede Repositioning Effort," *Folio,* April 1981, p. 15.

Some editors like the square-format look because they think it says "now." You can achieve the square look in an 8 1/2 × 11 magazine by adopting a consistent deep sink on the pages. That means making the "live area" of the pages—the part that does not include the margins—start low on the page. Instead of a one-inch sink, for instance, your magazine could carry a two- or three-inch sink. That does not keep you from printing anything above the sink. An occasional title may fit in that space. Or a piece of art may jut into it. Even a caption might appear there. But body copy would always be confined to the square or near-square grid that you have adopted.

Whatever size page a magazine adopts, if it contains advertising, it should provide column widths and lengths that are compatible with other magazines in the field. An advertising agency doesn't like to custom design each ad for every magazine scheduled to run it.

Lithopinion, the defunct graphic arts and public affairs quarterly of Local One, Amalgamated Lithographers of America, used to change its format from issue to issue to "illuminate the versatility of lithography by example." On the other hand, about the *only thing* that remained the same for *Kaiser News* was the page size: 8 1/2 × 11. It constantly changed design, frequency of publication, and printers. "What we are striving for is continuity through change," said Editor Don Fabun.[9]

The page size, of course, seriously affects the design. Most art directors feel that a *Life*-size book is easier to design than a *Time*-size book. Certainly a *Life* or *Time* page is easier to design than a *Reader's Digest* page. Ralph Hudgins, art director of *Westward* (5 1/2 × 7 1/2), found his pages rather difficult to work with, but he said that he derived satisfaction from coming up with effective layouts within the limitations of the format. His pages were sometimes crammed, but there was an excitement about them.

An advantage of the *Digest* size is that it is close to book format, and readers have more of a tendency to save the magazine. Portability, too, is an important consideration. The *Digest* size was adopted by magazines originally, of course, to fit the pocket.

The role of design

The history of journalism records the names of a number of editors who were able to build and hold audiences for publications that, from a design standpoint, had the grace of a row of neon signs or, at best, the monotonous, unadorned look of a telephone directory. One remembers Lyle Stuart's *Expose* and *Independent,* George Seldes's *In Fact,* and I. F. Stone's newsletter. One thinks of the typical cheap-paper journal of opinion. These are often radical sheets; yet their editors hold design views that can only be considered as reactionary. Northwestern University's Emeritus Professor Curtis D. MacDougall, who could identify with many of the causes of these publications, said that "Strong editorial material can overcome bad design. On the other hand, bad design can't kill good contents."

Another front page for *West Side Story,* three issues later. The style remains, but this time reverse type on a black page with rules and plenty of "black space" are art enough. The black is appropriate to the subject.

9. Don Fabun, "Dedicated to Human Questions," *DA: The Paper Quarterly for the Graphic Arts,* Second Quarter, 1970, p. 8. Fabun now writes a column, "Of Things to Come," for *Communication World.*

The Illuminator, published
monthly for employees of
Appalachian Power Company
and Kingsport Power Company,
comes in a tabloid format, but
with a difference: its main pages
consist of three unequal-width
columns. The body type runs
with unjustified right-hand
margins. The nameplate,
designed in letters that suggest
a neon sign, and the center story
both appear in wine-colored ink.
Heavy bars underline last lines of
the all-cap headlines. This is a
device seen on all the pages,
helping to unite them.

But why give editorial matter the additional burden of bad design? The job of communicating is already difficult enough.

Good design, by itself, can't make a publication useful or important; but combined with well-conceived, well-reasoned, and well-written content, it can make the printed page a joy rather than a chore.

And what is good design?

The answer is important. *Good design is design that is readable.* The key word is *readable.* Not *unique,* not *compelling,* not even *beautiful,* although all these qualities can play a part—but *readable.*

Some editors look upon design as a magic ingredient to be applied to an ailing publication, and Presto!—the publication's problems are solved. "A . . . reason for the confusion about design is the prevailing notion that it is a kind of frosting, an aesthetic overlay that makes humdrum objects more appetizing," says the eminent designer George Nelson. "No responsible designer believes this." Nelson adds that design models from nature "never show decoration that isn't functional, never show the slightest concern for aesthetics, and always try to match the organism with its environment so that it will survive."[10]

"Some publications work backwards, tailoring the editorial content to fit the graphics, but they won't live very long," adds design consultant Jan V. White. "They may make a big splash when they first appear because they are undoubtedly interesting to *look* at, but being nice to look at is not enough; if the shallowness of the content leads to reader dissatisfaction (as it must, when it becomes obvious) then the publication is on the road to oblivion."[11]

If ever there were rules to guide the designer in putting out a magazine or any printed piece, they were only vaguely accepted by some of those who did the work; and in the 1980s, with the changes in other aspects of our lives, the rules for design become even harder to pin down. What once struck many purists in design as abominable today seems to fit right in with what editors, art directors, and even readers want. Consider, for instance, the helter-skelter, patched, mortised look of the women's fashion magazines.

"There are no 'don'ts' that cannot be abridged, nor any design laws that are absolute," says Allen Hurlburt. "However, a designer should understand the nature of order and have some awareness of the framework from which he is departing."

Design and personality

How a publication looks should not be dictated by taste alone but by a knowledge of the personalities of typefaces and an understanding of how, when they are combined with the other elements on the page, they affect the mood and "color" of the page.

Here are some moods an editor might want and some suggestions on how an art director can achieve them:

   1. *Dignity.* Use old roman typefaces, centered headings and art,

10. George Nelson, "We Are Here by Design," *Harper's,* April 1975, p. 3.
11. Jan V. White, *Designing for Magazines,* R. R. Bowker Company, New York, 1976, p. x.

The second two pages of an eight-page article in *Forces*, Montreal, Quebec, Canada. The 3 1/4″ sink remains constant throughout the 9 × 12 magazine, with an occasional jutting of photos, titles, and copy blocks. The beautifully designed and printed magazine obviously follows a carefully worked out grid.

Two pages from another article, same issue, where the sink is ignored, but the basic three-column format holds steady. This spread, although it occurs after an opening spread, starts with a column of white space to set off the one column of art. A deep vertical piece of art contrasts with a wide horizontal piece. The horizontal photograph is airbrushed at the top to make a vignette out of it. The boldface subhead consists of three lines, the first one indented.

One more variation of the *Forces* grid. We are inside another article. The photograph at the left establishes the sink; the one at the right redefines it. The photos also share a common bottom axis. The copy in *Forces*, set in an unjustified sans-serif type, occasionally extends up into the sink area.

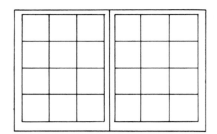

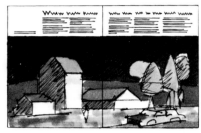

A grid consists of squares or rectangles that mark off areas for type and art. The three spreads shown in the rough sketches evolved from the grid shown at the top. There are hundreds of other possibilities.

generous amounts of white space, medium-size photos or paintings, or drawings made to resemble woodcuts.

2. *Power.* Use bold sans serif typefaces, boldface body copy, flush-left headings, large, black photos or drawings made with lithographic crayons.

3. *Grace.* Use italic with swash caps or script types, light-face body copy with unjustified (ragged edge) right-hand margins, carefully composed photographs or wash drawings, an uncrowded look.

4. *Excitement.* Use a mixture of typefaces, color, close cropping of pictures, an unbalanced and crowded page.

5. *Precision.* Use the newer sans serifs or a slab serif for headings and body copy, sharp-focus photos or tight line drawings, horizontal or vertical ruled lines, highly organized design based on a grid system.

These are only suggestions, timidly advanced. Obviously they may not always work; and as a designer you will discover other ways of creating similar moods on the page. For instance, you may develop a way of taking an old roman face, with its built-in dignity and grace, and enlist it to establish a mood of excitement or even power. What is being said in a headline or copy is always more important than the type chosen to deliver it or the art chosen to amplify or surround it.

The grid

For any kind of format some kind of a grid is almost mandatory. A grid, made up of vertical and horizontal lines, sets the limits of printing areas. It is usually a printed two-page spread with lines ruled in to show the edges of the pages, edges on the outside of the pages to indicate bleeds, the place for folios, and columns for body copy. The columns are often prepared with a series of ruled lines, one for the bottom of each line of type.

One grid system involves the dividing of the pages into squares, which in the design can be gathered into quarters, thirds, or halves of pages. Under this system, all headings rest on a line in the grid, and all photos and columns of copy occupy one or more squares.

The art director draws up a master grid in India ink, and the printer runs enough of them, in a light blue or gray ink, to last a year or two. The printed grids can be used for both rough layouts and finished pasteups.

For a more formal looking publication, with highly organized pages, a more detailed grid is called for. It is calibrated not only in columns and lines for copy, but also in areas for pictures and headings.

Many art directors enjoy working with a fully developed grid that establishes boundaries for every possibility. Within the restrictions of such a grid lie all kinds of challenges. The possibilities for variety in type and picture arrangements are still enormous. The grid no more spoils creativity than a net spoils the pleasure of a tennis game.

Width of the columns

How wide should a column of type be?

Well, any width, really. But the wider the column, the bigger the type should be.

An oft-stated rule for length of line is 1 1/2 alphabets of lowercase letters, or 39 characters. The rule is too restrictive. George A. Stevenson in *Graphic Arts Encyclopedia* (McGraw-Hill, 1968) lays down the 39-character rule and in a column of type which is itself more than 60 characters wide!

A column can be a little less than 39 characters wide, as in a newspaper, or even more than 60, as in some books. It depends to some extent on the age of the reader. It depends also on the mood the magazine is trying to create.

The fewer columns per page, the more bookish the look. A one- or two-column page looks more formal than a three-column page. A four- or more-column page begins to look like a newspaper page.

The look you want determines the number of columns per page.

There is no reason why a magazine can't have some narrow-column pages and some wide-column pages. A *Time*-size magazine, for instance, can run two columns per page for part of the book, and three columns per page for the remainder. Nor is there any reason an article can't start out at one width and, on another page, narrow down to another.

The lineup of magazine pages

The magazine designer arranges articles and stories as a baseball manager arranges a batting lineup. In baseball, the lineup has traditionally started off with a man who gets singles consistently. The second one up is a good bunter; the third one another consistent hitter, but one who more often gets extra-base hits; the fourth one a home-run king; and so on.

The lead-off article in a magazine may not be the blockbuster; it may be a more routine kind of an article. The second piece might be entertaining. The third piece might be cerebral. And so on. The editor—and art director—strive for change of pace from feature to feature.

When magazine articles and stories are not arranged by kind in the magazine proper, the arranging is usually done in the table of contents at the front of the book. There all the articles are grouped together; all the short stories are grouped together; all the regular departments or columns are grouped together. Some magazines even carry a separate table of contents of advertisements listed alphabetically at the back of the book.

Most readers read magazines front to back, but others—especially the browsers—read them from back to front. So far as advertisers are concerned, the best display impact is found in the first part of the magazine on right-hand pages; the best impact for the last part of the magazine, especially if it is side-stitched, is found on the left-hand pages. Most advertisers consider the first part of the magazine more important than the last half, and right-hand pages for them are highly desirable. They often accompany their insertion orders with the note: "Up-front, right-hand placement urgently requested."

Convinced that many readers work through the magazine from back to front, some editors start editorials or articles on a back page and continue them on preceding pages. *U.S. News & World Report,* when it ran its long editorials by David Lawrence, did this. So does one of the hunting and fishing magazines. *Esquire* followed a maddening practice of starting articles or stories in the middle or back part of the book and continuing them on pages near

The newsletter is the simplest and least expensive of the formats. No photos or drawings are needed to make it inviting, provided the designer uses enough white space and plans carefully the placing of the headings. The front page sets the style. Note that for this one the news items are blocked off into two-column rectangular units. The format works for either a printed or a duplicated piece. (Designed by the author.)

A person mentioned in *National Review* gets this decorative 3 × 9 card with the notation, "You are mentioned on page 00 of the attached issue of . . . NATIONAL REVIEW. Cordially, the EDITORS." James W. O'Bryan is the designer.

the front. Some of *The New Yorker's* best articles start in the last half of the magazine.

But articles and stories in most magazines begin in the first half of the book. Most editors and art directors, given a choice, prefer a spread (two facing pages) for each opening, but this is not always possible. When they start a feature on just the right-hand page, they favor giving a rather gray appearance to the tail end of the article before it. This assures the new opening more impact.

Page numbering

The reader will thank the art director for leaving room on every page for page numbers. The art director will make exceptions only for full-page bleed photos or advertisements. Even then, the reader would prefer the numbers. Right-hand pages are always odd-numbered, of course; left-hand pages are even-numbered.

An art director with a last-minute signature to insert into a magazine whose other pages are already printed with numbers can number the insert pages with letters. For instance: if the last numbered page in the signature before the new one is 48, the first page of the new signature would be 48a, the next page 48b, and so on. You see this numbering system used in the slicks with their regional editions.

Some magazines, embarrassed because of the thinness of the issues and not wanting the readers to realize they are reading only 24- or 36- or 48-page publications, start numbering the pages from the first issue of the year and carry through the numbering until the last issue of the year. The reader can pick up an issue in July, for instance, and find the issue beginning with, say, page 173. Some of the opinion magazines use this system. They might argue that they do it because the issues are part of a volume, and such numbering is an aid to the researcher.

Page numbering for some magazines starts on the cover and for other magazines on the first right-hand page after the cover. It is the embarrassingly thin magazine that considers its cover Page 1.

A magazine's thickness

Most magazines let the amount of advertising dictate the number of pages of any particular issue. The more ads the magazine gets, the more pages it runs. Its thickest issues are in late fall, before Christmas. Its thinnest issues are right after the first of the year and in the middle of the summer. The ratio of ad space to editorial space, ideally, runs 70:30. For some magazines, it runs closer to 50:50 or even 40:60. When the ratio gets that low, the magazine is in trouble. *Ms.,* though, deliberately keeps its ratio at that low level.

A few magazines offer readers the same amount of editorial matter issue after issue. Only the amount of advertising changes. A magazine that is highly departmentalized almost has to operate like that.

Magazines that do not contain advertising often run the same number of pages issue after issue. Company magazines fall into this category. And, because they contain so little advertising, so do opinion magazines.

The number of pages for most magazines runs to 32—two 16-page signatures. After the printing, the sheet is folded down to page size and trimmed. Signatures come in multiples of four, or eight, or sixteen, or thirty-two, depending upon the size of the page and the size of the press used to print the magazine.

If a magazine has a cover on a heavier stock—a separate cover—that's another four-page signature. Wrap it around two 16-page signatures and you have a 36-page magazine.

Handling advertisements

One problem that the art director of consumer and trade magazines faces will probably never be solved. That is the problem of ads and their intrusion into the editorial portion of the magazine. Advertisers do not have enough confidence in their ads to let them stand on their own merit. They do not want them buried in a sea of advertising. They insist that, instead, their ads be placed next to "reading matter" so that readers who otherwise would ignore the ads will wander into them, if only by mistake.

William Fadiman in an essay in "Phoenix Nest," a column in the *Saturday Review* for February 22, 1969, shows what it's like to begin a short story in a magazine and follow it through the ads. From his first paragraph: "Halfway up the steps . . . established since 1848 . . . he stopped to think of her . . . rugged endurance, dependable performance, and low operating costs. He finally knocked at the door determined to . . . ask for it by name. She opened the door slowly . . . and could not help admiring his manly form . . . built of mahogany and reinforced at the corners."

It was amusing comment on the design of American magazines made all the more striking by *Saturday Review* itself which, unintentionally, stuck a full-page ad in the middle of it, with this result: "Darling, he interrupted with a . . . Color Slide Art Lecture in Your Home for $1."

Floating ads and checkerboard ads and other odd shapes or placement add to the problems of magazine design. But because of their smaller page sizes and limited number of columns per page, magazines have not had to put up with the step-up half pyramid of ads that newspapers use on their inside pages. At least art directors on magazines almost always have rectangles to work with.

Modern Jeweler **makes available to advertisers a two-color calendar showing both editorial and advertising closing dates for each month of the year. The theme of each issue appears with the heading for each month. Skillful design puts all this on one 25 1/2 × 11 spread. The spread folds down to a handy 8 1/2 × 11 size so that advertisers can file it.**

Magazine bindings

By definition, a magazine is a bound publication of eight or more pages issued on a regular basis more often than once a year. Not all publications are bound. Newspapers consist of unbound sheets of paper folded and wrapped loosely around other folded sheets. Sometimes a newspaper carries a single sheet, printed on both sides, slipped inside one of the four-page "signatures."

At the least pretentious level a publication may consist of a single folded sheet of four pages. Or it may consist of a single sheet, unfolded, printed on both sides. Or it may consist of several sheets held together by a staple in one corner or by a couple of staples at the side.

There are several kinds of bindings, but only three really work for most magazines—saddle stapling (or saddle stitching), side stapling (or side stitching), and perfect (glued) binding.

The big advantage of saddle stapling is that the magazine opens up easily and lies flat on the table or desk. Readers can tear out pages they want to save.

And a saddle-stapled magazine may be easier to design. For instance, you can more easily run pictures and type across the gutter. When *Harper's* went from side stapling to saddle stapling, it said, in its announcement, it was doing it for design reasons. *The Atlantic* soon followed with a saddle-stapled format. Saddle stapling also allows for an uninterrupted center spread, as *Playboy* readers know.

Side stapling, on the other hand, makes for a more permanent binding. It suggests to the reader: this magazine ought to be kept. Editors wanting to make it easy for readers to tear out articles can have the pages perforated. Side stapling is especially recommended for magazines of many pages. Any reader can testify that the December issues of magazines like *Playboy, The New Yorker,* and *Sunset,* swollen with advertising, soon come apart in their hands.

After World War II *Reader's Digest* experimented with perfect binding—side binding without staples—and today the *Digest* and several other major magazines, including the women's fashion magazines, are bound in this way. Such magazines end up with spines, like books, on which their names can be printed. In 1978 the East/West Network, publishers of several in-flight magazines, went to perfect binding. The Network said that such binding made things more flexible. For instance, it could easily insert ad supplements in any size anywhere in the magazines.

Suggested further reading

Click, J. W. and Russell N. Baird, *Magazine Editing and Production,* Wm. C. Brown Company Publishers, Dubuque, Iowa, 1983. (Third Edition.)

Darrow, Ralph C., *House Journal Editing,* Interstate Printers & Publishers, Danville, Illinois, 1974.

Editors of Folio, *Magazine Publishing Management,* Folio Magazine Publishing Corporation, New Canaan, Connecticut, 1977.

Ferguson, Rowena, *Editing the Small Magazine,* Columbia University Press, New York, 1976. (Second Edition.)

Lattimore, Dan L. and John W. Windhauser, *The Editorial Process,* Morton Publishing Company, Denver, Colo., 1977. (A workbook.)

Mann, Jim, *Solving Publishing's Toughest Problems,* Folio, New Canaan, Conn., 1981.

Mayes, Herbert R., *The Magazine Maze: A Prejudiced Perspective,* Doubleday, Garden City, N.Y., 1980.

Mogel, Leonard, *The Magazine: Everything You Need to Know to Make It in the Magazine Business,* Prentice-Hall, Inc., Englewood Cliffs, N.J., 1979.

Rice, Don, *How to Publish Your Own Magazine,* David McKay, New York, 1978.

Williams, W. P. and Joseph Van Zandt, *How to Start Your Own Magazine,* Contemporary Books, Chicago, 1978.

Magazine Profiles: Studies of Magazines Today, Medill School of Journalism, Northwestern University, Evanston, Illinois, 1974.

Making Magazines, American Society of Magazine Editors, New York, 1978.

SOHO

spring '81

BOO! HISS! BUSINESS PLAYS THE VILLAIN

WALL STREET

WEDNESDAY FEBRUARY

News

Also featuring:
Murray Weidenbaum
on the economy
Give your child
the gift of music

EIGHT: THE MAGAZINE COVER

The ultimate goal for some people, it seems, is to make the cover of a national magazine. Dr. Hook and the Medicine Show did a song about getting on the cover of *Rolling Stone,* and a few weeks after the song hit the Top 40, Dr. Hook made it. A few weeks after that, as the song suggested he would do, Dr. Hook walked into the magazine's San Francisco office (it has since moved to New York), and bought five copies for his mother.[1]

The most prestigious cover spot, probably, is on the front of *Time.* Malcolm Muggeridge contemptuously called the *Time* cover spot "post-Christendom's most notable stained-glass window." At the end of each year *Time's* editors and letter-to-the-editor writers engage in a navel-contemplation maneuver as the decision is made about the "Man of the Year."

1977 saw a new low in magazine covers with the publication and national distribution of *Assassin.* The cover of the first issue showed a picture of President Carter with the crosshairs of a telescopic sight superimposed over his face. The blurb said: "How Would You Do It: See Special Entry Page." Inside the magazine also was information on how to blow up a car using a homemade bomb and how to build an atomic bomb.

What the cover does

No feature is so important to a magazine as its cover, no matter how the magazine is circulated.

A magazine cover does these things:

1. *It identifies the magazine.* The art director tries to come up with something in the cover design to set the magazine apart from all others.

2. *It attracts attention.* The art director must allure readers somehow—and then get them inside. Milton Glaser says a magazine cover can capture attention "by creating a tension between clarity and novelty."[2]

3. *It creates a suitable mood for the reader.*

And if the magazine is displayed on newsstands, the cover has one more function:

4. *It sells the magazine.*

In 1976, for the first time, the top general-circulation or consumer magazines—those with circulations of 300,000 or more—

(Opposite page)
Designer Janusz Einhorn of Herbick & Held uses a number of symbols to illustrate a blurb on a full-color *Sohio* magazine cover, a blurb which suggests how Hollywood deals with business people (they are always villains). The symbols are: a tough looking businessman in a striped suit, *The Wall Street Journal,* and a piece of movie film. In reverse letters in the film are two blurbs for other articles in the issue. *Sohio* is published quarterly by The Standard Oil Company of Ohio.

1. Peter A. Janssen, "Rolling Stone's Quest for Respectability," *Columbia Journalism Review,* January/February 1974, p. 59.
2. "The Importance of Being Rockwell," *Columbia Journalism Review,* November/December 1979, p. 40.

Long Lines

AUGUST/SEPTEMBER 1975

Before his day is over, he will make 25 phone calls, answer 15 others, travel 200 miles and read scores of reports and technical materials. He'll write a dozen memos (some of them to himself) and talk with his boss five times. He'll answer a hundred questions and ask twice as many. At microwave facilities, he'll make note of weeds that need uprooting and scratch his head about a sniper who's been taking potshots at a tower beacon, youths who are jumping a fence...

(continued on page 1)

Long Lines starts an article on the cover for this issue. The large-type lead continues on page 1 inside the magazine, then narrows down to regular-size columns. In the original, the logo appears in black, the lead in green, the silhouette art in full color. A thin line in red tops the story beginning. *Long Lines* is a slick-paper magazine for the employees of the Long Lines Department of the American Telephone & Telegraph Company.

Mark Andresen adopted futuris[t] and German expressionist styl[e] to create the art for this "Cleveland's Leftists" cover f[or] *The Plain Dealer Magazine.* Th[e] style had been popular in Bolshevik posters during the Russian Revolution. Greg Paul directed.

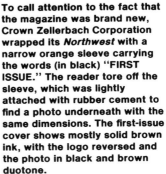

To call attention to the fact that the magazine was brand new, Crown Zellerbach Corporation wrapped its *Northwest* with a narrow orange sleeve carrying the words (in black) "FIRST ISSUE." The reader tore off the sleeve, which was lightly attached with rubber cement to find a photo underneath with the same dimensions. The first-issue cover shows mostly solid brown ink, with the logo reversed and the photo in black and brown duotone.

sold more copies on newsstands than they circulated through the mails. With postal rates so high, magazines were making a concerted effort to sell single copies. *TV Guide* set its subscription rate higher than a year's worth of single copies would cost.

What goes on the cover acquires added importance when a magazine depends mostly on newsstand sales. A magazine's circulation then rests on impulse buying. What is shown on the cover and how the blurbs are worded become vital editorial decisions.

But covers are important for non-newsstand magazines, too. Howard Paine, chief of editorial layout for *National Geographic,* says: "We may not have to compete on the newsstand but we do have to compete on the coffee table."[3]

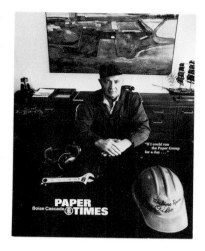

To call attention to an article on the results of an essay contest on how to run the company, *Paper Times* got a machine-room oiler to sit at the desk of a company executive and pose for a cover photograph. The equipment on the desk added to the novelty of the shot.

What goes on the cover

The typical magazine cover carries: a logo (the name, set or drawn in appropriate or impressive type); date of the issue and price per copy; art; the titles of major features, with names of authors.

Sometimes the art director has additional elements to contend with. *Freedom & Union* for a long time ran the name of the editor on its cover.

Major display on covers takes any of these forms:

1. *A photograph or illustration tied to a feature inside.* "Is Inflation Out of Control?" asks *Newsweek* on one of its 1980 covers. To illustrate the blurb, the magazine shows a full-color photograph of a dollar bill, larger than life-size, on fire, the flame reaching up to and under the logo.

2. *Abstract art or a photograph or illustration that stands by itself.* The art director may want to keep such art free of all type, including the logo, so that it will be suitable for framing. An explanation of the art can be carried in a caption on the title page.

The cover of the *Bulletin of the Atomic Scientists* accommodates a "doomsday" clock. The hands occasionally move back and forth as world conditions change. The hands, of course, are always close to midnight.

3. *Type only.* The type can be in the form of a title or two from articles inside, as in the case of most of the opinion magazines; or as a table of contents, a form *Reader's Digest* was instrumental in popularizing.

4. *The beginning of an article or editorial that continues inside.* The New Republic has used an occasional cover for this purpose. Some magazines—*Advertising Age* and *Billboard* for example—run several articles or stories on the cover, newspaper-style.

5. *An advertisement. Editor & Publisher* uses its cover for this purpose. A cover ad brings premium rates.

Making decisions about the cover

Covers require both a permanent decision on basic format and an issue-by-issue decision concerning art and typography.

For your basic format you must answer the following questions:

1. Should the cover be of the same stock as the remainder of the magazine? Or should it be of a heavier stock?

3. Quoted in *Folio,* March/April 1974, p. 58.

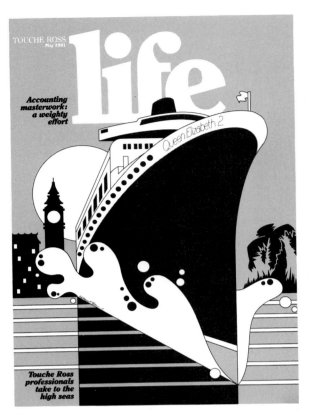

An earlier chapter shows a silhouetted photograph cover for *Touche Ross Life.* The monthly magapaper uses a variety of art forms for its covers. This one, in red and black, features abstract, Art Deco line art. (Reprinted by permission from *Touche Ross Life,* May 1981; published by Touche Ross & Co.)

(Opposite page)
This cover for *Inside,* a magapaper, features art and an introduction to an article inside on "The Two-Career Marriage." The two-paragraph opening of all-centered lines ends with "See story on pages 4 and 5." The clock establishes the fact that this well-dressed couple is up early to enjoy breakfast together before each person heads for work. *Inside* is a monthly publication for employees of Southern Company Services, Inc., Atlanta.

2. What process should be used to print the cover? The same as for the remainder of the magazine? Or some other?

3. What kind of a logo does the magazine need? Where should it go on the cover? Need it stay in the same place issue after issue?

4. Does the cover need art? Photograph or illustration? Must the art have a tie with an inside feature? Or can it stand on its own, like the old Norman Rockwell covers for *The Saturday Evening Post*?

5. Does the cover need color? Spot color or process color?

6. Are titles or blurbs necessary? Where should they go on the cover?

7. Will a regular cover do? Or is a gatefold called for? Or maybe an oversize cover, like those on the pulp magazines of the 1930s?

Newsstand considerations

A magazine sold on the newsstands, in contrast to one delivered only by mail, needs to (1) sell itself to the impulse buyer and (2) identify itself for the regular buyer. Where a through-the-mail magazine can run its logo anywhere on the cover and in different typefaces from issue to issue, the newsstand magazine needs a standard logo and in a standard position.

Most newsstand magazines are displayed in an upright position, often with only the left side showing. This is why many newsstand magazines have their logos crowded in the upper left. If the magazine is *Life*-size, it lies on its back, in stacks, often low in the stands.

What art and blurbs the art director puts on the cover seriously affect sales. "Trends in cover art change rapidly," said Norma P. Schoenfeld, when he was art director at *True.* "We have to keep close tabs on how a given cover sells on the newsstand. . . . Naturally, our circulation department takes a keen interest in our cover selection."

Bob Ciano, art director of the reborn *Life,* finds that his best-selling covers often break all the rules he learned at school. Even a mediocre photograph on a cover can work better than a photograph that might better please an art director. The subject matter makes a big difference.

Ciano told an American Society of Magazine Editors seminar in 1981 that no one has been able to identify a design pattern for the cover that will, automatically, boost sales. "I think we worry too much about what our readers want and don't want," Ciano said. "I think we all bring years of experience to magazines and don't often enough go with that experience and gut reaction."

John Volger, art director for *Business Week,* told the same seminar that for his magazine a black and white cover with just one color often does better than a full-color cover. A black and white cover can stand out on a newsstand aflood with color.[4]

Timing

A magazine that features people in the news on its covers may be deeply embarrassed as news changes while the magazine is being printed and delivered.

4. "Best Covers Often Defy the Rules of Good Graphics," *Folio,* July 1981, p. 6.

INSIDE

The Two-Career Marriage

Working couples are on the rise in the United States. The Department of Labor reports that more than 29 million women with children under the age of 18 are working today. What effect has the two-career marriage had on the once traditional roles of husband as breadwinner and wife as homemaker?

Four couples at Southern Company Services seem to be handling their marriage/career/family roles without too much difficulty, although "hectic" is a word that often crops up when they each describe their lives. *See story on pages 4 and 5.*

Geo, a handsome, slick-paper magazine, sees itself as "a living record of the Earth in magazine form." This cover keeps full-color art a nominal size, surrounding it with a box reversed in a field of green. The shortness of the name allows its being shown in large, classic capital letters. The blurbs, all with colons, are centered. Photograph by Maureen Bisilliat; © 1981 Geo.

An embarrassment on the cover is much more serious that an embarrassment inside. When choosing cover art you must give some thought to what a sudden turn of events might do to the message your cover art conveys. Perhaps the wording of the blurb can be adjusted to make it more flexible.

Another problem involves duplication. Editors (and art directors) come from similar backgrounds and hence tend to think alike. Often, then, they arrive at similar ideas for covers. Competing magazines like Time and Newsweek can't help but appear often with the same cover themes. It is not a matter of editorial leaks— one magazine does not want to copy the other. Nor is it a matter of taking precautions to avoid the duplication. If a story is there it gets the coverage. It is a matter of staying abreast of the times.

Jeff MacNelly in the comic strip Shoe shows the ultimate Time-Newsweek cover duplication. One character is reading a copy of Newsweek with a Time cover and logo printed on it; the other is reading Time, which carries a Newsweek cover and logo.

When you see a magazine for one week moving away from serious cover art to, say, art showing a well-endowed female entertainer, you can rightly suspect it is that time in the year when the magazine is attempting to step up newsstand sales to impress advertisers or make a good showing in a circulation audit.

The stock cover

Small-circulation magazines unable to afford original art and the printing of full-color covers can turn to a house which mass produces them for local imprinting. Editors simply choose from among a series of nicely produced if mundane scenes and order enough sheets to wrap around each of the copies of the magazines. Each cover acts as an extra four-page signature. The inside front cover, inside back cover, and back cover are blank. The editor works out copy for these and has the local printer run the sheets through a press to print appropriate material on the blank pages and the magazine's name over part of the full-color cover art. Monthly Cover Service, 400 North Michigan Avenue, Chicago, Illinois 60601 supplies stock covers.

What's in a name?

Picking a name for a magazine could be the single most important step a publisher or editor makes. Once decided upon, the name sticks, even when the formula for the magazine changes. That's why editors are well advised to avoid publication frequency in the name. Put Quarterly into the title, and what do you do when the publication becomes successful enough to go bi-monthly or monthly? What is the significance now of the Saturday in Saturday Review and Saturday Evening Post?

Your emphasis may seem permanent at the start, but in a few years, as times change, you may want your magazine to change. How can anyone take seriously a magazine that still goes by the name of Playboy?

You want to be clever in your name choice but appropriate, too. So how does The Avant Gardener strike you? Or Statutory Rap, a publication of the University of Dayton Law School? Or Rider's Digest, a publication of the Metropolitan Atlanta Rapid Transit Authority? Or The Eggsaminer, once published for egg producers?

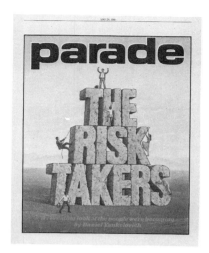

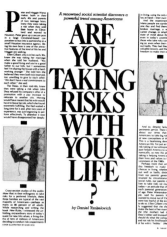

In *Annie Hall*, Woody Allen came up with a name for the merger of *Dissent* with *Commentary*: the name was *Dissentary*. *Atlas*, a digest of foreign press news, features, and comment, was named after the Titan who held up the heavens. "Our own more modest purpose," said the editors, "is to hold the world up to our readers." But *Atlas* changed to *World Press Review* in March 1980 because, its editors decided, "Atlas" suggested to would-be readers a book of maps or tables.

Magazines with long names can make references to themselves less cumbersome by going to initials. Hence, the Journal of the American Medical Association becomes *JAMA* and the Journal of the Association of Operating Room Nurses becomes the *AORN Journal*. *CA* was lucky enough in its initials that when it wanted to erase the commercial art image (it was originally called *Commercial Art*) it found its initials also stood for *Communication Arts*, the name by which it is now known. *National Review* sometimes features a big *NR* on its cover rather than its full name.

Few magazines would start off that way today, but some of the older magazines carry their founders' name: *McCall's, Forbes, Hoard's Dairyman, Best's Insurance News*. Sometimes this causes confusion. *Moody Monthly* is not a magazine for depressed persons; it is an evangelical magazine named after Dwight L. Moody.

A modifier seems useful to some editors who put a *Modern* or *Today's* in front of the title or an *Age* or *World* behind it, but often a single, straightforward word does the job: *Banking* or *Eternity*. Of course, a single name can be jarring to someone outside the magazine's readership. The student senate of the University of Louisville School of Dentistry publishes the perfectly serious *Abscess*.

Because it appears in the West, one important consumer magazine calls itself *Sunset*.

Often it is hard to find a name because all the possibilities seem to be taken. *Esquire* editors worked with "Trend," "Stag," and "Beaut" before getting a letter addressed with the quaint "Esq." after the recipient's name, and decided to try that word spelled out.

Prison publications have shown a feel for the ironic with such choices of titles as these: *Time & Tied, The Stretch, Bars & Stripes, Detour, The New Leaf, The Key,* and (are you ready for this?) *The Prism*.

Parade commissions a piece of art for a cover, then uses closeup details of it inside to decorate a spread. The thick, short bars inside that are used to set off the pieces of art match the thick strokes of the typeface in the article's title. The vertical bars on each side of the title match the thin strokes of those letters. Ira Yoffe is director of design at *Parade*.

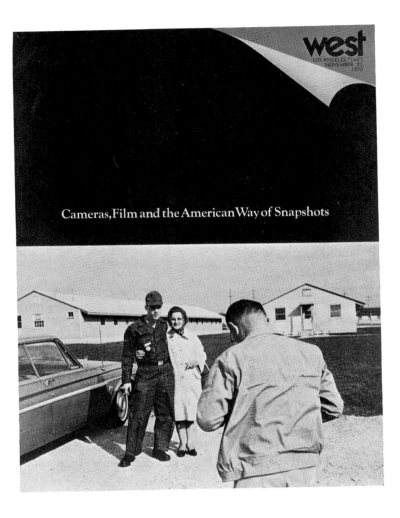

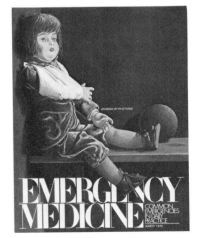

Company magazines have shown imagination in their choices of names, too. The company that makes Heath bars publishes *Sweet Talk*, Blue Chip Stamps publishes *Chip Chat*, Gulf Oil Corp. publishes *Gulf Oilmanac*, Wisconsin Electric Power publishes *The Outlet*, and Public Service Indiana puts out, er, *Watts Cookin'*.

The job of the art director is to come up with the right typeface to help say visually what the title says in words. But that does not mean that *Sweet Talk* should be dripping in chocolate or that *The Outlet* has to be in a script made from an electric cord.

The logo

The logo, a typographic rendering of the magazine's name, is much like a company trademark. Its adoption is a serious matter. Once selected, it settles in for many years of service. Its value increases to the point where its owner feels reluctant to abandon it even when its design becomes outmoded.

In designing a logo, then, you would avoid types or letterforms that soon will be out of date. Yet you would choose type that is distinctive. More important, you would select type that is appropriate. You might also decide on a typeface for the letters actually used, not for the beauty of the face as a whole. How a single letter looks might well influence your decision.

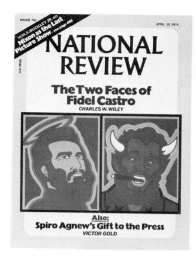  

The Sporting News is an example of a magazine with an inappropriate logo face: Old English. The editors would argue that their weekly publication is newspaperlike in its approach, and Old English has been used, historically, for newspaper logos. But Old English has an ecclesiastical feel; it is far removed from the roughness and vitality of the sports world.

Whatever face you choose, you have to decide whether you want all caps, caps and small caps, caps and lowercase, an initial cap and lowercase, all lowercase, upright and italics, solid or outline letters.

You may want to rough out the idea for your logo, but because of its specialized nature, its importance, and its permanence, you would call in a professional calligrapher or letterform artist to complete the job. You should not allow your logo to be hand-lettered by just anyone who knows how to draw. Illustrators as a rule are unfamiliar with type and letterform, and many of them do a poor job of lettering.

Settling for a regularly set typeface instead of hand lettering is the best solution when professional lettering help is not available or affordable. Without much ability as a lettering artist, you can do some innovating with type yourself. You can order reproduction proofs of the type and then cut the letters apart and respace them to bring to your logo a flair ordinary typography can't supply. Because logos involve only one or two words and because readers have a chance to study them issue after issue, you can do things with spacing that you wouldn't do when working on article and story titles. For instance, you can move two capitalized words together, with no space between.

LikeThis

You can doctor some of the letters, too, so that they would be unrecognizable were they not seen in context. Herb Lubalin, who designed *Sport's* tight-fitting all-cap logo, chopped off the bottom half of the main downstroke of the *R* and propped the letter up against the *O. Dare,* a magazine once published for barbershops, ran its logo in mirror reverse, so that it read from right to left. It was in keeping with the nature of the magazine; it "dared" to be different.

National Review, even though some of its circulation comes from newsstand sales, changes back and forth from a full logo to an initials logo with the full name in small type below. Usually, art director James W. O'Bryan uses full color, but for the cover at the far right a black and white photo seemed appropriate to illustrate William F. Buckley, Jr.'s review of *Scoundrel Time* inside. The photo is from a full-page ad for a fur coat that the author of *Scoundrel Time,* Lillian Hellman, had recently posed for. Often a *National Review* cover has a small diagonal banner running across a corner as a supplemental cover blurb, as on the Castro cover.

NewTimes

Family Circle

Steve Phillips, art director of the magazine, designed the *New Times* logo, using tightly spaced sans serifs and bringing the two words together by allowing the *T* to overlap the *w*. The *T* picks up the slant of the *w* for its left cross-bar; the right cross-bar does extra duty as the dot for the *i*. *New Times* is no longer published.

A logo designed by Herb Lubalin for *Family Circle*. This was one of the first of the "nestled" logos, with letters from one line fitting snugly against letters from another. The *C* actually overlaps the *m*. "Circle" is so placed that a couple of vertical axes are formed, one with the two *i*'s, the other with the *l* and *r*. The tail of the *y* is clipped to fit the tail of the *r*. And of course the letters are unusually close-fitting horizontally. All of which makes for a tightly knit *Family Circle*.

For its logo *Popular Photography* found it necessary to separate the word "Photography." (The "Popular" in the title is run small and up the side, an inconspicuous part of the logo.) The dictionary separates "photography" between the *g* and the *r*. But that doesn't read right. The magazine wanted "Photo" to stand out. So it went ahead and separated the word like this "Photo-graphy," even though the separation technically is wrong.

The logo can tolerate some tampering from issue to issue without hurting a magazine's identity. At the least, it can frequently change color. Many art directors move their logos around each time and change its size. Or they allow cover photographs to intrude a bit, hiding some of the type.

There comes a time in a magazine's growth when it must—it just must—change its logo.

Some magazines change suddenly, some gradually. *Newsweek* has made its changes gradually. *Family Circle,* on the other hand, changed its logo suddenly and dramatically.

Perhaps the rule should be: if the logo is salvageable, change it gradually, in order to retain what recognition value the logo holds for the reader. If the resistance to change has gone on too long and the logo is hopelessly outdated, go ahead and make a clean break.

The logo for *New York Life News,* a magapaper, incorporates an unusual amount of art, but the art—the New York skyline—is highly abstract and decorative. The final "S" becomes a cap to make it match the height of the "N" in "News" and to provide a well for "New York Life." The caps for "New York Life" are in a boldface version of the slab serif type to relate them to the boldness of the type used for "News." The logo is pushed to one side of a band of white running across the page, so it doesn't take as much room as its deepness might indicate. The designer was Joe Lombardo.

Art on the cover

The late Joe Ratner, after considering the various claims for one kind of cover over another, concluded that as far as the art was concerned, the ideal cover would show a nude woman sitting on a braided rug, with a dog at her elbow, a rose in her teeth, holding a baby, and eating apple pie. But cover art tends to be less predictable than in the past. It is more direct and less cluttered. Art directors of newsstand magazines think of their covers as posters to be seen from 30 feet away. They look for closeup art with a strong silhouette—art not dissimilar from the art on billboards.

Whether you should use photographs or illustrations depends again on the nature of the magazine and its audience. A journalistic magazine would normally use photographs, a literary magazine illustrations. It is probably not a good idea to switch back and forth.

Photographs have virtually replaced illustrations as cover art on magazines because photographs are more readily available on short notice and, in most cases, cheaper.

When working out your cover format you are wise to select a square rather than a rectangular hole for the photograph. Choosing a rectangle, you have to commit yourself to all horizontal or all vertical shots for your cover. By deciding on a square, you can, with judicious cropping, accommodate both horizontals and verticals, and of course you can run Rollei shots without any cropping. Whatever shape you choose, the photograph should dominate the page, perhaps even bleeding all around.

If you use art that ties in with something inside, you'll want to run a blurb on the cover pointing to that tie. If the art is independent, you'll have to separate the cover blurbs, if any, from the art to prevent the reader from making a wrong—and sometimes incongruous—connection.

While abstraction in cover art—both in photography and illustration—is making gains, realism still works best for certain magazines. Petersen Publications, publishers of magazines for car buffs, gun lovers, and hot rodders, experimented with arty covers but found they did not sell as well as covers crowded with type and illustrated with no-nonsense, sleeves-rolled-up paintings. Good design for Petersen audiences is not necessarily what good design would be for other audiences.

The use of offbeat art can unsettle the reader not accustomed to it. When *Time* for one of its covers ran a photograph of a papier-mache bust of Kenneth Gailbraith by Gerald Scarfe, one reader wrote in: "My five-year-old son looked at the cover picture and said: 'Well, I guess they did the best they could.'"

Titles on the cover

Article titles—or blurbs—on the cover are meant to lure the reader inside. Some magazines devote their entire cover to them. Others combine them with art. Obviously, the simpler the cover, the better. If titles and blurbs must be included, they should be held down to just a few words in two or three lines at the most.

With several blurbs on the cover, one right after the other, the reader may not see, immediately, where one stops and another begins. Four one-line blurbs may look like one four-line blurb. To solve this problem, you can set the blurbs in different sizes or in different faces. But this might hurt the consistency of your design.

Close-fitting sans serif letters make up the logo for *Print*. It is always run small and to the side at the top of the cover. Note that the *r* and *t* are designed to pick up the shape of the *n*. And note that the cross-bar on the *t* is elongated to give the letter better balance in context with the other letters.

For its logo, *Alma Mater*, publication for alumni directors, overlaps the two words of its name. The overlapping "ma" takes on characters of letters both at the left and at the right. The result is a logo made up of three kinds of letters. Yet the designer succeeds in making it all look like one tightly ordered unit.

"The Magazine of Winter" almost buries its logo in snow. But enough of the type shows so that the name stands out adequately on the newsstands.

REACH

Reach, published by the Church of God, Anderson, Ind., for its logo uses some trick typography to capture the spirit of the magazine.

The organization publishing this bimonthly newsletter is Public Employees Retirement System, or PERS. So "Perspective" was a natural as a name. Editor Bernerd Fred Park and graphic artist Arnold Albertson got together and worked out this logo that emphasizes the PERS initials. The small type at the top lines up with the *S* in "PERS," and the State of Oregon seal is placed to act as a sort of dot for the *I*.

STATE OF OREGON
Public Employees
Retirement System

Official Bimonthly Newsletter

PERSPECTIVES

A better answer might be to use punctuation—a period—after each blurb as advertisers use periods after lines of a headline. Or, if you have a second color available, you can run every other blurb in a color ink. That nicely separates them. With no second color, you could set every other blurb in italics. Or you could set one of the blurbs in a "slash."

A slash is a diagonal stripe at a top corner of the magazine usually printed in a color. The slash suggests immediacy. Or it says that the item in question is so important it has to be added, even though it clutters the design. *Good Housekeeping* found that a slash in 1979 announcing "165 color pictures" made the April issue especially hot at the newsstands. *Time* uses a variation of the "slash" with its "turned down" corner. That gimmick, a flat, almost abstract design, has been widely copied by other publications, especially by college and company magazines.

The beauty of the typeface and its arrangement on the cover are not nearly so important as the wording. The trouble with some blurbs is that people read them two ways. "Outlaw Pitchers" reads a blurb on the cover of *Inside Sports*. Is that a command? Does it mean pitchers should not be used in baseball? Or is the phrase simply a description of some pitchers now at work on mounds in the major leagues—pitchers who use spitballs or who attempt to bean the batters?

Most annoying to the reader is the practice of running a title on the cover and changing it when it appears over the article inside.

Color on the cover

Editors who don't use color anywhere else seem to feel they must use it at least on the cover. The possibilities include 3-D full color, ordinary process color, spot color, and one-color printing. If the cover is printed separately from the magazine itself, color on the cover is within the budget of most magazines even when they can't afford color throughout.

Small magazines usually go the second-color route, using a bright color that will contrast with the black-and-white photography. Often the second color consists of a band or block into which the logo or blurbs have been surprinted or reversed.

When only a second color is available, you are unlikely to come up with a more useful and powerful color than a red that is light enough to contrast with black but dark enough to carry reverse letters. Even when you have full color available, you want to have one color predominate. Colors tend to convey certain moods; and often the subject of the cover will dictate what color you want to stand out.

Editors and art directors—and circulation managers, too—have some rather firm ideas as to which colors work best for their mag-

Buildings, the construction and building management journal, moves its logo around each issue and completely changes its cover art. For this cover, art director John E. Sirotiak uses a montage of newspaper clippings behind two figures in full color. The logo and the blurb at the bottom are in bronze. The figures are arranged to match the logo in width.

azines. *House & Garden,* for instance, found that for its covers blue sold best, followed by green, then red.

Some magazines adopt a color and stay with it issue after issue, sort of as a trademark. *Time* uses a special red border. *National Geographic* similarly uses yellow.

Production matters

The art director puts a disproportionate amount of time on the cover, agonizing over the art, worrying about the placement of the type, checking the color proofs—and checking them again. Finally, it all fits. Everything is perfect. The magazine is printed. The circulation department takes over.

And what happens? The subscriber gets the magazine, and plunked down right over the type and art is a mailing sticker.

A unique case involved a 1969 issue of *Time,* which featured a cover portrait of Vice-President Spiro T. Agnew right after his first attack on the news media. About 320,000 copies of the magazine (only part of the press run) went out with the label pasted across Agnew's mouth. A spokesman for the magazine said it was "a production error."

Promotional considerations

The cover is important to both the circulation and advertising departments of a magazine.

The art and the blurbs on the cover strongly affect the number of copies sold on the newsstands. Sometimes the circulation department is not content with the cover as printed; it adds some promotional literature of its own.

To sell copies or subscriptions or to urge renewals, a magazine attaches slips of paper to the cover and sews or staples notices into the binding. This practice got out of hand in the 1950s and 1960s, as readers angrily ripped their magazines apart trying to dispose of all the come-ons. Now magazines show more consideration for their readers. They add stick-ons and stick-ins that, when removed, do not damage the magazine. *Time* and other magazines include a reorder card not bound into—simply slipped into—the magazine, so that it falls out when the magazine is opened.

The stick-ons are often localized for newsstand display. They call attention to articles high in local interest. Even though the magazine puts out several regional editions, covers themselves stay the same.

But for one of its issues *Esquire's* editor decided he needed seven different covers, one for most of the country, six others for selected large cities featured in an article. It was an experiment not often to be duplicated.[5] *Sunset,* which publishes four regional editions, has used two different covers for an occasional issue, better to set the stage for material inside.

Chicago in its December 1981 issues put Mayor Jane Byrne on its cover but used two different photographs. For half the copies the photograph showed the mayor smiling; for half, frowning.

5. It must have been a production and distribution nightmare. It was tried because a new editor didn't know any better. Reported the magazine: ". . . so in the end it turned out to be easier to do than to make him understand why it couldn't be done."

For his magazine called *Bird,* created for a Magazine Editing class, student William Lingle produces an all-lowercase logo with press-on Helvetica Bold letters. To make the logo appropriate to the subject matter of his magazine, he substitutes for the dot of an *i* a bird drawn in silhouette. It had to be a fat, squatting bird so it wouldn't be too different from the expected dot.

Change is made from a set of ligatures. This handsome type is based on a photolettering face which the magazine uses for titles inside.

New York's logo is adopted from an earlier one used by *New York* when it was part of the *Herald Tribune.* The original was in Caslon swash. Now, in a bolder version, it combines elements of both Caslon and Bookman. Designer: Tom Carnase. Art director: Walter Bernard.

The assignment: do a cover, including logo, for *Ethics,* a simulated new magazine with some newsstand distribution. (There is a real quarterly called *Ethics* published by the University of Chicago.) Feature on the cover an article on "Reporting Watergate: Some Second Thoughts" by John L. Hulteng. Full-color is available. Come up with a basic design that can be utilized in follow-up issues. Here are student solutions by (from left) Robin Andrea Teter, Anne Mangan, and Robin Perkins. Teter centers her bold logo, puts the blurb immediately below, and offers large art symbolic of the article. The colors are mostly green and brown. The strength of her design lies in the proportions. Mangan makes use of a blue border to match the extended-letter roman logo. The generous-size blurb, in red, superimposes itself over the simulated columns of a newspaper page. Perkins builds a Nixon out of newsclippings and puts a flag in full color behind. Instead of using standard type for her logo, she designs her own, coming up with letters that seem related. Note the ligature she builds out of the first three letters.

Newsstands had both versions. In the inner city, a frowning mayor sold best. In the suburbs the opposite was true. *New York* did something similar for its Dec. 28, 1981-Jan. 4, 1982 issue dedicated to the "Single in the City." The cover showed an arm reaching out of the shower for a "MINE" towel. Half the copies had it as a female arm, half as a male. "If your cover doesn't match your preference," said a cover note inside, "you can swap it with a friend or neighbor. It might turn into something."

When a magazine offers reprints of an article, it wraps the reprint with the cover for that issue. An advertiser requesting reprints of an ad for direct-mail use expects the cover to accompany the reprint. A picture of the cover may also be included in advertising directed to media buyers in advertising agencies. For that reason, the cover should be reproducible in a reduced size.

Covers to remember

Esquire's covers of the 1960s and early 1970s were among the industry's most memorable. They were the ideas of George Lois, the advertising executive and art director, with photography supplied by Carl Fischer—"The photographic magician," as Dugald Stermer called him. As "concept covers," they referred to lead articles inside the magazine. Lieutenant Calley posed with children looking very Vietnamese. Muhammed Ali posed with arrows stuck in his chest. Andy Warhol drowned in a can of Campbell's tomato soup. Many of the effects resulted from doctoring photographs, but some of them resulted from celebrities' willingness to pose.

Lois said that ". . . nobody ever refused to do anything, no matter how outrageous. . . ." "So why do they put up with it?" Dugald Stermer asked Lois. "Pure ego seems to be the answer; . . . people, at least many people, suffer any indignity to have their face out there in public."[6]

Rivaling *Esquire* with the uniqueness of its covers was a younger magazine, *New York,* like *Esquire* an exponent of the "new jour-

6. Quoted by Dugald Stermer, "Carl Fischer," *Communication Arts,* May/June 1975, p. 30.

nalism." For a cover promoting an article on ice cream, *New York* showed a nude woman holding out two ice cream cones, placed to look at first like a bra. The title, parodying a best-selling book at the time, went: "Everything You Always Wanted to Know About Ice Cream But Were Too Fat to Ask."

In a year-end issue, *New York* gave readers a 12-page handbook for consumers, telling them, among other things, "How to Break the Supermarket Code and Guarantee Your Food Is Fresh." The cover consisted of a drawing of a box one might find in the grocery store, gaudy in color, with a sunburst saying "Special" and a band with type running diagonally across the face. The designer even uglified the logo to make it appear as though it belonged on the package. The price for the issue was stamped on the top of the box in the familiar purple indelible ink under the printed words, "You pay only." The box carried the line, "Net weight 6 oz.," which was about what that issue weighed.

Even *The Atlantic* became more innovative in its covers. For one issue it ran a gatefold for the first time. It provided plenty of room to display a collage by Larry Rivers for a "Soldiers" feature. A title running across the bottom read: "The Army is the only damn thing [and then you had to turn the flap] holding this country together." To illustrate a "Trains in Trouble" blurb another *Atlantic* cover showed a drawing of an old-fashioned train engine chained to photographed railroad tracks with a circular inset of a woman in period costume, agonizing, asking "Will help arrive in time?"

National Lampoon came up with a much talked about cover when it showed a dog with a gun pointed to its head. The blurb read: "If You Don't Buy This Magazine, We'll Kill This Dog."

Mad magazine spoofed the universal product code on the cover of its October 1979 issue with a drawing of its mascot running a lawn mower up to it. The code represented the high grass about to be mowed.

The gatefold cover gives art directors their best chance for drama. The folded extra sheet not only makes possible a cover with a one-two punch but also an inside cover ad that stretches over three facing pages. A classic gatefold was *The Saturday Evening Post's* for April 28, 1962. It showed first a lineup of ball players looking pious while the "Star Spangled Banner" was being played, then a wild fight involving the players and umpires. Another classic gatefold was *Esquire's* cover for November 1966. Hubert Humphrey, then Vice-President, was shown saying, "I have known for 16 years his courage, his wisdom, his tact, his persuasion, his judgment, and his leadership." When you turned the page you found Humphrey was really sitting on President Johnson's lap. He was a ventriloquist's puppet! Johnson is shown saying, "You tell 'em, Hubert."

It took a magazine like *Psychology Today* to give the gatefold its ultimate impact. For July 1971 the magazine ran a *six*-page gatefold cover, which featured a game readers could play and also made possible an ad that spread over four side-by-side pages inside.

Some of the most admired covers in the industry appear on *The New Yorker*. They are subtle, beautifully drawn or painted, and they have nothing to do with what is inside the magazine. People wallpaper rooms with them.

The New Yorker once each February reruns its first cover designed in the early 1920s by the cartoonist Rea Irwin. It shows a

A nameplate doesn't have to carry art to make it distinctive. This bold nameplate for Seattle-First National Bank's semi-monthly magapaper for employees gets by with just a little merging of letters, causing ligatures to form. Note that "AF" and "NE" share the same basic down strokes. Gene Davis and Associates Graphic Design Group, Seattle, set up the format for this publication, a format that editor Ken Linarelli finds "easy to produce" each issue. Pasteup day is Wednesday; finished copies of the publication come back the next morning.

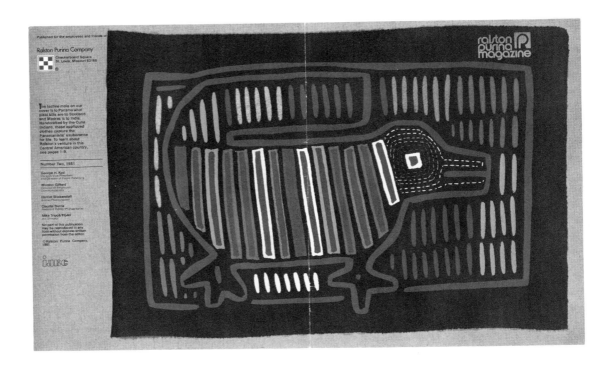

Published for the employees and friends of

Ralston Purina Company

Checkerboard Square
St. Louis, Missouri 63188

The festive mola on our
cover is to Panama what
plaid kilts are to Scotland
and Madras is to India.
Handcrafted by the Cuna
Indians, these appliqued
clothes capture the
Panamanians' exuberance
for life. To learn about
Ralston's venture in this
Central American country,
see pages 1-9.

Number Two, 1981

George H. Keil
Division Vice President
and Director of Public Relations

Winston Gifford
Director of Employee
Communications

Harriet Blickenstaff
Editor/Photographer

Claudia Burris
Assistant Editor/Photographer

Mike Tripoli/PGAV
Art Director

No part of this publication
may be reproduced in any
form without express written
permission from the editor.

©Ralston Purina Company,
1981

A general-circulation magazine editor doesn't have to worry about the back cover. That goes to an advertiser. But a company magazine editor does have to put something there. For one of its issues, *Ralston Purina Magazine* uses a wraparound, the art starting on the front cover (shown at the right in this spread) and carrying over to the back. Part of the back cover is given to masthead information. The art—an appliqued cloth—prepares the reader for a long piece on Panama.

foppish gentleman studying a butterfly. *The Saturday Evening Post* used to devote one cover each year to Benjamin Franklin, even after historian Frank Luther Mott assessed the magazine's tie to Franklin as tenuous.

Many magazines like to tie their covers to the seasons of the year. *McCall's* has used the *M* and *C* of its name to spell out "Merry Christmas."

The back cover

Editors of newsstand or trade magazines don't face the problem—the page belongs to the advertiser willing to pay a premium rate—but editors of company magazines must do something about it: the troublesome back cover. Too often the decision about what to put there is last-minute. And that's a shame. The space is too valuable for such cavalier treatment.

On a typical magazine the back cover ranks second only to the front cover in its impact on and its accessibility to the reader. It deserves the editor's thoughtful attention.

Logic suggests that the back cover be appealing—but not too appealing. It should not overshadow the front cover. The editor wants to encourage readers to start at the beginning of the magazine. Too many readers already seem inclined to start at the back and flip forward.

Whether the magazine is a self-cover or whether it wraps itself in a separate, heavy-stock, four-page signature makes a difference in the editor's plans. If the magazine is a self-cover, the editor might want to consider the back cover as just another page, as in a tabloid. An article on previous pages could carry over onto the back cover. But if it is built of firmer stock, the back cover should be a self-contained unit or at least part of a unit that is separate from the interior of the magazine. Whether the magazine is a self-mailer with a part of the back cover reserved for addressing affects the editor's plans, too.

Here are some ways in which editors with separate-stock covers—and with self-covers, too—can solve their back-cover problems.:

1. Choose horizontal art and wrap it around the spine. But make sure the art divides itself logically into two sections. The art on the back need not stretch all the way across the page.

2. Flop the front-cover art so that it reads right-to-left on the back.

3. Repeat the front-cover art, but without the logo. A variation of this has been tried by *Items,* published by the Federal Reserve Bank of Dallas. The back cover repeats the front-cover photo, but slightly cropped and in a smaller size, and includes a caption for the photo.

4. If the waste doesn't disturb you, leave the back cover blank. Or pick up one of the front cover colors and spread it across the back page.

5. Use a different photo or piece of art on the back cover from what you use on the front cover. *Reader's Digest* carries this idea to the extreme of using the *only* cover art on the back, reserving the front—or most of it—for a table of contents.

6. Put your table of contents on the back cover, as *Exxon USA* has done.

7. Use public-service material, as from the Advertising Council, National Safety Council, etc. There is enough of it around to give you plenty of variety.

8. Use a company ad designed originally for consumer magazines with a "This is how we're advertising" introduction.

9. Design ads specifically for your readers. Or use material the company might also use for plant posters.

10. Give the page over to cartoons, short humor pieces, poems, or other literary or art creations.

11. Use the page for a one-page feature that differs from features inside the book. A series of personality sketches of interesting employees has worked out well for some publications. The format should be somewhat standardized, but within that standardization is room for some variety: the title can go across the top or at the side; the art can be big or little, in a rectangular shape or in silhouette; sometimes you can go to two columns, sometimes three. But you would strive for consistency from issue to issue if only by retaining the same family of typefaces.

One of the interesting cover ideas of the past was developed by *Mad* in 1960. The day after the elections the newsstand browser was surprised to see a picture of John Kennedy, the newly elected President, and a congratulatory message. How could the magazine's production allow such planning? It was to be a close election. The answer lay with the back cover. There the reader found a picture of Nixon, with the same congratulatory message. All the dealer needed to do, it turned out, was to make sure the right cover was facing up when the magazine went on display after the election.

For its back cover, *Soldiers,* not bothered by advertising, promotes one of its inside features. Under this arrangement, both the front and back covers can be used to get the reader inside. Both covers for *Soliders* appear in full color.

Suggested further reading

Buechner, Thomas, *Norman Rockwell: Artist and Illustrator,* Harry N. Abrams, Inc., New York, 1970. (All 317 *Saturday Evening Post* covers plus other illustrations are reproduced.)

Finch, Christopher, *Norman Rockwell's 332 Magazine Covers,* Abbeville Press/Random House, New York, 1979.

Lois, George, *The Art of Advertising,* Harry N. Abrams, Inc., New York, 1977. (Some of the 92 covers he did for *Esquire* are included.)

Packer, William, *The Art of Vogue Covers: 1909–1940,* Crown Publishers, New York, 1980.

Pattison, Polly, *How to Design a Nameplate,* Lawrence Ragan Communications, Chicago, 1982.

any amendments to the Federal Election Campaign Act that would change the rules for corporate political activity.

In the political area, there are several paths a small business can take to become involved.

If the company doesn't want to establish its own political action committee (PAC), it can work through an already established and credible group, e.g. the Business-Industry Political Action Committee (BIPAC). A long-established group with high marks for electing pro-business candidates, BIPAC has established a program specifically aimed at small business. In this program, a company's employees are directly solicited for contributions to BIPAC. This relieves the company of the problems of establishing its own PAC, while helping to raise funds for pro-business candidates.

If individuals in the company would like to make contributions to pro-business candidates on an individual basis, there are publications with information to help. The **PAC-Manager,** published monthly by the NAM, places emphasis on political races involving pro-business candidates. Designed to help business-associated PACs keep better informed on candidates, it is also an excellent resource for a private individual.

Another resource small businesses shouldn't miss is state and local trade associations. While larger companies may hire their own staff, small companies can benefit from the manpower and information furnished by the NAM and other associations to which they belong.

It is critical that small companies give input into the decisionmaking process of the country. With minimal staff time, a small business can make its voice heard. ■

GARRY BRUTON,
NAM Public Affairs

WHERE TO GET FEDERAL DIRECTION

ARE YOU AWARE THAT EVERY FEDERAL AGENCY HAS ESTABLISHED GOALS FOR PARTICIPATION BY SMALL BUSINESS IN FEDERAL PROCUREMENT CONTRACTS OVER $10,000? IF YOU'RE NOT, YOU MAY HAVE MISSED SOME OPPORTUNITIES.

Under amendments to the Small Business Act in 1978, every agency is required to award a given percentage of procurement contracts to small business (exact figures are worked out between the agency and the Small Business Administration). Each agency also must establish an office with procurement powers, named the Office of Small and Disadvantaged Business Utilization. The director of such an office is responsible only to the ranking first or second person in the agency.

Today, these offices do exist and it's their responsibility to look after your interests. This includes making an annual report to the SBA on how well the agency has fulfilled its goals for small business participation in government procurement. The report then goes to both the Senate Select Committee on Small Business and the House Committee on Small Business for perusal and evaluation.

Though originally established just for purposes of procurement, these federal offices often assist small businesses with other actions involving their agencies. That's why we think it's worthwhile for you to know the appropriate person to contact in some of the more important agencies. NAM has put together a list of these contacts for your information. For a copy, write NAM publications coordinator, 1776 F St., N.W., Washington, D.C. 20006. Or phone (202) 626-3880. ■

Enterprise

SIZING IT UP

WONDERING WHAT HAPPENED TO THE NEW SIZE STANDARDS DEVELOPED BY THE SMALL BUSINESS ADMINISTRATION? THEY'RE DONE, HAVE BEEN REVISED AND WILL BE READY TO GO PUBLIC, ACCORDING TO THE SBA, AS SOON AS THEY GET THE GO-AHEAD FROM THEIR YET-UNKNOWN ADMINISTRATOR.

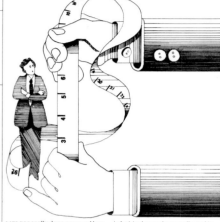

SBA first came out with a new set of size standards in March 1980, but they met with strong public criticism. The criticism took the form of complaints such as failing to take into account such factors as the "absolute size" of a firm and the implications of part-time temporary workers. In total, the SBA received more than 1500 comments on the proposed rules.

The comments have been "studied, reviewed and evaluated and are reflected in a considerable amount of changes" in the standards, said Kal Skeirik, chief of the SBA Size Standards Division. Nothing will be finalized, of course, until a new Reagan appointee to the SBA has given approval. Skeirik noted that the administration has already been briefed on the new size standards and the SBA has recommended the proposed changes should not only be implemented but as quickly as possible. The standards "are an important priority in the administration," Skeirik assured NAM.

SBA size standards originated in 1953 with the establishment of the agency. They were designed to determine which businesses were eligible—in other words, which were categorized as "small business"—to participate in SBA assistance programs. Though there were some revisions of the standards in the '60s, it was not a comprehensive review. Everything was generally done on an ad hoc basis up to now, with each industry lobbying for changes to standards in just its area of concern. The only exception was an across-the-board adjustment for inflation in the mid-'70s affecting only those industries, such as retail, on a dollar-basis eligibility. So new standards will presumably be good news to the nearly 800 industries they affect.

Chief among the new changes in the proposed standards is a conversion of all industries to a number-of-employees classification system. Though manufacturing industries have always adhered to this basis, this is new for retail and service industries. They formerly were categorized by income.

The SBA has also decided it would like to use a one-size standard for eligibility purposes in its assistance programs. In the past, each program—procurement, loans, security bonds, or Small Business Investment Co. funds—warranted its own size standard.

The SBA hopes to get the standards through Congress this spring. First, of course, comes a period of public comment and then a round of House and Senate hearings after the agency has finalized its proposals. NAM will continue to keep you up-to-date on the latest progress. ■

April 1981

NINE: INSIDE PAGES

The reader opens up a magazine and sees a left- and right-hand page together. It is up to you as the designer to arrange these two pages to form a single unit. You must do this and at the same time make each page readable of itself. You must create design within design.

The big problem is the gutter running between the pages of a spread, a psychological as well as a physical barrier. When left and right pages are complete in themselves, the gutter actually helps readers by acting as a separator; but for most spreads, you must build some kind of a graphic bridge to get the reader across.

You can be obvious about it, positioning a piece of art or a heading so that part is on one side of the gutter, part on another. Or you can do it more subtly, repeating on the right-hand page a style of art, a pattern, or a color from the left-hand page to help the reader make a visual association.

If you choose to run art across the gutter, you should do it at a natural break. If a face or figure is involved, you should not let the gutter split it in two. You should not split any art exactly down the middle, unless you want it to stretch all the way across the spread and bleed left and right. In most cases more of the art should be put on one side of the gutter than on the other.

Unaware of production limitations, you may make the mistake of running art across the gutter at a spot on the signature, or between signatures, where perfect alignment is impossible. It is a good idea to check with the printer to determine where across-the-gutter placement will permit the best production.

When you use a line of display type to bridge the gutter, you should use it in a large size. You should not separate the line between letters; you should separate it between words. You should also leave a little extra space at the point of separation, especially if the magazine is side stapled.

Designing facing pages so they go together is only part of the problem. You also have to arrange the spreads so *they* go together.

Some magazines like to have all pages related. Others are content to unify only those pages used for a specific article; the collection of article units making up a single issue can represent any number of design approaches.

As you unite your spreads, you may well think of yourself as performing a function similar to that of the *motion picture art director*. In fact a background in motion picture work would not be a bad preparation for a magazine art director. Asger Jerrild got his experience at Warner Brothers before he took over as art director of *The Saturday Evening Post*.

You can achieve a continuity for each spread by staying with the same typefaces and the same kind of art and by positioning

(Opposite page)
You see here two pages from an "On the Move" section of *Enterprise,* a monthly publication of the National Association of Manufacturers. The special section, printed in dark green ink on cream colored stock, deals in news and features about small and medium-size businesses. This spread shows the ending of one feature and two additional features with all-cap headlines and blurbs. The type throughout is slab serif, the columns are unjustified, and the bottom of the columns do not line up. The line drawings by Kim Johnson employ a consistent style for a highly unified look. Dean Gardei was art director.

This is the start of four-page article in *Sohio* on how Hollywood depicts business people (you've already seen the cover of the issue that carried the article). The title is reminiscent of the 1930s, an important decade for Hollywood. The spread puts silhouettes together with art from the cover and a rectangular photograph. The captions and title blurb are in the same boldface type. *Sohio* is published by The Standard Oil Company of Ohio.

A good way of tying two pages together is to run a photograph large enough to cover the pages completely and then to either surprint or reverse your type, both title and text. You have to be careful, of course, to pick a photograph that has the right amount of neutral area where the type can go and one that would not be bothered by a gutter running down the middle. The usual solution is to pick a scenic shot, but you can do the job as well with an informal portrait, as *Profile* does here for this article beginning. The article focuses on an individual, so that the art is appropriate, and it needs no caption. Notice that the art actually cradles the copy block. *Profile* is published monthly for employees of the Exxon Company, U.S.A., Houston.

these consistently on the pages. You can also set up a series of horizontal visual axes and relate each spread to them.

The opening spread

You achieve your most dramatic display when you use an entire spread—a left- and right-hand page facing one another—to open an article or story.

Sometimes it is necessary to start an article on a right-hand page. If the left-hand page is an ad, you will have an easy enough time of it making the opening look different from the advertisement so the two will not be read together. If the left-hand page is the ending of a previous article, you should keep art off that page, so that it will not compete with the new opening page.

To induce the reader to turn the page you should direct the thrust of the page to the right. You might want a slug saying "Continued" at the bottom of the page.

The two-openings spread

Sometimes it is necessary to run two article openers on one spread. The article on the left page is a one-pager. A new article begins on the right-hand page. Both articles contain illustrations. How do you keep them separated visually?

Some possibilities:

1. You run a wider-than-usual river of white between the two. You can, of course, separate them horizontally rather than vertically, running one across the top of the two pages, the other across the bottom.

2. If you separate the articles vertically, keeping one on the left-hand page and the other on the right-, you can hold the illustrations for the one on the right until later in the article.

3. You can make the heading of one article bigger than the other.

4. You can put one in a box or run a tint block over it.

5. You can set the articles in different types or set one in two-column format, the other in three-column format.

6. You can establish an optical gap by using and positioning artwork for both articles that pulls the reader to the outside edges.

When one of the articles or openers is to occupy more space than the other, you will want to make a special effort to close the gap at the gutter and establish a new gap between the articles. In addition to the devices already described for separating articles, you can use a rule or bar to separate the articles.

When you have to display *more* than two articles on a spread, especially when they are illustrated, you almost have to use boxes or ruled lines.

Magazines in Canada face the problem of presenting side-by-side columns of type in different languages. Unfortunately for the designer, type set in one language takes more space than type set in another. *Spargo,* published by Teleglobe Canada, Montreal, solves the problem by having the type in one language set wider than the type in the other. The columns in English come out in a 17-pica width; the columns in French in a 20-pica width.

Coming up with the right titles

The title of an article affects its design and the choice of art. Title and art must work in harmony.

A single issue of a magazine should offer a variety of title styles. Not all the titles should be phrased as questions, for instance. Some of the best titles are takeoffs on popular song, movie, or book titles or advertising slogans, or they comprise clichés and give them a surprising twist.

A good title often appears to be controversial. Only when readers get into the piece do they see that the idea advanced in big type makes sense after all.

Often a superlative is what's needed. The title promises that the

Four of the many interior logos used by *Boys' Life* to mark special sections or columns in the magazine. These go above whatever title or byline the features carry for that month. The depth changes a bit, but the width and basic format remains the same. In each case a bigger rounded rectangle with illustration sits atop a smaller rounded rectangle with type. The stencil type duplicates the stencil-type logo on the cover. Larry Ortino is the designer. *Boys' Life* is published by the Boy Scouts of America.

Final two pages of a six-page article in *San Francisco* on busing of school children. Art director Dan Marr uses Earl Thollander's line sketches—ten of them—throughout to tie the pages together and, of course, to make them visually alive. Drawings can be a refreshing change in a magazine, even for articles that seem to call for photographs.

design, *Regardless*, had won two races overall. Then the sea turned murderous, 15 racers died, six Holland boats lost carbon-fiber rudders, and Holland almost saw the bottom blow out of his life.

Holland's first office in Ireland was in a manor house on an ancient estate of several hundred acres, bordered on one River. The estate has become a compound for H His right-hand man, Butch Dalrymple-Smith, Drake's Pool, where Sir Francis hid from a pursui

Below is the ancient house in Currabinny that Laurel Holland is rebuilding one room at a time. The office is but a few paces away. Said Holland about the priorities in his life, "I don't have a living room, but I have a damn nice office. That's the priority in my life." That may be true, but the living

room is in better shape than when they bought the house; then there was a river running through it. That successfully dammed, there is now a set of killer drums, which the former drummer from Down Under beats to escape from the world constantly beating on his door. Left, two Irish draftsmen, Peter Sheehan and Pat Lynch, turn Holland's ideas into lines.

article deals with something or someone who is biggest, smallest, fastest, strongest, best, oddest—whatever. It might take accompanying abstract art to set the stage. What shape or texture, what medium of art, then, says "big," "small," etc.? Perhaps the concept can be covered with type choices and arrangements alone.

Another good title approach is to pit one word against its opposite. "The High Cost of Low _____ ." "Good News About Bad _____ ." "Tough Guys and Tender _____ ." "The Long Road to Short _____ ."

A bit of alliteration—but only a bit—helps some titles. Or some rhyme may be what a title needs. Every title benefits from rhythm. It is the designer's job to arrange the lines to take advantage of the rhythm.

As an editor you may want to let available art—photographs submitted by the author, for instance—dictate the approach you take with the title.

But words in a title must be selected with great precision. Pruning a title to make it fit can change its meaning. "Has Busing Worked?" suggests to the reader something quite different from "Has Busing Really Worked?"

When the title is accompanied by a blurb, the blurb should add a dimension; it should not merely restate the title at greater length. Blurbs can go above or below main titles in a face a smaller than what is used for main titles. They should be longer than titles—they can go on for several sentences—to provide some contrast. You can consider a blurb as a half-way step from the big type of the title to the small type of the body copy.

Varying the design approach

While you want the pages to work together, you also want to introduce some variety to keep readers interested. If you can't get them to take in the whole article, at least you can get them to read the title, look at the art, and read the captions and blurbs. Many magazines now don't let a spread go by without at least offering one blurb. A few magazines have tried running subsidiary features as part of the main features. For instance, *The Atlantic*, for an Arthur Hoppe article on tennis, showed a cartoon drawing on the spread following the opener. It was the first of a series of cartoons, one to a spread, until the article was over. As a reader you were caught up in the cartoon story, which was related to the theme of the article. You saw first a group of startled people at a tennis club. They had been drinking and relaxing. You saw the same group on the next spread, still drinking but puzzled. And you saw them again on the next spread. In the final cartoon a serious-minded player, now in the room, asked, "Tennis, anyone?" The people in the club were all dressed the part. They were even holding rackets (as well as drinks). But it was obvious they were there to socialize, not to play tennis. Into the spirit of the thing the reader presumably would turn back and get into Hoppe's prose.

Dealing with magazine editorials

We think of editorials as appearing only in newspapers. But magazines carry them, too. A magazine like *The New Republic* carries several of them at the beginning of each issue, before the articles.

(Opposite page)
Nautical Quarterly uses a unique approach to captions on this page. The caption for the large, partially silhouetted photograph starts with the large "B." The caption for the smaller photograph starts low in the second column with "Left, two Irish draftsmen. . . ."

How to sing your own song

Rev. Bill Little

The Rev. Bill L. Little is a minister, author, counselor, consultant, teacher, graduate student and family man. He counsels professional baseball players, cancer patients, ranking military officers, business executives, housewives, students, his church's parishioners, and listeners to his regular family radio program on the number one station in St. Louis.

Bill, as he prefers to be called, puts in his 19-hour days with a pace that would seem to exhaust Bruce Jenner.

What follows are highlights from a recent free-wheeling interview with Bill. As we spoke, his four-inch stack of telephone call slips mounted higher on his desk. As usual, however, Bill kept his cool and his mind on his goal at the moment: sharing some simple but eloquent truths with us in his special way. — W. G.

About living...

One of the things that I have learned in the last few years that has been very exciting to me about health is that there is only one valid reason for living.

The only reason for living is because you *want* to.

It's a love for life. There are three reasons people would like to live. One of them is fear of dying, one of them is a sense of obligation to others and the third one is that they just love to live and they want to sing their own song.

If you could look down into your body's immune system and the immune system looks back at you and your body's disease as you start getting sick, it may say, "Why do you want to defeat this?" And you say, "Because I'm afraid to die."

The immune system, in essence, says, "Big deal." So, in fact, fear is stress or stress-producing and retards our body's protection system. So, people who are fighting for their lives because they are afraid to die are really adding to their sickness.

The same thing is true of obligation and responsibility. You look in there and the immune system could say, "Why do you want to live?" And you say, "Because I

have obligations and responsibilities." The immune system says, "I'm sorry, I don't feel up to that."

I work with cancer patients a lot. The people who do best in cancer treatment are people who really love to live and just will not quit. They are not living because they are afraid to die. They are not living because they feel they have a responsibility to their family, though some of them say that. But the person who says, "I just like to live"...that person has a better than 50 percent chance of making it longer than the other people because that's a *good* reason to live.

That's the key. That you want so much of life that it frees you from intimidation, and it frees you from the stress that usually goes on around you.

Some people respond very well under a lot of pressure and stress and other people start to make bad decisions, use poor judgement, and become accident-prone under the same amount of stress or less. But one of the things that creates stress is not having joy in what you do.

You are not going to enjoy what you're doing if you don't fit with your job. It's going to be very difficult for you. That in turn generates disease. That makes people sick. It retards the immunization system. The body becomes more susceptible to disease.

About balance...

A healthy self-concept, if you're going to have one, must be balanced with a healthy concept of others. If you're going to spend time dealing with yourself you must balance that by dealing with other people as well. Balance is one of the keys.

You have to balance dependence and independence, balance thinking and acting, balance theorizing and practicality, you have to balance individualizing and socializing. Each person has to find his own balance.

On communicating with family...

By sitting down and talking with your family, it really saves time. You can have a family problem that takes 15 minutes to work out and hassle about it, instead, for 15 hours. Or, if you want to save time, you can sit down and discuss these things once or twice or three times a week with your family. You get input from other family members and you include them in the decision-making process. You include them in planning, you distribute responsibility during that time and then there is no more hassle.

We would save ourselves a lot of time if we would spend just 30 minutes three times a week talking with our families. We would also

save a lot of money in terms of divorce and sickness. We might save our families.

I talk to people who say, "I don't have time to spend an hour talking." I say, "How much time do you spend arguing with your wife or husband or your children about what you hadn't worked out with them before?" People may spend 10 minutes six times a day, five days a week doing that. And it adds up to about five to ten hours per week. You can do away with that. If you spend an hour you save nine. It's a good investment.

Even when they are communicating about problems, family members will also be wise to communicate about plans for pleasure outings and other things they can do together as a family...talking about old times and good times they have had in the past. If you only talk with your family when you have problems to work on, the focus of family life becomes a problem. So even in problem solving sessions I recommend that people spend part of that time discussing good things.

I wish I could convince this population to spend an hour twice a week or even once a week just sitting down with family members. I bet the divorce rate would go down by 40-50 percent right away. Just an hour. The average family spends about 15 minutes together seriously talking a week.

How many families do you know that even sit down together at dinner and talk? How many people sit down together without the TV going? How many people even talk to each other in the car, ride in the same car? We've gotten to the place where we are going in different directions from the time we get up in the morning till we come in at night. And we come in at different hours.

On goal-setting...

I happen to be a person who believes very strongly in setting goals. I don't believe that every person has to set them in exactly the same way. Some of us can set long range, general goals and really be motivated and pulled toward that in a sort of ideological way. I operate like that. That means I can live with a lot of ambiguity and confusion right now if I can see the eventual goal.

There are some people who function a lot better if the goal is closer to them. They look to have everything neat and ordered to get to that goal. But everyone functions better if they have some sense of direction and purpose. There are many people who have a gut feeling that short-term goals are important and their goal is to live.

to live fully *each* day. That's the way I look at things. I say let's plan as if we are going to live forever and live as if we are going to die today.

I have as my purpose to live my life to its fullest and to be as fully me as I can in a way that's consistent with everything else that I believe about God, about human beings, about the world, about relationships.

On Imagining

If you practice imagining a sickness long enough, you can induce real symptoms. One guy I talked about had convinced himself that his normal body temperature was 96.6. Every time he checked out with 98.6 he believed he had a fever of two degrees. He said, my gosh, when his body temperature went up to 101.6. He thought he was near death, burning up with fever, and nearly delirious because he had convinced himself that his normal was 96.6. Now there is a guy who created a symptom for himself.

About acceptance...

How do you feel when other people are doing things for you? There are a lot of us who do not mind at all doing things for other people, but we get as uncomfortable as hell when somebody else is doing something for us. If we are doing that, we're condescending. We have to be in a position of power. Let me hand it down to you, let me give you advice, but don't you give me any.

I think one of the hardest lessons I've had to learn in my whole life was how gracefully to accept advice and things from other people. I can give it and I thought I was doing it gracefully, but I never could give gracefully until I could receive it gracefully.

One of the things I have said on the air frequently is that when someone loves you, they want to give to you and it's alright to accept from someone like that. As a matter of fact, when I love someone I never feel more given to than when they take from me. When they accept they are really expressing love. I have to remember the same thing. It's easier for me to give than it is for me to receive. Receiving helps me keep balance in my life.

Ralston Purina Magazine **devoted one issue to a special report "dedicated to personal well-being." This spread of two oversize (11 × 15 1/2) pages deals with "An Expert's Suggestions on How to Sing Your Own Song." Solid blue and red blocks and initial letters help organize the materials into easy, boldface takes.**

U.S. News & World Report carries an editorial at the end. The general-circulation weeklies used to carry editorial pages about a third of the way into the publication.

A trade journal is likely to give an early page up front to an editorial and let the editor sign it. (Newspaper editorials are almost always unsigned.) A company magazine often carries as its "editorial" a letter from the president, along with a mug shot. The signing might better be done in type rather than in handwriting.

But the editorial, because it represents pure opinion, should be made to look different from anything else in the magazine. One way to set it apart is to present it in one wide column, heavily leaded, with extra white space on either side. The format should allow for a different length each time. An editorial writer should not be made to write to fit.

There is no reason why a magazine can't dress up its editorial or editorial page with an editorial cartoon, either drawn especially for the magazine or selected as a reprint from a newspaper or syndicate.

Man cannot live by bread alone...or carrots, peanut butter or even ice cream. Although a balanced diet is vital to good health, other factors are important, too, such as heredity, lifestyle, personality, mental attitude and environment. But good eating habits can improve your overall well-being.

Since the 1940's the United States has been trying to create a national nutrition policy. Yet after 40 years scientists are still investigating some areas.

Following are some basic recommendations which have been compiled from several sets of nutrition guidelines issued since 1980.

Eat a variety of foods

About 40 different nutrients are needed for good health. These include vitamins and minerals, amino acids, essential fatty acids and sources of energy.

Although most foods contain more than one nutrient, no single food item contains all the essential nutrients in the amounts that you need. Therefore, you should eat a variety of foods to assure an adequate diet.

Maintain ideal weight

Obesity is linked with high blood pressure, increased levels of fats and cholesterol in the blood and diabetes. These disorders are believed to be associated with increased risks of heart attacks and strokes.

It's hard to say why some people can eat more than others and still keep within their normal weight. But one thing is certain: to lose unwanted pounds you must burn more calories than you consume.

This means you should eat less, exercise more or both. One way to eat less is to change your approach to eating. Instead of gobbling and gulping, eat slowly, chewing each mouthful thoroughly. Keep your mouth empty after each bite to talk, then sit to take your time.

If you need to lose weight, do so gradually. A steady loss of one to two pounds a week is relatively safe and more likely to be maintained. It takes time to change your eating and exercise habits. Crash diets can be dangerous and usually fail in the long run.

Since a pound of body fat contains 3,500 calories, it is possible to lose one pound a week if you decrease your daily intake to 500 calories less than you require or increase activity to burn an additional 500 calories. Do not cut your food intake so low that it is impossible to get the nutrients you need.

Avoid too much fat, saturated fat and cholesterol

Much controversy surrounds this guideline. One guideline recommends that all persons reduce their intake of total fat, cholesterol and saturated fat. But other researchers suggest that only those people with major risk factors (such as diabetes or elevated blood pressure) monitor their intake. These scientists feel that there is no evidence strong enough to recommend that these restrictions be followed by all healthy adults.

To control your consumption of fat, saturated fat and cholesterol:
• Choose lean meat, fish, poultry, beans and peas for protein.
• Moderate your use of eggs and organ meats (such as liver).
• Limit intake of butter, cream, shortening, coconut oil and foods made from these products.
• Trim excess fats off meats.
• Broil, bake or boil rather than fry.
• Read labels carefully to determine amount and types of fat in foods.

Carbohydrates and fats are the major souces of energy in U.S. diets. So if you cut back on fats you should increase your carbohydrates to supply enough energy for your body's needs.

Carbohydrates contain less than half the number of calories per ounce than fats. Although simple carbohydrates as sugars provide calories for energy, they have few nutrients. Therefore, it is better to eat complex carbohydrates. These include beans, peas, nuts, seeds, fruits and vegetables, whole grain breads and cereals.

Increasing consumption of certain carbohydrates also can increase fiber in the diet. This tends to reduce symptoms of chronic constipation and irritable bowel.

Avoid too much sugar

Here again, researchers disagree. Many feel that most people do not need to reduce their sugar intake. The major health hazard from eating too much sugar is tooth decay. This risk of cavities is not just a matter of how much sugar you eat, but how often you eat it.

The risk increases if you eat sweets between meals and if you eat foods that stick to your teeth. Cutting down on sugar means eating less of all kinds, including white sugar, brown sugar, raw sugar, honey and syrups.

Avoid too much sodium

Although sodium is commonly associated with salt, it can be found in many other sources. Sodium is present in many foods and drinks such as condiments, sauces, pickled foods, sandwich meats and soft drinks. Baking soda, baking powder, monosodium glutamate and some medications contain sodium.

People with high blood pressure should be especially aware of the amount of sodium in their diets. About 17 percent of American adults have high blood pressure.

Americans tend to eat more sodium than they need but by using less table salt and eating sparingly of food with large amounts of sodium, they can reduce their intake.

Limit alcohol

Alcoholic beverages tend to be high in calories and low in nutrients. This makes it hard for people to drink a lot and lose or just maintain their weight and still get the nutrients they need.

Heavy drinkers may lose their appetite for certain foods with essential nutrients. Vitamin and mineral deficiencies, therefore, occur commonly in heavy drinkers. They also occur because alcohol alters the absorption and use of some essential nutrients.

Greek Tuna Salad
1½ quarts torn salad greens washed and drained
2 cucumbers, peeled and sliced
6 green onions, thinly sliced
Salt and pepper
⅓ cup olive oil
3 tablespoons lemon juice
13 ounces CHICKEN OF THE SEA solid white (albacore) tuna, drained
8 radishes, cleaned
3 tomatoes, quartered
16 pitted ripe olives
½ pound feta cheese, crumbled

In a salad bowl, combine greens, cucumbers and onions. Season to taste with salt and pepper. Combine oil and lemon juice; pour on just enough to coat greens. Break up tuna slightly. Arrange it, along with remaining ingredients, over top of salad. Toss just before serving.

Makes 6-8 servings.

Mushroom Chicken Bouillon
Light on the waistline

4 cups water
4 chicken bouillon cubes
½ teaspoon onion powder
Dash white pepper
½ pound COUNTRY STAND Fresh Mushrooms, cleaned and sliced
2 teaspoons chopped celery leaves

In large saucepan heat water, bouillon, onion powder and pepper until bouillon cubes dissolve. Stir in mushrooms and celery leaves. Heat to boiling. Reduce heat. Cover and simmer about 10 minutes or until mushrooms are tender.

Makes 4-5 servings.
(16 calories per cup)

Separating editorial matter from ads

Cortland Gray Smith, as editor of *Better Editing,* drew up a list of rules for separating editorial matter from advertising. Among them:

1. Make editorial matter look "as different as possible from the usual advertising pattern." Editorial usually has a quieter look.

This "EAT RIGHT" spread from the same issue, with bold splashes of red and blue artwork and with copy wrapping around some of the art, ends with some healthful recipes. Note that the title is buried partway down on the page. It is bold enough to take such treatment.

"Currents," a collection of short items, appears in the back of the 10 × 14 *Inside,* **the monthly magapaper for employees of Southern Company Services, Inc., Atlanta. The band running across both pages with the reverse title reminds readers what section they are dealing with (this spread is a carryover from a previous page). To further aid readers, the subheads are repeated at the tops of columns when appropriate, but in smaller type.**

Ordinarily you would avoid letters that run up and down, like "CHINATOWN," but the setup works well here because Chinese characters do run that way, and this highly organized and crowded page of rectangles makes such handling appropriate. The page uses three colors, with just a bit of the white paper showing. From *The Berkeley Monthly.* Michael Grossman, design director; Benjamin Ailes, photographer.

2. Adopt an editorial look or pattern that is *consistent* in its use of type styles and spacing. What Smith is saying, essentially, is that the formalized, highly ordered magazine has an easier time separating editorial from advertising than the more circuslike magazine.

3. Allow an extra measure of white space between editorial and advertising.

4. Concentrate ads *between* editorial features, not *within* them. He's asking here that the art director, representing the editorial department, work with the business and advertising department to establish a better lineup of page allocations.

Much has been written about how placement of an ad affects readership; and some advertisers pay premium rates for op-ed placement, "Campbell Soup" position, up-front placement, and so on. Recent studies tend to show that placement has less effect than was originally supposed. Ads do not necessarily have to be next to "reading matter." Editors have been moving away from the practice of continuing articles and stories in the back of the book so they will trail through ads. Perhaps eventually they will bunch the ads completely in one section of the book so that art directors can arrange editorial material into a unified whole.

Dealing with specially shaped ads

Some magazines offer advertisers space shapes other than rectangles, making life more complicated for their art directors. The ads may come into the magazine in stair-step or checkerboard arrangements. One part of an ad may be designed to appear on one side of a page, the other part to appear across the page. *Redbook,* for instance, allows Doral II to dominate a two-page spread with an across-the-gutter ad that features extended art breaking out of a rectangle, similar to what you see in the following rough sketch. The magazine even wraps editorial matter around the hands that dramatizes ". . . this much taste."

Such service to advertisers puts the magazine art director into collaboration with the magazine's advertising department, a position some art directors find uncomfortable. Ordinarily, magazine art directors (and editors) work with advertising departments only to the extent of making sure that an article with a strong theme does not appear next to advertising that makes an opposing point. For instance, an anti-smoking article would not be adjacent to a cigarette ad. It is true, though, that any magazine accepting advertising finds places for ads first and then asks the art director to weave articles and stories around them. Ad space is contracted for in advance; editorial material can more easily be manipulated at the last minute. But in most cases the editorial space left for the art director is in blocks or full pages that can be designed independently of advertising.

Some would criticize a policy that allows a Doral II ad to so completely dominate a spread. The feeling might be that with the copy block so faithfully tracing the contours of the ad, the reader is being forced to read it. On the other hand it could be argued that the ad breaks up the editorial matter into pleasant takes: a fairly long column at the left followed by four short columns, then a long column broken into two parts. Were all those sections put end to end on a page solid with copy, the reader might feel intimidated.

Of course the design of each ad, whatever its shape, is left to the advertiser and its agency. Only with small magazines catering to small advertisers who don't have agencies do magazine art directors become involved in advertising design. For magazines and most other print media, editorial art directors, like editors, separate themselves from the advertising departments of their publications.

Products pages

Some magazines put together products pages, which are a sort of a hybrid: part editorial matter, part advertising. The editor and art director work from press releases and photos supplied by manufacturers. For each item you have a headline, some description, and usually some art. Or maybe you just have a photograph and caption. A tag line invites the reader to circle a number on a "Reader Service Card" and send it in for further information.

The designing of these sections—and the cards, which are bound into the magazine—can tax the art director, because the items are short and numerous, while the art is uneven in quality.

One way to handle product pages is to run them with four or five columns instead of the usual three. You can get more on a page that way—narrow columns allow for smaller body type—and you don't have to run pictures so big.

The case for departmentalizing

Routine stories—of deaths, job changes, etc.—should be gathered under collective headings. This makes the design job much easier. It also makes related items easy for the reader to identify.

An obit column with a single heading makes unnecessary an editor's hunt for synonyms for death. The subheadings over each item can simply name the person.

On the letters-to-the-editor column it is not necessary to start each letter with "Dear Editor" or "To the Editor." The salutation is understood. Letters should be grouped by subject. Nor does each letter need a subheading. A new subheading is necessary only when the subject changes. Usually a group of letters respond to a particular article, agreeing with it or arguing with it. Author response to the criticism can be run in italics after each group.

You can add interest to letters columns by supplying illustrative cartoons occasionally, or by taking sample quotes from letters and

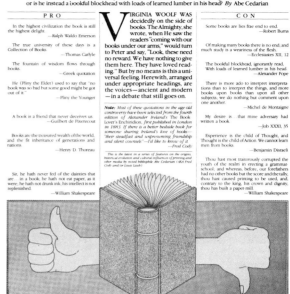

In this back-of-the-book feature, *The Berkeley Monthly* centers everything: kicker, title, blurb, introductory copy, author's note, and art. The line art makes use of two different Zipatone patterns. Michael Grossman, design director; Suzanne Anderson, designer/illustrator.

In this single-page feature, *Jordan,* the quarterly published by the Jordan Information Bureau, Washington, D.C. uses white space effectively to unify the title, art, and copy. The white space stays in two places, essentially: at the top and at the lower right.

One of the best-read sections of a company magazine is the section dealing with job changes and other personnel matters. Names appear frequently in bold face, so they will stand out, and mug shots decorate the page. It is a problem, sometimes, to gather the information. Some departments or plants cooperate with the editor, some don't. This is one answer: running a special box on the page. It does have the disadvantage of making people who appear on the page look like publicity seekers.

"Nutritional Terms. Easily Digested," is a sometimes feature in _The Body Forum_. The art carrying the feature's title juts out from the box containing the definitions. As a visual pun and to dramatize the "Digested" in the title of the feature, an artist does a little retouching on an ordinary photograph of a book.

playing them up in display type—one for each page or column of letters. The type for this display can be simulated typewriter type. You can also occasionally show a small reproduction of a letter as written, as when you receive a cute note from a semi-literate youngster.

You probably would want to run a box or legend at the end of the column giving the magazine's address and explaining the policy of editing and publishing letters.

At one or two spots inside the magazine you might want to run a smaller version of the cover logo: on the table of contents page and, if you have a number of advertising pages intervening before you get to your article section, at the head of the opening article. How well a cover logo will take reduction should be a consideration in its design.

You do researchers a favor when you keep the name of your magazine consistent. A number of magazines, unfortunately, use a term like "Weekly" or "Monthly" on the cover but drop it when the magazine is named inside on the table of contents page and in the masthead. You also do researchers—and readers—a favor when on each spread you name the magazine in a folio line and include the date and page number.

Interior logos

Editors tend to think of their material as falling into two categories: special departments or columns and articles or features. One of the jobs of the art director is to segregate the two. The special departments or columns appear either early or late in the publication, and standing heads mark them. Ideally, these heads share a design approach that ties them to the logo on the cover. We call them _interior logos_. Some magazines manage with type alone; others incorporate art. Like regular logos, interior logos work best with a flat, almost abstract look that over the months does not grow tiresome. And they must be kept small—smaller, certainly, than the logo on the cover.

They often incorporate bylines and mug shots of the writers and a bit of art that tells what the writing deals with.

NUTRITIONAL TERMS. EASILY DIGESTED.

Metabolism — A number of separate processes are always taking place for different purposes within the human body. Protoplasm or cell material, for example, has to be built up and broken down, and energy must be provided within the body for the vital functions. The total, or sum of all the processes by which the body functions is called metabolism.

Behavior Modification—Although this is a psychological term, it relates directly to nutrition and diet through eating habits. Genetic structure, past learning experiences, and present situations combine to produce the behavior of a person. Behavior modification works on the theory that we learn and follow behaviors because they

are of positive benefit to us. Overeating, for instance, gives some people more benefits than drawbacks even though they may be test being overweight. Behavior modification attempts to influence behavior by changing our learning patterns. We find that new behaviors have more rewards than the old behaviors, thus the behavior, buying two pounds of chocolate chip cookies, for instance, changes.

Chelate—This is a combination of a metal, such as zinc, for example, and an amino acid. Certain types of chelates may be absorbed very readily by the body, while others are so completely tied up by the chelating agent that no absorption is possible.

Carbohydrate — Carbohydrates, compounds of carbon, hydrogen and oxygen, are found in

sugars, starches and celluloses. Carbohydrates are the nucleus of many current debates regarding proper diet.

Endocrinology— This is the science that studies how the endocrine glands (such as thyroid or pituitary) produce secretions that are carried throughout the body via the bloodstream.

Glucose — Produced mainly by carbohydrates consumed in a diet, glucose is a primary source of energy for humans and other animals. It is a syrupy liquid that travels through the bloodstream to all parts of the body in need of energy.

Glycogen — The principal type of carbohydrate that is stored in humans and converted to glucose as needed is glycogen. It is usually found in the liver—its primary place of origin—and to some degree in the muscles.

Hypoglycemia— One of the big question marks in current dieting studies revolves around hypoglycemia, a disease characterized by an abnormally low amount of glucose in the blood. Among the numerous symptoms are tremulousness and headache. The degree of glucose insufficiency, and its effects on human feelings and behavior at various levels, is the center of the question.

Transfollicular Percutaneous Absorption—Refers to the process by which a substance applied to the skin passes down a hair follicle and into the bloodstream. By using the follicle as an entrance, and crossing into the bloodstream at the hair root, the substance can bypass the normal impenetrability of the skin. This is thought to be a possible route of access for Keratin protein into the body.

20

CZ's Clallam Managed Forest, the company's second largest Northwest timber holding

Near the top of the peninsula is CZ's Clallam Managed Forest, at 90,000 acres the company's second largest Pacific Northwest timber holding and an economic mainstay of the Sekiu-Neah Bay region. Here at the Makah Indian Reservation fishing village of Neah Bay, only a couple of miles from the most northwesterly point on the United States mainland, is CZ's Neah Bay Boom, where Clallam logs begin a voyage inland to the company's Port Angeles and Port Townsend pulp and paper mills and other regional markets along the beautiful Strait of Juan de Fuca waterway.

ENTERING MAKAH INDIAN RESERVATION THE NORTHWEST TIP OF THE CONTINENTAL UNITED STATES

The logs reach Neah Bay by truck over the company's 285-mile network of logging roads through the Clallam Managed Forest, the huge western hemlock and other native species rumbling in from the sorting yard on three-trailer "mule trains."

Lifted, lowered, and maneuvered . . .

Here they are carefully lifted from the trucks by a crane capable of hoisting up to 60 tons and then gently lowered into the water, where agile, snorting little boom boats maneuver them into selected areas for temporary storage. Then they are cabled together in large tow rafts, or booms, to be towed up the choppy strait by tugboats. CZ installed the boom in 1945 to achieve more efficient, lower cost log transportation by utilizing the strait's natural waterway to reduce highway truck travel.

Staff of nine men

The Neah Bay Boom staff consists of a nine-man crew. They work mostly in cold, usually wet and often windy conditions, but they're little concerned about the climate.

"We work every day regardless,"

"We work every day, regardless," said Fred Norman, boom foreman, one hand firmly gripping the bill of his hardhat to keep it from being blown off by a chill wind whipping in from the Pacific. "That is, except when one of our winter storms sends waves over the dike and raises all kinds of trouble with our boat operators. She does get rough, plenty rough, sometimes."

The only visitors, besides the truck drivers, are the seagulls that circle almost continually overhead. For the seeker of solitude, this is the place.

Jim McLean, whose "straw boss" job title seems perfectly suited to his tough, stocky, football lineman build, has 20 years-plus of continual Neah Bay Boom service under his water safety belt.

Bill Mahone

Don Haltom   Dean Francis   Bill Mahone

21

Coming up with column names

You give your imagination a brisk workout as you try to come up with names for your standing columns. What you settle for is important when you consider that you will be using the names for months, maybe years.

Some magazines use no-nonsense names, like "Letters" for the letters-to-the-editor column, and that may be the safer course. But other magazines are more inventive. *Trans-action,* before it changed its own name, came up with "Feedback from Our Readers," which was appropriate for its social scientist readers. *Essence,* the high-fashion magazine for black women, for a time called its letters column "Write On!" *Campus Life* called its letters column "Assault & Flattery." Sears and Roebuck calls its letters column in *Pacific Coaster* "Seariously Speaking."

JAMA, the Journal of the American Medical Association, used "AMAgrams" for its column of short news items: "AMA" for the American Medical Association; "gram[s]" from a Greek word meaning "written." The art put each letter in a block, and the blocks were slightly scattered to represent blocks used in the game of anagrams. *Fitness for Living* headed its column of short news items on fitness with "All the News That's Fit," a takeoff on the slogan of the New York *Times. Tennis USA* has used "Net Results" for a column of match scores.

The title for a record column in *Senior Scholastic* was "DIS-Cussions." The all-cap beginning was art enough. The title for a record column in *Harper's* was "Music in the Round." *Oak Leaves,* Oak Park, Illinois, called its birth announcement column "Hello World." (A good title, but it needed a comma after "Hello.")

National Review for years has put a "RIP" over its obit-editorials and although the acronym is perfectly proper ("Rest in Peace"), it startles the reader somewhat because of a recent meaning "rip" has acquired.

A two-page spread (the article starts on the previous spread) from Crown Zellerbach's first issue of *Northwest.* It combines square-finish and silhouette halftones (all in duotone) with copy and blurbs. The blurbs, set off with thin horizontal rules, are really like subheads, picking up wording from the paragraphs immediately following.

New York

New York Faces Future Shock
By Alvin Toffler

"... Future shock may turn out to be the most devastating urban disease of tomorrow, and millions of New Yorkers are first in line, as usual. The challenge: how to control change ..."

To accommodate the new urban millions, we would have to build a duplicate city for each of the hundreds that already dot the globe. A new New York, Tokyo, London, a new Rome and Rangoon —all in 11 years.

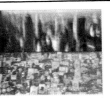

The lead time for adjustment to new discoveries is slashed. The lead time between introduction and peak production of the refrigerator was 34 years, for the electric fry pan eight years, for transistor radios even shorter.

"... It is impossible to understand what is happening to human relationships in America unless we examine their duration ..."

"... Instead of conversations, we send high-speed communiqués and search for all sorts of magic to accelerate friendship ..."

Technology leads to physical objects that are cheaper to throw away than to repair, objects that pass into and out of our lives at a rapid clip. From birth on, our children are in a throwaway culture.

Even our ties with architecture, that part of the environment that has contributed most heavily to man's sense of permanence, are now more short-lived. We tear down neighborhoods at a mind-numbing rate.

New social forms erupt into being—urban communes, free universities, Black Panther-run day nurseries. New movements, each shorter-lived than the last, leap into headlines.

"... To depressurize the city—to moderate tensions between Hard Hat and student, black and white—we must avoid future shock ..."

The main illustration develops right before the reader's eyes spread after spread in this 10-page *New York* article. An accompanying boldface blurb changes position on each two pages as the illustration changes, adding to the feeling of movement. The original is in full color. Like many magazines, *New York* runs a small-size reproduction of its logo at the beginning of the main article in each issue to remind readers after plowing through pages of advertising what magazine they are reading.

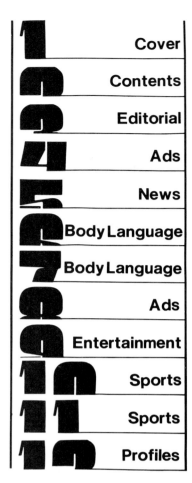

	Cover
	Contents
	Editorial
	Ads
	News
	Body Language
	Body Language
	Ads
	Entertainment
	Sports
	Sports
	Profiles

West Side Story, a lively newsmagazine in tabloid form published by West High School, Iowa City, Iowa, for a time used huge numbers on each page. So, asked its editors, why not capture the flavor of the numbering by using part of the huge numbers in the table of contents run on page 2? This is a sample table, shown in a greatly reduced size.

This is the inside front cover for the 9 × 12 *Teller.* The magazine reproduces its logo and (in a small size) its cover and combines them with a masthead and a table of contents printed in reverse letters on a black background. Note that the editor has really made a real *table* out of the table of contents. The blackness of the page complements a black border around art on the cover.

The table-of-contents page

For many years the table of contents was only an afterthought on American magazines. No longer. Now the table of contents—and the entire table-of-contents page—is a magazine showpiece.

Saul Bass made a high art of motion picture titles and credits. Today many motion pictures run an additional credit line at the beginnings or ends: "Titles by _____ ." Magazines haven't gone that far, but their art directors have given more thought to the table-of-contents page than ever before.

What goes on that page varies from magazine to magazine, but on most magazines, the page includes (1) the table of contents, (2) the listing of staff members, (3) the masthead, and (4) a caption for the cover picture along with a miniature version of the cover. There may also be some copy on the page, as, for example, an editorial, a preface to the issue, a statement from the publisher or editor, or an advertisement.

For some reason *The New Yorker,* alone among major magazines, did not for many years run a table of contents. For that matter it did not—nor does it yet—run bylines, except at the ends of articles and stories. Nor do many of the opening spreads carry art. Perhaps the magazine expected readers to start at the beginning

and read straight through. Perhaps it felt readers didn't have to be lured. Competition from *New York* and a general change in readers' attitudes changed *The New Yorker,* at least to the extent that in the late 1960s it began to carry a regular table of contents.

The table of contents for a magazine lists the titles of articles and stories, the names of authors, and the page numbers where the articles and stories start. If the table is extensive, the editor divides it into sections, like "Articles," "Stories," and "Departments." *The New Yorker* and *Saturday Review* list the full names of cartoonists appearing in each issue—a worthwhile service when you consider the unreadability of most cartoonists' signatures.

For their tables of contents art directors increasingly are taking parts of illustrations inside their magazines and reproducing them with the tables of contents. Some art directors take whole pages or spreads from inside their publications and reduce them way down to put on table of contents pages.

A magazine of fewer than 16 pages probably doesn't need a table of contents. There isn't enough hunting around for the reader to do. Certainly for a small magazine you wouldn't want elaborate treatment or much space devoted to a table of contents.

The masthead

The masthead (not to be confused with the logo) may be too long or too involved to go on the table of contents page. It may go at the bottom or side of some other page (on the back cover of some company magazines). With the masthead often goes a list of staff members.

The listing of staff members should feature the members in the order of their rank and in parallel terminology. It should not, for instance, use "editor" for one staff member and "production" for another. Many magazines find it desirable to list principal staff members in one size type, lesser staff members in another. Editorial staff members are usually run separately from business staff

The reproduced *Ms.* contents page and *Touche Ross Life* spread are shown alongside the following captions:

Many magazines dress their contents pages with sections of art taken from inside the issue. *Ms.* magazine, for its contents page, organizes material under across-the-page headings: Features, Departments, Fiction & Poetry, Reading, and The *Ms.* Gazette. With this kind of an arrangement, listings can vary in length. Columns do not line up at the bottom. (© The Foundation for Education and Communication, 1981. Reprinted with permission.)

The blurb in this spread is set in type almost as big as the title type and is decorated with flag art to make it into a rebus. The article consists of four short pieces, with authors' portraits starting them off. The heavy bars are in green. (Reprinted by permission of *Touche Ross Life,* December 1980; published by Touche Ross & Co.)

A table of contents page (inside front cover) for *Resource,* monthly publication of Crown Zellerbach Corporation, San Francisco, uses gray all over and, for contrast, bright, full colors with white in the art. Thin lines and one thick line help organize the material. Some basic information at the top is centered, to give the page a *formal* look, and the columns of copy are staggered at the bottom, to give the page an *informal* look. This sophisticated design is the product of Sidjakov & Berman & Associates.

A right-hand page has already introduced this article in *Resource.* That's the opening paragraph of copy at the upper left. The article continues on another spread. This spread features one large across-the-gutter full-color photograph in contrast with two small ones. The large photograph carries its caption inside one un-busy corner. Design by Sidjakov & Berman & Associates.

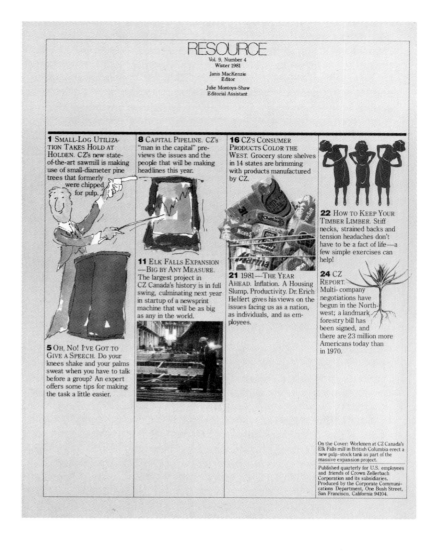

members. On many magazines, the three top editorial staffers are the editor, the managing editor, and the art director. The listing need not be in the form of a table; it can be "run in" to save space.

The masthead should make it easy for the contributor and subscriber to find the correct addresses (editorial offices often have addresses different from circulation offices). It might be a good idea to introduce each address with a boldface line: "If you want to submit a manuscript" for one and "If you want to subscribe to the magazine" for the other. Perhaps a third will be needed: "If you want to place an advertisement." Every editor should take time once each year to rethink the masthead to better organize the material it contains.

The masthead carries basic information about the magazine: date of issue, volume number, frequency of publication, name of publishing firm, editorial and business addresses, information on submitting manuscripts, information on circulation, price per copy, and annual subscription rate. It may also briefly summarize the magazine's history and philosophy.

Set in agate or small type, masthead information is necessary for record-keeping and even legal reasons, but it doesn't have to

THEY SAY THAT THOSE WHO CAN, DO. THOSE WHO CAN'T, TEACH.... BUT AT TOUCHE, THOSE WHO CAN, ALSO TEACH.

Another *Touche Ross Life* spread, with white space wisely concentrated in just a couple of areas. The magapaper resists the urge to crop the "unnecessary" area in the large photograph. The uncropped photograph provides a marvelous sweep from the title and small photographs at the left to the beginning of the article at the right. The second-color horizontal bars are in orange. (Reprinted by permission of *Touche Ross Life,* November 1980; published by Touche Ross & Co.)

"Play Back" is a back-of-the book feature in *Mobil World.* The balloons-in-tintblock format makes the feature stand out from other items on an oversize page. Questions from employees are in boldface, answers in regular-weight type, all sans serif.

be dull. This from the masthead of the tabloid *Uncle Jam,* "the world's best free paper" published in Long Beach, Calif.: "All rights reserved. No portion of *Uncle Jam,* the neat articles, the high quality photos, our handmade ads, nothing, may be reproduced in whole or in part without the written permission of the publishers. So please don't rip us off—we work too hard!"

And just below that: "*Uncle Jam* is published whenever we get enough people in the room to do it, usually TWICE a month by Fragments West. . . . *Uncle Jam* comes from the Sumerian "Un Kell Jom," meaning, you have just stepped on a toad. For advertising rates or a good time call. . . ."

Mad lists its attorney's name in the masthead.

The American Spectator in its masthead briefly traces its origins: "*The American Spectator* was founded in 1924 by George Nathan and Truman Newberry over a cheap domestic ale in McSorley's Old Ale House. . . ." The name was changed to *The Alternative: An American Spectator* in 1967, "but by November 1977 the word 'alternative' had acquired such an esoteric fragrance that in order to discourage unsolicited manuscripts from florists, beauticians, and other creative types" the magazine took back its original name.

The magazine does not even take seriously its house advertising. An ad inviting subscriptions "quotes" H. L. Mencken: "If I were alive today, *The American Spectator* would be my favorite magazine."

Suggested further reading

Dorn, Raymond, *How to Design & Improve Magazine Layouts,* Brookwood Publications, P.O. Box 1229, Oakbrook, Illinois, 60521, 1976.

Hill, Donald E., *Techniques of Magazine Layout and Design,* Donald E. Hill, Huntsville, Alabama, 1970.

McLean, Rauri, *Magazine Design,* Oxford University Press, New York, 1969.

Smith, Cortland Gray, *Magazine Layout: Principles, Patterns, Practices,* published by the author, Plandome, New York, 1973.

When it runs a Q. and A. article, *Johns Hopkins Magazine* reproduces one question and one answer in large type as a title. This has the advantage of getting the reader right into the article. Here you see two opening spreads using this approach. One utilizes a photograph that became only part of the opening page; the other utilizes a bleed photograph, with surprinted display type, and a smaller photograph mortised in.

White, Jan V., *Editing by Design,* R. R. Bowker Company, New York, 1982. (Second Edition.)

————, *Designing for Magazines,* R. R. Bowker Company, New York, 1982. (Second Edition.)

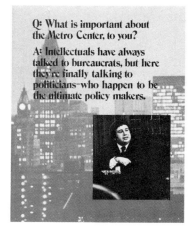

It would be nice to report that because it tried harder the Avis of New York newspapers was able to catch up with the then stodgy New York *Times*. Unfortunately, the *Herald Tribune* not only failed to catch up; it failed to survive. And yet, in its last days, it was, by all odds, America's best-designed newspaper.

Once a near-equal to the *Times* in circulation in the New York morning field, the *Herald Tribune* by 1963 had fallen far behind. In desperation its management considered a number of editorial changes and—more important to the readers of this book—a number of design changes. Long a pacesetter in typographic excellence among newspapers, the *Herald Tribune* decided a *radical* change was in order.

The look of the late Herald Trib

The man management turned to was a stranger to newspapers: Peter Palazzo, an advertising and graphic designer. With no preconceived notions of what a newspaper should look like, Palazzo conducted a study and was surprised to find that newspapers—all newspapers—had scarcely changed at all in format over the years. The typical daily or weekly was not designed, really; its parts were merely fitted together. They were usually combined in such a way as to fill in all the available space—to the top, the sides, the bottom of the page, somewhat like a jigsaw puzzle.

It was a format that, not seriously challenged in several centuries, was not being challenged much in the 1960s, not even with all the technological changes going on. The late Bernard Kilgore, editor of *The Wall Street Journal,* represented the thinking of many newspaper people when he said, "The market wraps fish in paper. We wrap news in paper. The content is what counts, not the wrapper."

Convinced, however, that in competition with magazines, newspapers, from the standpoint of quality, were running a poor second, Palazzo recommended changes for the *Herald Tribune* in design and even editorial content. To improve itself the paper would have to coordinate its editorial and design operations. And yet Palazzo asked for nothing revolutionary. He worried, rightly, about reader habits.

"One must be very careful about tampering with habits which have built up over a long period of time," he said. Perhaps he was thinking of the storm that followed the about-face made by *The Saturday Evening Post* in the early 1960s.

What Palazzo asked for and got, essentially, was a magazine look for the paper. He concentrated on the Sunday issue, especially

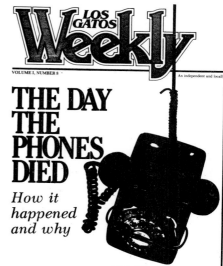

To illustrate the feature, "The Day the Phones Died," the Los Altos (Calif.) *Weekly* on its front page showed a phone using its own cord to hang itself.

the Sunday magazine section and the front pages of the other sections. He insisted that more thought be given to selection, editing, and placement of pictures. Cropping of pictures was often needed, he admitted, but he reminded his client that when you crop a picture you change what it says. Cropping does more than simply "move the reader in close."

For its headlines the *Herald Tribune* had been using Bodoni Bold, an "in" face among the better-designed newspapers in America. Palazzo requested Caslon, which, as far as management was concerned, was a face for advertising and book typography. Anyway, did it have the quality Palazzo ascribed to it? To convince the skeptics, Palazzo lettered a four-letter word, first in Bodoni, then in Caslon. And, by golly, in Caslon the word looked almost respectable!

Print, the prestigious magazine of graphic design, applauded the new *Trib* look, saying the change has been "widely hailed as

The Chico (Calif.) *News & Review,* a tabloid, devotes two full pages here to an interview, and *shows* that the piece is an interview by enclosing it in giant quote marks. There is not much white space on this spread; but it concentrates itself in two or three places, giving itself more impact than it would have if it were scattered.

a milestone in newspaper design." But other papers were not willing to emulate it because it was, essentially, a *magazine* look. Only in their locally produced magazine sections did the new look take hold. Most editors of these sections recognized *New York,* the Sunday magazine of the *Herald Tribune,* as the most beautiful in the industry. Some of these editors, moved by what they saw, shortly after the appearance of the new *Trib* began to make greater use of white space, heavy and light horizontal rules, old-style roman headline faces in lighter-than-usual weights, and even italic swash capitals where appropriate. *West,* the Sunday magazine of the Los Angeles *Times,* took on the look of the *Herald Trib.*

By the end of 1966 the New York *Herald Tribune,* its design already compromised through merger with other papers earlier in the year, gave up altogether. Good design—and some fine writing, especially in the magazine section—could not save the paper.

Following his experience with the *Herald Tribune* Palazzo redesigned a number of other papers, including the Providence *Journal* and the Winnipeg (Man.) *Tribune.*

When the New York *Times* was making plans in 1975 to go from eight to six columns for page one, *New York* asked Peter Palazzo, as an exercise for that magazine, to redesign the *Times'* page one. You can see his solution in a two-page sequence in the April 1975 issue (pages 45 and 46).

One criticism Palazzo had for the eight-column paper was that it didn't tell readers clearly enough which stories were really important. "Why must page one be a do-it-yourself kit?" Another criticism centered on the use of pictures more to break up blocks of type than for the information the pictures themselves carry.

Palazzo argued against the concept of bylines. They are great ego boosters for reporters, he said; but they are a design nuisance. He suggested "tag lines" at the ends of stories instead.

Palazzo also quarreled with the use of condensed, all-cap headlines, the overuse of decks for headlines (although he did not advocate doing away with them altogether), and the arbitrary appearance of an occasional all-italics headline.

His redesigned page had more of a horizontal look; with multi-column rather than single-column headlines; photographs clustered rather than scattered; pictures and captions presented as self-contained units; a summary column of news which, with page numbers, served as general table of contents for what was inside; better displayed stories but fewer of them; and consistent typographic devices to segregate "hard" from "soft" news.

The Herald of Everett, Wash., uses both thick and thin horizontal rules on front and inside pages. It also outlines photographs with thick rules and sets off bylines with thin rules. The day of the week gets prominent display with the nameplate.

Get the ball rolling for the week in today's **Herald Calendar**

Ejected
After all the bumping and shoving, the Sonics had another win. Page 1C.

WEDNESDAY
February 10, 1982

The Herald

EVERETT AREA EDITION

Jodi Walters leads a cheer at Valley High School (below). But before the game, she has to put on her artificial left leg (right) at home. "I go through false legs so fast you wouldn't believe it," she says.

AP photo

Marine firm may move to Mukilteo

By JIM FULTON
Herald Economics Writer

Snohomish County's dwindling employment may get a needed boost, but not until 1983 and beyond.

Honeywell Inc. confirmed today it is negotiating to purchase a 40-acre site as part of the Daon Corp.'s Harbour Pointe development south of Mukilteo.

The company plans to move its 1,100-employee Marine Systems Operation from its present location in Seattle's Ballard area to the new site, where total employment could reach about 1,300 to 1,600 by 1990, said Jim Durand, manager of facilities planning for the Marine Systems Operation. Durand said Honeywell is still not begin the move until late 1983.

Her only worry is seeing her leg sail into stands

By THE ASSOCIATED PRESS

ABERDEEN — "You shouldn't be afraid to do what you want to do," says one-legged cheerleader Jodi Walters. "If you're afraid, you won't do anything."

El Salvador torture not down, says group

By THE ASSOCIATED PRESS

NEW YORK — The U.S. branch of Amnesty International has rejected the State Department's contention that violence is on a "downward trend" in the Central American nation of El Salvador.

So send me to jail, Watt dares his foes

By THE ASSOCIATED PRESS

WASHINGTON — Interior Secretary James Watt predicted victory today in his battle over a possible contempt of Congress citation, but he said he would be willing to go to jail to uphold the principle of executive privilege.

James Watt at today's news conference: "This is a constitutional issue."
AP photo

Lawmakers shift Everett to 1st District

OLYMPIA — In a surprise move, the Legislature early this afternoon approved a redistricting plan shifting Everett residents to the Seattle-oriented, 1st Congressional District.

Inside

Rain?
Increasing chance rain tonight and Thursday. Warmer tonight. Highs in 40s. Lows tonight in 30s. Details on Page 2G.

Index

Astrology	3-8C
Classified	5-8C
Comics	5C
Community	5C
Crossword	5C
Dear Abby	16A
Economy	1-4B
Entertainment	11-12A
Food	1-14C
Forum	5C
Jumble	5C
Leisure	11-12A
Movie listings	12A

Northwest Area
Opinion	1G
People	14-15A
Sports	9B
Television	13A
Tides	2G
Time Out	2G
Vital statistics	2C
Weather	2G

Our phones
Information
Everett	339-3000
Lynnwood	672-3000
Classified	
Everett	339-3100
Lynnwood	672-3003
Circulation	
Everett	339-3200
Lynnwood	672-3000

County Council hikes garbage rates by 75%

By ROBERT T. NELSON
Herald Staff Writer

The Snohomish County Council increased garbage rates by 75 percent today in a move that will cost residential customers at least an extra $1.38 each month by mid-April.

See GARBAGE, Page 4A

The look of the New York Times

In the 1970s and into the 1980s, the New York *Times* gradually improved its appearance so that today, besides being the nation's "newspaper of record," it is quietly handsome (if you discount the poor printing quality). Especially it has made strides in the redesign of its special sections, especially those carried in the Sunday issues. The crisp typography there, the horizontal rules, the white space, and the imaginative art have inspired newspapers all over the country to reexamine their dress. The *Times* special-section look now is widely imitated.

And on its news page the paper's use of photography has been outstanding. A writer in the *Columbia Journalism Review* notes that the "good, gray *Times*" publishes more pictures than the *Daily News* does.

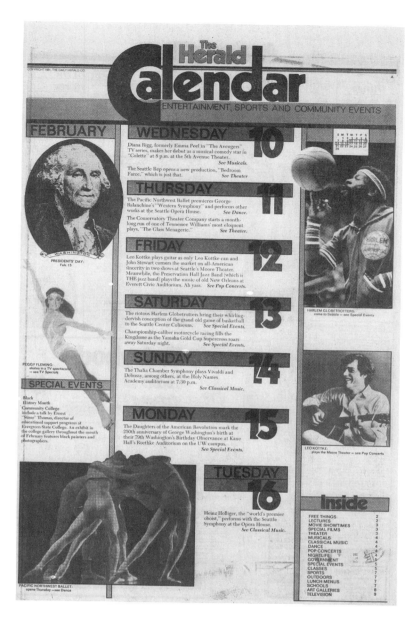

The Herald's "Calendar" section (run in Wednesday's paper) uses big numbers on the front page to make it serve as a table of contents. Art takes all kinds of shapes to bring plenty of display to the page. There is lots of color, too.

Like many other newspapers, the *Times* has gone to a six-column format, not so much to improve the looks of the front page as to save money. In changing from eight narrow to six wider columns, the paper was able to chop off a modest three-quarters of an inch from the page and save itself $4,000,000 a year in newsprint costs.[1]

Observing the changes at the *Times* and other papers going for the six-column format, a writer in *Columbia Journalism Review* expressed some second thoughts. The changes, he said, would mean a shrinkage of news content. Wider columns meant an increase in

1. Clive Irving, "Does God Care What the Times Does with Page One?" *New York,* April 14, 1975, p. 47.

Newspaper design and layout **187**

type size.[2] Even Clive Irving had misgivings about what was going on. That its front page had always looked a bit intimidating added to the paper's greatness, he thought. "I have learned to read its codes and to respect it as a basic American institution. At a moment when nothing else seems to hold together, why add to the confusion?" He suspected that the changes would result in less material being presented. "And you won't know how good the old page one is until it's gone."[3]

What good layout does for a newspaper

Talk about modernizing newspapers—making them more attractive and maybe more magazine-like—fails to take fully into account the problems of daily and even hourly deadlines, production limitations and challenges, quick news decisions, and word- rather than visual-oriented management. There is something to be said for the "newspaper look" that for so many years dominated newsroom operations. Traditional layout practices—even "makeup" practices, to go back to a term prevalent during the days of letterpress—can accomplish more than today's critics may be willing to acknowledge. Newspaper makeup helps the reader "go through the newspaper and find stories of interest or skip those with no appeal," writes Martin L. Gibson, associate professor of journalism at the University of Texas. "Proper makeup, in this sense, includes a big dose of what we used to call 'good editing.' It includes grouping by subject or geography, perhaps, and arranging the pages in some orderly progression from one kind of news to another."[4]

On the typical daily newspaper, the city editor, in charge of local news produced by reporters, and the news editor, in charge of national and international news from the wire services, meet with the news editor and whoever does the layout to discuss what should be played on the front page. These negotiations often go on near deadline time, which means that the actual laying out must be done in a matter of minutes. The scene differs from the scene in a magazine office, where deliberation between editor and art director can go on for hours.

On some papers it is the news editor who lays out the pages. On others, the managing editor. On still others, the copy chief, who also supervises the work of the copy editors. The idea of full-time art directors or design directors has taken hold only at large newspapers.

Even with an art director, a paper may allow certain sections to go their own way in design. The various editors do their own layout work. Unfortunately the result is often an inconsistency.

On a big daily, the front page changes several times a day as each new edition is issued. The newsstand edition published to attract commuters on their way home from work, for instance, would have a more urgent look than the home delivered edition. As the laying out takes place, a new lead for a story may come in, or a new story may break that cries out for prominent placement. Above all, a newspaper layout editor must be flexible.

2. Fred C. Shapiro, "Shrinking the News," *Columbia Journalism Review*, November/December 1976, p. 23.

3. Clive Irving, *op. cit.*, p. 47.

4. Martin L. Gibson, *Editing in the Electronic Era*, The Iowa State University Press, Ames, Iowa, 1979, p. 215.

Whoever lays out the page usually starts out with a piece of paper on which is printed a grid of the page showing columns across and inches running down the sides. These sheets, sometimes called dummies, are usually a quarter of the actual size. Working in miniature speeds things up. What the layout editor creates is no work of art, merely a piece of visual shorthand clear enough to show the pasteup artist what to put where. On some papers editors roughly paste galley proofs onto full-size layout sheets. (The printer makes available simultaneously two sets of proofs: one to proofread, the other to clip and paste.) Using a pencil, the editor marks the number of the galley across the face of every story—perhaps every paragraph—then with scissors or razor blade cuts away excess paper, making a unit out of each story.

THE OREGONIAN

TUESDAY FEBRUARY 24 1981 / 20¢

NATIONAL   LOCAL   SPORTS   SCENE

Doctor's lover convicted

Reagan cautious on El Salvador

Spanish rebels end coup bid

Charles to wed Lady Diana

Where to look

the Junction City
times

Junction City's hometown paper since 1891
Junction City, Oregon   vol. 89 no.22
thursday, february 26, 1981   price 20¢

Closed campus urged

Four seek J.C. school board posts

City mulls 11% pay raises

today

Safeway construction approved

Student Brooks Dareff tries his hand at modernizing the front page of Portland's big daily, *The Oregonian,* moving away from the traditional Old English for the nameplate, putting an across-the-page index under the nameplate, and allowing pieces of art to congregate in an uneven line at the bottom. He also combines silhouette art with regular rectangles and varies the widths (and type sizes) of the columns of body copy. The headlines tombstone, but at no expense to readability because the typefaces are different sizes. It is not a practical page because it does not crowd in enough stories and in sufficient length, and it doesn't provide for cutlines, but it shows, anyway, one way to bring newspaper design up to date.

Student Stacy Mellem chooses a small-town weekly to redesign, and comes up with this clean, handsome front page. She suggests one story be set in a different width. She clusters her art at the top but runs a screen-tint box at the bottom to enliven the look there.

The final pasteup, as distinguished from the rough pasteup or layout, involves careful placement of type and art on a full size page so that it can be photographed for platemaking.

The horizontal look

Until recent years the vertical look predominated among newspapers. Single-column, multiple-deck headlines plunged deep into each page, while unbroken black lines fenced off each column from its neighbor. Today on an increasing percentage of papers, the horizontal look prevails.

The first break with the past came with the extension of headlines across one column and into the next. Not only were multicolumn heads better looking; they were also more readable. That the headline writer had more space to work with meant he could avoid some of the headline clichés—those miserable three-, four-, and five-letter words that only a deskman could love.

Another break came with the elimination of column rules. They had made pages monotonously vertical. But it was impossible to eliminate column rules without adding extra white space. Without rules, you needed as much as a full pica of space between columns. Otherwise, you sometimes had more space between words than you had between columns.

Where was the extra space to come from? Newspapers couldn't very well make their pages wider. Nor could they make their columns narrower. Columns were too narrow as it was. The standard column measured out at 11 or 12 picas, too narrow for good readability, even with copy set in small news type. Two Minnesota researchers showed that columns set in 7- or 8-point types, common then, would be more readable if the columns were 15 or even 18 picas wide. Yet at the close of World War II, publishers, facing rising newsprint costs, trimmed another pica from their narrow columns. (It was a painless way to raise advertising rates; a column inch was still a column inch, even when it took up less space.) To compound the felony against readability, they increased body-type size to 9 points.

The logical step was to cut down on the number of columns—from nine or eight columns to seven or six. Edmund Arnold saw value in the "7 1/2" format, in which one column was slightly wider than the other six. The slightly wider column could be used for a feature column or a news roundup. Eventually publishers accepted the idea of the wide column for newspapers. Today the six-column format is common.

The case for wider columns

It would be a mistake to write off the narrow column altogether. In some circumstances, in limited doses, the narrow column serves the reader well, especially when it is set with an unjustified right edge. But when columns stretch from top of page to bottom, row on row, page after page, narrow measure puts too much of a burden on readers.

A study conducted by Jack Nuchols, Jr., working under the direction of J. K. Hvistendahl, associate professor of journalism at South Dakota State University, showed that 9-point Imperial, a news face, could be read 4.1 percent faster in a 15-pica width than in an 11-pica width.

The Dispatch of Lexington, North Carolina, uses traditionally narrow columns and caps-and-lowercase headlines and yet achieves a today look. Notice the "Good Afternoon" greeting at the top, accompanying the prominent dateline; the nicely-drawn modern-roman nameplate with its "A" jutting up higher than the other letters to compensate for its pointed shape; the heavy rules used in conjunction with lighter rules; and the unheadlined 3-unit table of contents at the lower right.

Monday, October 11, 1976/Good Afternoon

THE DISPATCH

Lexington, N.C. Volume 95 Number 137/ 15¢ a single copy

S. Main Train-Car Wreck Kills Man

BRIEFS

Poisoned At Church

Historic Event Re-Enacted

Three Die In Fire

PEOPLE

Happy In Russia

HHH 'Doing Well'

Good Will Tour

WEATHER

Sunny And Cool

Workmen move from train tracks the car that was struck by a work train (background) at about 7 A.M. today. The driver, Gary Gordon Countryman, was killed. (Staff photo by Henry Farber)

LEXINGTON
By HENRY FARBER

Ethnic Vote Courted Today

The Associated Press

Neal, Mizell Swap Charges; Neal To File Complaint

LEXINGTON
By WILLIAM MARCH

Liz Taylor To Wed. See page 2.

School Tax Report Due At Board Meeting Tonight

HOLLY GROVE
By ROBERT PAGE

(Continued on Page 12)

Information Charges Begin

LEXINGTON
By ROBERT PAGE

Page 4

Page 5

Page 19

When the weather takes an unusual turn, a newspaper may doctor its nameplate to make it appropriate. Here's a doctored nameplate and a front-page story you are not likely to see again coming out of Miami. Yes, Miami! The year was 1977. Note the snow-flakes and the snow-covered tree in and around "The Miami News."

Moreover, narrow columns take longer to set. Albert Leicht, also working under the direction of Professor Hvistendahl, found that Linotype operators, using the same face, could set matter with 15-pica lines 35 percent faster than matter with 11-pica lines.

Wider columns mean fewer lines, less hyphenation at the ends of lines, and more consistent spacing between words.

Of all the suggestions for improvement of newspaper format made in recent years by Arnold, Hvistendahl, and others, the wide column stands the best chance for universal adoption. Despite what Arnold calls "the reluctance of the industry as a whole to break out of timeworn habit," newspapers one by one are adopting a six-column format for the regular eight-column-size sheet. *The Wall Street Journal* has long used the wide-column, six-column format. The Louisville *Courier-Journal* and the Los Angeles *Times* were among the first dailies to make the conversion.[5]

5. J. Clark Samuel, editor of the Foxboro, Massachusetts, *Reporter,* a weekly, wrote to *The American Press,* January 1966 to point out that, so far as he knows, his paper has used the six-column format since its founding in 1884.

By the mid-1970s papers everywhere were making the move to six columns, if not on all pages at least on their front pages. And those that did go to an all-six-column format for news/editorial material went in the opposite direction for advertising: from eight to nine columns. This meant some adjusting to line up six-column news/editorial formats with nine-column advertising formats on a page, but it was a way of painlessly raising advertising rates. In addition, some newspapers went from nine columns to ten columns for their classified advertising sections.

Meanwhile, national advertisers were troubled by too much format variety in newspapers, and the industry was forced to standardize somewhat in order to encourage agencies to buy space.

The San Francisco *Examiner* uses some typographic imagination in readying this feature for publication. It deals with the obliquity of calling San Francisco "Frisco." For each mention of the hated word, a "Censored" mark appears. (Reprinted by permission.)

The case for unjustified lines

People who went to small high schools that couldn't afford printed newspapers may remember the problems of getting stencils ready for mimeographed papers. The mark of a smart paper in these schools was the justification of right-hand margins. Copy had to be typed twice, once to find how many extra spaces were needed to fill out each line and once to actually add the spaces. The result was some spotty copy, but to the young editors the paper somehow looked really printed.

The young editors could not accept the fact that ordinary typewriters are not flexible enough to produce natural-looking justified

In the Winnipeg (Man.) *Tribune*, before its demise, stories appearing on the front page, where ads did not interfere, formed rectangles. This page could almost represent the blocked-in canvas for a Mondrian painting. The nameplate floats partially down on the page and takes a shape similar to what could be occupied by a news story. You see no "ears." The continued lines under three of the stories refer to the first words of headlines inside. (Reprinted by permission of the Winnipeg *Tribune*.)

Controls will end Oct. 14, says paper

TORONTO (CP) — The Star says wage and price controls will start to be lifted Oct. 14 this year.

The newspaper says confidential documents, now being circulated by Ottawa to provincial finance ministers, set out a point-by-point argument for ending controls on Oct. 14, exactly two years after they were imposed.

Under current law, controls are not scheduled to come off until December, 1978.

The Star says Jean-Luc Pepin, chairman of the anti-inflation board, told provincial labor ministers this week that the October date is most likely.

It says the documents refer to "the equity among different groups of workers which would be obtained if the starting date for closing out the program was Oct. 14, 1977."

This date "implies that most workers would have been subject to control for two years," the newspaper quotes the documents as saying.

"In general, those groups which were first in, would be first out," the documents continue.

Federal Labor Minister John Munro denied that Ottawa has decided to begin lifting anti-inflation board wage and price controls on Oct. 14, a year earlier than planned.

"I can state unequivocally that no discussions in that area have been made in cabinet," Munro told Montreal reporters asking him about a published report that Ottawa had plans for phased withdrawals from controls beginning on that date.

Speaking Saturday after attending a conference on multiculturalism, Munro said, "We have discussed various techniques for decontrol . . . what policies would be fair."

Amin warns against rescue try

No. 49   Monday, February 28, 1977   ★ ★   Final Edition

NAIROBI, Kenya (AP) — President Idi Amin has moved his meeting with U.S. citizens in Uganda to Entebbe Airport, delayed it until Wednesday and warned the United States not to emulate its Israeli allies with an attempted commando rescue.

In Washington, President Carter said the U.S. government is watching the situation "closely, trying not to upset President Amin; and trying to take advantage of his good wishes that he has expressed."

Radio Uganda reported on Sunday that Amin postponed the meeting to 8 a.m. Wednesday from 11 a.m. Monday at the request of the U.S. nationals in his East African country, who are estimated by the state department to number about 240.

Amin is apparently summoning Britons as well as U.S. citizens to a meeting with him Wednesday. British diplomats said they were checking reports that members of the 200-strong British community were ordered to attend.

Sunday's broadcast said the location of the meeting has been changed from the International Conference Centre in Kampala, the capital, because the main lounge at Entebbe is the only facility in the country large enough to accommodate the 2,000 persons who were to attend. However, there was no indication who would be present beside the Americans and Amin.

The official radio also warned Ugandans to be alert for signs of an invasion. It said after the Israeli raid on Entebbe last July,

the presence of U.S. naval vessels off the Kenyan coast "must be taken seriously."

Quoting a "military spokesman," believed to be Amin himself, the broadcast said: "In the event of an invasion, the invading force will be disintegrated by the Ugandan armed forces."

The United States said the nuclear-powered aircraft carrier Enterprise and its escorts are cruising in the Indian Ocean off East Africa following a goodwill visit to Kenya last week.

Police arrest 35 strikers

About 35 strikers were arrested this morning outside the Griffin Steel Foundries Ltd. plant in Transcona.

The strikers were attempting to prevent the plant, which has been closed since Sept. 19, from opening today with new employees.

The strikers warned last week that they would resist efforts by the company to hire strikebreakers and break the 23-week-old strike.

The strikers, who sat with arms linked in an effort to

block traffic to the plant, were removed forcibly by police. They were taken in paddy wagons to the police station in the Transcona district.

Police said no charges had been laid late this morning, but that the attorney-general's office was being consulted.

No injuries were reported. Police said about 35 new employees and management personnel passed through the gates to the plant.

Separate Quebec viable, but disastrous: Trudeau

By Ben Tierney
Southern News Services

WASHINGTON — Prime Minister Trudeau conceded here Sunday that Quebec has all the "essential requirements" of nationhood, but insisted it would be both pointless and disastrous for the province to separate from the rest of Canada.

In a nationally televised interview with U.S. newsmen which was videotaped at the completion of Trudeau's three-day visit to Washington last Wednesday, the prime minister said Quebec Premier Rene Levesque was right when he told a three-nation businessmen in New York last month that Quebec could be a viable nation.

"But," said Trudeau, "what I don't think he realizes is that his argument boomerangs so beautifully.

"So what! I mean Quebec has exist-

ed in this way for hundreds of years and it has progressed and it has existed freely under our federal form of government.

"It has had its language, it has had its civil laws, it has had its educational system, it has had its territory which was largely aggrandized at the beginning of the century courtesy of the federal government.

"And my answer to Mr. Levesque is, 'Well, a good point, but why separate?'"

Trudeau claimed separation would be disasterous for Quebec when asked why, during his three-day visit to the U.S. capital, he had emphasized the danger of a Quebec separation to the U.S. and left the impression that it would not be all that serious for Canada.

Trudeau replied: "Don't misunder-

stand me. I don't think it wouldn't be grave for Canada. I think it would be very grave. And as a French-Canadian myself, as a Quebecer, I think it would be disastrous for Quebec to separate.

"As a French-Canadian I think it would be terrible if we sort of ghettoized ourself rather than use the whole country as a sounding board for the French reality in Canada and so on."

At other points during the interview, which was 90 per cent taken up with Quebec, Trudeau:

• Argued that last November's Quebec election result was not a vote for separation, and that in the two previous Quebec elections, in which the Parti Quebecois campaigned openly as a separatist party, the voters of Quebec had overwhelmingly rejected it.

See QUEBEC, Page 5

Tribune photo by Gregg Burner

The lost tread on the jetliner's tire is barely visible on the outside left wheel.

Retread forces jet landing

An airliner with 119 people aboard made an emergency landing at Winnipeg Saturday with landing gear problems.

The Transair jet, a Boeing 737, landed without incident at Winnipeg International Airport. A faulty tire was replaced and the charter flight to Mazatlan, Mexico, re-started three

hours after the touchdown.

Bob Scott, public relations director for Transair, said the plane, designated flight 803 from Winnipeg, lost the tread from a re-capped tire during its take-off run.

The pilots noticed vibrations and, once aloft, looked out a viewing port and saw the missing cap, he said.

Departure time was 7 a.m. and the plane, which has no provision for fuel dumping, circled the region for three hours to burn off nine tons of fuel and land at the proper weight.

Transport Canada's emergency plan went into operation during the wait. Hospitals were notified, ambulances

See TIRE, Page 5

Bill planned in Que.
Language limit eyed

QUEBEC (CP) — Legislation being prepared by the Parti Quebecois government will restrict freedom of choice in the language of education to citizens whose mother tongue is English.

Sources close to Cultural Development Minister Camille Laurin say there is general agreement in the cabinet on the new policy but many details have yet to be worked out before the proposed legislation is tabled in the Quebec national assembly in the session beginning March 8.

The sources said the criterion used to determine the language of education will be that recommended by the Superior Council of Education before the adoption of the Official Language Act, commonly known as Bill 22.

Under the proposal the language of education would be French for all children except those whose mother tongue is English. In doubtful cases checks would be made of

civil documents such as birth certificates to determine the mother tongue of a child.

However, the council, made up of representatives of both French and English speaking communities, also recommended that children with brothers or sisters already in English schools be allowed into the English school system.

The sources said the government is divided on that recommendation because some ministers do not want to leave the doors of English schools open to brothers and sisters of children whose mother tongue is not English.

The PQ government wants to avoid at all costs regulations such as English proficiency tests required under Bill 22.

Premier Rene Levesque easily overcame demands from within the party that English-language schools be abolished immediately and replaced by a unilingual French education system, sources said.

Why they go West

You've heard about the good life in British Columbia.

So have many Manitobans.

Each year, hundreds of Manitobans retire, decide they've had enough of Manitoba's ice and snow, and head west to B.C.

We thought you'd like to know how they're faring, so we sent Dave Cross, assistant managing editor, to Victoria, Penticton, Kelowna and Burnaby, to interview ex-Manitobans.

He tells about his visit in a five-part series entitled Westward-Ho, starting today on Page 10.

Students organize cleanup
Grim lesson learned

By Anne Marie Travers
Tribune Education Reporter

Students at Sisler High School don't eat their lunches in dirty washrooms anymore.

They don't fill sinks and toilets with gum and cigarette butts or strew their garbage on washroom floors like they used to.

They learned a grim lesson this month when one of their 15-year-old classmates died of hepatitis.

It was a lesson they are not likely to forget.

Up until the girl's death Feb. 10, some students were congregating in school washrooms for lunch.

While there is no evidence the girl contacted hepatitis this way, the school administration has since warned students against such habits, citing possible health hazards.

Medical officials say insanitary practices like those at Sisler increase the risk of spreading disease.

In an interview Friday, Dr. John Waters, deputy provincial epidemiologist, said "you're talking about an increase in a small risk but it is increased, there's no question about that." The circumstances would be conducive to the transmission of all sorts of germs and viruses, he said, noting however, that hepatitis is most often spread through close and prolonged physical contact.

There is no evidence the girl contacted hepatitis by eating in the school washrooms. In fact, her friends said she never did. But the potential danger is real and other children admitted to eating there under filthy conditions.

The Tribune visited Sisler Friday in response to parents' charges that there was mass growing on the walls of the boys' shower stalls, girls smoking and eating in the washrooms; sinks full of butts and a dirty lunchroom.

Pop cans, wet socks, tissue paper and a jock strap were found scattered on the floor of the boys' change room. The blue-green shower stall walls were peeling and almost all shower heads were missing. There was no evidence of moss but rust-colored splotches gave the impression of growths.

All but one of the girls' washrooms were locked for the lunch hour. The girls described them as "condensed," implying they were off limits.

In the one open washroom, girls were smoking but there was no sign of food.

Hand-printed signs on the walls read "Clean up operation now in progress"; "Welcome to the can . . . enjoy," and a third which urged students to flush cigarette butts

See STUDENTS, Page 5

Ashtrays now replace sinks in school washrooms.

Inside your Tribune

News summary	2
Local news	3, 4
World news	42
Editorials	6
Comics	43
Crossword	37
Sport	13-19
Lifestyle	20-41
Business	38-21
Deaths	3, 11
Movies	47
TV	26
Classified	13-23

Don't miss reading today's Trib Classified to catch such "best buy" items as . . .

It all starts on page 23 of today's Trib. To place your Free Private Party Want-Ad phone us today at 956-8780.

The weather: Sunny this morning, clouding over this afternoon with a high near -7. Low tonight near -18. Tuesday, clear with a high near -5.

Printed and published daily except Sunday by Southam Press Limited, at 257 Smith Street, Winnipeg, Manitoba.

Daily 15 cents, Friday, (with TV-Times) 20 cents. Saturday (Weekend Edition) 20 cents.

---

lines. Nor could they see that the 10- or 12-point typewriter typefaces (elite or pica) were too large for their narrow columns. They made a mistake all too common in the graphic arts: they tried to make one medium fit the mold of another. Young artists for letterpress papers made a similar mistake. In the days when linoleum blocks were used for line art (photoengraving was too expensive for some school-paper budgets), these artists did everything they could—including the heating of the linoleum to make cutting easier—to make the block look like a regular line engraving. They failed to realize that the inherent crude, strong, black look of a linoleum block could be the look of graphic art of a high order.

Ironically, while the young editors of mimeographed papers were trying to emulate regular printed newspapers by justifying their columns, regular printed newspapers for their news columns were toying with the idea, already established in advertising, of ragged-right edges.

The advantages of unjustified lines appear to be these: complete consistency of spacing between words, less need for hyphenation

Portugal devalues currency

LISBON (Reuter) — Portuguese tightened their belts Saturday after the announcement of a 15-per-cent devaluation of their currency and the most wide-ranging package of economic measures since the 1974 military coup which ended almost a half century of rightwing dictatorship.

The austerity drive—combined with incentives to investment and exports—is designed to rescue and revive the country's ailing economy and boost its chances of joining the European Common Market.

It is the first official devaluation of the escudo since the Bank of Portugal began fixing the rate in 1931, although its weakness on international markets has been evident for some years.

Other main measures contained in the package are:

• A price freeze for a year on four foods
• Tighter control on non-essential imports and an extension of a 60-per-cent surcharge on such goods
• An increase in the bank rate from 6¾ to eight per cent
• Tax concessions to boost Portuguese exports
• Higher postal charges and telephone rentals

Detective dusts for fingerprints on remains of bank safe

Burglars pulled boner, empty safe destroyed

RYAN, Okla. (AP) — Would-be robbers almost reduced the People's Bank of Ryan to a mass of rubble early Sunday in an attempt to steal a 1,000-pound safe that turned out to be empty.

"Just driving up here, you would have thought they used explosives," said Jefferson County Sheriff Don Allen. He said no damage estimate had been made.

Someone pried open the bank's front doors and ran a cable from a winch truck to the steel safe in a far corner of the bank, Allen said. The thieves then activated the winch and began pulling the safe toward the door.

"The safe tore and pushed through the door," he said. "About two feet of the front of the bank is brick veneer and the rest is glass. When it went through the door, it pulled frame, door and all out."

When police arrived, they found the safe in the middle of Main Street, about 60 feet from what used to be the front of the bank. The cable was still attached to the safe.

A winch truck was found abandoned near the Red River, a few miles south of here.

Allen said the truck probably was stolen and the bandits were strangers to the area.

"Everybody around here knew it wasn't used any more."

37 N.B. hockey fans hurt when arena roof collapsed

ST. BASILE, N.B. (CP) — Thirty-seven people were taken to hospital at nearby Edmundston, N.B., for treatment of injuries suffered when a portion of the roof of the arena here collapsed Sunday during a hockey game.

A hospital spokesman said early today that 10 of the 37 were being kept in hospital, one was under further observation, eight had been released and the remainder were awaiting examination or x-rays.

He said none of the injuries appeared to be critical although several people were suffering from broken bones.

Roger Aubfrey of St. Basile, an off-duty RCMP constable who attended the hockey game with his wife, said about a quarter of the arena was covered with debris when the roof collapsed

during an intermission in a game between St. Basile Aces and Riviere du Loup, Que., Three La of the Republican Hockey League.

About 800 people attended the game in the arena which can hold about 2,000.

Guy Lebel, a photographer who was attending the hockey game, said some people were badly cut by aluminum from the arena roof.

If the accident had happened when all the fans were in their seats "it would have been a massacre," he said.

Constable Aubfrey said several people were trapped under the metal roofing, between large beams, making it difficult for rescuers to get to them. Others, including the constable's wife, were thrown out of the danger area when the seats collapsed.

Mrs. Aubfrey had bruised her leg but, like many others, did not go to hospital for treatment.

Lebel said the arena is about 25 years old.

Mayor Edmund Theriault of St. Basile said he believed the weight of people in the stands—not the snow on the roof—caused the wall which supported the roof to give way.

He said the collapsed portion was about 120 feet square.

The crowd of Sunday's game was considered unusually large for this village of 3,500. An extra attraction was a presentation for Jean-Louis Lavoie, a long-time goaltender for the St. Basile Aces.

Lebel said attendance was double the number that usually attend Republican League games.

Quebec holiday could further relations: Clark

OTTAWA (CP) — Progressive Conservative Leader Joe Clark has suggested that more English Canadians vacation in Quebec to help improve mutual understanding with French Canadians.

Speaking on how individual English Canadians may help defeat Quebec separatism, Mr. Clark said "it would not hurt" if "more English Canadians made it a point to, for example, take their holidays in the province of Quebec."

"It might sound minor—I think it isn't," he said in an interview for broadcast on CTV's Question Period on Sunday.

Commenting on Prime Minister Trudeau's Washington speech that "a small majority" of Quebecers support separatism, Mr. Clark said it is a minority but "I don't know how small it is."

"It would be wise, prudent for us, for federalists, to assume" that the 40 per cent of the Quebec voters who elected the Parti Quebecois government "have at least taken a first step towards separatism," Mr. Clark said. And they have to be persuaded to choose one Canada.

Mr. Clark, who became leader of his party a year ago, called his first year as leader a period of "organisation and identification."

"I think the second year is probably consolidation and definition. That's my political task as I look ahead."

Answering a question, Mr. Clark said that he doesn't intend to "get into the wholesale vending of specific policy matters because I really believe that's irresponsible."

"I expect to be taken seriously when I articulate a policy and so I'm only going to do it when I know we're able to lay something we can act on later."

However, Mr. Clark said he expects that "over the next several months, we will be indicating, I hope, more clearly the areas in which we differ" with the Trudeau government.

Mr. Clark acknowledged that historically the Conservative party has not done as well as the Liberals in Quebec, but said his party's problems are much less severe in Quebec than the problems of the Liberal party are in other parts of the country.

Missing man's car found

Winnipeg police today were thoroughly examining a car owned by Henry David Elkomuk, 70, who disappeared Jan. 28

The car was found by a snowmobiler Sunday about 300 feet from the Red River near the end of Drury Road, half a mile south of the Perimeter Highway, a police spokesman said.

Mr. Elkomuk failed to return a month ago to his home at 268 Minnehaha Ave. in West St. Paul, after seeing his son off at Winnipeg International Airport. His dog returned home two days later.

The police officer said the car was found off the end of the road, just over the riverbank incline, about 4:45 p.m.

"We're keeping an open mind on it and having a good look at it today," he said.

Coffee laced with acid

PHILADELPHIA (AP) — A 16-year-old student, reprimanded the previous day, served his photography teacher a cup of coffee laced with hydrochloric acid, school officials said.

Bailey Dean, 31, said he felt ill after taking only a sip of the coffee Friday. He reported to the school nurse, then was taken to hospital where he was treated and released.

"Being a teacher, you can take the obvious kind of assault," Dean said.

Police were rushed to the school and Dean, following procedures suggested earlier this year by city school Supt. Michael Marcase, pressed charges against the youth.

The boy, whose name was not released, was charged with reckless endangerment and two counts of assault.

Was top Nevada labor leader kidnapped?

LAS VEGAS, Nev. (AP) — Nevada labor leader Al Bramlet telephoned the Dunes Hotel shortly before he disappeared and asked a hotel executive to deliver $10,000 to a Las Vegas casino, said Bramlet's wife.

Bramlet, 60, has not been heard from since late last Thursday when he did not return home from a business trip to Reno. Authorities have no leads, and his union has posted a $25,000 reward for information leading to his whereabouts.

His wife of two months, Barbara, 27,

said Bramlet made the telephone call to the Dunes on Thursday night and asked that the money be delivered immediately to a downtown casino.

The call was the last word from Bramlet, head of Local 226 of the Culinary Workers Union for the past 24 years and president of the state AFL-CIO for more than a decade.

"I hope we don't have a Hoffa case on our hands," said an investigator, referring to the disappearance of former Teamsters boss James Hoffa 18 months ago.

Mrs. Bramlet said the unidentified executive called the casino where the money was to have been delivered and found that officials there knew nothing of the planned delivery.

Mrs. Bramlet said the Dunes didn't deliver any money but the casino agreed to make $10,000 available to anyone who came in asking for it. No one did, she said.

Mrs. Bramlet said she still believes her husband is alive and is being held by kidnappers. "I'm just really hanging on to

hope. Now as time goes on, the scales tip the other way, but I think it's still too early to give up hope."

Bramlet, who started his culinary career as a potwasher in Peoria, Ill., in the mid 1930s, rose to power in 1953 by taking over leadership of the local here when the strip was not much more than a two-lane highway. Since then he has pushed the local to a membership of 22,000, giving him the power to meet and bargain with the state's top politicians and businessmen.

Having trouble keeping up with all the news? Don't miss The Tribune's News of the Week in Review every Saturday in the Focus section.

Students clean up own mess

(Continued)

down the toilet instead of leaving them on the floor and in the sinks.

The girls claim they congregate there to smoke because there is nowhere else to go. (Smoking is not permitted in the school.)

They launched a clean-up campaign in early February when they became fed up with the filthy conditions.

"It was really bad in here," said one girl. "You name it and it was on the floor and in the sinks.

Students accepted full responsibility for the conditions. As one girl put it: "We all made the mess and we all cleaned it up."

Everyone pitched in one day and washed the walls, swept the floors and scoured the sinks and toilets, she said.

The timing of the campaign — just after their friend took sick — was merely coincidental, they said.

J. D. MacFarlane, the school principal, attributed the volunteer clean-up to "feelings of pride and shame on behalf of fellow students that the school they live in day to day was in that condition."

Shortly after the girl's death, he said, the student council proposed a student patrol to monitor behavior in the washrooms, lunchroom and corridors.

The patrol, which started Feb. 21, consists of 10 senior and 10 junior high school students who assume their duties through the lunch hour.

Student president Gary Dolski said the patrol can either warn a student or take him to the principal's office. He said four students have been reprimanded in the past week.

Mr. MacFarlane said the patrol idea came in direct response to the girl's death. "It shocked the kids and they figured it's time we corrected some of the things that need correcting. There was no feeling that picking up soft drink cans would stop someone from dying, but there was a feeling that there were some conditions in the school that should be changed," he said.

Asked why the administration had failed to take action about children eating in the washrooms, he called it repulsive and said he wasn't aware it was being done on such a large scale.

"There was no feeling there was any serious health hazard. If kids are going to smoke you can't stop them. Sometimes it takes something like this to bring it home to everyone."

"With high school kids you prevent them doing things that will be harmful to others but if they're going to do things that are harmful to themselves, what can you do?"

Smoking is a case in point," he said.

He said students receive instruction about good health practices and are especially warned about the dangers of smoking.

As for the dangers of eating in the washroom, he said he didn't think it was ever the subject of a health lesson. "It's

Boys' shower room at Sisler High.

one of those things where hindsight is better than foresight."

He said school facilities for lunch are more than adequate and rarely full. Grade 13 students "were provided with a separate lunchroom last year, he added, but it was closed because of vandalism.

As for the boys' shower room, Mr. MacFarlane said he asked the school board some time ago to tile it but no action was taken. However, he said, he has been promised it will be repainted, and equipped with shower heads and a ventilation system.

Dr. Waters said the condition of the shower room was more an aesthetic problem than a health hazard.

Mr. MacFarlane said a daily health inspector gave the school a clean bill of health the day after the girl's death.

Sisler High school, with a student population of more than 1,300, is one of the city's largest schools.

Winnipeg school trustees discussed the unsanitary conditions at the school at an in-camera board meeting Feb. 22.

The discussion was not public because it touched on matters relating to personnel, a source said.

Tire forces jet landing

(Continued)

were on standby and crash trucks were stationed near the point of touchdown.

In the terminal building itself, there was no evidence of alarm; very few people were aware that airport officials were dealing with a critical situation. Up to the last few seconds before touchdown, flights departed normally and a pair of aged DC-8s continued their tedious touch-and-go landing practices.

The twin-engined 737, registered CF-TAQ and named "Fort Rouge," made a low, slow pass in front of the control tower to allow controllers a visual check of the tire, then went into its approach circuit.

The 60-ton aircraft eased down the glide path and touched gently on to the runway, slowing down gradually

as the thrust reversers on its engines roared. The crash trucks, beacons flashing, sped after it, then stood by as the plane eased to a halt.

The jet was towed to the Transair ramp but neither the 131 passengers nor the six crew members were allowed to speak with reporters about the incident.

Mr. Scott said it was a "fairly routine" incident, but conceded it had only occurred about three times in Transair's last five years of operations.

Passengers were told about the problem just after takeoff, and they remained calm throughout, he said.

Re-capped tires are common on company aircraft and comply with Transport Canada regulations, he said. Two of the four tires on the main landing gear were new and two were re-treads — one on each of the two main wheel assemblies.

Tires are inspected daily by Transair maintenance crews as part of the routine safety check. As well, aircrews do visual checks before each flight, said Mr. Scott.

Transport Canada is investigating the incident, a standard procedure for such occurrences, said a spokesman.

Quebec viable separate: PM

(Continued)

• Reiterated that he would accept separation if the people chose it democratically, and that he would not use force to keep Quebec within Confederation unless force was being used to take it out.

• Repeated his view that the November election in Quebec has forced English-Canada to face the reality of the French fact in Canada and confronted it with the choice of responding maturely to that reality or allowing Quebec to go.

• Restated his view that the break-up of Canada would present more of a threat to the U.S. than the Cuban missile crisis, suggesting, without specifically saying so, that Quebec could become another Cuba.

Dealing with his contention that last November's vote was not a vote for separation, Trudeau said the Parti Quebecois "had two general elections in the province where it tried to get elected on a separatist plank ... and it was very, very roundly defeated.

"This time they said, 'We are not going to campaign on separatism, we are going to campaign on good government.' We want to provide an alternative to the third government." And they insisted separation was not the issue.

"Whenever separatism was put to them (the voters of Quebec) as a question, 'Do you want a separatist government?', they said no, and they said no very roundly ... when given a choice they rejected it."

Commenting on the use of force to keep Quebec within Confederation, Trudeau noted that there is no provision in the Canadian constitution for the peaceful recession of a province.

"But," he added, "my attitude is that a democratic country like Canada should only hold together because the people want to hold it together."

---

at ends of lines, less chance of readers losing their places as they move from line to line, less expense in setting copy and making corrections. Research has not confirmed all these advantages, but Professor Hvistendahl, one of few persons to do any work in this area, suggests that you can read unjustified lines "a little faster" than you can read justified lines. But when you call the lack of justification to the attention of readers, they are likely to say they prefer the lines justified.

Varying the look

Radio and television news programs present their stories with a sameness that makes it difficult for listeners and viewers to sort out the important from the unimportant. Newspapers allow readers to skip and choose, and when something is really important, newspapers can turn up the visual volume. Newspapers with a usually quiet, subdued front page especially serve their readers in times of crises. When crisis comes, an across-the-page banner announces

To see if there are "other ways to design newspapers so they'll be more exciting and interesting," the Louisville (Ky.) *Times* brought 30 editors and designers together for a seminar in 1974. Each designer redesigned the front page of the *Times*. This one, by Paul Back of *Newsday*, struck participants as the most promising. Back uses a device here of emphasizing the first word of each headline, helping the reader speedily choose stories to read.

Louisville Times

SATURDAY EVENING   JUNE 1, 1974 / 10¢

Secretary of State Henry Kissinger brought back good news from his 34-day Middle East peace mission. Yesterday he spoke with President Nixon in the White House Rose Garden about the talks.

Prisoners exchanged by Israel and Syria are greeted by joyous throngs

Associated Press

[body text]

See JOYOUS
Back page, col. 3, this section

It's a long, slow ride from Chicago to Louisville, Mrs. Etta Faber, of Chicago, and fellow Floridian passengers relied on reading and sleeping to help pass the time on a train that usually averages only 25-30 m.p.h.

Trains that once flew now crawl along the tracks

By ROB KASPER
Louisville Times Staff Writer

[body text]

See TRAINS
Page A6, col. 1

Drinking on credit doesn't go down well with the state

By LES WHITELEY
Louisville Times Staff Writer

[body text]

See DRINKING
Back page, col. 1, this section

Kathleen Orndorff and her son Brennan, 4, snuggled down comfortably on the River City Mall pavement yesterday afternoon to hear the friendly sounds of bluegrass music. The Bluegrass Music Festival continues today and tomorrow on the River City Mall and the Riverfront Plaza.

Bluegrass festival brings downhome music to downtown

By ROB KASPER
Louisville Times Staff Writer

[body text]

See DOWNHOME
Back page, col. 2, this section

Sunday may really be sun-day

[body text]

Full weather data on Page A6

Where to look

VOL. CLXXI—No. 55 IN 46 PAGES
Copyright 1974 The Louisville Times
FINAL HOME

it, and the readers understand. An always screaming newspaper, on the other hand, has no typographic device to turn to.

Logic tells you that a front page on a normal or quiet news day should look quite different from a front page on an assassination-of-a-public-official day. A newspaper should not adopt a standard pattern to use regularly. News should not be fitted to a pattern. Instead, news should *dictate* the pattern.

Of course, a layout artist could work out a series of patterns to cover various conditions, and call one into play as the news unfolds. For instance, one pattern could fit a day with two moderately important events to play up, another to fit a day with one big event and two smaller ones, etc. But the best procedure is to create design on the spot, taking into account the nature of the story and especially the quality and number of photographs.

You can do a lot in design working with the front page of a newspaper and certain special pages inside, but much of your work involves pages cluttered with ads arranged by the ad staff, so that your territory not only is cramped but also is non-rectangular. On such pages the best you can hope for is some visual order, a bit of graphic relief, an obvious separation of news-editorial matter from advertising.

Basic formats

The newspaper editor has two basic format choices: the full-size sheet, approximately 15 inches wide by 23 inches deep, usually with 6 and sometimes 7 or 8 columns to the page; and the tabloid sheet, approximately 11 inches by 15 inches, with 4 or 5 columns to the page. The oversize newspaper page—or broadside—was originally a tax dodge. Beginning in 1712 British papers were taxed by the page. Taxes eventually disappeared, but by then editors and readers had gotten used to the oversize page.

The tabloid, a half-size paper, was developed to serve the straphangers on mass transit systems. It became less popular with the demise of mass transit systems and because it became associated with the discredited sensational press in some big cities. But interest in the tabloid format has revived in recent years.

The format has the advantage of making a small paper look thicker. A four-page broadsheet turns into an eight-page tabloid.

Peter Palazzo at the Louisville _Times_ seminar offered several possibilities to consider. You see them here. Note especially his handling of the nameplate. Some of his pages make use of a three- rather than a six-column format. The _Times_ is a full-size newspaper.

It is easier to departmentalize in a tabloid. You can give one full page over to business news, another to religious news, another to entertainment news, etc. You have a better chance, too, of creating ad-less pages. The smaller size pages allow you to segregate ads on pages of their own without burying them.

One problem with a tabloid is that it doesn't easily break into separate sections so that, say, the sports section can be read apart from the remainder of the paper. Another problem is that you must limit the number of pages. A tabloid that is too thick becomes hard to handle. The small, unbound pages too easily slip out of place as you turn the pages.

Some two dozen dailies and many other weeklies are now using the tabloid format. One of the best is Long Island's *Newsday,* which is providing "a well rounded package of original reporting and features to a large, densely populated suburban area."[6]

Kinds of newspaper layouts

"In theory, all front pages begin as blank paper," observes Clive Irving. "In fact, they all have a preordained basic structure: the vertical division imposed by the columns, and less visible horizontal boundaries which determine the placing of stories—in descending order of importance."[7]

Authors dealing with newspaper design and layout (or makeup) tend to categorize it under five headings:

1. *Symmetrical.* You'll be hard pressed to find examples of symmetrical newspaper pages today. Even the New York *Times* has abandoned them.

2. *Informal balance.* This is far more common and sensible; all the other kinds of layout are really nothing but variations. One variation goes by the name *Quadrant,* where informal balance is achieved on a page cut into imaginary quarters; each quarter has some art and some heavy typography.

3. *Brace.* Liberal use is made of stories that start out with multicolumn heads and leads, funneling down to single-column tails. One *L*-shaped story fits snugly into another; or a picture fits into the *L.* Stories look like braced wall shelves, hence the name. Brace layout is regarded by some critics as dated, although in Great Britain, where it is widely used on tabloids, it results in some lively looking pages.

Edmund Arnold defends the use of L-shaped stories because of the variety and flexibility they bring to newspaper design. "Some editors are slavishly devoted to so-called 'modular makeup.' This requires every story to be in a square or rectangle. That imposes an unwanted and unnecessary handicap. . . ."[8]

4. *Circus.* Such layout is loudly informal and gimmick-ridden. Otto Storch gave it magazine respectability on the pages of *McCall's* in the late 1950s.

5. *Horizontal.* This informal layout has many multicolumn heads and pictures, with stories blocked off into horizontal rectangles several columns wide. Horizontal, but not vertical, column rules are used.

To these Arnold has added *functional* layout, with its increased emphasis on readability. Crowding is out; white space is in. Furthermore, the nature of the news determines the look of the page.

Which is as it should be.

"All bad newspaper layout is bad because the process is performed backwards; somebody dreams up some pretty shapes and then the poor material is massaged to fit," says Clive Irving.

6. "Stooping to Conquer in Boston," *Time,* Sept. 21, 1981, p. 53.

7. Clive Irving, *op. cit.,* p. 44.

8. Edmund C. Arnold, "Horizontal Layouts—Whittling at Apparent Length," *Publishers' Auxiliary,* April 13, 1981, p. 5.

(Opposite page)
To illustrate a speech he was to make to a group of newspaper executives, Dan Kelly, senior vice-president and creative director of the Chicago office of Foote, Cone & Belding, asked art directors at his agency to redesign some newspaper front pages, two of which are shown here. Original pages are shown at the left, redesigned pages at the right. Although the art directors admitted that their suggested formats might be impractical, they did feel that newspapers can be more inviting, more interesting, and more relevant to their readers. The designers are Dave Hunter (Knoxville *Journal*) and Pat Sindt (St. Louis *Post-Dispatch*).

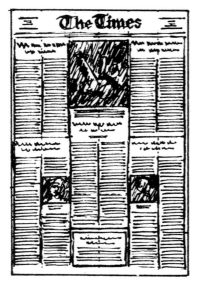

Prof. Roy Ockert of Arkansas State University warns that design, as important as it is, should not be a first consideration. "The news always should be, and therefore design must be functional. Art in the newspaper business must take a back seat to timeliness and practicality. It's easy for an artist (or good make-up man) to produce a more attractive page when he is not pressured by a deadline, as news editors on dailies always are."

Whatever kind of layout you use, a crucial decision you must make is whether to crowd as many stories as possible on the front page or to limit the selection to just a few. Using many stories increases the chance that every reader will find at least *something* of interest on the page. A page with only a few stories, on the other hand, makes for less clutter, allows for more white space, and makes possible full development of the stories on that page. Fewer jumps to inside pages are needed.

Edgar T. Zelsmann, president of Carl J. Nelson Research Corp., Chicago, says surveys show that half the readers are lost when a story jumps from one page to another. Furthermore, when readers follow a story to another page they may not get back to the page where they started the story. For these reasons newspapers try to develop their stories as complete units on a page. They break a long story into two stories and put the second on an inside page.

Newspapers that jump stories make finding them as easy as possible for readers. Carrying all jumps to a single page inside is one approach, giving that page a general "Continued" label. Repeating or partially repeating the original headlines helps, too. The repeated headline can be smaller, or in a screened version of the type used for the original headline. Some papers make sure last paragraphs of stories to be continued are complete. Readers, then, do not have to carry partial sentences with them. The new jump headlines may be based on what is contained in those last paragraphs on the front page.

When stories jump they should jump to a page in the section they start in, ideally on the back page of that section. Then the reader can easily return to the front page.

You signal the reader that a jump is ahead with a "Continued on" or "Please Turn to" line. But when a story simply carries over to another column you do not need such a line. In a magazine you don't need such a line when an article carries over to the next page or spread.

Whether using jumps or not, editors look for ways to make long stories appear to be shorter than they are. A one-column by 15″ story, for instance, goes down easier as a three-column 5″ story. And whether the story stays in one column or moves along to several, subheads can break it into more pleasant takes. Some papers set occasional paragraphs in boldface type and maybe narrower measure as a change of pace, but such paragraphs cheapen a page and give arbitrary emphasis to parts of stories.

Making things easy for the reader

Readers appreciate a news digest on the front page, boxed or otherwise set aside, perhaps over the nameplate, with single paragraphs devoted to each of the major stories. But the editor should be stingy with details here so as not to spoil the reader for the whole story. When page numbers follow each entry, the digest serves, too, as a special table of contents.

For large papers, there should be a general table of contents pointing the reader to regular features. The thoughtful editor runs standing features and pages in the same position, issue after issue.

Obits should be gathered in one section of the paper under a standing heading or between symbolic black bars. Obits need no individualized heads. How many ways can you say—would you want to say—that a person has died, anyway? The full name by itself is headline enough. Besides, you avoid awkward part-present tense, part-past tense heads like this: JOE SMITH DIES TUESDAY. (Sounds as if poor Joe is set to face a firing squad.)

The Indianapolis *News* solves the problem of obit headlines by using subjects and predicates but putting them in past tense. The past tense, contrasting with the present tense elsewhere in the paper, says "death" by implication: "Joe Blank Ran Car Agency" or "Carol Cook Taught at Jefferson." The Denver *Post* bunches its obits under a column heading that includes an abstract drawing of a sunset.

Similarly, engagements and weddings can be gathered together under standing headings and run with label, name-only heads.

Readers also appreciate an arrangement of material—possible only with large newspapers—that makes separate sections out of sports pages, financial pages, and other special pages. That way the whole family can enjoy the paper at the same time. Some papers have printed special sections, like sports sections, on a tinted stock.

The question of emphasis

Newspaper layout is largely a matter of assigning proper emphasis to stories. Usually, one story receives greater emphasis than any other. On some days, however, the page may have two stories of equal significance. Maybe three.

It is a good idea to think of stories as falling into three general categories of importance—major stories, important stories, and fillers—and assign emphasis accordingly.

You can emphasize through placement. You can also emphasize through story length, headline size, body copy size, art boldness, color.

Until recently, the No. 1 spot on the front page was always the top of the last column, because that was where the banner headline ended. With decreased emphasis on newsstand sales, the banner is less important and not often used; there is no reason, then, why the No. 1 story can't go at the top left of the page, where the eye normally first settles.

At one time, all the emphasis was confined to the top half of the page. Now the entire page is considered; editors take specific steps to get some typographic display "below the fold." Edmund Arnold talks about "anchoring" all four corners of a page with something heavy. Run dark headlines, boxes, picture, or other typographic weights to "define" each corner, he advises. One wonders, though: what's so important or mysterious about corners that they need defining?

Inside the paper

Most design of newspapers concentrates on the front page. But, as Arnold tells his seminars on newspaper design, "We have to make sure there isn't an immediate and dramatic letdown in quality when a reader turns to Page Two."

These rough sketches— thumbnails—show examples of each of five basic newspaper layout approaches: symmetrical, informal balance, brace, circus, and horizontal.

Laying out inside pages you might want to see them as front pages but with ads at the bottom and at the side. You can treat the ads as though they were unrelated photographs. Of course, if there are so many ads that the triangular shaped newshole turns out to be only a small portion of the page, there is nothing you can do to make it attractive and precious little you can do to make it even readable.

The ads are already marked for placement when you receive an inside page to lay out. But chances are, you won't see the ads. There may be only boxes there. You won't know what kind of art or headline a story next to an ad will be competing with. It is a good idea to run solid columns of copy next to ads, keeping news/editorial art safely away from the ads. This gives both your art and the advertising better display. It also helps keep the lines drawn between news/editorial and advertising.

Ads arranged in a half pyramid make difficult the designing of inside pages of a newspaper. How to give the news-editorial material a look of its own? Often there is no room for art. Nor is art always a good thing. Editorial art may fight advertising art for attention. The St. Cloud (Minn.) *Daily Times* solves the problem nicely on this page from "3rd Tuesday," a monthly full-newspaper-page magazine section. The three features, all set in unjustified type with column rules, use same-size type for the headlines. You see three different body-copy widths. A small "Home entertainment" kicker acts as a heading for the entire page.

Many newspapers prohibit advertisers from using in their ads the same typeface used in headlines for news stories.

Editorial and op-ed pages

The late William Loeb, the crusty, outspoken, ultraconservative publisher of the Manchester (N.H.) *Union Leader,* ran some of his editorials on the *front page* of his paper, and in boldface type and all caps to give them urgency. Loeb delighted in name calling: Democrats were "left-wing kooks," President Eisenhower was "a stinking hypocrite," President Kennedy was "the No. 1 liar in the United States."

Loeb dictated rather than wrote his editorials to give them a "plain talk" feel. And where better to alert readers than on the front page? Other powerful newspaper editors and publishers used

"Now, really . . . do I look like the sort who'd meddle in the affairs of El Salvador?"

An editorial page of the Louisville *Courier-Journal* features Hugh Haynie's Ronald Reagan-looking-like-Teddy-Roosevelt editorial cartoon at the upper left instead of the upper right, where most papers would put it, and a photograph to accompany the lead—or at least the top-of-the-page—editorial. That editorial is long enough for its third leg to get a subhead. The letters section gives one letter a multi-column headline. (Copyrighted, the *Courier-Journal.* Reprinted by permission.)

For its editorial page, *The Dispatch* uses the nameplate type for "OPINION" with bold lines across the top, as on page 1. The neatly designed masthead (the box that names the top officers and gives other information) is centered in the area carrying the editorial (for this issue, an editorial from another paper), with the Oliphant editorial cartoon just below. Mug shots of columnists are cropped unusually close and made into horizontals instead of the usual verticals. Perhaps the design theme would be better served on this page if the double-ruled lines above the "Letters" column, the Jack Anderson column, and the Patrick Buchanan column and under the cartoon were filled in to make single lines as bold as the ones at the top of the page.

OPINION

No More ECU

THE DISPATCH

October

L.A. MARTIN

LETTERS

Carter On Pride

JACK ANDERSON

Bottling The Air Bill

BILL NOBLITT/TODAY IN NORTH CAROLINA

Education For Offenders

THE DISPATCH

PATRICK BUCHANAN

Last Of The New Frontiersmen

---

their front pages for editorializing, too. So far as most journalists are concerned, though, editorials belong on an inside page set aside for them. It is usually the next-to-the-last left-hand page in the first section.

That page needs a design treatment to make it different from other pages in the paper. Because of its essentially serious nature, it is, as a rule, more subdued typographically. On some papers the headline face is a classic one—say Caslon or Garamond—to contrast with a sans serif head schedule elsewhere. Columns often are wider. The one illustration, usually, is a multi-column editorial cartoon to the right of the column of editorials, which occupy the first column or columns.

The more innovative editorial pages try illustrative photographs or drawings as inserts in editorials. The syndicated columns may use art as part of their headings. The letters column may use cartoon drawings.

As the world has become more complex and more in need of explaining, as syndicated columnists and cartoonists have multiplied, and as people have written more letters, newspapers have allowed the contents of their editorial pages to expand to the adjacent right-hand page, called the op-ed page.

Some newspapers are experimenting on their editorial pages, giving them a more horizontal thrust, running editorials across the top, for instance, rather than down the side. It is a good idea to make the format flexible enough so that the amount of space you give to editorials each day can vary. On some days there might not be much to editorialize about. You can give over most of the space to columns and other syndicated features.

Whatever basic design is adopted, it must fit into the design of the paper as a whole. If the page uses a different type for headlines, for instance, at least the body type would remain the same, although it could go to a larger size. The interior logo on the page would use the same type the front-page logo uses, but the interior logo would be smaller.

Newspaper typography

The character of the publication, the kind of paper it's printed on, the amount of space available—these considerations affect the designer's choice of typefaces. That the typical newspaper is published for persons of varying backgrounds and ages suggests body faces should be simple and familiar. That the paper stock used is cheap, absorbent newsprint suggests these faces should be open and somewhat heavy. That space is at a premium suggests they should be somewhat condensed with a large x-height.

For headline type, newspapers use sans serif, slab or square serif, or modern roman in display sizes. A few use old style or transitional romans, provided they are on the heavy side, like Cheltenham. Most editors prefer a condensed face so that they can get a better "count" for their headlines. Among the sans serifs, Spartan is popular; among the slab serifs, Stymie; among the moderns, Bodoni bold. Countless new romans and sans serifs are available to give newspapers a more contemporary look.

Edmund Arnold has recorded two important dates in the use of headlines: September 1, 1908, and December 4, 1928. On the first date, the Minneapolis *Tribune* became what Arnold believes was the first newspaper to use caps-and-lowercase headlines. Until then, all newspaper headlines had been all-caps; and for years afterwards—on through most of the 1920s—most newspapers continued to use all-caps headlines. Unreadable though they are, they find favor on a few newspapers even today.

On that second date, the *Morning Telegraph,* a specialized newspaper in New York, became the first newspaper to use flush-left headlines. Until then, all newspaper headlines had been contorted into inverted pyramids, hanging indentions, and other stringent and crowded shapes. A few newspapers in the East today continue to use hard-to-read and hard-to-write heads.

The argument now is over the adoption of all-lowercase heads. These are heads with only the first word and all proper nouns capitalized. Magazines have long since adopted such heads—or "titles," as they are called in that medium; newspapers gradually are coming around. A headline contains a subject and predicate. It is a sentence picked out from among the first few paragraphs and enlarged. It follows, then, that it should *look* like a sentence. That each word should be capitalized does not help.

The modern newspaper has dropped the idea, too, of the mul-

Now *here* is a masthead! The Louisville *Courier-Journal* runs a box like this inside the paper every day, sometimes arranged to fit a different space, but always complete. This one is 4 1/2" wide by 11" deep. It is no work of art; but notice how sensibly things are arranged to help the reader. Main headings are "For Information," "Managing Editor," "To Report a News Item or Story Idea," "Have a Complaint?" "To Advertise," and "To Subscribe." (Copyrighted, the *Courier-Journal.* Reprinted by permission.)

Columns

	units per pica	1	2	3	4	5	6
14 R	1.794	24	50				
14 I	1.704	23	47½				
18 R	1.395	18½	39	59	79½		
18 I	1.326	18	37	56	75½		
24 R	1.046	13½	29	44	59½		
24 I	.9945	13	27½	42	56½		
30 R	.8372	11	23	35½	47½	60	72
30 I	.7856	10½	22	33	44½	56	67½
36 R	.6977	9½	19½	29½	39½	50	60
36 I	.663	9	18½	28	37½	47½	57
42 R	.5978	8	16½	25	34	42½	51½
42 I	.5755	7½	16	24	32	41	49½
48 R	.5233	7	14½	22	29½	37	45
48 I	.4973	6½	14	21	28	35½	42½
60 R	.4186	5½	11½	17½	24	30	36
60 I	.3978	5	11	17	22½	28½	34

The head chart worked out by Dave Emery for the Eugene (Oreg.) *Register-Guard*, an offset daily newspaper. The large numbers running down the side represent type sizes for upright letters (the "R" is for "roman") and italics. The uprights happen to be Cheltenham; the italics Goudy. The big numbers running across the top represent widths in columns (columns are 13 1/2 picas wide). Hence, for a two-column head set in 18-point Cheltenham, the count would be 39. The units-per-pica column takes care of odd-width headings. Emery designed a lamp-shade-like box to hang down over the copy desk with the head chart reproduced on all four sides. The box is built to be bigger at the top so that the chart slants at an angle for easy reading. No head chart works all the time because the count is based on average widths of letters, but this one works 95 percent of the time.

The logo for *The Floridian*, a Sunday magazine published by the St. Petersburg *Times*, uses a second color for the filled-in "O" and allows the beginning and ending letters to drop below the baseline to partially enclose a couple of blurbs. Richard A. McCormick and Cliff Snuffin designed the logo.

tiple-deck headline. Today, on most papers, a headline consists of one or, at the most, two decks of two or three lines each. Headlines are not so deep as they were; but they are wider. They spread across several columns, adding to the horizontal look.

The head schedule

All papers draw up a "head chart" or "head schedule," which reproduces sample heads in various sizes and arrangements, gives them numbers, and tells what the maximum count is per line. The count can only be approximate; it is based on a system which puts all letters, numbers, and punctuation marks into four width categories: 1/2, 1, 1 1/2, and 2. With some exceptions, punctuation marks are 1/2; lowercase letters, 1; numbers and capital letters, 1 1/2; and lowercase letters *f, i, j, t,* and *l* usually count as 1/2, lowercase *m* and *w* as 1 1/2; caps *I* and *J* as 1. The space between words can be 1/2 or 1 unit, but it should be consistently one or the other.

The advantage of a head chart is this: Referring to it, the copyreader can pick quickly a "stock" style and size appropriate to the story, scribble the code number at the top of the sheet, shoot it over to the headline writer. The code tells the headline writer what style is wanted, how wide in columns the head is to be, how many decks are wanted, how many lines are wanted in each deck—and what the maximum count is. This can't exceed the maximum count, but it can stay under it. Some newspapers insist that each line take up at least two-thirds of the maximum count and that in a multi-line headline the longest lines be kept at the top.

The computer equipment now in use in newsrooms make the counting less of a chore than before.

The few newspapers that remain faithful to the geometric-shaped heads of an earlier era—flush-left-and-right, cross-line, step-line, hanging indention, inverted pyramid—require an *on-the-button* count. Fortunately, the flush-left heads now so universally used do not so seriously restrict the headline writer. The heads are more readable. And they are better looking, too.

Ideally, headlines should be written to be wholly appropriate to stories, not to fit assigned spaces. The lines in a headline should not be separated according to count; they should be separated according to sense. If that means a one- or two-word line followed by a six-word line, so be it. Whenever possible, the whole headline should go into a single line.

It should not be necessary to vary the weight of the headline according to the length of the story. A same-size headline face in several column widths is variety enough. Additional variety can be achieved through picture sizes and shapes, placement of white space, and use of ruled lines.

Nor should headlines be subject to arbitrary editorial rules that say they must always have a subject and a predicate, be written

in present tense, be free of words like "and" and "the." Headlines should be given more flair than today's head schedules allow.

That's *ideally*. No doubt the exigencies of newspapering will keep headline writing and display pretty much as they have been.

The nameplate

From journalism's beginnings, editors felt names of their newspapers should stand out as copies were peddled and hawked on city streets. About the only dark type known or available was the blackletter, a face we know today as Old English. Even today, partly because of tradition, partly because of what editors consider the "dignity" of the face, many nameplates still appear in that same unlikely face. But most papers now have adopted faces for nameplates more in keeping with the times and with their headline and body types. Plenty of boldface types are available; and we know today that even small faces can stand out provided they are displayed with a generous amount of white space.

If a paper can't bring itself to give up Old English for its nameplate, it can at least simplify the type. The New York *Times* did this, greatly improving the looks of the nameplate. Compare it to that of the Washington *Post,* also Old English, but in an inline version.

Two versions of a heading for the letters column of the Minneapolis *Tribune,* shown here actual size. When the column spreads over onto two pages, the paper runs one of these on the editorial page, the other on the op-ed page.

Headings for regular columns in the *Tribune* are look-alikes: each carries a line-conversion portrait, balanced at the right by a heavy bar that forms a near-box. Samples are shown here in actual size. Note that one heading only names the columnist; the other does that and carries a column title, too. Still, the headings clearly are related.

An efficiently organized page of information about goings-on in Portland, Oregon, the area served by *Willamette Week*, an interpretive newspaper. The roman type for headlines remains constant, except for size changes. The combination of thick and thin rules nicely segregates the material. Outlined photographs combine with small line sketches to give the page some areas of visual relief.

The typeface in a nameplate can be in strong contrast to the headline face, or it can be in the same face, say in all caps where headlines are caps and lowercase.

Actually, a newspaper's nameplate is almost always drawn, and in the days of letterpress it was photoengraved—that's why it's called a name*plate*. A nameplate is to a newspaper what a logo is to a magazine. The drawing often incorporates a line sketch of an insignia or some local scene. An effective nameplate can be made of reproduction proofs of type cut and repasted and retouched by an artist familiar with letterform.

Many newspapers use a single design in more than one size. The nameplate may "float" to any location from issue to issue.

Newspaper photographs and illustrations

Phil Douglis has called the daily press "a photographic disaster area." What bothers Douglis and other critics is the preponderance of staged shots and meeting pictures that can interest only those persons who arrange for the shots or pose for them. News-

paper editors have always put photographs in a role secondary to copy. Editors use pictures to fill holes.

And the cutlines that accompany the photographs strain credibility. J. C. Donahue, Jr., editor and publisher of *Suburban Trends,* Butler, New Jersey, complained about the photographs that followed up the call-in show put on by CBS radio for President Carter shortly after he took office. "In paper after paper," Donahue said, "there appeared photos of people with telephones, ostensibly elated at being one of the elect to reach the President.

"It doesn't take much to figure there was no way of knowing in advance who was going to get through, in order to assign a photographer to record the moment. Yet not one cutline among those I saw identified the photo as a posed, after-the-fact set-up, or reenactment. In fact, they seemed designed to mislead."[9]

The constant search for novelty or irony or humor leads sometimes to embarrassments. A prestigious small daily, to accompany a news story about the state senate's passing a bill to allow terminally ill persons to direct the withdrawal of life-support systems, uses a photograph of the bill's co-sponsor that happens to include an exit sign in the background. So the paper crops the photograph into a dramatic deep vertical that shows only the state senator and the sign. The cutlines say that the senator "co-sponsored the bill passed by the Senate Wednesday that would allow Oregonians to exit with dignity." No doubt the cutline writer was happy with the visual pun.

A swearing-in ceremony does not offer much chance for innovative photography. Nor would Eugene (Oreg.) *Register-Guard* photographer Paul Petersen place this shot among his best photographs. But compared to what an unimaginative photographer would do with an assignment like this, Petersen's photograph is a nicely designed piece of art.

9. In a letter to the editor of *Editor & Publisher,* March 19, 1977, p. 7.

Certain changes have taken place on newspapers since editors have become more visually alert and more willing to take advantage of offset lithography's ability to reproduce photographs. Photographers taking pictures for newspapers now move in close on their subjects. If they don't, picture editors crop the pictures to emphasize small portions of the originals. Even then, picture editors run photographs large. Most editors agree with their photographers that the paper is better off with fewer but larger pictures.

Peter Haley for the San Francisco *Chronicle* captures the drama of fighting a three-alarm fire at Berkeley. The rainbow stream of water adds an artistic note to the urgency of the scene. It takes many frantic shots on location to come up with a photograph as effective as this one.

Some photographs lend themselves to severe horizontal or vertical cropping. Such odd rectangular shapes, shown large on the page, bring variety to newspaper makeup. In this example of a county commissioners' meeting, run in the *Daily Tidings* of Ashland, Oregon, photographer Peter Haley was able to capture some interesting and perhaps revealing expressions as one commissioner was making a point.

Bill Kuykendall for the Worthington (Minn.) *Daily Globe* captures Ralph Nader in a memorable photograph. The story accompanying the photo describes Nader on the platform: "As he speaks, his eyes lift up to meet the crowd, his back arches up, his voice gains in volume and authority. He does things with his hands. He folds them into prayer position. . . ."

A wash drawing is executed by this author in India ink. The ink was used in its original state for outlines and in a watered down state for tones. Such a drawing calls for highlight-halftone reproduction. The Eugene (Oreg.) *Register-Guard* ran the drawing to illustrate a feature on a local crackdown on fathers who had deserted their families. It had to be a drawing; the story didn't lend itself to photographic coverage.

As newspapers added photographs to their ranks they reduced their staffs of illustrators. Before the turn of the century the typical daily newspaper employed a dozen or more staff artists whose job it was to supply illustrations for feature stories, maps and charts for news stories, cartoons for columns, editorial cartoons, and other visual delights. When photography and the syndicates came along, the need for local staff artists shriveled.

A paper today might employ one or two illustrators for the news/editorial department, and a few more for the advertising department; but the art factories that once existed on newspapers have closed down. Artists employed by newspapers now are more likely doing pasteups. And nobody spends a lot of time retouching photographs anymore.

Newspapers have a wealth of syndicated material to draw from. Syndicated editorial cartoonists, for instance, supply caricatures along with their regular features. Editors can drop these into their stories and columns about public figures. There are also plenty of stock-art services, as chapter 6 points out. What editors must guard against is reaching over into the advertising stock-art services for editorial art. The art from there has an advertising look which the knowledgeable reader would be able to spot.

Newspaper color

Newspapers pride themselves these days on the quality of color they get on their offset presses compared to what they used to obtain in letterpress operations. They look for excuses to run full-color photographs on the front page. If there is no full color, then at least there is a ribbon of a single color somewhere, or perhaps a nameplate or banner headline in solid red or blue.

Indiscriminate use of process color does nothing to improve the communication. In fact, color can hurt rather than help. Why hold

out for a washed-out, too-purple color halftone when a less-costly-to-produce black-and-white halftone shows up clearer? Nor does *flat* color necessarily improve the communication. Type in a too-light color becomes hard to read. Halftones in a too-light color lose their detail. Flat color is best when laid out in reasonably large areas in solid or screened tones to contrast with nearby type or art.

Process color should be reserved for times when you have transparencies with plenty of closeup detail. Flat or spot color is best when laid out in reasonably large areas in screened or solid tones to contrast with nearby type or art.

A page of news items from *Shield*, a monthly tabloid — a newsmagazine — published by A. N. McCallum High School, Austin, Texas. On this page from *Shield* editors arrange photos to form a single, irregular-shaped unit. Randy Stano is publications adviser.

Newspaper magazines and special sections

Several nationally syndicated magazines once were available to newspapers for Sunday distribution. Does anyone remember *American Weekly* and *This Week?* Two big ones are left: *Parade,* going to 130 papers with a total circulation of about 22,000,000, and *Family Weekly,* going to 356 smaller papers with a total circulation of more than 12,000,000. A few papers on Sundays include one or the other of these with a locally-produced magazine section.

Locally produced magazine sections get the same kind of design thinking that regular magazines get. But the pages are bigger. The sections are almost always tabloids. The designer has plenty of room to make an impact with art and type. The design of a locally produced magazine section does not have to bear a relationship to the design of the newspaper itself.

Locally produced Sunday magazines do not always receive parent support editors would like to have. Often there is little contact between the regular reporters and the people who work on the magazine. The magazine editor may work more with freelancers than with staff writers. Getting enough advertisers for the magazine section can be a problem, too; one reason is that the magazine needs more lead time.

A paper needs a circulation of 150,000 or more to make a locally-produced Sunday magazine pay off. One count in 1981 put the number of locally edited newspaper magazine sections at fifty. Few of the magazines now are printed by rotogravure. The printing process usually is offset lithography, as it is for the remainder of the paper. And pages, as in the regular paper, are unbound.

The fattest of the locally produced magazines is *The New York Times Magazine,* a rotogravure publication, saddle stapled, which some weeks expands to 200 pages. Other newspaper magazines are as thin as 16 pages.[10]

Some newspapers publish special sections or tabloids, in addition to or in place of a locally edited magazine. Special sections lure advertisers who otherwise would stay away to the paper. The sections concentrate on recreation, or the outdoors, or entertainment, or "lifestyles." Some special sections are designed to appeal specifically to youthful readers.

The proliferation of tab sections caused some critics to wonder if newspapers were losing sight of their basic reason for existence: to present the news so that the people can be informed and make intelligent decisions on important matters.

10. Elise Burroughs, "Sunday Mags, Long Neglected, Begin to Glow," *Presstime,* February 1981, pp. 48–50.

Newspapers, like magazines, get into subsidiary publications: publications for advertisers and for employees, for instance. Publications for employees or near-employees can become specialized, as this one for 13,000 carriers shows. It is a quarterly publication of the Detroit *News*. Coming in a 12-inch square (roughly) format on newsprint, the 12-page publication presents its news of awards and circulation drives in lively fashion. The front cover serves as an illustrated table of contents.

Some newspapers put out publications not included in regular editions. The New York *Times* publishes *Large Type Weekly,* with type about twice as large as that of the regular paper, for people with limited vision or those whose eyes tire easily. The 32-page *Weekly* prints material from the regular paper, including news, feature stories, and columns.

How research helps

After the Rapid City (South Dakota) *Journal* discovered, through research, that its readers wanted more information they could use in their daily lives, the paper in 1976 became more consistent in its placement of items, making them easy to find, and more willing to put national and international news on inside pages, devoting the front part of the paper mainly to local news. A "Lifestyle" section each day concentrated on a single subject. For instance, on Monday the subject was "Money."

Research can be useful in helping designers make up their minds about which course to take. And if the newspaper itself can't conduct the research, plenty of studies exist that can be consulted.

The American Newspaper Publishers Association, Washington, D.C., in the 1970s sponsored a series of News Research Bulletins on newspaper design and typography. One, by J. W. Click and Guido H. Stemple III, showed that readers, young and old, prefer newspapers with "modern" front pages. By "modern" the authors meant six-column instead of eight-column pages with a horizontal rather than a vertical emphasis. David K. Weaver, L. E. Mullins, and Maxwell E. McCombs found that there was a tendency in competing situations for the second newspaper to adopt a more modern format: no column rules, six rather than eight columns to the page, fewer stories on the front page, larger photographs and color photographs, smaller headlines. J. K. Hvistendahl and Mary R. Kahl found that newspaper readers prefer roman to sans serif body types.

The Carl J. Nelson Research Corp. reported that headlines four or more columns wide attract twice as many readers as one-column headlines do.

Relying on research findings like these makes more sense than pushing ahead on the basis of personal preference.

Newspapers and the new technology

It was after World War II that the old letterpress process began giving way to offset as the ideal method for printing newspapers. The smaller papers, with less investment in old equipment, took up the new process first. The big papers followed. The new process allowed cheaper and better reproduction of halftones and cheaper and more flexible typography.

But it took years before newspapers broke away from the design restrictions imposed on them by hot type and photoengraving. The typical newspaper format still looked as though someone in the back shop, arranging metal type and cuts on a stone, did the designing. Then experimentation took hold, and some papers began to look as though high school art students anxious to be different were in charge. Design finally grew up to take advantage of the offset without sacrificing readability.

The big idea now is to take advantage of the computer and the new technology. Since 1960 the computer has had some use—in

some newsrooms—in justifying right-hand margins. Now it becomes the key to all the new systems used by newspapers: video display terminals, optical character readers, and direct-input typewriters.

On many of today's newspapers, reporters become directly involved in typesetting as they sit in front of video display terminals and punch out their stories. "Today's reporter is his own typesetter," observes Prof. Mario R. Garcia of the University of South Florida, "and for all practical purposes, he develops a strong link with the page designer."[11] The makeup of the paper goes on in editorial offices, not in the print shop or backshop of letterpress days.

And increasingly, papers are experimenting with or actually using pagination, a computer system by which makeup can be done on a screen. Once pagination is established, proofs of type and prints of art no longer will have to be moved around by hand and fastened to a gridded layout sheet.

Joseph M. Ungaro, executive editor of the Westchester-Rockland (New York) Newspapers, sees the elimination eventually of all walls between the newsroom and the production department. A number of papers will be put together by going directly from computer to plate, with laser beams used to create the plates.[12]

But change comes slowly.

Clive Irving a number of years ago, before the computer had taken over in the newsrooms, wrote: ". . . Printing advances are being introduced whose potential is not even recognized [by newspapers] let alone exploited." Editors, he said, use offset and phototypesetting to produce papers that look just like the old standby letterpress papers. "Yet the mechanical restraints imposed by the use of hot metal and rotary presses are no longer there. The prison door has been opened but the prisoner refuses to leave the cell."

Two examples of center spreads in *The Christian Science Monitor*. That two pages are on a sheet encourages the use of across-the-gutter art and headlines. The *Monitor* makes dramatic use of this space, varying the approach from issue to issue. The center spread almost always has a strong horizontal thrust. Note especially the handling of the "Halting the Desert" feature and the way the sifting sand partially covers the headline. For some of the photographs on these spreads the editors use a textured screen. (Reprinted by permission from *The Christian Science Monitor*. © 1977 The Christian Science Publishing Society. All rights reserved.)

11. Mario R. Garcia, *Contemporary Newspaper Design*, Prentice-Hall, Inc., Englewood Cliffs, N.J., 1981, p. 226.

12. "Copy Editors to Feel Automation Impact," *Editor & Publisher*, March 19, 1977, p. 16.

Redesigning the newspaper

The new technology has prompted newspapers to think about design overhauls. In many cases, papers have called in outsiders to set up new patterns and new routines that staff layout people and editors could follow.

In a redesign program, every detail is considered, down to what you might think were the most insignificant measurements. The redesign program anticipates every problem that may arise.

Redesign takes into account a newspaper's personality. The changes that occur should enhance that personality. The designer usually tries to strengthen the personality and make it more obvious without drastically changing it.

Redesign especially should consider production capabilities, including paper availability and press capacity. The goal should be to simplify procedures by standardizing them and to encourage economies in an age of rapidly rising prices and continuing shortages.

The look to come

Newspaper design will change as newspapering itself changes. TV will help. It already has. Most journalists admit now that the electronics media do a better job with spot news than the print media. The trend in newspapers will have to be away from the "what" to the "why." TV and radio stimulate the appetite; newspapers deliver the details, the background. The interpretive newspaper will dispense with the hodgepodge and take on more and more the look of permanence and stability and, at the same time, vitality.

The computer will continue to make a difference. Reporters have already come to terms with it. Now it is the designers' turn. ". . . The new technologies available to artists and designers are overwhelming in their complexity and sheer numbers," says *U&lc.* The publication adds: "The best of the typesetters, color scanners and paginators, laser printers, slide-makers, and graphic display terminals are only as good as the people manipulating them. And therein lies the dilemma." The dilemma is that senior designers are turned off by the new devices instead of being stimulated by them. And young designers, excited by the devices, don't have much of a chance to acquaint themselves with them because their schools find them too expensive to install. *U&lc.* calls for a program through which schools and industry can come together to share their various facilities.[13]

Suggested further reading

Alexander, James P., *Programmed Journalism Editing,* Iowa State University Press, Ames, Iowa, 1980.

Allen, Wallace, *A Design for News,* Minneapolis Tribune, 425 Portland Ave., Minneapolis, Minn. 55488, 1981.

Arnold, Edmund C., *Designing the Total Newspaper,* Harper & Row, New York, 1981.

Baskette, Floyd K. and Jack Z. Sissors and Brian S. Brooks, *The Art of Editing,* Macmillan Company, New York, 1982. (Third Edition.)

Berner, R. Thomas, *Editing,* Holt, Rinehart and Winston, New York, 1982.

13. "Now is the Time . . .," *U&lc.,* September, 1981, p. 3.

Click, J. W. and Guido H. Stempel III, *Reader Response to Modern and Traditional Front Page Make-up,* American Newspaper Publishers Association, Washington, D.C., News Research Bulletin No. 4, June 4, 1974.

Copperud, Roy and Roy Paul Nelson, *Editing the News,* Wm. C. Brown Company Publishers, Dubuque, Iowa, 1983.

Crowell, Alfred A., *Creative News Editing,* Wm. C. Brown Company Publishers, Dubuque, Iowa, 1975. (Second Edition.)

Editors of the Harvard Post, *How to Produce a Small Newspaper,* The Harvard Common Press, Harvard, Mass., 1977. (With chapters on "Typography," "Pasteup," and "Design and Layout.")

Evans, Harold, *Editing and Design,* a five-volume manual dealing with English usage, typography, and layout, put together by the editor of *The Sunday Times,* London. Useful for American as well as British editors. Volume 1: *Newsman's English;* Volume 2: *Handling Newspaper Text;* Volume 3: *News Headlines;* Volume 4: *Picture Editing;* Volume 5: *Newspaper Design.* Holt, Rinehart and Winston, New York, 1973.

Fidler, Roger F., comp., *Newspaper Design/1981,* Source Publications, Inc., 700 N.E. 61st St., Miami, Florida 33137, 1981.

Garcia, Mario R., *Contemporary Newspaper Design: A Structural Approach,* Prentice-Hall, Inc., Englewood Cliffs, N.J., 1981.

Gibson, Martin L., *Editing in the Electronic Era,* Iowa State University Press, Ames, Iowa, 1979.

Gilmore, Gene and Robert Root, *Modern Newspaper Editing,* Bond & Fraser Publishing Company, San Francisco, 1976. (Second Edition.)

Hollstein, Milton and Larry Kurtz, *Editing with Understanding,* Macmillan Publishing Co., Inc., 1981.

Hulteng, John L. and Roy Paul Nelson, *The Fourth Estate: An Informal Appraisal of the News and Opinion Media,* Harper & Row, Publishers, New York, 1983. (Second Edition.)

Lown, Edward, *An Introduction to Technological Changes in Journalism,* University Microfilms International, 300 North Zeeb Road, Ann Arbor, Michigan, 48106, 1977. (By the world news editor, Newburgh [New York] *Evening News.*)

MacDougall, Curtis D., *News Pictures Fit to Print—Or Are They?* Oklahoma State University Press, Stillwater, Oklahoma, 1971.

Newsom, D. Earl, ed., *The Newspaper,* Prentice-Hall, Englewood Cliffs, N.J., 1981.

Riblet, Carl, Jr., *The Solid Gold Copy Editor,* Aldine Publishing Company, Chicago, 1972.

Westley, Bruce, *News Editing,* Houghton Mifflin, Boston, 1980. (Third Edition.)

Computer-Assisted Layout of Newspapers, American Newspaper Publishers Association, Reston, Va., 1977.

Newspaper Design, American Press Institute, Reston, Va., 1978.

A certificate, diploma, or award does not have to take the usual horizontal shape with calligraphic or script type, each line centered. Ernst Aufseeser designed this powerful certificate of sports achievement in the early 1930s.

With a magazine or newspaper your design becomes cumulative. You see your mistakes in one issue and begin to correct them in the next. Eventually you finely tune your design to a point where, at least for the moment, it really works for you. With miscellaneous publications you never know. You make your mistakes and create your triumphs, but they work only once. On the next assignment you start all over again.

Of course, some miscellaneous publications come out frequently enough that you can get a handle on the design, but for these you would probably have a budget so limited that you couldn't do what you want anyway.

Miscellaneous publications can take regular magazine and newspaper formats and, in addition, these:

1. leaflets (single sheets) or cards, loose or stapled;
2. folders (sheets folded one or more times);
3. broadsides (extra large sheets like maps that are folded down for easy reading or handling);
4. booklets (similar to saddle-stapled magazines, but usually smaller—small enough, say, to fit into a No. 10 business envelope);
5. brochures (extra fancy booklets with oversize covers, die cuts, pockets, etc.);
6. books (paperback or hardbound), catalogs, directories, and manuals.

Moving from one format to the other

Corporate, governmental, educational, political, and other kinds of organizations using miscellaneous publications do plenty of switching back and forth among the formats. In the 1970s, a number of company magazines decided that the traditional magazine format did not lend itself very well to news items. Something closer to a newspaper format would work better. If the magazine consisted primarily of news, it went to a newspaper format or, more commonly, to a tabloid format. Such a format represented savings not only in paper costs (the editor could use newsprint rather than book stock) but also in binding costs. To affect further savings, some editors went to a newsletter format.

If a company magazine consisted of both feature material and news, editors—some of them—went to two formats: the magazine continued to carry feature material; the new tabloid or newsletter, perhaps issued more frequently, carried the news and chit-chat associated with the typical magazine for employees.

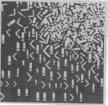

For publications used as sales tools, you see much experimentation with format. Sometimes the job seems to call for a simple folded sheet, sometimes something bound. A department store, for instance, instead of settling for one of those numerous tabloids we see nowadays inserted in our daily newspapers, decides on something that looks like a cheaply bound paperback book to go through the mails. Anything to get a jump on the competition.

Corporate design programs

Business and industrial concerns and nonprofit organizations, too, put more emphasis than ever before on the design of their publications. They have bought the concept, put forth by the firms which specialize in corporate identity programs, including redesign of corporate symbols, that all printed and televised materials as well as signs on and in the company buildings should bear a family relationship and convey the impression that the firm is innovative and contemporary. It would not do, for instance, for a company to work out a beautifully designed and coordinated set of stationery and business forms and then allow the employee relations department to issue an internal magazine, newspaper, or newsletter that looks as though it were laid out by someone who couldn't make the art staff of a padded-cover yearbook put out by a rural high school.

When a company goes through a program of redesign, from trademark to company magazine, it often introduces the changes through ads and direct-mail pieces. To cite one example: when Republic Steel redesigned its logo it issued a booklet to all employees so that they could share "the sense of pride and excitement" management felt "at the introduction of our forceful, distinctive and wholly modern appearance which portrays Republic Steel as the dynamic, forward-looking, growth-minded company we all know it to be."

As the booklet explained, the new corporate identity program revolved around the company name. It stayed the same, but "Republic" grew bigger in the design "Because there are many other steel companies, but only one Republic. . . ." The company also adopted a special color— "Republic Blue"— "for unique and dramatic expression. . . ." Of course, the blue was used as a second color throughout the booklet.

For management people and others involved in corporate communications, companies undergoing corporate identity redesign programs issue manuals telling exactly how to use the new symbols and signs. Placement must be just so, the manual cautions. Colors must be exact. Reading one of these manuals you feel as intimidated as when reading one of those mattress labels warning that "removing this label is punishable by. . . ."

Designer James W. O'Bryan in a booklet promoting *National Review* to advertisers uses small, square pieces of abstract art as sort of chapter headings. The pieces shown here illustrate, left to right, a page saying *NR* readers are "extraordinarily activist," they are "uniquely motivated by the magazine," they travel a lot, they "entertain with zest," and they "consume books voraciously."

"Did you ever see a calculator with a rotary dial?" asks Pacific Northwest Bell in a letter inviting phone users to switch from rotary dialing to Touch-Tone service. The rotary-dial calculator shown at the top of the letter was a good example of double-take art: an attention getter.

The Potash Corporation of Saskatchewan, Canada, makes a coloring book of company scenes available to school children. This is one of the 8 1/2 × 11 pages with its heavy-outline art. "Keep your crayons nearby," advises an introductory page. "The Potash Corporation of Saskatchewan is a very busy—and very colorful—part of life in Saskatchewan." The book points out that potash is used mainly in the production of fertilizer.

Where pictorial symbols are involved in corporate design, the designer simplifies, settling for abstract shapes rather than realistic portrayals. Sometimes initials-only do the job. A simplified logo can be reduced and repeated in a wallpaper pattern to be used as a backdrop for a booklet cover or annual report cover.

With simplification, however, goes the risk that you are repeating someone else's design. It is almost impossible sometimes to come up with a design not used before, as NBC, to its embarrassment, discovered when it decided on its *N* logo in 1975. NBC had to settle out of court with the tiny Nebraska Educational Network, which had in use an *N* that was almost exactly the *N* that Lippincott & Margulies invented for NBC.

People who work in corporate design often face greater frustrations than in other design jobs, because so much is at stake and so many people are involved in decision making. Officials all along the route to production can change their minds about what may appear to be trivial matters. Each change can result in hours of additional work and revision.

Even freelancers are affected. Photographers, for instance, find that they have considerable less freedom working on annual reports than they would have, say, working for newsstand magazines or newspapers. But at that International Association of Business Communicators meeting in New York (mentioned in an earlier chapter), William Rivelli said that "What can make corporate work satisfying is working within . . . [the] restrictions to come up with better material, finding new ways to do that portrait, to get that machine, or to pose the board [members]." Some corporate assignments can be better than journalistic assignments. The three panelists recalled an assignment given to corporate photographer Jay Maisel, who spent two years traveling for Heinz photographing harvests around the world. And rates for the corporate photographer can go way beyond what they would be for the photojournalist. They can run as high as $2,000 a day.[1]

One-shots

Sometimes a magazine of rather broad appeal gathers enough material on one of its areas of interest to put out a special issue apart from the regular issues. A shelter magazine, for instance, may put out a publication about furniture and distribute it to newsstands as the magazine itself is distributed. This special publication may gather together material that has already appeared in the magazine, or it may present all new material. We call the publication a one-shot, even though it may catch on and become, say, an annual publication.

Designing a one-shot could involve taking the basic design of the magazine and applying it to the special issue; or it could require a brand new design approach appropriate to the subject matter.

Any publisher can bring out a one-shot. A publisher can specialize in producing one-shots. That publisher then acts much as a book publisher would act, but the product takes on the look of a magazine instead of the look of a book.

1. Robert A. Parker, "A Panel Discussion of Corporate Photography," *Communication Arts*, January/February 1982, pp. 80–82.

Direct-mail pieces

The term "one-shot" can be stretched to include direct-mail pieces. Direct-mail pieces are produced by every conceivable kind of company or organization to do a public relations or selling job, and they appear only once; then they are forgotten. Unlike other one-shots, they are meant mostly to be given away, not sold. The term "direct-mail" comes from their usual method of distribution; but many direct-mail pieces are handed out at doors or from counters. Another term for these pieces is "direct advertising." Still another term is "direct marketing."

The sketch above shows some of the most common direct-mail pieces, beginning with the lowly leaflet (a small single sheet, unfolded) and ending with the booklet. Items 2, 3, 4, and 5 show different folds for three-fold (eight-panel) folders. Item 4 is called a "gatefold," item 5 an "accordian fold." The next item is a "French fold," used widely for Christmas cards; printing on one side of the sheet only, you have an image on each of the four panels that show. The next-to-the-last item is a "broadside." It can fold down to folder size.

You don't have to think of the folder as strictly a vertical piece. You can turn it sideways and design the panels as horizontals. The sketch that follows shows a regular two-fold and three-fold folder turned sideways. The third horizontal folder, a two-fold, opens from the side.

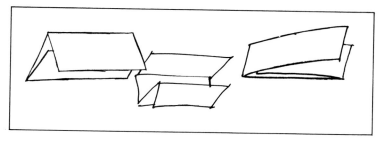

In producing a folder or any direct-mail piece, the designer starts from scratch. Paper stock, format, type for body copy, even the printing process has to be selected. The designer in effect launches a new publication whenever designing and producing a direct-mail piece.

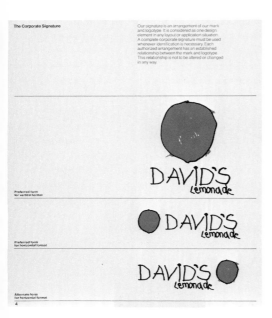

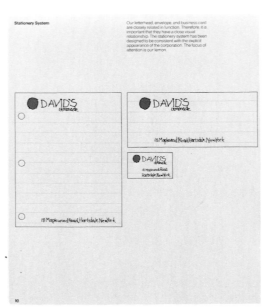

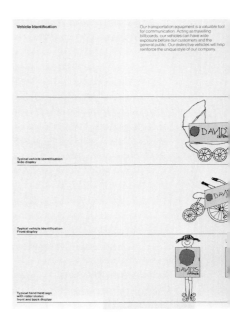

When you think of all the folders you see advertising and promoting products and causes and institutions, all the leaflets you see in packages, all the booklets you pick up at counters, and all the mailings you get urging you to subscribe to magazines, you begin to appreciate how massive a medium this is. In dollars spent on advertising, direct-mail ranks right up there with newspapers and TV. Certainly in dollars expended it is ahead of magazines and radio. Magazines themselves—many of them—could not exist were it not for direct-mail advertising to gain and hold subscribers.

The trend in direct mail as used by magazine and book publishers is to overwhelm the potential purchaser with a variety of separate pieces crammed into one large envelope. Lately the full-color broadside has become popular to carry the principal message. The typical mailing consists of the broadside, a letter, a return card and envelope, and an extra letter wondering how on earth you can afford to pass up this bargain. All must be designed to build up to a sale. Sometimes the pieces are unified in design; sometimes the designer purposely produces a hodgepodge to overwhelm the recipient.

The biggest job of a mailing is to get the reader to open the envelope. Writers and designers of direct-mail pieces try all kinds of tricks: manila envelopes with Copperplace Gothic type to look like official government business, roughly stamped "Urgent"s, real stamps instead of postage meter prints, handwriting instead of typewriting. Sometimes a piece of intriguing art does the job. *Harper's* mailings to potential subscribers have used a question printed on the envelope, without the name of the magazine: "Should you be punished for being born with a high IQ?" Can persons who value their intelligence resist finding out what this is all about?

The advantage of direct mail is that the recipient, theoretically, reads all this material without distraction from other printed material. It is a selective medium in that a direct-mail piece can be designed and sent to a specific class of persons. But most important to the designer, the medium is flexible; it can utilize any printing process, any paper, any format, any design style. And gimmickry is limited only by the designer's lack of ingenuity.

Folders

The folder is probably the most common form of direct mail. A single cut sheet, it can be folded once, twice, three times, or more after printing; and several different kinds of folds can be used, as the previous sketches have shown. What results from the folding are panels; you would have six panels to design in a two-fold folder, three on each side of the sheet. You would have eight panels to design in a three-fold folder. The trick is to design the panels to take advantage of the sequence of the folding.

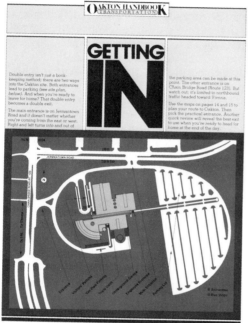

To help employees make the move when it changed its headquarters from Washington, D.C., to nearby Oakton, Virginia, AT&T *Long Lines* produced an "Oakton in a Nutshell" kit that included a handsome full-color 48-page 8 1/2 × 11 saddle-stitched booklet. This two-page spread shows the lively but orderly design created by Michael Gibbs. A light touch is provided by the noose (right page) that forms the "O" in "NOT."

Among the items included in the help-employees-to-move kit was this envelope containing cards to fill out. This illustration shows only a few of them.

This seven-fold accordian-folder publicizes Bayler University Medical Center's TelMed service, which allows people in the Dallas area to phone in for free information about medical problems and be plugged into any one of 300 available tapes. You see here the dark brown cover (with title in reverse) and the inside spread of the folder. The other side consists of just the dark brown color. The opened out phone-with-cord helps unite the panels and give them visual impact.

Some designers try to design folders so that each panel works separately. Other designers try to make spreads out of the panels.

A folder is cheaper to produce than a booklet because no binding costs are involved. But the design of the two involves similar problems.

Paper choice makes a big difference to the design. For instance, some papers fold well only with the grain. Size, quality, opacity, bulk, and durability desired all figure in the paper choice. So do mailing factors, printing process to be used, and the nature of the contents. An all-type piece may call for an antique (rough surface) stock, for instance, while a mostly-photography piece would call for a slick, coated stock. The size of the piece would be determined by how economically it cuts from the sheets or rolls available to the printer.

Whether the folder is to be a self-mailer or a piece to be put inside an envelope makes a difference. A self-mailer needs one panel—or part of one panel—left blank.

As a folder designer, you would do your rough layout or comprehensive to size, trimmed and folded as the piece is to appear in print. That way the client can actually hold it, study it for design and color, and get the feel of how it folds before okaying its final printing.

Before choosing a printer you would want to obtain some estimates of costs. For a big job, you would go to two or three printers. Be sure that each printer bases a bid on the same set of specifications and the same rough layout. Price alone should not necessarily determine the successful bidder. Sometimes a higher bid turns out to be more of a bargain.

Sometimes the designer presents camera-ready copy to the successful bidder, sometimes just the rough layout. If the printer is expected to furnish the pasteup, the cost is likely to be higher.

The design of direct mail falls usually to the advertising department of the company producing it or to its advertising agency. In almost every city freelancers take on direct-mail designing assignments, too, making anywhere from $50 to several hundred dollars per item, depending upon whether or not they furnish camera-ready copy or just a rough. Freelancers can also work with printers or engravers or platemakers.

Booklets

A booklet is a bound volume of eight or more pages, often with a page size that fits a No. 10 business envelope. In an 8 1/2 × 11 size, a booklet looks like a magazine or an annual report. It is usually saddle stapled. The cover stock often is heavier than the inside pages.

Cover stock comes in a greater range of colors and surfaces than regular book stock. Some of these papers come with one color or surface on one side and a different combination on the other.

Designing a booklet is much like designing a book, a subject covered in the concluding chapter.

Catalogs

It used to be that when we thought of catalogs we thought only of the massive "wish books" issued by Montgomery Ward, Sears Roebuck, and a few other big stores. But catalogs now come from all kinds of retailers, including those dealing in exotic and expen-

The Washington Park Zoo, Portland, reverses all type and boxes and uses some full-color photographs as rectangles, others as closeup silhouettes in this five-fold (12-panel) accordion fold. You see one side of the sheet here, the cover at the far right.

Two spreads from a full-color 8 1/2 × 11 booklet published by the Toledo Chamber of Commerce show how a grid, used throughout, can bring consistency to a publication. The pattern is always evident, even with slight variations in placement.

...for 20 years we've been making a world of difference.

For 20 years now Peace Corps has been sending Americans to the Third World, building a tradition of people - to - people cooperation. And when you consider how the world has changed in the last two decades, that makes Peace Corps pretty special.

Today, in a single month, more than one million lives are directly affected by Peace Corps volunteers at work in over 60 countries. They treat malnourished children. Bring water to deserts. Plant forests. Help build schools and bridges.

But just as important are the bridges Peace Corps volunteers build between people. By living and working in local communities, they offer people around the world a chance to learn about Americans. And vice versa.

By becoming a member of a neighborhood, village or town, Peace Corps volunteers don't just share their work with the people they live with. They share themselves. That means they return home with a unique knowledge of other peoples and cultures. And their experiences help our nation better understand what's happening in today's world.

It also helps make the hard work, long hours and personal sacrifice worth it. Despite the rigors of Peace Corps life, more than 9 out of 10 volunteers say they'd do it again. Sound remarkable? It is. But then, so are the people who have become Peace Corps volunteers. Since 1961 more than 80,000 Americans have served—including the 6,000 who serve today.

Twenty years ago Peace Corps was a great idea—a program that could help other nations meet their needs for skills. It was a program to promote better understanding of Americans abroad and greater knowledge of the Third World here at home.

In 1961, these were worthy objectives. But today—in an era of dwindling global resources, scarcer energy, rising international tensions and troubled economies—these Peace Corps goals have grown into prerequisites for a peaceful future.

Twenty years later, we're much more than just a good idea. We're helping to make the world work better.

fected by short-term national foreign policy objectives. Peace Corps is the only U.S. agency that places its people in the communities of developing nations to work and live with the people they're helping.

Volunteers represent the American people. They receive a monthly allowance that enables them to live at the level of their hosts. Often, in fact, they live with a host family. At the end of their service—usually two years—they get a readjustment payment of $125 for each month of service.

Peace Corps is looking for volunteers with practical experience. You don't need a special degree; we'll teach you the specific skills you don't have, or help you discover talents you do have, but don't know about. During your 8-12-week training you'll study the culture of the people with whom you'll be living, and learn to converse in the local language.

What volunteers have in common is motivation. They have a desire to work in a way that suits the local setting,

and to understand and be accepted by their hosts. A volunteer might be a mid-career plumber, or a grandmother who has taught three generations of children to read and write, or a recent college graduate with a sociology degree; a printer, a lawyer, a nurse, a farmer, a doctor, a teacher.

In return you get experience—valuable professional and personal experience—and expertise in the Third World, an important asset to almost any career in the 1980s. You get a chance to travel and broaden yourself as you interact with other people, other cultures, other lifestyles. You get as much responsibility as you can handle. You get plenty of independence. You get more challenges than most people face in a lifetime. And you get a unique opportunity to see yourself, your country and the world from a new perspective.

So, then: What does Peace Corps offer? We're ready to offer you the world.

These two spreads from a Peace Corps booklet show how art can be used to cross the gutter to unite two facing pages. It is important to pick art—or crop it—so that nothing important falls at the gutter, where binding occurs.

sive merchandise. If you've ever bought anything by mail you find yourself swamped for years afterwards with all kinds of catalogs, especially at Christmastime. Some firm sold your name to a mailing list broker. You became a known buyer.

Some customers or potential customers find it necessary to *pay* for their catalogs—to *pay* for being advertised to. Gucci in an ad in *The New Yorker* for the 1981 Christmas season asked $8 for its catalog, plus another $1.50 for "handling and postage."

Designing a catalog involves presenting merchandise in the best possible lights and in the most favorable settings. Pages are necessarily busy; a theme of some kind often helps to unite them.

Catalogs help sell more than mere merchandise.

College catalogs (or "bulletins," as they are often called) sell courses rather than merchandise, but they have some of the same problems. They may look more like a book than a catalog. The cover is particularly important. To the designers of some school catalogs, cover art boils down to the latest shot of a good looking student reading a book, sitting under a tree with campus buildings in the background. And if the campus itself does not yield scenery attractive enough to go on the cover, the designer may choose to reproduce a picture of a nearby stream or mountain that students have been known to frequent on slow spring afternoons. Sometimes an in-classroom shot shows up with enough natural light to make good reproduction possible. Or perhaps the designer settles for a montage of faces of happy but serious-minded students, with the expected ratio of men to women and minority to majority students, of course.

For one of its catalogs Cooper Union eschewed the art stereotypes and went with all-type, using the type to create the illusion that the reader was stumbling onto a conversation among students. It was an example of theater-of-the-mind design.

Down the left side of the cover ran a series of conversational paragraphs, set in various typefaces to approximate the nature of the conversation and the character of the speakers. It was all highly imaginary but perfectly appropriate. And to help with the illusion that the reader was coming by in the middle of things, the quotations bled off the top and bottom. In this respect, it was an example of wallpaper design.

Some of the quotes read:

"Fine art—what good is that? People will need an art form that communicates! That's why I'm in graphic design."

"Would you listen to that now—an altruistic commercial artist."

And:

". . . you miss the point. The real problems are crowding, energy, scarcity, pollution, the population crunch. And they all fall on the architect's shoulders."

Then:

"I don't agree. . . ."

And so on.

Annual reports

People read annual reports to find out about companies they have invested in or want to invest in, to check them out as places to work, to see if they are good credit risks as buyers of services, parts, and supplies.

This cover for a Nordstrom "Indian Summer" catalog features a diamond-shaped painting by Neil Parsons, a noted American Indian artist. Designer Claudia Milne uses triangular corners to put the art in context. The largely maroon, olive, and gold colors reflect the colors of the merchandise advertised inside. Nordstrom, Inc., is a Seattle-based fashion specialty store.

A spread from the same catalog mortising four photographs inside a two-page bleed photograph. All the rich color photographs in the catalog were taken at Santa Fe, New Mexico.

Another page from the Nordstrom catalog. This is a good example of framing people in a photograph.

The front and back cover of an annual report issued by Doyle Dane Bernbach, the advertising agency. The original was in full color. The montage represented the various products and companies that were the agency's clients.

The full-color cover of the 1979 annual report of H. J. Heinz Company shows that you don't have to resort to large type for a title. This small title is reversed in a solid-color area of a closeup photograph. Corporate Graphics Inc., New York, designed it.

This spread represents a
continuation of a long article on
"The Year" in an H. J. Heinz
Company annual report. All the
way through, columns are
separated by thin lines, with
heavy, broken bars at the top.
Each spread is interrupted—and
decorated—with an illustrated
sidebar, with a different type
printed in a dark color.
Corporate Graphics Inc. did the
designing.

**Page 1 of an H. J. Heinz
Company annual report presents
a table of contents, a description
of the company, and a lineup of
company logotypes, all displayed
with a generous amount of white
space.**

Annual reports rank among the most elaborate of the direct-
mail forms. For a big company, copies of an annual report in the
early 1980s ran to an average of $3 each, and that did not include
postage to mail it out (another $1.50 or so). With that kind of an
investment, design had to be carefully thought out. Annual reports
often dazzle readers with quality art and expensive paper. Some
companies, like Emhart Corporation, put out reports in videotape
form.

Annual reports of most corporations must conform to regulations set up by the Securities and Exchange Commission. A designer's first job here is to understand current regulations, which
change from time to time, then deal with such matters as what
content must be included and what type size must be used.

But even companies not bound by such regulation, and non-
profit organizations, too, issue annual reports. Beginning in April
of each year, which is about as early as anyone can get all the
figures and features together and publish them, these booklets, some
pretentious, some rather commonplace, go into the mails or over
counters to people interested in what these organizations are doing.

Albany General Hospital, Albany, Oregon, gives citizens of the
town an "Annual Review" as a tabloid supplement to the Albany

**Special annual reports, for
employees rather than
stockholders, have become
popular with some large
corporations. ITT Rayonier used
a series of big-photograph,
small-photograph pages for one
of its employees' annual reports,
the photographs and headings in
black, the boldface, italic, sans
serif body copy in red.**

Democrat Herald. Like any annual report it carries revenue and expense statements and various statistical information as well as feature material. It is generously illustrated. Saint Joseph Hospital, Joliet, Illinois, gives its annual report an added dimension and additional use by putting it in a spiral binding and making a calendar out of each two-page spread.

While annual reports for profit-making organizations are designed primarily for stockholders, most of the nation's large manufacturing companies distribute annual-report information to employees, too. From some companies the employees get the same annual report stockholders get; from others, regular annual reports with special sections inserted; from still others, specially prepared annual reports simplifying all those tables and financial reports. Sometimes the company magazine devotes one issue a year to the annual report.

Omark Industries, Portland, for its 1980 annual report to employees issued a kit with loose 7 1/2″ × 5 1/2″ cards, one side asking a question and featuring a photograph of a worker, the other side giving an answer. The kit carried the title: "[President] Ted Smith Answers Tough Questions About: Pay, the Economy, Omark's Future, and More."

Few companies or organizations are willing to resort to humor in annual reports—annual reports are serious business—but in recent years the reports have offered readers feature material and informal photography as well as the expected statistics and financial statements. A number of them revolve around themes, as yearbooks do. For instance, Time-Life, Inc., designed an annual report to look like a magazine.

Some organizations are getting away from the usual 8 1/2 × 11 saddle-stapled look. Their reports come in oversize or undersize formats or folders. These are fine, provided they can be filed conveniently by the recipient.

The cover can be a decisive factor in drawing the reader into the annual report and even in setting the mood. The theme, if there is one, starts here. Special papers and inks can be chosen that are appropriate to the report and the organization. Often the cover comes from a heavier stock than what is used on inside pages. And the cover can come in the form of a gatefold or with an extra tissue-paper or acetate wrapper. Die cuts can also be used.

Like magazines, annual reports can carry bound-in signatures of different paper stock and even of different page sizes.

Nowhere in graphic design is white space more important. White space helps carry the concept of quality, something stockholders and members of an organization can appreciate.

Color is an important consideration. If used, it should be planned from the beginning. Color becomes especially useful in dramatizing charts and graphs. But Professor Bob Anservitz of the University of Georgia School of Journalism observes that in many charts and graphs color is used only decoratively, whereas it could be used to key the information.

In recent years many companies have cut back on color, art, inserts, and other production niceties. Other companies continue to dazzle readers. "Research done by my students and me has shown that there is no direct relationship or predictability between the poshness or austerity level of the annual report and the p & 1 [profit and loss] statement," reports Professor Anservitz. ". . . In a poor year, a company may forego worrying about some share-

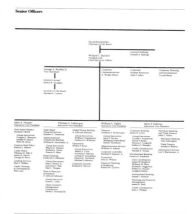

This Chase Manhattan Corporation annual report uses nothing but type on the cover, but type tastefully arranged, in two colors plus black, with plenty of white space. A full interview with David Rockefeller and Willard C. Butcher appears inside. Design by Corporate Graphics Inc., New York.

This organization chart—a full page—from an annual report of The Chase Manhattan Corporation shows that you don't have to resort to boxes and gimmicks to show relationships of officers in an organization. The thick and thin lines here (some of them in an olive second color) pleasantly organize the spaces and help make the chart readable.

Safety Scoreboard

Beginning with this issue,
PAPER TIMES will list
the continuing safety performances
of Boise Cascade's
14 North American pulp
and paper mills.

LOCATION	NUMBER OF LOST-TIME CASES	NUMBER OF WORK DAYS LOST	TOTAL OF REPORTED CASES
PERIOD COVERED		JAN.-SEPT. 1976	
BRATTLEBORO	0	0	5
CALCASIEU	2	15	19
DeRIDDER	13	373	19
FORT FRANCES	18	316	173
INTERNATIONAL FALLS	16	89	64
KENORA	5	307	81
MIRAMICHI	20	202	26
RUMFORD	39	1897	49
ST. HELENS	2	47	47
SALEM	19	205	34
STEILACOOM	10	478	19
VANCOUVER	1	19	13
WALLULA	7	76	23
WEST DUDLEY	2	21	2

If you must use a table, give it some design and surround it with a little art. This from *Paper Times,* a magazine for employees of Boise Cascade Paper Group. The original occupied a full 8 1/2 × 11 page.

The Official District Seven

House 7 Organ

FEBRUARY, 1977

This is an association publication for editors of company magazines. A number of these are published in the United States and Canada by chapters of the International Association of Business Communicators. They take a newsletter format. This one is a four-pager, with a pre-set logo and body copy simply typed out on a typewriter, with no attempt made to justify the right-hand margin.

holders grumbling about the gloss and heft of any obviously costly report and may issue a particularly Sybaritic report to satisfy the felt need to bolster the egos of another genre of shareholders and financial analysts."

Company magazines

Previous chapters have already dealt with company magazines, but because they come in so many varieties, some additional attention seems appropriate here. Company magazines are omnipresent, and they appear in every format imaginable. The saddle-stapled 8 1/2 × 11 magazine is standard. Students looking forward to magazine careers no doubt will find most opportunities lie with company magazines. In most cases, the editor does it all: writes, edits, takes photographs, designs, lays out, and even pastes up. The bigger books leave the designing to an outside art director. In some cases the editing and art directing are done by the company's advertising agency.

Few company magazines carry ads. The publications are themselves advertisements—institutional advertisements—for the companies publishing them. In that respect, they fall under the heading of direct-mail advertising. Some company magazines communicate mostly with employees; others communicate mostly with customers, potential customers, dealers, and opinion leaders on the outside; some try to serve both internal and external audiences.

Just as general-circulation magazines have grown specialized, so have company magazines. The big companies publish a whole series of magazines, each concentrating on one aspect of the business or addressing itself to one level of employees or customers.

Association publications

An estimated 40,000 associations exist in this country to promote the interests of industrial, professional, educational, charity, religious, social, and other groups; and almost all of them are involved in publishing activities. They produce magazines, newsletters, directories, manuals, annual reports, and direct-mail pieces of all descriptions.

Most of the regularly issued publications exist to educate members and keep up the funding of the organizations. Until recently these publications carried material of interest only to persons associated with or sympathetic to the associations. But they are broadening their appeal now and concerning themselves with the world outside.

The magazines issued by associations look like any other magazines, except that usually they try harder to keep costs down. Many association magazines accept advertising. In that respect, they differ from company magazines.

Newsletters

Talking about the design of company publications, you tend to think only in terms of saddle-stapled 8 1/2 × 11 magazines or larger tabloid newspapers. You forget about a third important format, unless you happen to read or edit a publication that uses it: the newsletter.

Corporate profits: a pretty thin slice

Profit is not a four-letter word. It's the ingredient that makes our free-market system work. Dinwiddy's Diner—and Boise-Cascade—are part of that system.

Paper Times gives dimension and realism to a pie chart. The chart illustrated an article that establishes the fact that "The average American manufacturer earns a net profit of less than *five cents on the sales dollar*. But the man on the street thinks profits are much higher."

And even among newsletters, there is a variety of subformats, ranging from pages inside regular magazines through loose sheets on up to folded and even bound sheets. The binding can take the form of a single staple in one corner or the saddle stapling used by magazines. The distinction between newsletters and magazines, especially when you get up to eight pages, becomes blurred.

One of the most popular formats for newsletters now is the two-fold folder with a total of six 8 1/2 × 11 pages (three on each side of an 11″ × 25 1/2″ sheet). The format allows the reader to turn back an illustrated cover to reveal three facing pages of important information. Then there are two more pages on the back. The newsletter becomes a sort of unbound magazine.

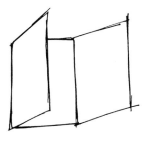

Chocolate News is printed with chocolate-scented ink on brown stock. It goes out bi-monthly to 10,000 people who just love chocolate. It is published, of course, to make money. Other newsletters are published for public relations reasons. Every kind of organization issues newsletters. Politicians find them an ideal medium to reach constituents.

In one of his newsletters, Sen. Daniel Patrick Moynihan (D.,

THE YEARS OF NEGLECT

This is the back page of a full-size, full-color newspaper (or magapaper), *RF Illustrated*, published by the Rockefeller Foundation. You see here an article, "The Years of Neglect," and a sidebar inside and another right below. At the bottom is a house ad about some Foundation "working papers." The initial letters start out large and get progressively smaller as you read through the article. Each is an outline letter with full-color illustrations inside. The initials are of the kind that extend up from their paragraphs rather than down into them.

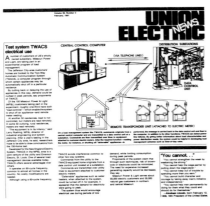

This monthly *Union Electric News* consists of one 33 × 11 sheet folded twice to make six pages (three on each side). Editor Deborah J. Walther uses black and one color on a tinted stock. That's the cover above. The inside spread (below) shows how bars and lines and a consistent sink can be used to organize material.

N.Y.) used the line: "I would . . . welcome comment about this adventure into newslettering." Prof. James Q. Wilson of Harvard was displeased with the use of "newsletter" as a verb. "If my good friend, the Senator, continues to newsletter me, I shall ask my post office to deadletter him."[2]

Among these publications are newsletters on newslettering, among them *The Newsletter on Newsletters* (44 West Market Street, Rhinebeck, New York 12572). There is also *The Newsletter Yearbook/Directory,* a Newsletter Clearinghouse, and a Newsletter Association of America.

Prof. Albert Walker of Northern Illinois University calls newsletters "the number one print medium among business communicators." He estimates that 50,000 companies and organizations issue newsletters. The typical newsletter acts as a means of internal communication between management and members or employees of an organization, and it is distributed free; but 2,000 newsletters dealing with specialized information circulate to business and professional persons who are willing to pay a high price to subscribe, in some cases several hundred dollars a year.

"Readership surveys reveal that subscribers to newspapers and magazines are scanners and skimmers," reports Professor Walker. "In fact, one survey revealed that many subscribers to magazines may not get around to reading some issues of the magazine they pay for.

"On the other hand, subscribers to newsletters are likely to read every issue from cover-to-cover."[3]

2. Quoted by William Safire, "Safety Nets," *The New York Times Magazine,* March 29, 1979, p 10.

3. Albert Walker, "Newsletters: Fastest Rising Print Medium," *Journal of Organizational Communication,* 1977/1, p 22.

From a design standpoint, it is not always easy to draw a line between a company magazine and a newsletter. The monthly management newsletter published by W. R. Grace & Co. is a handsome but no-nonsense sheet folded to four 8 1/2 × 11 pages. Sometimes an extra 8 1/2 × 11 sheet (two pages) slips inside. You see here a four-page issue. The publication uses a second color (orange) for horizontal rules, an occasional duotone, and (screened with black) the "NEWS" in the logo. The headline schedule calls for sans serif faces, with the body copy set in a light face slab serif. Note the abstract art used to decorate the column headings.

The inside two pages of the four-page oversize newsletter *Re:cap*, a Mobil Corporation publication, use boxes and bars and a deep sink to nicely organize a variety of features. Only one headline face is used. Body copy is unjustified. The two line drawings add visual interest to the spread.

A spread just inside the cover of an eight-page saddle-stapled 9 × 11 newsletter, *Alum News,* published by Bristol-Myers for its retired and former employees. The front page—and all pages—look very much like these sample pages: all the stories carry headlines in a single typeface. This nicely unifies the publication. Thin horizontal rules above and below the headlines give them added display. Lines of the headlines are centered. Boxes surround some of the stories. *Alum News* is one of several publications produced by Editorial Services, a division of Bristol-Myers, New York.

Provided you don't do it too often in a yearbook, you can sometimes get dramatic effects by playing around with photographs. An issue of *The Trojan Epic* puts together parts of two students—a female and a male—and adds extra legs to show the fashions for the year. "From overalls, to painter pants, to high waisted wool cuffs, to quilted patchwork jeans, to cotton cuffs or just plain levi's . . . all styles could be seen at West High," says the caption. West High School is in Iowa City, Iowa. Ben Van Zante is publications adviser.

He adds: "Increased reader confidence [in newsletters] may . . . be due to the newsletter's simplified format. . . ." There is much to be said for keeping it simple. Too often designers try to make of a format something that it is not. Perhaps they try to make a newsletter look like a newspaper or magazine. The very nature of a newsletter dictates that the copy not be cluttered with useless ornamentation. A single wide column of copy, typed on a typewriter, unjustified, with extra space between paragraphs and with typed, all-caps heads at the top or at the side should do the job. Keeping the items short and separating them with extra space, stars, or something similar works well in most cases. A preprinted logo at the top of the first page starts things off.

The standard newsletter format works well enough to be copied by magazines that run "newsletters" as pages of late news in their regular issues. To duplicate the tinted-stock look that many newsletters carry, the magazines often run the items over a tint block or a color.

A newsletter often is the product of a duplicating rather than a printing process. In contrast to printing, duplicating produces only a few hundred copies per master, with quality inferior to printing but good enough to serve the purposes of the publication.

Chief among the duplicating processes, so far as publications are concerned, are spirit duplicating and mimeographing. In spirit duplicating, also called fluid duplicating, the image is typed or drawn on a master backed by an aniline-dye carbon sheet. A deposit of dye is transferred to the back of the master, which is used to do the printing. In mimeographing, a stencil permits ink to pass from a cylinder to the paper.

Paul Novitski, who art directed the *Pacific Northwest Review of Books* and who, on the side, produced a fanzine (see glossary), defends one of the duplicating processes, mimeographing, for its image softness as well as its economy. He points out that electronic stenciling in mimeographing can reproduce art with excellent fidelity.[4]

There is a process that lies somewhere between duplicating and printing, but closer to printing, called Multilith. If yours is a duplicated publication, you should investigate its possibilities, for it can reproduce photographs and art and print in color just as its big brother—offset lithography—can.

And of course for really short runs ordinary office copying machines, so readily available now, can be the quickest and cheapest and most efficient reproduction system of all.

Western Electric, New York, produces an electronic newsletter. On the day of "publication," which occurs six times a year, the editor roughs out copy in the morning and has a secretary code it into the company's computer system, then proofs it on a terminal. By afternoon it is teleprinted and available to field representatives in 35 offices across the country. There are no printing or mailing costs, of course; just the cost of software and computer time.[5]

Yearbooks

As a print medium, yearbooks fall somewhere in between magazines and books. Because they are permanently bound and because they serve both historical and reference purposes, they have many qualities of the book. But because they are issued periodically, they also fit the magazine category. Increasingly, they have taken on the look of the magazine.

Many kinds of organizations issue yearbooks, but schools and colleges are the most familiar users of this medium. While interest in yearbooks may be only moderate in the large state universities, it continues strong in the smaller colleges, and especially in high schools, where students identify more with each other and their institutions. Most junior high schools and many elementary schools publish yearbooks, too.

The yearbook's main offering is the photograph: the informal shot, the group shot, the mug shot. Over the years as visual sophistication has increased, editors have given more attention to the informal shot, less to the group and mug shots. But they ignore the latter at the peril of decreased sales. Yearbooking these days turns out to be a constant battle between the editor's and designer's urge to be creative and the reader's desire to have an album of portraits to file away for later perusal. There is room for experimental typography and design in the front of each book, of course, but the real challenge to the designer is to work out a readable, orderly, and attractive display of the routine lineup of same-size pictures in the back.

Settling on a theme proves to be a first hurdle for most editors and designers. *The Haliscope* published by Halifax County Senior

The first issue of a four-page (one folded sheet) newsletter, printed in black on quality light brown paper. Each three-column page features art similar to what you see here on page 1. The art butts up against the horizontal rules and bars in some cases; in other cases it juts up over them. *Media* is a publication for the staff and clients of Campbell-Ewald Advertisng.

A full-page high-contrast photograph used to set a mood for a feature section in the *Round Table,* yearbook published by Northwest Classen High School, Oklahoma City, Oklahoma. The well-composed photograph nicely places its figures and brilliantly displays its textures. The caption appears in the upper-left corner, well away from the image area of the photograph. M. E. Burdette is adviser.

---

4. From a letter to the author from Paul Novitski, Seattle, Wash., June 15, 1978.

5. "Electronic Newsletters Offer Speed, Flexibility," *IABC News,* February 1982, p 11.

That's not really an old lady sitting there. It's a plastic casting by Duane Hanson on exhibit at the University Art Museum, Berkeley. Photographer Peter Haley for the yearbook at the University of California nicely captures the expressions of incredulity on the faces of the onlookers.

High School, South Boston, Virginia, one year started out with 80 themes, boiling them down, finally, to six really promising ones. "But further reduction was impossible," the editors wrote in the back of their book. "There wasn't one major story of the year. The story was multiple. What seemed to be happening in student life wasn't happening in academics. Clubs had their own story; so did sports." So the yearbook presented six themes, each with its own section. Each section had its own design style, too, with the unifying force in the book coming from standard caption and headline type styles.

The theme, singular or plural, should be appropriate to the school and to the year. It should not simply evolve from some special interest of the editor. It should not be a typographic and visual gimmick used as an excuse to bombard the reader with a lot of verbal or visual puns.

Tune In Tomorrow

The massive, crowded *Volunteer* of the University of Tennessee, one of the nation's few impressive college yearbooks, offers special features in addition to the usual sections on academic affairs, housing, graduation, etc. This two-page feature deals with soap operas. ". . . alongside tennis and skipping class, soap operas have to be one of a student's favorite pastimes." The captions for the small photos at the extreme left and extreme right serve also as blurbs because a larger, bolder typeface is used. Les Hyder is adviser.

Special Report

Another spread from the *Volunteer* showing a variation in the basic design. In this case, copy spills onto the next page. The "Special Report" deals with news items for the year.

A theme too blatantly developed can do more harm than good in unifying a book. It takes over, calling attention to itself rather than to the book's real content. Some designers manage to put out yearbooks without themes or rather with themes that are only typographic: for instance, the type remains consistent throughout the book.

All publication designers have a tendency to imitate one another; yearbook designers carry imitation to an extreme. Because most of the designers are inexperienced and unsure of themselves, they gather all the yearbooks they can from other schools and borrow liberally from them. It is a sort of blind-leading-the-blind operation. If not that, they engage in wild typographic experiments which succeed only in making the text difficult to read and the pictures hard to identify.

As an alternative, the imitation of major magazines or books

High school yearbooks, once a repository of examples of what *not* to do in graphic design, have become much more design conscious. This is the title page spread and a spread from the introduction to the *Eugenean,* yearbook of South Eugene High School, Eugene, Oregon. The example is from 1968, but the highly ordered, modular look holds up well.

from commercial publishers, where design is more subtle, is encouraged by yearbook advisers and judges of organizations that rate yearbooks.

Uppermost in the designer's mind is—or should be—the use to be made of the book years after it has been purchased. To read the book later, the reader must be helped along by captions.

Some thought should be given to the durability of the binding. And if a yearbook has only a limited number of pages, the editor is not likely to make it look bigger by giving it a padded cover. A padded cover only signals that the book is small.

Nor need the cover necessarily present some striking art or carry the school colors or symbol. The best covers sometimes are those that carry only the name in a good looking, well spaced and placed type.

Whether or not the yearbook includes special division pages, the editor and designer should organize the material into divisions or departments and include a table of contents to make things easy for the reader. An index at the back helps readers find people they want to see and read about. That means that all non-bleed pages should be numbered. On the title page or right near it should go a paragraph of information about the school, its location, and frequency of publication. The principal staff members should be listed, too. The title of the book should remain constant on the cover, title page, and wherever else it is mentioned. If "The" or the year is part of the title, it should always appear in formal references to the book.

Dedications, acknowledgements, and colophons are only optional; and certainly preoccupation with the staff and its problems should be discouraged. Too often yearbooks end up with orgies of printed self-congratulations.

Suggested further reading

Alexander, Shirley B., *An Inside Look at the Newsletter Field: Report on Survey of Newsletters,* Newsletter Clearinghouse, 44 W. Market Street, Rhinebeck, New York 12572, 1975.

Arnold, Edmund C., *The Student Journalist and Editing the Yearbook,* Richards Rosen Press, New York, 1974.

Beach, Mark, *Editing Your Newsletter: A Guide to Writing, Design and Production,* Coast to Coast Books, 2934 N.E. 16th Ave., Portland, Oreg. 97212, 1982. (Second Edition.)

Brann, Christian, *Direct Mail and Direct Response Promotion,* Halstead Press, John Wiley & Sons, Inc., New York, 1973.

Brigham, Nancy, *How to Do Leaflets, Newsletters and Newspapers,* The New England Free Press, 60 Union Square, Somerville, Mass. 02143, 1976.

Denton, Mary Raye, *A Blueprint for Yearbooks Today,* Crescendo Publications, Inc., P.O. Box 28218, Dallas, Texas 75228, 1976.

Hodgson, Richard S., *Direct Mail and Mail Order Handbook,* Dartnell, Chicago, 1976. (Second Edition.)

Jones, Gerre, *How to Prepare Professional Design Brochures,* McGraw-Hill Book Company, New York, 1976.

Kliment, Stephen A., *Creative Communications for a Successful Design Practice,* The Whitney Library of Design, New York, 1977.

Maas, Jane, *Better Brochures, Catalogs and Mailing Pieces,* St. Martin's Press, New York, 1981.

Moore, Charles B. and William F. Blue, Jr., *Editing and Layout Techniques for the Company Editor,* Ink Art Publications, P.O. Box 36070, Indianapolis, Ind., 1979.

Patterson, N. S., *Yearbook Planning, Editing, and Production,* Iowa State University Press, Ames, Iowa, 1976.

Pritchett, Elaine H., *The Student Journalist and the Newsmagazine Format,* Richards Rosen Press, New York, 1976.

Ragan, Lawrence, *The Organizational Press,* Lawrence Ragan Communications, Chicago, Ill., 1981.

Raines, Gar, *How to Design, Produce, and Use Business Forms,* North American Publishing Company, Philadelphia, 1971.

Schuh, Colleen, *Newsletters: Designing and Producing Them,* Division of Program and Staff Development, University of Wisconsin-Extension, Madison, Wis., 1978. (Revised Edition.)

Stone, Bob, *Successful Direct Marketing Methods,* Crain Books, Chicago, 1975.

Sutter, Jan, *Slinging Ink: A Practical Guide to Producing Booklets, Newspapers, and Ephemeral Publications,* William Kaufmann, Inc., Los Altos, Calif., 1982.

Wales, LaRae H., *A Practical Guide to Newsletter Editing & Design,* Iowa State University Press, Ames, Iowa, 1976.

Creative Newsletter Graphics, Creative Communications, Suite 530, One Dupont Circle, Washington, D.C. 20036, 1976. (Expensive.)

Oxbridge Directory of Newsletters, Oxbridge Communications, Inc., New York. (1979 edition lists 5,044 newsletters.)

A page from the index of *The Haliscope* published by Halifax County Senior High School, South Boston, Virginia. Each page of the index features at least one photograph to provide visual relief from the list of names. The photos, like the boxes that surround each page, have rounded corners. Richard J. Fitz, Jr., is publications adviser.

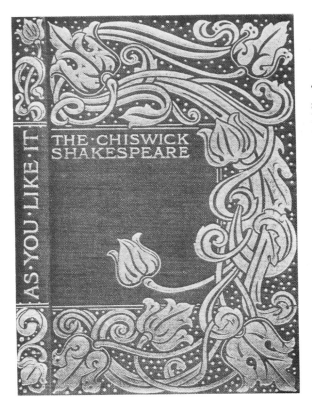

This handbound turn-of-the-century book uses an art nouveau design for its front cover and spine. Small dots, picked up from the basic design, separate words in the titles. The small, all-caps title on the cover snuggles up in one corner of the rectangle that contains it. The designer was Gerald Moira.

A number of years ago books used classic roman faces, in rather large body sizes, letterpressed skillfully on off-white, antique paper stock. In some cases the paper's edges were deckled. Spacing was tightly controlled, and any artwork or decoration was subtly integrated. The understated beauty came largely from the careful craftsmanship. Costs today put such beauty beyond the reach of most publishers, although Alfred A. Knopf, Random House, and a few others still make stabs at it.

With less luxury to work with publishers can still produce books that have the look if not the feel of quality.

This final chapter explores aspects of book design, typography, art, and production that have not been treated in previous chapters.

Understanding book publishing

Think of a book publisher as essentially a middleman between the writer and the reader. It is the book publisher who arranges the details of publication and distribution of the manuscript and who finances the project. The publisher's job is to make money for both the company and the writer.

Under the standard contract between writer and publisher, the writer gets 10 percent of the retail price of every book sold, a little more if the book goes into high sales figures. The other 90 percent is used to pay for the editing, design, production, printing, promotion, and distribution of the book, and other business expenses, and to provide some profit to the publisher.

More disorganized, more hazardous than most businesses, book publishing is unique in that its product constantly changes. Each book published—some houses publish 600 or 700 titles a year—must be separately designed, produced, and promoted. ". . . [Book] publishing has adapted to visual demands," say R. D. Scudellari, corporate art director at Random House. "Books are now much more graphic, more product oriented. So where we used to have only author relationships, we now have more pure product development."[1]

The book publishing industry tends to divide most of its output into two broad categories: tradebooks and textbooks. Textbooks are those volumes, mostly nonfiction, published to meet the specific needs of students at all levels. Sales depend upon adoptions by teachers, departments, and boards of education. Tradebooks in-

1. "Interview: R. D. Scudellari," *Art Direction,* March 1979, p. 34.

clude most other books, fiction as well as nonfiction. They do not serve a captive audience; sales must be made on an individual basis, and they often depend upon impulse buying. For this reason, tradebooks, unlike textbooks, require jackets as an aid in selling. Sales are made through retail stores, through mail order, through book clubs.

Textbooks and tradebooks use different pricing structures. The difference between the list price and the dealer's cost for a trade book is 40 percent. For textbooks, the difference is only half that, which explains why textbooks, like this one, are hard to get at regular bookstores. Textbooks for college students must be sold by college bookstores where large numbers are ordered for classes.

Reference books (dictionaries and encyclopedias) and children's books ("juveniles," as trade calls them) are in categories of their own. They require different kinds of selling methods as well as different design and production approaches.

Some publishers specialize in one kind of book, some in another; and a few publishers produce books in all categories. Several hundred book publishers in the United States produce among them close to 40,000 different titles each year.

The typical first printing of a book comes to 5,000 to 10,000 copies. If a book sells well, the publisher may go back into a second printing, a third, and others as needed. This is not the same thing as putting out a new *edition* of a book. A new edition involves an updating and rewriting of all the chapters and probably a rearrangement of them. It may mean dropping certain chapters and adding new ones. It involves new typesetting and design. In short, it means a brand new book but one that draws on the goodwill and promotional buildup of the first edition. The book you are reading is the third edition of a book that went through several printings in its first and second editions. Textbooks go to new editions more frequently than trade books. Publishers decide to bring out new editions to update the material and, frankly, to fight the market in used books.

In the early years of book publishing, the publisher, printer, and seller were one and the same. As the industry grew, each became a business by itself. Today few publishers do their own printing; and, except for mail order sales, the retailing of books is also a separate business.

Bookplates, printed or hand-drawn labels pasted in the front of books by book owners, show pride of ownership and identify books in case they are borrowed. Some people collect bookplates as a hobby. This turn-of-the-century art nouveau example is by Howard Nelson.

What design does for books

Does design spur the sale of a book? Probably not, admits Marshall Lee, a book design and production specialist. But poor design can hurt sales. "The general public's reaction to book design is, in most cases, subconscious," he writes. "Except where the visual aspect is spectacular, the nonprofessional browser is aware of only a general sense of pleasure or satisfaction in the presence of a well-designed book and a vague feeling of irritation when confronted by a badly designed one."[2]

Only the large houses, those publishing more than 100 books a year, seem able to employ full-time art directors and designers.

2. Marshall Lee, *Bookmaking: The Illustrated Guide to Design and Production,* R. R. Bowker Company, New York, 1965, p. 13.

These four spreads from the fourth edition of this author's heavily illustrated *The Design of Advertising* show how a grid, with single columns of copy pushed consistently to left and right outside edges, provides a concentration of white space at the gutter for a variety of arrangements of art and captions.

Some houses don't even have production departments, turning that job over instead to independent shops and studios.

A few houses—Alfred A. Knopf is one—use the same designer or group of designers to develop a "house style," making books from that house easily recognizable. Publishers bringing out a series of related books, for example, books covering various aspects of the law or a "college outlines" series, tie the books together with the same basic cover and interior design. The pattern on the cover may change from title to title only in the colors used.

The typical book designer is a freelancer who works for a number of houses, designing books for as little as $200 or $300 each. For a jacket, a designer may get even less. The book publishing industry is not noted for its lush commissions to freelancers. But there is a satisfaction in this work, designers tell themselves, that can't be found in the much higher paid area of advertising or even in the slightly higher paid field of magazine journalism.

The book designer's approach

The typical book comes in a 6 × 9 size, centers its display-type lines, uses Times Roman for body type, and maybe Helvetica for titles, runs chapter numbers up large, starts opening paragraphs of chapters flush left, and puts most margin space at the bottoms of pages. All of which works well enough. As a designer you would want to have reasons for varying this approach.

When you vary the approach you engage in what Stanley Rice calls "design by exception." So much of book design is routine, he points out, and designers would prefer not to be bothered with some of it. There are just so many ways to take care of page after page of text material. Designers, he says, are beginning to ask printers and typesetters to follow standard formats except where the designers specify something else. "Design by exception can be most useful to the designer when it is conscious, systematic, and implemented by computer-controlled composition using stored format controls."[3]

3. Stanley Rice, *Book Design: Systematic Aspects*, R. R. Bowker Company, New York, 1978, p. 221.

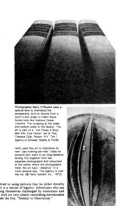

You can also look at book design as involving two basic approaches, as all graphic design does. One is the *transparent* approach (Marshall Lee's term), where the design does not intrude. The designer makes reading as effortless as possible.

The other is the *mood* approach, in which the designer sets a stage for the reader. The choice of typefaces and illustrations amplifies what is in the text. In some cases, they call attention to themselves. Obviously, this second approach is the more spectacular, perhaps even the more desirable. But it has to be good.

The first approach is safer. The second approach—more fun.

When dealing with mood, the designer takes into account not only the subject matter but also the nature of the audience. Certain typefaces, for instance, are more appropriate for children than for adults (although, ironically, it is the child, whose eyes see best, who gets the larger, bolder faces). The kind of pictures used depends to a large extent on the kind of reader the book seeks to reach.

Some of the best design in publishing—certainly some of the best art—can be found in children's books.

Textbooks present a special problem to the designer because they are selected or purchased, not by the readers but by teachers or, worse, by committees. The designer then must satisfy two different audiences.

In textbook design, writers play an important role if not in design then in art selection. Art and copy must be integrated, and the author is in the best position to help along that integration. ". . . Ideally, there should be no separation of author, illustrator and designer," says Alexander J. Burke, Jr., president of McGraw-Hill Book Company. "Communication through word, picture and design is, or should be, a simultaneous act of creation. Where it is, we get better education and better bookmaking."[4]

With textbooks reaching new highs in cost to students, good design becomes even more important. This is especially true in the United States where, according to Ed McLarin, vice president of international sales for McGraw-Hill Book Company, college text-

4. Quoted in "New Research, Team Approach Needed in Textbook Design," *Publishers Weekly*, January 3, 1977, p. 54.

books are the best designed and most attractively produced in the world.[5]

Color is almost mandatory for textbooks designed for high school audiences or for courses in college with large enrollments. The competition here is fierce.

How-to books also represent another challenge to designers. Usually, there are several available on the same subject on the bookstore shelves. Potential readers have only a short time to make their decisions. The name of the author is not likely to be decisive. The appearance of the book may make all the difference. Obviously, a heavily illustrated how-to will look more inviting than one with only a few illustrations. And color may also be crucial.

As a book designer you would be particularly concerned about unity. You achieve unity by keeping to the same typeface throughout, preferably for both titles and text; using the same "sink" for the beginning of each chapter; placing the page numbers and running heads at the same spot on each page; and establishing a standard copy area and staying with it throughout the book. You should insist that the printer honor your placements and measurements.

New designers hired by book publishers tend to overdesign the books assigned them. Most books cannot afford an avant-garde treatment. "Our design problem in the book industry today is not a lack of creativity—we have more creativity than we can use," reports Scudellari. "Rather, we need quality in execution, and our problem is to discipline young designers to the proper execution of routine tasks on which their creativity must rest if it is to produce quality end results."

Production and the book designer

On magazines the art director turns over the more routine chores to a production editor who follows through on fitting type, ordering halftones, and doing pasteups. In book publishing, the art director—or the designer—plays a more subservient role. Often a production editor hires the designer and supervises the work.

The production editor, along with the editor, imposes upon the designer a number of limitations: a proposed number of pages for

5. "Marketing Managers Tell AIGA Clinic How Design Influences Book Sales," *Publishers Weekly,* April 4, 1977, p. 74.

the printed book, some art that will have to be included, a budget. The designer goes to work from there.

Sometimes the designer is involved in planning of the book. In a few cases, the book is designed first and the text then written to fit, or the design evolves as the book is written. The subject may dictate an unusual format. A book about wines may be shaped like a wine bottle, a book on how to stop smoking like a pack of cigarettes, a kid's book like a house. Sometimes a toy or other unit is attached to the book. Die cuts and special packaging are enormously expensive, but they are novel enough to catch the most jaded book browser's attention.

A few books—juveniles and art books—are written, designed, and even illustrated by the same person. A few nonartist writers like to get in on the act, too. For instance: John Updike. "We don't always agree with him," says Scudellari, "but usually his ideas are followed."

In the course of the work the designer soon becomes an expert in production, learning how to cut costs without lowering the quality of the book. By confining color and art to certain signatures, by slightly altering page size, by omitting head and tailbands (they pretty a book a bit but add nothing to the strength of the binding), by having process color reproductions tipped on rather than printed on the signatures, by avoiding multiple widths of the text—by doing many of these things the designer can save the publisher money and still produce a handsome book.

Ernst Reichl of Ernst Reichl Associates has observed that a designer is worth the cost to a book publisher in that "the charge for design, measured against the plant cost (composition and plates) of a book, is extremely small; and a well-planned book costs so much less to produce than an unplanned one. . . . [The designer's] most obvious value is that of a safeguard against unpleasant surprises."

The time needed for putting a book through production varies from as little as three weeks, for "instant" paperbacks based on news or special events, to six months, for complicated picture books. Of course, for the author, the time lag is more; because before the production department gets the job, the manuscript has to be accepted, approved, and copyread—processes that can take more time than actual production.

Publishers of elementary and high school textbooks follow production guidelines set up by the Book Manufacturers Institute in collaboration with the National Association of State Textbook Administrators. These guidelines affect paper choice, binding, and margins. A textbook designer should check into these guidelines, which change from time to time.

Book design as problem solving

So far as the designer is concerned, a book represents a problem with several possible solutions. As a book designer you would choose the solution that seems to work best, bearing in mind the theme of the book, the nature of the book's audience, and the method by which the book will be sold.

If the book is to sell mainly in bookstores, it should have an attractive jacket, a thick or hefty appearance, and, if possible, lots of pictures. If it is a gift book, it should look large and expensive, even if it isn't. If it is a mail order book, it should be printed on

A spread from *American Furniture: 1620 to the Present* by Jonathan L. Fairbanks and Elizabeth Bidwell Bates (Richard Marek Publishers, New York, 1981) shows one way to handle illustrations in a book that is rich with them. The chairs are presented in silhouette form, with copy blocks handled as though they were captions, but captions developed as short essays. Andor Braun designed the book.

lightweight paper, to save postage costs. If it is designed primarily for library sales, it should have a strong binding. If it is a textbook for elementary and high school use, it should have lots of color.

In choosing typefaces and illustrations you should avoid satisfying your own taste at the expense of what the author's approach calls for. The design should be appropriate to the book.

In every case, you would read the manuscript rather carefully before starting your design. You must stay within your budget, but at the early stages you can forget the budget and come up with the ideal solution even though it is beyond what the budget can support. You can then modify the design to fit the budget.

University presses often can experiment more than commercial publishers can. A small book Muriel Cooper designed for MIT Press, *File Under Architecture,* was set in various typewriter fonts, printed on kraft paper, and bound in covers made of corrugated boxboard. All of this was appropriate because the book challenged many architecture principles.

As it has to other units of the print-medium industry, the computer has come to book publishing. Many book publishers use computer typography, which they buy from outside, just as they buy their printing from outside. The type may be set in one part of the country; the printing may go on in another—or in some other country, for that matter. For less important books—say for instructors' manuals that accompany textbooks—the type may set "in house" with "strike on" composition. Much "in house" typography is dreadful; and the computer has added some quirks in typography that old-line designers do not like. But Ernst Reichl, a book designer for 50 years, says that ". . . it is possible to get a decent, attractive, even beautiful type page out of the computer if you insist on the standards you learned in using hot metal composition." Some designers would go further than that. They would say that the computer actually *improves* your chances of producing a beautiful book.

The grid in book design

The best book designers have always insisted on exact placement of columns of type page after page. The margins have to be consistent. The idea started in the days of letterpress when the hard impression of type had a tendency to bulge the other side of the sheet. Printing columns of type exactly back to back covered this.

New American Library for its paperback release of *The Rockefellers* designed the book with two different covers so that two copies of the book put next to each other on display in bookstores would act as a sort of poster, with a book title looming large to catch the browser's attention. ". . . A revolutionary new cover treatment," claimed the publisher's promotion department. The book was written by Peter Collier and David Horowitz.

The fussiness carries over into offset because often the thinness of the paper allows show-through. Again, true back-to-back columns of type cover up the problem.

The quest for exactness makes the use of a grid in book design especially desirable.[6]

"There is no reason why book design should go on indefinitely with multiple proofs, piecemeal corrections, and pasted bits and pieces that mark the pattern of contemporary bookmaking," Allen Hurlburt declares in *The Grid.* "A properly planned grid with appropriate encoded specifications should be able to guide most trade books through a properly equipped photocomposition terminal and return the printouts in completely paginated form."[7]

Guides to book design

Nothing helps the beginning designer so much as studying contemporary and even classic books to see how these matters are handled. It makes sense to borrow spacing ideas that have already worked and leave experimentation to those better equipped to handle it and pay for its mistakes.

To help designers make their decisions, Stanley Rice in *Book Design: Text Format Models* (R. R. Bowker Company, New York, 1978) offers a range of models "that incorporate most of the variations commonly required." The book, Rice says, "can be thought of as an order catalog of text typography. You order what you need from the variety you see, assuming only that both publisher and typesetter can refer to the book as necessary." Each example has a code to facilitate any discussion between the editor or designer and the printer or typesetter.

In *Book Design: Systematic Aspects* (R. R. Bowker Company, New York, 1978) Rice offers additional advice on non-artistic as-

6. Allen Hurlburt, *The Grid,* Van Nostrand Reinhold Company, New York, 1978, pp. 68, 69.

7. *Ibid.,* p. 80.

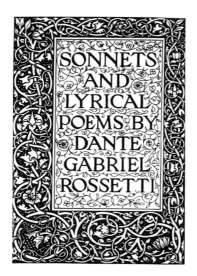

A title page designed by England's William Morris in 1894. Morris was influenced by incunabula books. He devoted himself to fighting cheapness and standardization brought on by the industrial revolution.

pects of book design: record keeping, dealing with freelance artists, production, etc. "In the last few years book designers have been so mercilessly assaulted by technology and other winds of complications and change that, in fact, they . . . require help, in the form of some usable strategies and weapons," he says.

Another guide that could prove useful is *One Book/Five Ways: The Publishing Procedures of Five University Presses* (William Kaufmann, Inc., Los Altos, Calif., 1978). Published originally as a workbook for use at the 1977 annual meeting of the Association of American University Presses, it documents and illustrates action taken by each publisher, including the handling of design, for a mythical book called *No Time for House Plants* by Purvis Mulch. "Here one can see how a book is published," writes Joyce Kachergis in the Foreword, "compare the procedures of five professional scholarly publishers, and see differences and similarities between equally valid and startlingly different solutions."

A lot of other nagging problems having to do with consistency are covered in *A Manual of Style* (University of Chicago Press) and *Style Manual* (U.S. Government Printing Office).

The lineup of book pages

Once in a while a designer gets a book like Stephen Schneck's *The Night Clerk* (Grove Press, 1965) to design. That book started right out on page 9, in the middle of a sentence. People who bought the book thought they had defective copies. The publisher had to send a notice around to booksellers assuring them the book was meant to be that way.

The usual book is a little more logically planned. In fact, the lineup of pages stays pretty much the same, book after book.

Here's the lineup of pages for a nonfiction book:

"Half" title (this page goes back to the time when books were sold without covers; the real title page was thus protected).

Advertising card (list of the author's previous works or of other books in the series.

Title.

Copyright notice and catalog number.

Dedication.

Acknowledgments (or they can follow the table of contents).

Preface or foreword (it's a preface if written by the author, a foreword if written by someone else).

Table of contents.

List of illustrations.

Introduction (or it can follow the second "half" title).

Second "half" title.

Chapter 1.

Additional chapters.

Appendix.

Footnotes (if not incorporated into the text).

Bibliography (or it can follow the glossary).

Glossary.

Index.

Colophon (a paragraph or two giving design and production details about the book).

This list does not take into account blank pages in the front and back of the book. Nor does it show whether these are left- or right-hand pages. Customarily, main pages, like the title pages, are given right-hand placement.

Up through the second "half" title page, the numbering system used is small roman. From chapter 1 (or from the introduction, if it follows the second "half" title page) the numbering is arabic.

How far to carry the design

As a book designer you do not design all the book's pages. That would be repetitious; most of the pages are essentially the same. You design only the opening and strategic pages and set basic standards for the others.

Among the pages you design are the title, table of contents, a chapter opening, and two facing pages inside a chapter (to show how running heads, subheads, and page numbering will look).

You also provide the printer with a specification sheet on which you list or describe the following:

1. trim size of pages,
2. size of margins,
3. size of copy area,
4. size and style of type and amount of leading,
5. amount of paragraph indentation,
6. handling of long quotes (set in different type or size? narrower width? centered or flush left or flush right?),
7. handling of footnotes,
8. size and placement of page numbers (folios),
9. handling of chapter titles, subheads, running heads, and initial letters,
10. amount of drop between chapter titles and beginnings of chapters,
11. handling of front matter, including title page and table of contents,
12. handling of back matter, including bibliography and index.

The printer goes ahead and sets some sample pages according to your specifications to enable you to check them to make sure all instructions are understood and that your design works. You can change your mind better at this point than after the entire book is set. The setting of the front matter of the book is deferred until last.

If the book is highly illustrated and the illustrations are integrated with the text, you would, of course, design every page.

The necessary steps

You start with an office-machine copy of the manuscript. The first order of business is to "cast off"—count the number of words or, better, the number of characters in the manuscript and, using standard copyfitting techniques, determine how many pages of print the characters will occupy. The longer the manuscript, the more likely you are to choose a small typeface, but you do not go smaller than 10 point, unless you choose to set the book in narrow columns. If the manuscript is short, you may use a larger face and more leading than usual, and you may choose a high-bulk paper to give extra thickness to the book. Whenever possible, you arrange the book so that the final number of pages, including front and back matter and blank pages, comes to a multiple of 32.

A Will Bradley-designed page of 1896. Bradley was one of the American book designers influenced by William Morris.

After the editor approves your type selection and sample page layouts, the original manuscript, now copyread, goes to the printer or typographer for setting. When proofs are ready, you receive one set to use to prepare a dummy of the book. The extra number of pages remains somewhat flexible as you wrestle with fitting problems. You may have to increase or decrease some of your spacing in order to come out even on signatures. You may find it necessary to add or subtract a signature.

You prepare your dummy by cutting and pasting the proofs roughly into place, along with copy prints of the art. That's as far as you carry the pasteup, unless the book is to be printed offset or gravure; then you or someone in production does a camera-ready pasteup, using reproduction proofs rather than galley proofs. The dummy serves as a guide, then, either for the printer, if the book is letterpress, or for the pasteup artist, if it is offset or gravure.

Book paper

As much as 25 percent of the retail price of a book goes to pay for production and printing. According to an estimate by Marshall Lee, one-fifth of that 25 percent goes for paper.

More so than other designers, the book designer must know the special qualities of papers. Where a magazine designer usually needs to make a choice only once, the book designer must make a choice for every job. These are the four basic kinds of paper used for book printing:

1. *Antique stock.* There are many textures, finishes, and weights, but essentially these papers are soft, rough, and absorbent. They are especially good for books made up wholly of text matter; that they are nonglare makes them easy on the eyes. For quality books, the designer may choose an antique stock with deckle edges.

2. *Plate or English-finish stock.* Essentially, these are antique papers that have been smoothed out, making possible sharper reproduction, especially for pictures. Paper used for the big magazines falls into this category.

3. *Coated stock.* Simple polishing (calendering) may not suffice to give the paper a finish that is smooth and slick enough. The designer, then, can choose a coated stock, smooth to the feel, rich looking, and highly desirable where maximum fidelity is desired in picture reproduction. But coated stock is expensive.

4. *Offset stock.* The offset printing process needs special papers that will resist moisture. (Offset, you'll remember, makes use of plates that carry both moisture and ink.) Were paper not treated, it would stretch, shrink, and curl. Offset papers come in a variety of textures and finishes, but the most common is the rather smooth, severely white stock used for so many company magazines and for books that carry numerous halftones.

In addition to these basic papers the designer should know about the special papers, including kraft, available for end sheets.

Doubleday once brought out a book, *The Sleeping Partner,* in a great variety of papers, a different one for each 32-page signature, causing William Jovanovich, president of Harcourt, Brace & World (now Harcourt Brace Jovanovich), to remark: "This is, no doubt, a way to clear out one's inventory in the name of Art."

These days books come in a greater variety of sizes than ever, but the most common trim sizes still are 5 3/8 × 8, 5 1/2 ×

8 1/4, and 6 1/8 × 9 1/4. Mass paperbacks come usually in 4 1/8 × 6 3/8 or 4 1/8 × 7 sizes. As in magazine publishing, there is a trend toward the square format, especially for volumes dealing with the fine arts. As for all printing, the designer should check with the printer on paper sizes available and choose a page size that can be cut with a minimum of waste.

Establishing the margins

It may not seem that way, but the nontype area of a book—the white space—accounts for close to 50 percent of the total area. For art books and highly designed books, white space may account for as much as 75 percent of the total area.

Where you put this white space counts heavily in your thinking. For your all-type pages, you concentrate white space on the outside edges of your spreads, but not in equal-width bands.

The idea is to arrange the copy on facing pages so that the pages will read as a unit. For the typical book you establish margins that tend to push the copy area of the two pages together. Book margins are like magazine margins. The narrowest margin on each page is at the gutter (but the combined space at the gutter is usually wider than other margins). The margin increases at the top, increases more at the outside edge, and increases most at the bottom. You should be careful to keep the margin at the gutter wide enough (never less than 5/8 for books in the 6 × 9 range) so that the type does not merge into the gutter when the book is bound. When you run a headline or title across the gutter, you leave a little extra space at the gutter to take care of space lost in the binding.

Book Typography

For many books, design is almost wholly a matter of type selection and its careful, consistent spacing. But even that requires many agonizing decisions. For instance: how big should the paragraph indentations be? How much space between words? How should lists, tables, footnotes, captions, credit lines, the table of contents, bibliography, glossary, index be handled?

Your showplace pages are the title page and the pages with chapter openings.

The trend is toward a two-page title spread. Why should the left-hand page be blank and the right-hand page be crowded with all the information that makes up a title page? The title, or elements of the title page, cross the gutter to unify the two pages. The effect can be dramatic. It may seem to say: "This book is important."

Type for the chapter headings usually matches the type for the title pages. The headings seldom go over 18 or 24 points, and often they are smaller. Small-size type displayed with plenty of white space has just as much impact as large-size type that is crowded.

Text type in books ranges from 8 points to 12 points, depending upon the width of the column, the length of the book, the face used, the amount of leading between lines, and the age level of the reader. Body copy is leaded from one to three points. Space between words is usually 1/4 em or, at most, 1/3 em.

"Widows"—last lines of paragraphs—shouldn't be any narrower than 2/3 of a column when they begin a column or page. Some publishers do not want widows of any width at the tops of pages or columns. That means that as a designer you'd have to bring the widow and at least one line before it to the top of a page or column when you lay out a book.

You also have to make a decision about how to handle long quotations. Should they be integrated with the text or should they be segregated, perhaps in smaller, indented type? Then how much space should go above and below them? Do you indent opening lines? Or do you handle opening lines of excerpts as you would opening lines of first paragraphs in each chapter?

Now consider the matter of how to begin the first paragraph of a chapter. There are all kinds of possibilities, with or without the use of an initial letter. For many books the first paragraph of each chapter is not indented. The display type used for the chapter title acts as the "indentation," announcing to the reader a beginning. An indentation, some book designers feel, is redundant. At the other extreme, the opening paragraph may begin half way or more across the column. All or part of the opening line can be in all caps or small caps.

Paragraphs following subheads often go without indentations, too.

For nonfiction books, and especially for textbooks, subheads are important. They help the readers organize the material as they read. Subheads also break up large areas of gray type into convenient takes.

Subheads are best when kept close to the size of the body type. Sometimes they are in bold face, sometimes in all caps, sometimes in italics. They should be accompanied by some extra white space (both above and below) to make them stand out.

Handling subheads can be a problem when they occur near or at the bottom of a page or column. Publishers like to see two or three lines of text matter under those low lying subheads. Otherwise the subheads become isolated. Subheads can begin pages or columns, but when they are only *near* the top at least two or three lines of text matter should go above them.

The author of a book supplies subheads with the manuscript and usually establishes the level of importance for each. Subheads can occupy up to four levels of importance. From a design standpoint, the fewer the levels the better. This book has a single level.

The designer determines the type size for each level, often choosing to keep subheads all in the same size type, centering those of the first-level, running the second-level ones flush left, and indenting those of the third-level. The fourth-level ones could go in italics. Sometimes the designer runs subheads at the side of rather than inside the text.

You also have to decide how to handle running titles—small lines at the tops or bottoms of inside pages—along with page numbers. You want to make things easy for the reader, who should be able to see, always, the book's title, the chapter's title, and the page number. The book title usually goes on left-hand pages, the chapter title on right-hand pages. In some books the page numbers go to giant sizes as a design affectation.

Book art

In the well-designed book the style of the art complements the style of typography. Boldface types; powerful art. Graceful types; fanciful art.

Impressionism, German Expressionism, Surrealism, Pop Art—all the various art movements have had their influence on book illustration. And with today's printing techniques the designer is free to call in artists who work in any technique or any medium. Still, the predominant art form for books seems to be the line drawing done in the manner of Frederic Remington, Charles Dana Gibson, Howard Pyle, A. B. Frost, E. W. Kemble, and Rockwell Kent. One reason is that such art is the easiest to reproduce under any printing conditions. The author may supply the art, sometimes finished, sometimes only in rough form for use as a guide for a professional artist picked by the publisher.

In works of nonfiction, the photographer has taken over from the illustrator, but perhaps not to the same degree as in newspaper and magazine publishing.

To give photographs and illustrations the display they need, you either bleed them or surround them with white space. You do not crowd them up against copy blocks. Where art occupies all or most of a page, you omit the page number and the running heads, because these tend to detract from the art. If you feel the paper used is not opaque enough, you may decide to leave blank the side backing the printed art. For some books you might put all the art on a single signature, perhaps a glossy-stock signature, without text matter but with captions.

Book captions

Earlier chapters pointed out that newspaper people call the descriptive text under or adjacent to a piece of art "cutlines." Magazine people call it a "caption." Book people—some of them—call the material a "legend," and reserve "caption" for the tag line or small headline that accompanies it. We'll use the more common "caption" here as magazine people use it.

Publishers like to have each caption preceded by a "Fig." number. This aids greatly in the makeup of the pages. If the text refers

After the Civil War, Howard Pyle became one of America's most influential magazine illustrators. Pyle both wrote and illustrated books. His style was rich, his design carefully controlled. This illustration is from *The Wonder Clock,* a book published in 1887.

specifically to a picture "above" or one "below," the designer has to keep in painfully close touch with each line of copy while laying out pages and readjust material to make "above" and "below" really work. When the text instead refers to, say, "Fig. 5," Fig. 5 can go anywhere nearby.

As in magazine design, captions for books usually are set in a face smaller, lighter, or bolder than the body copy or in italics or sans serifs if the body face is roman.

Some book editors and designers avoid including credit lines in the captions, putting them instead in tiny type immediately below the art or running up the side. Or, if they can get away with it, editors may choose to bunch all credit lines and bury them somewhere in the front or back of the book.

The binding

Books come in four kinds of bindings:

1. *Sewn binding.* For this kind of binding signatures are placed next to each other. They are not nested, as for saddle-stitched magazines. Open up a book and look at the binding from the top or bottom, and you can see how the signatures fit together.

Two kinds of sewing are available: (a) Smythe sewing, in which the sewing is done through the gutter of each signature and then across the back; and (b) side sewing (less common), in which the thread goes through the entire book about 1/8 from the back. A side-sewn book does not lie flat when opened. But the binding is sturdy. Libraries, when they find it necessary to rebind a book, frequently use side sewing.

2. *Stapled binding.* The staples can go in through the spine, if signatures are nested; or they can go in through the side. Such binding is reserved for low-budget books.

3. *Adhesive binding.* Sometimes called "perfect binding," this system brings together loose pages rather than signatures. The binding is accomplished by applying glue across the back. Cheap, mass audience paperbacks use this kind of binding. Unfortunately, the pages have a tendency to separate when subject to constant use.

4. *Mechanical binding.* The most common mechanical binding is *spiral binding,* in which loose pages are held together by a wire that spirals along a series of punched holes. The covers of such a book can be heavy paper, cardboard, or boards covered with paper. Pages can be torn out easily. With some mechanical bindings, new pages can be inserted. Mechanical binding is used for books with short press runs—books written for technical- or practical-minded audiences.

The first three binding processes—the main binding processes—can be used for paperback as well as hardbound books. Most hardbound books, however, come with sewn binding since it permits a book to lie flat when it is opened.

The cover

Let's assume you are designing a hardbound book. With the kind of binding decided, you turn your attention to the cover.

You must decide whether you want the boards of the cover to be wrapped fully in cloth, partially in cloth and partially in paper, or fully in paper. If the boards are to be wrapped in cloth, should the cloth be all of the same color and texture? Or should you seek a two-tone effect? And what color or colors should you use?

For many books the cover consists merely of wrapped boards with the name of the book, author, and publisher printed or stamped on the spine. But even that small amount of type should be coordinated with the other elements of the book.

The type used can be printed on the cover material before it is wrapped around the boards, or it can be stamped on afterwards.

Many hardbound books require design on the cover proper as well as on the jacket. Textbooks by and large get by with cover design only. There are no jackets.

Dark colors in cloths used for hardbound books show wear at the corners more quickly than light colors do. But light-colored cloth soils more quickly. The lighter colors have the advantage of making books look bigger, suggesting to readers that they are getting a lot for their money. Textbooks tend to come out in lighter colors.

The design on hardbound covers can be printed or stamped. The stamping process, not recommended for intricate designs or small type, can make use of foils for a metallic look. The designer can also specify blind stamping, which simply depresses the surface.

For their cover material publishers once used animal skins—vellum or leather—but now they use cloth, vinyl, or paper. Cloth gained popularity as book cover material in the latter part of the nineteenth century. The cloth used today is often a cotton impregnated or coated with plastic. Paper became popular during World War II when cloth was scarce. The paper most commonly used is kraft.

The cloth, vinyl, or paper is wrapped around binder's board (found in most textbooks), chip board (found in cheaper books), pasted board (found in most trade books), or red board (found in limp books meant to be carried around in pockets).

To keep the top edges of the book's pages from soiling, you may decide to have them stained. You can choose a color that complements the endpapers.

Designing the cover for a paperbook is a little like designing the jacket for a hardcover book. Here are the front cover, back cover, and spine for *The Tales of Rabbi Nachman* by Martin Buber (Discus Books, New York: Barbara Bertoli, art director). The publisher evidently feels that the name of the author, "one of the great thinkers of our time," is more important than the name of the book. The type and illustration form one unit. The original is in black, grayed red, and light olive.

Endpapers in hardbacks serve more of an aesthetic than structural purpose. Their main function is to hide folded cloth and stitching. Endpapers used to be nothing more than tan kraft paper, but increasingly they have taken on color and even art.

For *sets* of books, hardbound as well as paperback, publishers often supply *slipcases,* which unite and encase the books, leaving only their spines exposed.

The cover for a *paperback* book represents a special challenge to the designer in that it is both a jacket and a cover. Because paperback sales are so dependent on impulse buying, the cover art must be particularly compelling. Like the jacket for a hardbound book, the cover for a paperback is as much an exercise in advertising design as in book design. "After all, aren't book covers packages, and isn't packaging a function of advertising?" asks Ian Summers, executive art director of Ballantine Books.

As a book publisher art director, Summers works on 150 titles at a time (Ballantine publishes 400 titles a year). As an advertising art director, by way of contrast, he worked on 10 projects at a time. Summers looks upon book covers as similar to two-page advertising spreads in magazines. But the front cover is the most important part of each design. "We are in the business of making posters that are only four by seven inches tall," Summers says.

While Ballantine tries to be innovative, some of its covers never change. People who buy gothic novels, for instance, do not respond to anything but frightened women running from castles. The only way to upgrade such covers is to hire the very best illustrators. "My ability to put the right book together with the right illustrator is probably my most important contribution," Summers declares.

Science fiction offers some of the best possibilities for high-level illustration. You look for super-realism here. "The science fiction fans are probably the only category of readers who really care about the quality of art on their books. They know their artists and consider them heroes."[8]

With their heavy-paper covers, paperback books have experimented with various devices to get casual browsers inside. They have used both real and fake embossing on their covers, xographs (three-dimensional pictures), and die-cuts that expose part of the title page. Still, covers are largely a matter of chance. "No scientific principles guide the decisions [at Bantam Books, world's largest paperback publisher]," writes Clarence Petersen in *The Bantam Story.* "Past experience helps, but mostly publishing executives call the shots by a sort of gut reaction. Bantam knows, for instance, that the color red sells books. It is the boldest of the primary colors, which in turn are the boldest of all."[9]

The trouble is, everybody knows this, so that many publishers, including Bantam, go to other colors to make their books stand out from the sea of red. Soon all publishers seem to settle in on some other color. In many seasons, white becomes a favorite principal cover color.

Sometimes a publisher puts a book out with different covers to appeal to different buyers. Bantam's *Future Shock* by Alvin Toffler came out with six different covers. One advantage, Bantam

8. Ian Summers, "Selling a Book by Its Cover," *Art Direction,* October 1976, pp. 59–62.

9. Clarence Peterson, *The Bantam Story,* Bantam Books, New York, 1975, p. 65.

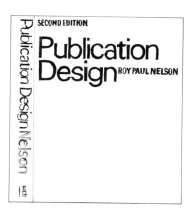 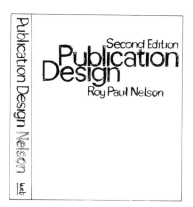  

discovered, was that some booksellers put all six versions on display, giving the book a big advantage over books from other publishers that had a single cover.

A single paperback book, if it enjoys a long life, may go through several different cover designs before it finally goes out of print.

For some covers or jackets, type alone, carefully selected, tastefully if not unusually arranged, with strong colors, is enough to do the job. For other covers art is vital. Often that art becomes a visual pun. Milton Glaser's illustration for Germaine Greer's *The Female Eunuch* was a standing pair of scissors, spread open, with a woman's muscular legs for the blades.

The jacket

Books didn't always come with jackets. The introduction of modern distribution methods required that books be protected, and the idea of the "dust" jacket was born. At first the jacket was nothing more than a plain wrapper. It did not become a display piece until after World War I. Then it helped sell the book as well as protect it.

Jacket design probably is less important to hardcover books than cover design is to paperbacks. For a hardcover book, poorly designed jackets discourage buying but well designed jackets do not necessarily stimulate buying, says Alan Kellock, a sales manager at Harcourt Brace Jovanovich. Still, the jacket is where a book's design starts.

Once you know for sure how many pages the book will take, you ask for a bound dummy, with pages blank, so that you can get the feel of the book and so that you can properly fit the jacket.

Ideally, you should know a great deal about a book before attempting to design its jacket. But often there is no time to give the manuscript or page proofs the reading they deserve.

The typical jacket features the name of the book and the name of the author on the front; a picture of the author on the back; and a description of the book and biographical information about the author on the inside flaps. The names of the book, author (often last name only), and publisher run from left to right at the top of the spine, if the book is thick enough; if the book is too thin, the names run in a single sideways line, from top to bottom.

A jacket should emphasize a single idea, reflect the mood or character of the book, and lure the reader inside. Sometimes the name of the author is featured most prominently, sometimes the title of the book.

Three rough layouts submitted by the author/designer to his publisher for consideration as the cover or jacket for the second edition of this book. The publisher decided on a fourth idea, feeling it looked more contemporary. The narrow panels at the left represent the spine of the book.

Book design   **257**

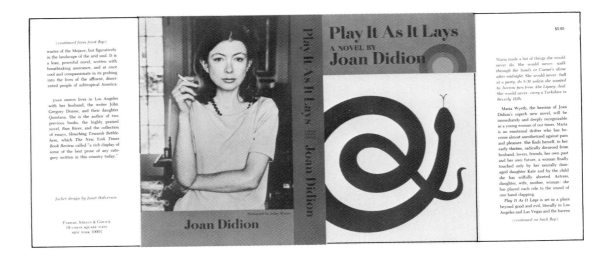

Play It As It Lays
A NOVEL BY
Joan Didion

$5.95

Joan Didion

Janet Halverson's jacket for Joan Didion's novel about "an emotional drifter" who has played her various roles "to the sound of one hand clapping." In black, magenta, orange, and yellow. (Reprinted by permission of Janet Halverson and Farrar, Straus & Giroux, Inc.)

A question of ethics comes in when the designer gives undue play to a popular earlier work of the author, perhaps deceiving readers into thinking that is the work they are buying. Ethics also become involved when the designer uses an illustration that promises other than what the book actually delivers.

Because jackets serve as advertisements, advertising designers rather than book designers often create them. Sometimes the authors have a say in their design.

For one of his zany books Alexander King got his publisher to wrap each copy with two jackets, an inner one, staid and conservative, and an outer one featuring one of his somewhat vulgar paintings. Tongue-in-cheek, he invited any reader who was easily offended to dispose of the outside jacket.

Grove Press, for a novel called *Commander Amanda,* produced three different jackets, all designed by Kuhlman Associates. Sets were sent to booksellers; they were invited to pick the one they wanted on copies they would be selling. This involved booksellers in the book's production and presumably made them more interested in the book. Alfred A. Knopf brought out Edward Luttwak's *Coup d'Etat* with jackets in two different color combinations: half the copies had one jacket, half the other. Booksellers were encouraged to make what in effect was a two-tone display of the books to help sell them.

Most jackets come in black plus a second color. The black is for the author's portrait on the back. To save costs, some publishers run their jackets in a single color on a colored stock. The paper used is coated or varnished only on the side on which the printing is done. The side next to the book itself is rough-finished so the jacket will cling to the book.

Publishers run off more jackets than are needed to cover their books; they use the extra copies for promotion and as replacements for jackets worn and torn in shipping and handling.

First things first

All of these considerations add to the reader's enjoyment of a book, but they are as nothing compared to the Big Three contributions the designer can make.

Designer/illustrator Fred Marcellino for his jacket for *Neighbors* depicts venetian blinds, which make a nice pattern on which to reverse the novel's title and the name of the author. The blinds also help say "Neighbors." A hand pulls the blinds just enough to show a moving van and part of a house. You see here the jacket front and spine. (By permission of Delacorte Press/Seymour Lawrence. © 1980 by Fred Marcellino.)

1. Picking a paper that does not bounce the light back into the reader's eyes.

2. Picking a typeface big enough to be read without squinting.

3. Printing the text of the book far enough in from the gutter so the reader does not have to fight the binding to keep the book open.

Readers do not buy publications—books, magazines, newspapers, whatever—to admire the versatility of their art directors. They buy publications so that they can be informed; they buy them for

PAUL RENNER

In the 1920s the Bauhaus in Germany was establishing the principle that design should be simple, geometric, and above all functional. Still, some important designers of that period continued to bring to design the decorative quality of an earlier era. This is a Paul Renner book cover, so rich in personality and texture that, as designer, he was allowed to sign it.

guidance; they buy them to relax with. What they expect—what they must have—are headings and columns of type arranged for effortless assimilation, with large, clear pictures unencumbered by visual scars and typographic clutter.

What art directors must do, then, more than anything else, is make their publications useful to their readers. Design should help readers; it should not get in their way. This is not to say that art directors should shy away from imaginative approaches. Far from it. It takes imagination—more of it—to truly organize the pages of a publication than merely to decorate them.

Suggested further reading

Bailey, Herbert Smith, *The Art and Science of Book Publishing,* University of Texas Press, Austin, 1980.

Balkin, Richard, *A Writer's Guide to Book Publishing,* Hawthorn Books, New York, 1977.

Bodian, Nat G., *Book Marketing Handbook,* R. R. Bowker Company, New York, 1980.

Bonn, Thomas L., *Undercover: An Illustrated History of American Mass-Market Paperbacks,* Penguin Books, New York, 1982. (With reproductions of the 170 book covers.)

Coser, Lewis A.; Charles Kadushin, and Walter W. Powell, *Books: The Culture and Commerce of Publishing,* Basic Books, New York, 1981.

Dessauer, John P., *Book Publishing: What It Is, What It Does,* R. R. Bowker Co., New York, 1974.

Greenfield, Howard, *Books: From Writer to Reader,* Crown Publishers, New York, 1976.

Hanson, Glenn, *The Now Look in the Yearbook,* National Scholastic Press Association, Minneapolis, Minnesota, 1971.

Henderson, Bill, ed., *The Publish-It-Yourself Handbook: Literary Tradition and How to,* Pushcart Book Press, Box 845, Yonkers, New York 10701, 1973.

Jennett, Sean, *The Making of Books,* Faber, London, 1973. (Fifth Edition.)

Judd, Karen, *Copyediting: A Practical Guide,* William Kaufmann, Inc., Los Altos, Calif., 1982. (Written from a book publisher's perspective.)

Klemin, Diana, *The Illustrated Book: Its Art and Craft,* Clarkson N. Potter, Inc., New York, 1970.

Lee, Marshall, *Bookmaking: The Illustrated Guide to Design and Production,* R. R. Bowker Company, New York, 1980. (Revised Edition.)

Peppin, Brigid, *Dictionary of Book Illustrators 1800–1970,* Arco, New York, 1980. (Covers 1200 artists, with samples of their work.)

Peters, Jean, ed., *The Bookman's Glossary,* R. R. Bowker, New York, 1975. (Fifth Edition.)

Rice, Stanley, *Book Design,* R. R. Bowker Company, New York, 1978. (Two volumes.)

Salter, Stefan, *From Cover to Cover: The Occasional Papers of a Book Designer,* Prentice-Hall, Englewood Cliffs, New Jersey, 1970.

Thompson, Susan Otis, *American Book Design and William Morris,* R. R. Bowker Company, New York, 1977.

Wong, Wucius, *Principles of Three-Dimensional Design,* Van Nostrand Reinhold, New York, 1977.

Guide to Book Publishing Courses, Peterson's Guides, Princeton, N.J., 1979.

One Book/Five Ways, William Kaufmann, Inc., Los Altos, Calif., 1978.

GLOSSARY

Terminology in journalism and art varies from publication to publication and from region to region. This glossary gives meanings of terms as the author uses them in this book and in his other books on graphic design.

abstract art   simplified art; art reduced to fundamental parts; art that makes its point with great subtlety. Opposite of realistic or representational art.

agate type   5 1/2-point type.

airbrush   tool that uses compressed air to shoot a spray of watercolor pigment on photographs or artwork. Used for retouching.

all caps   all-capital letters.

antique paper   rough finish, high-quality paper.

area composition   composition that provides a printout or proof with copy, headlines, subheads, and even illustrations in place, as opposed to composition that provides a printout or proof of copy only.

art   all pictorial matter in a publication: photographs, illustrations, cartoons, charts and graphs, etc.

Art Deco   the look of the 1920s and 1930s: simple line forms, geometric shapes, pastel colors, rainbow motifs.

art director   person in charge of all visual aspects of a publication, including typography.

art editor   see *art director*.

ascender   part of lowercase letter that moves above the x-height.

asterisk   small star used as a reference mark or as a footnote.

author's alterations   changes made on proofs not necessitated by errors made by typesetter or printer. The author or the publisher pays for them.

axis   imaginary line used to align visual elements and relate them.

back of the book   section of a magazine following the main articles and stories and consisting of continuations of articles and stories, ads, and filler material.

balance   stability in design; condition in which the various elements on a page or spread are at rest.

bank   see *deck*.

banner   main headline running across the top of a newspaper page.

bar chart   art that shows statistics in bars of various lengths.

baseline   imaginary line that forms the base or bottom of letters. Some letters have descending strokes that dip below the baseline.

Bauhaus   school of design in Germany (1919–1933). It championed a highly ordered, functional style in architecture and applied arts.

Ben Day   process by which the engraver or printer adds pattern or tone to a line reproduction.

Bible paper   thin but opaque paper.

binding   that part of a magazine or book that holds the pages together.

bird's-eye view   view from above.

blackletter   close-fitting, bold, angular type that originated in Germany. Also known as *Old English* and *text*.

bleed   a picture printed to the edge of a sheet. Use also as a verb.

blind embossing   embossing without printing.

blueline see *Vandyke.*

blurb follow-up title for a magazine article, longer than the main title and in smaller type. Also, a title displayed on the cover. Also, copy on a book jacket.

blowup enlargement. *Blow up* when used as a verb.

body copy column or page of type of a relatively small size.

body type type 12 points in size or smaller.

boldface type black type.

bond paper crisp paper used for business stationery, often with rag content.

book bound publication of 48 pages or more, usually with a stiff or heavy cover. Some magazine editors call their publications *books.*

book paper paper other than newsprint used in the printing of books and magazines. Includes many grades and finishes.

box design element composed usually of 4 rules, with type or art inside.

broadsheet standard-size newspaper sheet or page.

broadside direct-mail piece that folds out to a large sheet.

brownline see *Vandyke.*

bullet large dot used as an attention getter or to set off a unit in a series.

byline the author's name set in type, usually over the story or article.

CAD computer-aided design by which a computer processes and manipulates the design elements.

calender to polish, as in the making of paper.

calligraphy beautiful handwriting or drawn type.

camera-ready copy a pasteup ready to be photographed by the plate-maker.

Camp art so bad it's good.

caption textmatter accompanying a photograph; newspapers use *cut-lines.*

caricature drawing of a person that exaggerates or distorts the features.

cartoon humorous drawing, done usually in pen or brush and ink, or in washes.

casebound hard cover for a book.

cast off estimate the amount of copy in a book. In magazines, it's *copyfit.*

center fold center spread that opens out for two more pages.

center spread two facing pages at the center of a magazine or newspaper.

character any letter, number, punctuation mark, or space in printed matter.

circulation number of copies sold or distributed.

cliché something used too often, hence boring and no longer effective.

clipbook pages of stock art usually on slick paper, ready for photographing by the platemaker.

clip sheet see *clipbook.*

coated paper paper to which a smooth, hard coating has been applied.

cold type type composed by typewriter, paper pasteup, or photographic means.

collage piece of art made by pasting various elements together.

colophon paragraph or paragraphs of information about a book's design and typography, carried at the end of the book.

color separation negative made from full-color art for use in making one of the plates.

column section of a book's or magazine's text that runs from top to bottom of the page. Also, regular editorial feature in a newspaper or magazine, usually with a byline.

column inch area that is one column wide by one inch deep.

column rule thin line separating columns of type.

combination cut printing plate made from both a line and halftone negative.

comic strip comic drawing or cartoon that appears in a newspaper on a regular basis as a series of panels.

commercial art art prepared for editorial or advertising purposes, for any of the media.

comp   short for *comprehensive layout*.

company magazine   magazine published by a company for public relations reasons, not to make money.

compositor   craftsman who sets type.

comprehensive layout   layout finished to look almost as the printed piece will look.

condensed type   type series with narrow characters.

continuous-tone art   photograph or painting or any piece of art in which tones merge gradually into one another. Requires halftone reproduction.

contrast   quality in design that permits one element to stand out clearly from others.

copy   article, story, or other written material either before or after it is set in type.

copy area   see *type page*.

copyedit   see *copyread*.

copyfit   estimate how much space copy will take when it is set in type.

copyread   check the manuscript to correct errors made by the writer or reporter.

copyright   protection available to the owner of a manuscript, piece of art, or publication, preventing others from making unfair use of it or profiting from it at the expense of the owner.

copywriting   writing copy for advertisements.

cover stock   heavy or thick paper used as covers for magazines or paperback books.

credit line   the photographer's name set in type, usually right next to the photograph.

crop   cut away unwanted areas in a piece of art, usually by putting marks in the margins.

CRT   cathode ray tube. Part of the typical VDT.

cursor   small block of light on VDT screen that locates characters being activated by keyboard.

cut   art in plate form, ready to print. For the letterpress process.

cutlines   see *caption*.

deck   portion of a headline, consisting of lines set in the same size and style of type.

deckle edge   ragged, feathery edge available in some of the quality paper stocks.

descender   part of a lowercase letter that dips below the baseline.

design   organization; the plan and arrangement of visual elements. A broader term than *layout*. Use also as a verb.

designer   person who designs pages or spreads.

die-cut   hole or other cutout punched into heavy paper.

direct-entry typesetter   a single-unit system that transmits type from a keyboard directly to a printout.

direct-mail piece   folder, leaflet, booklet, or other printed item issued on a one-time basis.

display type   type larger than 12-point, used for titles and headlines.

double truck   newspaper terminology for *spread*.

downstyle   style characterized by the use of lowercase letters wherever possible.

drop   see *sink*.

dropout halftone   see *highlight halftone*.

drybrush   rendering in which partially linked brush is pulled across rough-textured paper.

dummy   the pages of a magazine in its planning stage, often unbound, with features and pictures crudely sketched or roughly pasted into place.

duotone   halftone printed in two inks, one dark (usually black), one lighter (any color).

duplicator   machine that reproduces a limited number of copies of a publication. Large press runs require regular printing presses.

dust jacket   see *jacket*.

Dutch wrap   in newspapering, continuation of body copy to adjacent columns not covered by the headline.

ear paragraph, line, or box on either side of a newspaper's nameplate.

edit change, manage, or supervise for publication. Also, as a noun, short for *editorial*.

editing the process by which manuscripts and art are procured and made ready for publication.

edition part of the press run for a particular *issue* of a publication.

editorial short essay, usually unsigned, stating the stand of the publication on some current event or issue. Also used to designate the non-business side of a publication.

editorial cartoon single-panel cartoon of opinion found on the editorial page of a newspaper.

element copy, title or headline, art, rule or box, border, spot of color— anything to be printed on a page or spread.

elipses three periods used to indicate omitted words.

em width of capital M in any typesize.

emboss print an image on paper and stamp it, too, so that it rises above the surface of the paper.

en width of capital N in any typesize.

endpapers sheets that help connect the inside front and back covers to the book proper.

English finish smooth finish. English-finish papers are widely used by magazines.

expanded type type series with wider-than-normal characters.

face style or variation of type.

family sub-category of type. The name of the face.

fanzine privately circulated amateur magazine devoted to science fiction and art, often highly illustrated with imaginative art but usually cheaply printed.

feature any story, article, editorial, column, or work of art in a publication. Also used as a verb: play up.

filler short paragraph or story used to fill a hole at the bottom of a column of type.

fine art art created primarily for aesthetic rather than commercial purposes.

first pass first proof of set copy.

fixative clear solution sprayed onto a drawing to keep it from smearing.

flag see *logo*.

flash forms signatures of four, eight, or more pages held out by the editor until the last minute. Often they are printed on different paper stock from what is used in the remainder of the magazine.

flat color see *spot color*.

FlexForm ad newspaper ad in other than the usual square or rectangle shape.

flop change the facing of a picture. If a subject faces left in the original, he will face right in the printed version. Not a synonym for *reverse*.

flow chart art showing a manufacturing process.

flush-left aligned at the left-hand margin.

flush-left-and-right aligned at both the left- and right-hand margins.

flush-right aligned at the right-hand margin.

folder a printed piece with at least one fold.

folio page number. Also, a sheet of paper folded once.

font complete set of type of a particular face and size.

foreshorten exaggerate the perspective.

format size, shape, and appearance of a publication.

formula editorial mix of a publication.

foundry type hand-set metal type.

fourth cover back cover of a magazine.

four-color red, yellow, blue, and black used to produce effect of full color.

freelancer artist, photographer, designer, or writer called in to do an occasional job for a publication.

French fold a fold that allows printing on one side of a sheet to create the illusion that all the pages are printed.

gag cartoon humorous drawing, usually in a single panel, with caption, if there is one, set in type below.

galley tray on which type is assembled and proofed.

galley proof long sheet of paper containing a first printing from a tray of type.

gatefold magazine cover that opens out to two additional pages.

gingerbread design design with an overabundance of swirls and flourishes; cluttered design.

glossy print photograph with shiny finish.

gothic term applied in the past to various typefaces that have challenged the traditional. Currently, modern sans serifs.

graphic design design of printed material.

graph see *bar chart, line chart,* and *pie chart.* Also, short for *paragraph.*

gravure method of printing from incised plate. For publications, a rotary press is involved, hence *rotogravure.*

grid carefully spaced vertical and horizontal lines that define areas in a layout; a plan for designing pages.

gutter separation of two facing pages.

hairline very thin rule or line.

halftone reproduction process by which the printer gets the effect of continuous tone, as when reproducing a photograph. It's done with dots.

hand lettering lettering done with pen or brush.

hanging indent the second and all subsequent lines of a unit indented a set amount, as in this glossary.

hard copy printed record produced as tape is punched. Also: printout from computer.

head short for *headline.*

headband piece of rolled, striped cloth used at the top of the binding to give a finished look to the book.

heading headline or title. Also, the standing title for a regular column or section in a publication.

headline display type over a story, feature, or editorial in a newspaper.

headline schedule chart of different headline sizes and arrangements used by a newspaper.

hed short for *head,* which is short for *heading* or *headline.* Mostly a newspaper term.

high Camp see *Camp.*

highlight halftone halftone in which some parts have been dropped out to show the white of the paper.

horizontal look lines of type, rules, and art are arranged to make the page or spread look wide rather than deep.

hot type type made out of metal.

house ad advertisement promoting the publication in which it appears.

house organ see *company magazine.*

house style style that is peculiar to a publisher or that remains the same from issue to issue or publication to publication.

hung punctuation punctuation placed outside the copy block.

illustration drawing or painting.

illustration board cardboard or heavy paperboard made for artists, available in various weights and finishes to take various art mediums.

imprint run printed piece through another press to add information. Use also as noun.

incunabula books printed before 1501.

index alphabetical listing of important words and names in a book or magazine, accompanied by page numbers. Found in the back of the publication. The table of contents is found in the front.

India ink permanent drawing ink.

India paper see *Bible paper.*

initial first letter of a word at the beginning of an article or paragraph, set in display size to make it stand out.

initial cap and lowercase the first word and all proper names begin with caps; all else is lowercase.

insert separately printed piece that can be bound into a magazine with its other signatures.

intaglio see *gravure.*

interabang combination exclamation mark and question mark.

Intertype linecasting machine similar to Linotype.

issue all copies of a publication for a particular date. An issue may consist of several *editions*.

italic type type that slants to the right. Used for emphasis, for captions, for names of publications, etc.

jacket paper cover that wraps around a book.

jump continue on another page.

justify align the type so it forms an even line on the right and the left.

kerning fitting letters together tightly so that parts of some appear in the space of others.

keyline drawing drawing done partly in outline to use in making plates for spot color printing.

kicker short headline run above main headline, often underscored.

kraft paper heavy, rough, tough paper, usually tan in color.

lay out put visual elements into a pleasing and readable arrangement.

layout noun form of *lay out*.

lead (pronounced *lead*) put extra space between lines of type.

leaders repetition of a period, spaced or unspaced, to fill out a line.

leading extra space between lines of type.

legend book publishers' term for *caption*. Also, magazine term for information about an author.

legibility quality in type that makes it easy for the reader to recognize individual letters.

letterpress method of printing from a raised surface. The original and still widely used printing process.

letterspace put extra space between letters.

letterspacing extra space between letters.

libel published defamatory statement or art that injures a person's reputation.

ligature two or more characters on a single piece of type that join or overlap.

line art in its original form, art without continuous tone, done in black ink on white paper. Also, such art after it is reproduced through *line reproduction*.

linecasting machine see *Linotype* and *Intertype*.

line chart art that shows trends in statistics through a line that rises or falls on a grid.

line conversion continuous-tone art that has been changed to line art.

line feed same as *leading*, but for photocomposition.

line printer unit that produces a printout for copyediting or proofreading, but not in the typeface that eventually will be produced.

line reproduction process by which the printer reproduces a black-and-white drawing.

linespacing see *leading*.

Linotype linecasting machine that produces type for letterpress printing or type from which reproduction proofs can be pulled.

lithography process of making prints from grease drawing on stone. See also *offset lithography*.

logo short for *logotype*. The name of the publication as run on the cover and sometimes on the title or editorial page. On a newspaper it is called the *flag* or *nameplate*.

lowercase small letters (as opposed to capital letters).

Ludlow machine that casts lines of display-size letters from matrices that have been assembled by hand.

magapaper magazine with a newspaper format. Or newspaper with a magazine format.

magazine publication of eight pages or more, usually bound, that is issued at least twice a year. Also, storage unit for mats for linecasting machine.

mass media units of communication: newspapers, magazines, television and radio stations, books, etc.

masthead paragraph of information about the publication. It is run on an inside page, under the table of contents, for a magazine, and on the editorial page for a newspaper.

mat short for *matrix*. Cardboard mold of plate, from which a copy can be made. Also, brass mold from which type can be cast.

matrix see *mat*.

matte finish dull finish.

measure width of a line or column of type.

mechanical see *camera-ready copy*.

mechanical spacing non-adjusted spacing between letters; the opposite of *optical spacing*.

media see *mass media*.

medium singular for *media*. Also, paint, ink, or marking substance used in drawing or painting. In this context, the plural of medium is *mediums*.

mezzotint halftone made with special texture screen.

modular design highly ordered design, marked by regularity in spacing.

moiré undesirable wavy or checkered pattern resulting when a halftone print is photographed through another screen.

Monotype composing machine that casts individual letters. Used for quality composition.

montage combination of photographs or drawings into a single unit.

mortise a cut made into a picture to make room for type or another picture. Use also as a verb.

mug shot portrait.

Multilith printing process similar to offset lithography, but on a small scale.

nameplate see *logo*.

"new journalism" journalism characterized by a highly personal, subjective style.

news hole non-advertising space in a newspaper.

newsprint low-quality paper lacking permanence, used for printing newspapers.

nonlining numerals numbers with ascenders and descenders as found in some oldstyle romans.

OCR optical character reader. It converts typewritten material to electronic impulses and transmits them to a tape punch or computer. It is also called a "scanner."

offset lithography method of printing from flat surface, based on principle that grease and water don't mix. Commercial adaptation of *lithography*.

offset paper book paper made especially for offset presses.

Old English see *blackletter*.

one-shot magazine-like publication issued only once. Deals with some area of special interest.

Op Art geometric art that capitalizes on optical illusions.

op-ed short for "opposite the editorial page." The page across from the editorial page.

optical center a point slightly above and to the left of the geometric center.

optical spacing spacing in typesetting that takes into account the peculiarities of the letters, resulting in a more even look.

optical weight the visual impact a given element makes on the reader.

organization chart art that shows how various people or departments relate to each other.

outline letters letters in outline rather than in solid-black form. Also called *open face*.

overlay sheet of transparent plastic placed over a drawing. The overlay contains art or type of its own for a plate that will be coordinated with the original plate.

overset type set wider than the given measure. Also, excess copy that won't fit into the layout.

page one side of a sheet of paper.

page proof proof of a page to be printed letterpress.

paginate to number pages.

pagination photocomposition system that produces complete pages of type and art, with no pasteup of elements necessary.

painting illustration made with oil, acrylic, tempera, casein, or water color paints. Requires halftone reproduction; if color is to be retained, it requires process color plates.

paper stock paper.

pastel colors soft, weak colors.

pastel drawing drawing made with color chalks.

pasteup see *camera-ready copy.*

paste up verb form for *pasteup.*

pencil drawing drawing made with lead or graphite pencil. Usually requires halftone reproduction.

perfect binding binding that uses glue instead of stitching or stapling.

perspective quality in a photograph or illustration that creates the illusion of distance.

photo essay series of photographs that make a single point.

photocomposition composition produced by exposing negatives of type characters on paper or film.

photoengraving cut or plate made for letterpress printing.

photojournalism photography used in the mass media to report news, express opinion, or entertain.

photolettering display type produced photographically.

phototypesetting text matter produced photographically.

pic short for *picture.*

pica 12 points, or one-sixth of an inch.

Pictograph a chart or graph in picture form. A term coined by *U.S. News & World Report.*

picture photograph, drawing, or painting.

pie chart art that shows statistics—usually percentages—as wedges in a pie or circle.

pix plural for *pic.*

plate piece of metal from which printing is done. See also *cut.*

PMT photo-mechanical transfer. Duplicate print of the original line art.

point unit of measurement for type; there are 72 points to an inch.

Pop Art fine art inspired by comic strips and packages. See also *Camp.*

Pre-print ad in a sort of wallpaper design printed in rotogravure in another plant for insertion in a letterpress newspaper.

press run total number of copies printed during one printing.

printer craftsman who makes up the forms or operates the presses.

printing the act of duplicating pages and arranging or binding them into copies of publications.

process color the effect of full color achieved through use of color separation plates; way to reproduce color photographs, paintings, and transparencies.

production process that readies manuscripts and art for the printer. Can also include the typesetting and printing.

progressive proofs proofs of process color plates, each color shown separately, then in combination.

proofread check galley and page proofs against the original copy to correct any mistakes the compositor made.

proportion size relationship of one part of the design to the other parts.

psychedelic art highly decorative art characterized by blobs of improbable colors, swirls, and contorted type and lettering.

publication product of the printing press.

publishing act of producing literature and journalism and making them available to the public. Printing is only part of publishing.

race major category of typefaces.

ragged left aligned at the right but staggered at the left.

ragged right aligned at the left but staggered at the right.

readability   quality in type that makes it easy for the reader to move easily from word to word and line to line. In a broader sense, it is the quality in writing and design that makes it easy for the reader to understand the journalist.

readership   number of readers of a publication. Larger than the *circulation.*

ream   500 sheets of printing paper.

recto   a right-hand page, always odd-numbered.

register   condition in printing in which various printing plates, properly adjusted, print exactly where they are supposed to print. Use also as a verb.

relief   raised printing surface.

render   execute, as in making a drawing.

repro   short for *reproduction proof.*

reproduction   a copy.

reproduction proof   a carefully printed proof made from a galley, ready to paste down so it can be photographed.

retouch   strengthen or change a photograph or negative through use of art techniques.

reverse   white letters in a gray, black, or color area. Opposite of *surprint.* Mistakenly used for *flop.* Use also as a verb.

rivers of white   meandering streaks of white running vertically or diagonally through body copy, caused by bad or excessive word spacing.

roman type   type designed with thick and thin strokes and serifs. Some printers refer to any type that is standing upright (as opposed to type that slants) as "roman."

rotogravure   see *gravure.*

rough   in cartooning, the first crude sketch presented to an editor to convey the gag or editorial idea. Also, *rough layout.*

rough layout   crude sketch, showing where type and art are to go.

rout   cut away.

rule   thin line used either horizontally or vertically to separate lines of display type or columns of copy.

run-in   let the words follow naturally, in paragraph form.

run-around   area of body copy that wraps around an inset piece of art.

running head or title   heading that repeats itself, page after page.

saddle stitch   binding made through the spine of a collection of nested signatures. Also *saddle staple.*

sans serif type   typeface with strokes of equal or near-equal thicknesses and without serifs.

scale   quality in a photograph or illustration that shows size relationships.

schlock   vulgar, heavy, tasteless.

score   crease paper to make it easier to fold.

scratchboard drawing   drawing made by scratching knife across a previously inked surface.

script   type that looks like handwriting.

screen   the concentration of dots used in the halftone process. The more dots, the finer the screen.

second color   one color in addition to black or the basic color.

second cover   inside front cover.

sequence   series of related elements or pages arranged in logical order.

series   subdivision of a type family.

serif   small finishing stroke of a roman letter found at its terminals.

set size   the width of the characters, which, in computer-controlled CRT typesetting systems, can be controlled separately from the vertical point size. The set size can be expanded or condensed. For instance, 10-point type can have a set size of 9 points, meaning the type is narrower than usual.

set solid   set type without leading.

shelter magazine   magazine that deals with the home and its surroundings.

sidebar   short major story related to story and run nearby.

side stitch   stitch through side of publication while it is in closed position. Also *side staple*.

signature   all the pages printed on both sides of a single sheet. The sheet is folded down to page size and trimmed. Signatures usually come in multiples of 16 pages. A magazine or book is usually made up of several signatures.

silhouette   art subject with background removed.

sink   distance from top of page to where chapter begins.

sinkage   see *sink*.

slab serif type   type designed with even-thickness strokes and heavy serifs. Sometimes called "square serif" type.

slash   diagonal stripe on magazine cover, put there to advertise an article inside.

slick magazine   magazine printed on slick or glossy paper. Sometimes called simply "slick."

slug   line of type from linecasting machine. Also, 6-point spacing material.

slug line   significant word or phrase that identifies story. Found usually on galley proofs.

small caps   short for *small capitals*. Capital letters smaller than regular capital letters in that point size.

sort   what a printer calls a piece of type.

SpectaColor   ad printed in rotogravure in another plant for later insertion in a newspaper. Unlike a Pre-print ad, a SpectraColor ad has clearly defined margins.

spine   back cover of a book or magazine, where front and back covers join.

spot color   solid color used usually for accent. Less expensive, less involved than *process color*.

spot illustration   drawing that stands by itself, unrelated to the text, used as a filler or for decorative purposes.

spread   facing pages in a magazine or book.

stereotype   plate made from mat that in turn was made from photoengraving or type.

stock   paper or other material on which image is printed.

stock art   art created for general use and stored until ordered for a particular job.

straight matter   text that is uninterrupted by headings, tables, etc.

strike-on composition   text matter produced on typewriters or typewriter-like composing machines.

style   distinct and consistent approach to art or design.

subhead   short headline inside article or story. Also *subhed*.

surprint   black letters over gray areas, as over a photograph. Opposite of *reverse*. Use also as a verb.

swash caps   capital letters in some typefaces with extra flourishes in their strokes, usually in the italic versions.

swatch   color sample.

swipe file   artist's or designer's library of examples done by other artists, used for inspiration.

Swiss design   design characterized by clean, simple lines and shapes, highly ordered, with lots of white space; based on a grid system.

symmetric balance   balance achieved by equal weights and matching placement on either side of an imaginary center line.

table   list of names, titles, etc.

tabloid   newspaper with pages half the usual size.

tailband   piece of rolled, striped cloth used at the bottom of the binding to give a finished look to the book.

tape merger   in typesetting, a method of combining the original tape with a second tape containing corrections to produce a third tape.

technique   way of achieving style or effect.

text   see *body copy*.

text type   see *blackletter*.

third cover   inside back cover.

thumbnail   very rough sketch in miniature.

tint   weaker version of tone or color.

tint block   panel of color or tone in which something else may be printed.

tip-in   sheet or signature glued onto a page.

title   what goes over a story or article in a magazine. On a newspaper, the term is *headline.*

tombstone heads   same size and style headlines, side by side.

tone   the darkness of the art or type.

trade magazine   magazine published for persons in a trade, business, or profession.

transparency   in photography, a color positive on film rather than paper.

type   printed letters and characters. Also, the metal pieces from which the printing is done.

typeface   particular style or design of type.

type page   that part of the page in which type is printed, inside the margins. Sometimes called "copy area."

type specimens   samples of various typefaces available.

typo   typographic error made by the compositor.

typography   the type in a publication. Also, the art of designing and using type.

unity   design principle that holds that all elements should be related.

universal characters   characters not of any particular typeface that can be used with any of them. For instance: mathematical signs.

upper case   capital letters.

Vandyke   photographic proof from a negative of a page to be printed by the offset process. Sometimes called *brownline or blueline.*

VDT   video display terminal. It has a keyboard with a TV-like screen above. Stories can be set and corrected on VDTs.

Velox   photoprint with halftone dot pattern in place of continuous tone, ready for line reproduction.

verso   a left-hand page, always with an even number.

vignette   oval-shaped halftone in which background fades away gradually all around.

visual   having to do with the eye.

visualization   the process by which an artist or designer changes an idea or concept into visual or pictorial form.

wash drawing   ink drawing shaded with black-and-white water color. Requires halftone reproduction.

watermark   faint design pressed into paper during its manufacture.

waxer   device or machine that deposits thin coat of wax on backs of proofs so they can be attached to the pasteup.

white space   space on a page not occupied by type, pictures, or other elements.

widow   line of type less than the full width of the column.

woodcut   engraving cut in wood. Also, the impression made by such a plate.

word processor   computer with keyboard, screen, and printer that produces copy or business letters. More sophisticated than an ordinary electric typewriter.

worm's-eye view   view from low vantage point.

wrong font   letter, number, or character in a different size or face from what was ordered.

x-height   height of lowercase *x* in any typeface.

Zipatone   transparent sheet on which is printed a pattern of dots or lines. Fastened over part of line drawing, it gives the illusion of tone. See also *Ben Day.*

INDEX